Get the eBook FREE!

(PDF, ePub, Kindle, and liveBook all included)

We believe that once you buy a book from us, you should be able to read it in any format we have available. To get electronic versions of this book at no additional cost to you, purchase and then register this book at the Manning website.

Go to https://www.manning.com/freebook and follow the instructions to complete your pBook registration.

That's it!
Thanks from Manning!

Tiny C Projects

Tiny C Projects

Dan Gookin

MANNING

SHELTER ISLAND

For online information and ordering of this and other Manning books, please visit www.manning.com. The publisher offers discounts on this book when ordered in quantity. For more information, please contact

> Special Sales Department
> Manning Publications Co.
> 20 Baldwin Road
> PO Box 761
> Shelter Island, NY 11964
> Email: orders@manning.com

Manning Publications Co.		
20 Baldwin Road	Development editor:	Becky Whitney
PO Box 761	Technical development editor:	Christopher Haupt
Shelter Island, NY 11964	Review editor:	Aleksandar Dragosavljević
	Production editor:	Andy Marinkovich
	Copy editor:	Pamela Hunt
	Proofreader:	Keri Hales
	Technical proofreader:	Frances Buontempo
	Typesetter:	Dennis Dalinnik
	Cover designer:	Marija Tudor

ISBN: 9781633439825
Printed in the United States of America

brief contents

1 ■ Configuration and setup   1

2 ■ Daily greetings   17

3 ■ NATO output   38

4 ■ Caesarean cipher   50

5 ■ Encoding and decoding   68

6 ■ Password generators   93

7 ■ String utilities   109

8 ■ Unicode and wide characters   141

9 ■ Hex dumper   164

10 ■ Directory tree   191

11 ■ File finder   223

12 ■ Holiday detector   245

13 ■ Calendar   273

14 ■ Lotto picks   312

15 ■ Tic-tac-toe   331

contents

preface xiii
acknowledgments xv
about this book xvi
about the author xix
about the cover illustration xx

1 Configuration and setup 1

1.1 The C development cycle 2

Editing source code 2 ▪ Compiling, linking, building 3

1.2 The integrated development environment (IDE) 4

Choosing an IDE 4 ▪ Using Code::Blocks 5 ▪ Using XCode 7

1.3 Command-line compiling 9

Accessing the terminal window 9 ▪ Reviewing basic shell commands 10 ▪ Exploring text screen editors 11 ▪ Using a GUI editor 12 ▪ Compiling and running 12

1.4 Libraries and compiler options 13

Linking libraries and setting other options in an IDE 14 Using command-line compiler options 15

1.5 Quiz 16

2 **Daily greetings   17**

2.1   The shell starts   18

*Understanding how the shell fits in   18 ▪ Exploring various shell
startup scripts   18 ▪ Editing the shell startup script   20*

2.2   A simple greeting   21

Coding a greeting   21 ▪ Adding a name as an argument   22

2.3   The time of day   23

*Obtaining the current time   23 ▪ Mixing in the general time
of day   25 ▪ Adding specific time info   26*

2.4   The current moon phase   27

*Observing moon phases   28 ▪ Writing the moon phase
algorithm   29 ▪ Adding the moon phase to your greeting   30*

2.5   A pithy saying   31

*Creating a pithy phrase repository   31 ▪ Randomly reading a pithy
phrase   32 ▪ Adding the phrase to your greeting code   37*

3 **NATO output   38**

3.1   The NATO alphabet   38

3.2   The NATO translator program   40

*Writing the NATO translator   41 ▪ Reading and converting
a file   42*

3.3   From NATO to English   43

*Converting NATO input to character output   44 ▪ Reading NATO
input from a file   47*

4 **Caesarean cipher   50**

4.1   I/O filters   51

*Understanding stream I/O   51 ▪ Writing a simple filter   54
Working a filter at the command prompt   56*

4.2   On the front lines with Caesar   57

*Rotating 13 characters   58 ▪ Devising a more Caesarean
cipher   60*

4.3   Deep into filter madness   63

*Building the hex output filter   63 ▪ Creating a NATO filter   64
Filtering words   65*

5 Encoding and decoding   68

5.1 The concept of plain text   69

*Understanding ASCII   69 ▪ Exploring the control codes   71
Generating noncharacter output   74 ▪ Playing with ASCII
conversion tricks   76*

5.2 The hex encoder/decoder   79

*Writing a simple hex encoder/decoder   79 ▪ Coding a better hex
encoder/decoder   82 ▪ Adding a wee bit of error-checking   87*

5.3 URL encoding   89

*Knowing all the URL encoding rules   89 ▪ Writing a URL
encoder   90 ▪ Creating a URL decoder   91*

6 Password generators   93

6.1 Password strategies   94

*Avoiding basic and useless passwords   94 ▪ Adding password
complexity   95 ▪ Applying the word strategy   96*

6.2 The complex password jumble   97

*Building a silly random password program   97 ▪ Adding conditions
to the password program   98 ▪ Improving upon the password   99*

6.3 Words in passwords   101

*Generating random words, Mad Libs style   101 ▪ Building a
random word password generator   106*

7 String utilities   109

7.1 Strings in C   110

*Understanding the string   110 ▪ Measuring a string   112
Reviewing C string functions   114 ▪ Returning versus modifying
directly   115*

7.2 String functions galore   116

*Changing case   117 ▪ Reversing a string   118 ▪ Trimming a
string   121 ▪ Splitting a string   124 ▪ Inserting one string into
another   125 ▪ Counting words in a string   128 ▪ Converting
tabs to spaces   130*

7.3 A string library   132

*Writing the library source and header file   133 ▪ Creating a
library   134 ▪ Using the string library   135*

7.4 A kinda OOP approach   136

*Adding a function to a structure   137 ▪ Creating a string
"object"   139*

8   *Unicode and wide characters   141*

8.1   Text representation in computers   142

Reviewing early text formats   142 ▪ *Evolving into ASCII text and code pages   145* ▪ *Diving into Unicode   147*

8.2   Wide character programming   148

Setting the locale   149 ▪ *Exploring character types   150 Generating wide character output   152* ▪ *Receiving wide character input   156* ▪ *Working with wide characters in files   160*

9   *Hex dumper   164*

9.1   Bytes and data   164

Reviewing storage units and size mayhem   165 ▪ *Outputting byte values   169* ▪ *Dumping data   170*

9.2   Dump that file!   175

Reading file data   175 ▪ *Fixing uneven output   178*

9.3   Command-line options   179

Using the getopt() function   180 ▪ *Updating the dumpfile program code   182* ▪ *Setting abbreviated output   185* ▪ *Activating octal output   187*

10   *Directory tree   191*

10.1   The filesystem   192

10.2   File and directory details   194

Gathering file info   194 ▪ *Exploring file type and permissions   197* ▪ *Reading a directory   203*

10.3   Subdirectory exploration   207

Using directory exploration tools   208 ▪ *Diving into a subdirectory   210* ▪ *Mining deeper with recursion   212*

10.4   A directory tree   217

Pulling out the directory name   218 ▪ *Monitoring directory depth   220*

11   *File finder   223*

11.1   The great file hunt   224

11.2   A file finder   225

Coding the Find File utility   225 ▪ *Understanding the glob   228 Using wildcards to find files   232*

11.3   The duplicate file finder   234

Building a file list   235 ▪ *Locating the duplicates   239*

12 Holiday detector 245

12.1 The operating system wants its vig 246

*Understanding exit status versus the termination status 246
Setting a return value 246 ▪ Interpreting the return value 247
Using the preset return values 249*

12.2 All about today 250

Getting today's date 250 ▪ Obtaining any old date 251

12.3 Happy holidays 254

*Reviewing holidays in the United States 254 ▪ Discovering
holidays in the UK 255*

12.4 Is today a holiday? 256

*Reporting regular date holidays 256 ▪ Dealing with irregular
holidays 261 ▪ Calculating Easter 266 ▪ Running the date
gauntlet 270*

13 Calendar 273

13.1 The calendar program 274

13.2 Good dates to know 275

*Creating constants and enumerating dates 276 ▪ Finding the day
of the week 277 ▪ Calculating the first day of the month 280
Identifying leap years 282 ▪ Getting the time zone correct 283*

13.3 Calendar utilities 285

*Generating a week 286 ▪ Showing a month 292 ▪ Displaying a
full year 295 ▪ Putting the full year into a grid 299*

13.4 A calendar in color 303

*Understanding terminal colors 303 ▪ Generating a tight-but-
colorful calendar 306 ▪ Coloring holidays 309*

14 Lotto picks 312

14.1 A tax for those who are bad at math 313

*Playing the lottery 313 ▪ Understanding the odds 313
Programming the odds 315*

14.2 Here are your winning numbers 317

*Generating random values 317 ▪ Drawing lotto balls 320
Avoiding repeated numbers, another approach 322*

14.3 Never tell me the odds 324

*Creating the lotto() function 325 ▪ Matching lottery picks 327
Testing the odds 328*

15 *Tic-tac-toe*   331

15.1   A silly kids' game   331

Playing tic-tac-toe   332 ▪ Approaching the game mathematically   333

15.2   The basic game   334

Creating the game grid   334 ▪ Adding game play   337 Limiting the input to free squares   339 ▪ Determining the winner   340

15.3   The computer plays   344

Choosing the number of players   344 ▪ Coding a dumb opponent   346 ▪ Adding some intelligence   348

index   353

Is C programming still relevant?

Every time I read that C is becoming obsolete, another article pops up on how C continues to be one of the most popular, in-demand programming languages—even as it passes its 50th birthday. Disparagement aside, C is the primary language used for system programming, networking, gaming, and coding microcontrollers. Even those trendy languages that the cool kids boast about most likely have their core originally written in C. It's not going away any time soon.

I often refer to C as the Latin of computer programming languages. Its syntax and even a few keywords are borrowed heavily by other languages. Just as knowing Latin helps you understand and learn French, Italian, Spanish, and other languages, knowing C allows you to easily understand and learn other programming languages. But don't stop there! Honing your C skills is just as important as exercising a muscle. And what better way to work on and perfect your C programming abilities than to continually write small, useful programs?

Why did I write this book?

I feel the best way to learn programming is to use small demonstration programs. Each one focuses on a specific part of the language. The code is short and easy to type, and it drives home a point. If the little program can do something impressive, inspiring, or silly, all the better.

My approach contrasts with other programming books I've read. These tedious tomes often list a single, huge program that drives home all the concepts. Typing 100 lines of code when you have no clue what's going on is discouraging, and it misses one of the more delightful aspects of programming: instant feedback.

Somehow, the habit of writing tiny programs sticks with me, even beyond when I'm writing a C programming book or teaching an online C programming course. For years, I've been coding tiny programs on my blog at https://c-for-dummies.com/blog. I do so to provide supplemental material for my readers and learners, but also because I enjoy coding.

Of course, to make small programs meaningful, they must dwell in the ancient command-line, text-mode environment. Graphics are limited. Animation is dull. The excitement, however, remains—especially when something useful is presented all within only a few lines of code.

My approach echoes the way I code: start small and grow the code. So, the programs in this book may begin as only a dozen lines of code that output a simple message. From there the process expands. Eventually a useful program emerges, all while remaining tiny and tight and teaching something useful along the way.

Who knows when the mood will hit you and you decide to code a handy command-line utility to improve your workflow? With a knowledge of C programming, the desire, and a few hours of your time, you can make it happen. It's my hope that this book provides you with ample inspiration.

acknowledgments

I set out to be a fiction author. At one point, I was engaged in personal correspondence with a magazine editor who liked my stuff, but nothing was ever published. Then along came a job at a computer book publishing house, CompuSoft. There I combined my self-taught skills in programming with my love of writing to help craft a series of technical books. It was there I learned how to write for beginners and inject humor in the text.

Six years and 20 titles later, I wrote *DOS For Dummies*, which revolutionized the computer book publishing industry. This book showed that technological titles could successfully impart information to a beginner by using humor. The entire industry changed, and the *For Dummies* phenomenon continues to this day.

Computer books have diminished as an industry, thanks to the internet and humanity's disdain for reading printed material. Still, it's been a great journey and I have many people to thank: Dave Waterman, for hiring me at CompuSoft and teaching me the basics of technical writing; Bill Gladstone and Matt Wagner, for being my agents; Mac McCarthy, for the insane idea of *DOS For Dummies*; and Becky Whitney, for being my long-time, favorite editor. She has taught me more about writing than anyone—or perhaps just taught me how to write in a way that makes her job as editor easy. I appreciate all of you.

Finally, to all the reviewers: Adam Kalisz, Adhir Ramjiawan, Aditya Sharma, Alberto Simões, Ashley Eatly, Chris Kolosiwsky, Christian Sutton, Clifford Thurber, David Sims, Glen Sirakavit, Hugo Durana, Jean-François Morin, Jeff Lim, Joel Silva, Joe Tingsanchali, Juan Rufes, Jura Shikin, K. S. Ooi, Lewis Van Winkle, Louis Aloia, Maciej Jurkowski, Manu Raghavan Sareena, Marco Carnini, Michael Wall, Mike Baran, Nathan McKinley-Pace, Nitin Gode, Patrick Regan, Patrick Wanjau, Paul Silisteanu, Phillip Sorensen, Roman Zhuzha, Sanchir Kartiev, Shankar Swamy, Sriram Macharla, and Vitosh Doynov, your input helped make this a better book.

about this book

Who should read this book?

This book assumes that you have a good knowledge of C. You don't need to be an expert, but a raw beginner may struggle with the pace. Though I explain the techniques used and my approach for writing these small programs, I don't go into detail regarding how the basic aspects of C work.

The operating system I chose is Linux. Though I've run the code on a Linux box, I developed the programs on Ubuntu Linux running under Windows 10/11. The programs also run on a Macintosh. All the programs in this book are text mode, which requires a terminal window and knowledge of various shell commands, though nothing too technical or specific. Chapter 1 covers the details of coding and building in the command-prompt environment.

Bottom line: this book was written for anyone who loves the C language, enjoys programming, and takes pleasure from writing small, useful, and interesting programs.

How this book is organized: A road map

This book is organized into 15 chapters. The first chapter touches upon configuration and setup to ensure that you get started properly and are able to code and create the programs without going nuts.

Chapters 2 through 15 each cover a specific type of program. The chapter builds upon the program's idea, often presenting a simple version and then expanding the program to offer more features. Sometimes other programs are introduced along the way, each of which follows the main theme or otherwise assists the primary program in its goal.

Software/hardware requirements

Any modern version of a C compiler works with this book. The code doesn't touch upon any of the newer C language keywords. Some functions are specific to the GNU compiler. These are mentioned in the text, with alternative approaches available if your C compiler lacks the GNU extensions.

No third-party libraries are required to build any of the programs. Variations in Linux distributions or between Windows 10/11 and macOS play no significant role in creating the code presented here.

Online resources

My personal C programming website is c-for-dummies.com, which is updated weekly. I've been keeping up my habit of weekly C language lessons since 2013, each one covering a specific topic in C programming, offering advice on coding techniques, and providing a monthly Exercise challenge. Please check out the blog for up-to-date information and feedback on C, as well as more details about this book.

I also teach various C programming courses at LinkedIn Learning. These courses range from beginner level to advanced topics such as using various C language libraries, pointers, and network programming. Visit www.linkedin.com/learning/instructors/dan-gookin to check out my courses.

About the code

This book contains many examples of source code both in numbered listings and in line with normal text. In both cases, source code is formatted in a `fixed-width font` `like this` to separate it from ordinary text.

In many cases, the original source code has been reformatted; we've added line breaks and reworked indentation to accommodate the available page space in the book. In rare cases, even this was not enough, and listings include line-continuation markers (➥). Additionally, comments in the source code have often been removed from the listings when the code is described in the text. Code annotations accompany many of the listings, highlighting important concepts.

You can get executable snippets of code from the liveBook (online) version of this book at https://livebook.manning.com/book/tiny-c-projects. The complete code for the examples in the book is available for download from the Manning website at www.manning.com and from GitHub at github.com/dangookin/Tiny_C_Projects.

liveBook discussion forum

Purchase of *Tiny C Projects* includes free access to liveBook, Manning's online reading platform. Using liveBook's exclusive discussion features, you can attach comments to the book globally or to specific sections or paragraphs. It's a snap to make notes for yourself, ask and answer technical questions, and receive help from the author and other users. To access the forum, go to https://livebook.manning.com/book/tiny-c -projects/discussion. You can also learn more about Manning's forums and the rules of conduct at https://livebook.manning.com/discussion.

Manning's commitment to our readers is to provide a venue where a meaningful dialogue between individual readers and between readers and the author can take place. It is not a commitment to any specific amount of participation on the part of the author, whose contribution to the forum remains voluntary (and unpaid). We suggest you try asking the author some challenging questions lest his interest stray! The forum and the archives of previous discussions will be accessible from the publisher's website as long as the book is in print.

about the author

DAN GOOKIN has been writing about technology since the steam-powered days of computing. He combines his love of writing with his gizmo fascination to craft books that are informative and entertaining. Having written over 170 titles with millions of copies in print and translated into more than 30 languages, Dan can attest that his method of creating computer tomes seems to work.

Perhaps his most famous title is the original *DOS For Dummies*, published in 1991. It became the world's fastest-selling computer book, at one time moving more copies per week than the *New York Times* #1 best-seller list (though as a reference, it couldn't be listed on the NYT best-seller list). From that book spawned the entire line of *For Dummies* books, which remains a publishing phenomenon to this day.

Dan's popular titles include *PCs For Dummies*, *Android For Dummies*, *Word For Dummies*, and *Laptops For Dummies*. His number-one programming title is *C For Dummies*, supported at c-for-dummies.com. Dan also does online training at LinkedIn Learning, where his many courses cover a diverse range of topics.

Dan holds a degree in communications/visual arts from the University of California, San Diego. He resides in the Pacific Northwest, where he serves as councilman for the city of Coeur d'Alene, Idaho. Dan enjoys spending his leisure time gardening, biking, woodworking, and annoying people who think they're important.

about the cover illustration

The figure on the cover of *Tiny C Projects* is captioned "Femme de la Carniole," or "Woman from Carniola," taken from a collection by Jacques Grasset de Saint-Sauveur, published in 1797. Each illustration is finely drawn and colored by hand.

In those days, it was easy to identify where people lived and what their trade or station in life was just by their dress. Manning celebrates the inventiveness and initiative of the computer business with book covers based on the rich diversity of regional culture centuries ago, brought back to life by pictures from collections such as this one.

Configuration and setup

1

This first chapter is purely optional. If you already know how to build C code, especially if you're familiar with working at the command prompt, stop wasting time and merrily skip up to chapter 2. Otherwise, slug it out and

- Review the C language development cycle
- Use an integrated development environment (IDE) to build code
- Explore the excitement of command-line programming in a terminal window, just like Grandpa did
- Review options for linking in libraries and supplying command-line arguments

The purpose of this material is for review, though if you've never used a command line to program, you're in for a treat: I find command-line programming to be fast and easy, specifically for the tiny programs created in this book. This code is well suited for the command-line environment.

Still reading? Good. This chapter serves as a review when your C programming skills are rusty or if you just want to confirm that what you know is up to par for successfully navigating the rest of the book. I appreciate that you're still here. Otherwise, these pages would be blank.

And why do skills get rusty? Is it the iron and oxygen? The field of computer jargon needs to plant new terms for poor skills, something highly offensive and obnoxious to the point of being widely accepted. I'll ruminate on the topic, and maybe add a quiz question along these lines at the end of the chapter.

1.1   *The C development cycle*

According to ancient Mesopotamian tablets currently on display in the British Museum, four steps are taken to develop a C language program. These are illustrated in figure 1.1, where you can plainly see the C development cycle written in cuneiform.

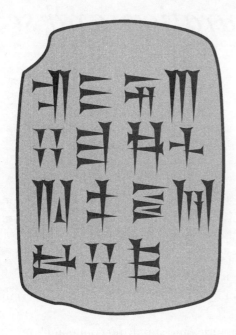

Figure 1.1   The C development cycle, courtesy of the British Museum

As a review, and because neither of us knows Babylonian, here is the translation:

1 Start by creating the source code file.
2 Compile the source code into object code.
3 Link in a library to create a program file.
4 Finally, run the program for testing, disappointment, or delight.

Step 4 is a rather liberal translation on my part. The original reads, "Run the program and rejoice by consuming a cow." I have also omitted references to pagan deities.

These steps present a simple overview of the process. The steps are more numerous due to inevitable errors, bugs, booboos, and lack of cows. The following sections describe the details.

1.1.1   *Editing source code*

C language source code is plain text. What makes the file a C source code file and not a boring ol' text file is the .c filename extension; all C source code files use this filename extension. Eyeball code uses the .see extension. Naval code uses .sea. Know the difference.

Use a text editor to craft your source code. Do not use a word processor, which is like using a helicopter to prune a tree. Don't let the exciting visual image dissuade you; your goal is to use the best tool for the job. Any plain-text editor works, though the good ones offer features like color-coding, pattern matching, and other swanky features that make the process easier. I prefer the VIM text editor, which is available at vim.org. VIM is available as a both a text mode (terminal window) program and a GUI or windowed version.

IDEs feature a built-in text editor, which is the point of the I in IDE: integrated. This editor is what you're stuck with unless an option is available to change it. For example, in Visual Studio Code, you can obtain an extension to bring your favorite editor commands into the IDE.

As a tip, the .c file extension defines a C language source code filetype, which is often associated by the operating system with your IDE. On my system, I associate .c files with my favorite VIM text editor. This trick allows me to double-click a C source code file icon and have it open in my text editor as opposed to having the IDE load.

1.1.2 *Compiling, linking, building*

After writing the source code, you build the program. This process combines two original steps that only a handful of programmers at the Old Coder's Home remember: compiling and linking. Most code babies today just think of compiling, but linking is still in there somewhere.

After the source code file is as perfect as you can imagine, you compile it into object code: the compiler consumes the text in the source code file, churns through it, and spews forth an object code file. Object code files traditionally have a .o ("dot-oh") filename extension unless your compiler or IDE opts for the heretical .obj extension.

Items in your source code that offend the compiler are flagged as warnings or errors. An error terminates the process with an appropriately rude but helpful message. A warning may also thwart the creation of object code, but often the compiler shrugs its shoulders and creates an object code file anyway, figuring you're smart enough to go back and fix the problem. You probably aren't, which is why I admonish you to always take compiler warnings seriously.

Object code is linked or combined with the C library file to build a program. Any errors halt the process, which must be addressed by re-editing the source code, compiling, and linking again.

These days, the original separate steps of compiling and linking are combined into a single step called *building*. Compiling and linking still take place. No matter how many steps it takes, the result is the creation of a program.

Run the program.

I'm quite nervous when my efforts survive the building process with no warnings or errors. I'm even more suspicious when I run the program and it works properly the first time. Still, it happens. Prepare to be delighted or have your suspicions confirmed.

When things go awry, which is most of the time, you re-edit the source code file, compile, link, and run again. In fact, the actual C program development cycle looks more like figure 1.2.

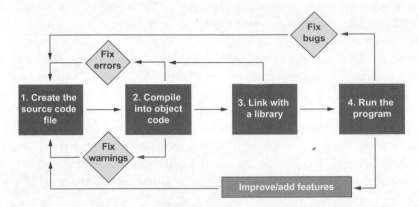

Figure 1.2   The true nature of the program development cycle. (Image courtesy of the California Department of Highway Safety.)

For trivia's sake, the original C compiler in Unix was called *cc.* Guess what it stands for?

The original Unix linker was named *ld*. It probably stands for "link dis." The *ld* program still exists on today's Linux and other Unix-like systems. It's called internally by the compiler—unless the code is riddled with errors, in which case the compiler calls its friend Betsy to giggle about how horrible your C code reads.

Okay. The *ld* program most likely is short for Link eDitor. Please stop composing that email now.

1.2   *The integrated development environment (IDE)*

Most coders prefer to work in an *integrated development environment,* or *IDE*—this program is software used to create software, like a toaster that makes toasters but also makes toast and bread.

The IDE combines an editor, a compiler, and a running environment in a single program. Using an IDE is a must for creating GUI programs where you can build graphical elements like windows and dialog boxes and then add them to your code without the toil of coding everything by hand. Programmers love IDEs.

1.2.1   *Choosing an IDE*

You don't need an IDE to craft the programs presented in this course. I suggest that you use the command prompt, but you're stubborn and love your IDE—and you're still reading—so I'm compelled to write about it.

The IDE I recommend for C programming is Visual Studio Code, available at code.visualstudio.com. It comes in Windows, macOS, and Linux flavors.

Visual Studio Code can be overwhelming, so I also recommend Code::Blocks, available at codeblocks.org. Its best version is available only for Windows. Ensure that you obtain a version of Code::Blocks that comes with a compiler. The default is MinGW, which is nice. Better, get *clang* for Windows, which can be obtained at the LLVM website: llvm.org. You must manually cajole Code::Blocks into accepting *clang* as its compiler; details are offered in the next section.

If you're using Linux, you already have a compiler, *gcc*, which is the default. Even so, I recommend obtaining the LLVM *clang* compiler. It's incredibly sophisticated. It features detailed error messages plus suggestions for fixing your code. If I were a robot, I would insist that *clang* be used to compile my brain's software. Use your distro's package manager to obtain this superb compiler at once!

1.2.2 Using Code::Blocks

Though I prefer Visual Studio Code, I recommend Code::Blocks if you're just starting out. Before you build your first program in the Code::Blocks IDE, confirm that the path to the compiler is correct. For a standard installation, the path is:

```
C:\Program Files (x86)\CodeBlocks\MinGW\bin
```

Ensure that this address is specified for Code::Blocks to locate the default compiler, MinGW, which I just mentioned. Or, if you've disobeyed the setup program's suggestions, set the proper path to your compiler. For example, be spicy and use LLVM *clang* as your compiler. If so, set the proper path to that compiler so that Code::Blocks doesn't barf every time you click the Build button.

To set the path, heed these directions in Code::Blocks. Don't be lazy! The missing compiler error message is one of the most common email complaint messages I receive from readers who can't get Code::Blocks to work. Follow these steps in Code::Blocks:

1 Choose Settings > Compiler.
2 In the Compiler Settings dialog box, click the Toolchain Executables tab.
3 Write (or paste) the compiler's address into the Compiler's Installation Directory text box.
4 Click OK.

The IDE should be happy with the compiler after you work through these steps. If not—yep, you guessed it—get some cows.

Once the compiler is set, you use Code::Block's built-in editor to create your code. The editor uses color-coding, matches parentheses and other pairs, and features inline context assistance for C library functions. All good.

After creating—and saving—your source code, Code::Blocks uses a Build command to compile and link the source code. Messages are output in another part of the window where you read whether the operation succeeded or failed.

Figure 1.3 shows the Code::Blocks workspace. Its presentation can be customized, though in the figure look for the callout items of the buttons used to build or run or do a combined build-and-run.

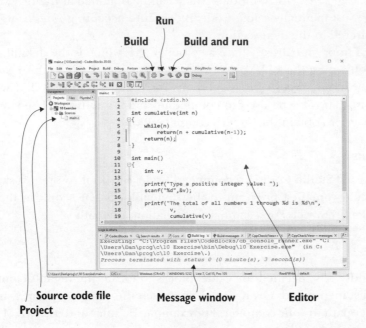

Figure 1.3   Important stuff in the Code::Blocks IDE window

Like all IDEs, Code::Blocks prefers that you create a new project when you start to code. The process works like this:

1 Click File > New > Project.
2 From the New From Template window, select the Console Application icon, and then click the Go button.
3 Select C as the programming language, and then click Next.
4 Type a title for the project, which is also the name of the project folder tree.
5 Choose the folder in which to create the project.
6 Click Next.
7 Select to create a Release configuration. You don't need the Debug configuration unless you plan on using the Code::Blocks debugger (which is really quite cool, but no).
8 Click Finish to create the project skeleton.

Code::Blocks spawns all kinds of folders and creates a prewritten source code file, main.c. You can replace the contents of this file with your own stuff. I find this entire process tedious, but it's how an IDE prefers to work.

As an alternative, you can use the File > New > Empty File command to open a new source code file in the editor. Immediately save the file with a .c filename extension to activate the editor's nifty features. You can then proceed with creating an individual program without enduring the bulk and heft of a full-on project.

Existing files—such as those you steal from GitHub for this book or for other, nefarious purposes—can be opened directly. The point of opening any file directly is that you don't need the bulk and overhead of creating a project to create such small programs.

To perform a quick compile and link in Code::Blocks, click the Build button. This step checks for warnings and errors but doesn't run the created program. If things go well, click the Run button to view the output in a command prompt window, such as the one shown in figure 1.4.

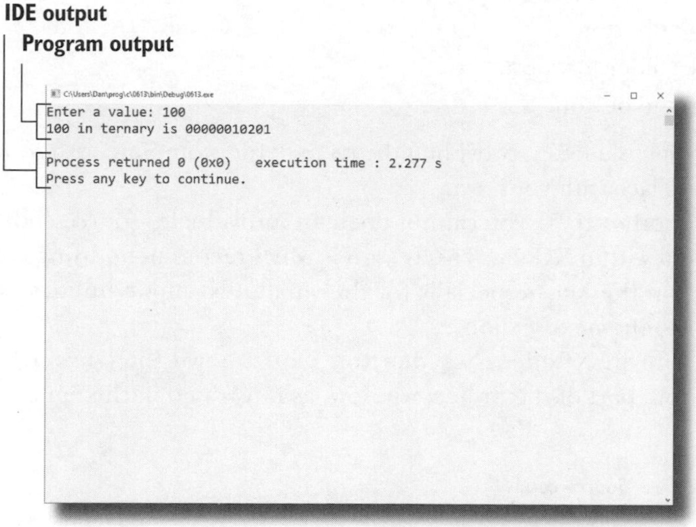

IDE output

 Program output

```
C:\Users\Dan\prog\c\0613\bin\Debug\0613.exe                    –  □  ×
Enter a value: 100
100 in ternary is 00000010201

Process returned 0 (0x0)    execution time : 2.277 s
Press any key to continue.
```

Figure 1.4   The command prompt window

Close the command prompt window when you're done. Remember to do this! A common problem some people have with Code::Blocks is that they can't see the output window. This dilemma most likely occurs because an output window is already open. Ensure that after test-running your programs, you close the wee li'l terminal window.

If you're feeling cocky, you can use the combo Build-and-Run button (refer to figure 1.3) instead of working through the separate Build and Run commands. When you click Build and Run, the code builds and immediately runs, unless you riddled the thing with errors, in which case you get to fix them.

1.2.3   Using XCode

The XCode IDE on the Macintosh is a top-flight application used to build everything from macOS programs to those teensy apps that run on cell phones and wristwatches for the terminally hip. You can use this sophisticated tool to write the simple command-line, text mode utilities offered in this book. It's kind of impractical, given the power of XCode, but this hindrance doesn't prevent millions of Apple fans from doing so.

If your Macintosh lacks XCode, you can obtain a copy for free from the App Store. If prompted, ensure that you choose to add the command-line tools.

To create a text mode C language project in XCode, heed these directions:

1 Choose File > New > Project.
2 Select the Command Line Tool template for the project.
3 Click Next.
4 Type a name for the project.
5 Ensure that C is chosen as the language.
6 Click the Next button.
7 Confirm the folder location.
8 Click the Create button.

XCode builds a project skeleton, providing the `main.c` file, complete with source code you can gleefully replace with your own.

Alas, unlike with other IDEs, you cannot open an individual C source code file and then build and run it within XCode. This reason is why I recommend using command-line programming on the Mac, especially for the small, text mode utilities presented in this book. Refer to the next section.

To build and run in XCode, click the Run icon, shown in figure 1.5. Output appears in the bottom part of the project window, as illustrated in the figure.

Run icon   **Source code**

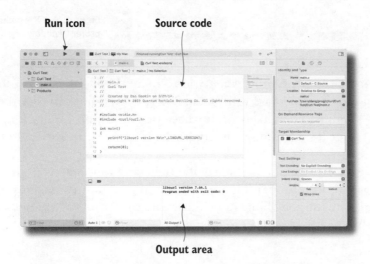

Output area

Figure 1.5   XCode's window. (Squint to view clearly.)

While the project files may dwell in the folder you chose earlier in step 7, the resulting program is created and buried deep within XCode's folder system. This attempt at concealment makes it inconvenient for running and testing command-line programs demonstrated in this book. Specifically, to set command-line options or perform I/O redirection at the prompt requires jumping through too many hoops. To me, this awkwardness makes using XCode as your IDE an option limited to masochists and the fanatical Apple type.

1.3   Command-line compiling

Welcome to the early years of computing. It's nostalgic to edit, build, and run C programs in text mode, but it works well and is quite efficient. You must understand how the command line works, which is something I believe all C programmers should know innately. Truly, it's rare to find a C coder worthy of the title who lacks a knowledge of text mode programming in Unix or Linux.

1.3.1   Accessing the terminal window

Every Linux distro comes with a terminal window. MacOS features a terminal program. Even Windows 10 comes with a command shell, though it's better to install the Windows Subsystem for Linux (WSL) and use an Ubuntu bash shell for consistency with the other platforms. Never have the times been so good for text mode programming. Crack open a Tab and kick off your sandals!

- To start a terminal window in Linux, look for the Terminal program on the GUI's program menu. It may be called Terminal, Term, Xterm, or something similar.
- On the Mac, start the Terminal application, which is found in the Utilities folder. Access this folder from the Finder by clicking Go > Utilities from the menu or by pressing the Shift+Command+U keyboard shortcut.
- In Windows 10, open the Microsoft Store and search for the Ubuntu app. It's free to download, but to make it work you must also install the WSL. Directions for installing the subsystem are splattered all over the Internet.

The Windows 10 Ubuntu app is shown in figure 1.6. Like all other terminal windows, it can be customized: you can reset the font size, the number of rows and columns, screen colors, and so on. Be aware that the traditional text mode screen supported 80 columns by 24 rows of text.

If you plan on using the terminal window for your program production, I recommend keeping a shortcut to the Terminal program available for quick access. For example, in Windows, I pin a shortcut to the Ubuntu shell on the taskbar. On the Mac, I have my Terminal window automatically start each time I sign into OS X. Directions for accomplishing such tasks are concealed on the internet.

```
communications$ ls -l
total 0
-rwxrwxrwx 1 dang dang 13331 May 24 07:40 'C Communications.docx'
-rwxrwxrwx 1 dang dang  8712 Apr 13 12:54  a.out
-rwxrwxrwx 1 dang dang  8712 Apr 13 12:54  client
-rwxrwxrwx 1 dang dang  1044 Apr 13 12:54  client.c
-rwxrwxrwx 1 dang dang   355 Mar 31 11:45  cliserv.h
-rwxrwxrwx 1 dang dang   213 Mar 30 18:45  fifo1.c
drwxrwxrwx 1 dang dang  4096 May 25 09:53  networking
-rwxrwxrwx 1 dang dang   521 Mar 27 10:13  pipe1.c
-rwxrwxrwx 1 dang dang   697 Mar 27 10:21  pipe2.c
-rwxrwxrwx 1 dang dang  8696 Mar 29 09:37  pipe3
-rwxrwxrwx 1 dang dang   697 Mar 29 09:20  pipe3.c
-rwxrwxrwx 1 dang dang  8440 Mar 29 09:37  pipe4
-rwxrwxrwx 1 dang dang   409 Mar 29 09:37  pipe4.c
-rwxrwxrwx 1 dang dang   761 Mar 30 17:38  pipe5.c
-rwxrwxrwx 1 dang dang   596 Mar 26 10:18  posix_test.c
-rwxrwxrwx 1 dang dang  8736 Apr  4 20:55  server
-rwxrwxrwx 1 dang dang   967 Apr  4 20:55  server.c
drwxrwxrwx 1 dang dang  4096 Apr 25 10:48  sockets
communications$ _
```

Figure 1.6   Linux in Windows—such sacrilege

1.3.2   *Reviewing basic shell commands*

I bet you know a few shell commands. Good. In case doubt lingers, table 1.1 lists some commands you should be familiar with to make it easy to work at the command prompt. These are presented without context or further information, which helps maintain the command prompt's mysterious and powerful aura.

Table 1.1   Shell commands worthy of attention

Command	What it does
cd	Change to the named directory. When typed without an argument, the command changes to your home directory.
cp	Copy a file.
exit	Log out of the terminal window, which may close the window.
ls	List files in the current directory.
man	Summon the manual page (online documentation) for the named shell command or C language function. This is the most useful command to know.
mkdir	Make a new directory.
mv	Move a file from one directory to another. Also used to rename a file.
pwd	Print the current working directory.
unlink	Delete the named file.

Each of the commands listed in table 1.1 has options and arguments, such as filenames and pathnames. Most everything is typed in lowercase and spelling errors unforgivable. (Some shells offer spell-check and command completion.)

Another command to know is *make*, which helps build larger projects. This command is covered later in this book. I'd list a chapter reference, but I haven't written the chapter yet.

Also important is to know how the package manager works, though with many Linux distros you can obtain command-line packages from the GUI package manager. If not, familiarize yourself with how the command-line package manager works.

For example, in Ubuntu Linux, use the *apt* command to search for, install, update, and remove command-line software. Various magical options make these things happen. Oh, and the *apt* command must be run from the superuser account; onscreen directions explain the details.

My final recommendation is to understand the file-naming conventions. Spaces and other oddball characters are easy to type in a GUI, but at the command prompt, they can be nettlesome. For the most part, prefix spaces with the backslash character, \, which acts as an escape. You can also take advantage of filename completion: in *bash*, *zsh*, and other shells, type the first part of a filename, and then press the Tab key to spew out the rest of the name automatically.

File-naming conventions also cover pathnames. Understand the difference between relative and absolute paths, which helps when running programs and managing your files.

I'm sure you can find a good book somewhere to help you brush up on your Linux knowledge. Here is an obligatory plug for a tome from Manning Publications: *Learn Linux in a Month of Lunches*, by Steven Ovadia (2016). Remember, it's free at the library.

1.3.3 *Exploring text screen editors*

To properly woo the command prompt, you must know how to use a text mode editor. Many are installed by default with Linux. Those that aren't can be obtained from your distro's package manager. On the Mac, you can use the Homebrew system to add text mode programs that Apple deems unworthy to ship with its operating system; learn more about Homebrew at brew.sh.

My favorite text mode editor is *VIM*, the improved version of the classic *vi* editor. It has a terminal window version that runs in text mode as well as a full GUI version. The program is available for all operating systems.

The thing that ticks off most coders about *VIM* is that it's a modal editor, which means you must switch between text editing and input modes. This duality drives some programmers crazy, which is fine by me.

Another popular text mode editor is *Emacs*. Like *VIM*, it's also available as a text mode editor as well as a GUI editor. I don't use *Emacs*, so I am unable to wax eloquent upon its virtues.

Whatever text editor you obtain, ensure that it offers C language color-coding as well as other helpful features like matching pairs: parentheses, brackets, and braces. With many editors, it's possible to customize features, such as writing a startup script that properly contorts the editor to your liking. For example, I prefer a four-space tab stop in my code, which I can set by configuring the .vimrc file in my home directory.

1.3.4   *Using a GUI editor*

It may be scandalous, but it's convenient to use a GUI editor while you work at the command prompt. This arrangement is my preferred programming mode: I write code in my editor's glorious graphical window and then build and run in the dreary text mode terminal window. This arrangement gives me the power of a GUI editor and the ability to examine text mode output at the same time, as illustrated in figure 1.7.

Text editor window (VIM)   **Terminal window**

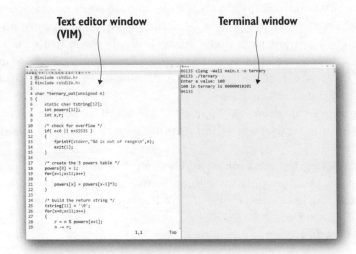

Figure 1.7   A desktop with an editor and a terminal window arranged just so

The only limitation to using a GUI editor is that you must remember to save the source code in one window before you build in the other. This reminder isn't as much of an issue when you use a text mode editor running in the terminal, because you save when you quit. But when bouncing between two different windows on a desktop, it's easy to forget to save.

1.3.5   *Compiling and running*

The command-line compiler in Linux is *gcc*, which is the GNU version of the original *cc* compiler from the caveman days of Unix. As I wrote earlier, I recommend using the *clang* compiler instead of *gcc*. It offers better error reporting and suggestions. Use your distro's package manager to obtain *clang* or visit llvm.org. For the remainder of this chapter, as well as the rest of this book, my assumption is that you use *clang* as your compiler.

To build code, which includes both the compiling and linking steps, use the following command:

```
clang -Wall source.c
```

The compiler is named *clang*. The -Wall switch activates all warnings—always a good idea. And source.c represents the source code filename. The command I just listed generates a program file, a.out, upon success. Warnings may also yield a program file; run it at your own peril. Error messages indicate a serious problem you must address; no program file is generated.

If you desire to set an output filename, use the -o switch followed by the output filename:

```
clang -Wall source.c -o program
```

Upon success, the previous command generates a program file named program.

The compiler sets the program's executable bit as well as file permissions that match those for your account. Once your program is created, it's ready to run.

To run the program, you must specify its full pathname. Remember that in Linux, unless the program exists in a directory on the search path, a full pathname must be specified. For programs in the current directory, use the ./ prefix, like so:

```
./a.out
```

This command runs the program file a.out, located in the current directory, as shown here:

```
./cypher
```

This command runs the program name cypher, again located in the current directory.

The single dot is an abbreviation for the current directory. The slash separates the pathname from the filename. Together, the ./ forces the shell to locate and run the named program in the current directory. Because the program's executable bit is set, its binary data is loaded into memory and executed.

1.4 Libraries and compiler options

As someone who aspires to improve the craft, you must be aware of the assortment of compiler options—specifically, those that link in libraries. These libraries expand a mere mortal C program into realms of greater capabilities.

All C programs link in the standard C library. This library contains the horsepower behind such functions as *printf()*. Yet, it's a common misconception among beginning C programmers that it's the header file that contains the oomph. Nope. The linker builds the program by combining object code (created by the compiler) with a C language library.

Other libraries are also available, which are linked in addition to the standard C library to build complex and interesting programs. These libraries add more capabilities to your program, providing access to the internet, graphics, specific hardware, and a host of other useful features. Hundreds of libraries are available, each of which helps extend your program's potential. The key to using these libraries is to understand how they're linked in, which also raises the issue of compiler options or command-line switches.

As you may expect, methods of adding options and linking libraries differ between the IDE and command prompt approaches to creating programs.

1.4.1   *Linking libraries and setting other options in an IDE*

One area where using an IDE becomes inconvenient is the task of setting compiler options or specifying command-line arguments. Setting the options includes linking in a library. You must not only discover where the linking option is hidden but also confirm the location of the library on the filesystem and ensure that it's compatible with the compiler.

I don't have the time, and it's really not this book's subject, to get into specifics for each IDE and how they set command-line arguments for the programs you build or how specific options are set, such as linking in an extra compiler. After all, I push command-line programming enough—get the hint! But if you insist, or you just enjoy seeing how difficult things can be, read on. For brevity's sake, I'll stick with Code::Blocks because I know it best. Other IDEs have similar options and settings. I hope.

Compiler options in Code::Blocks are found in the Settings dialog box: click Settings > Compiler to view the dialog box, shown in figure 1.8. This is the same location where you specify another library to link.

Compiler Settings tab   **Linker Settings tab**

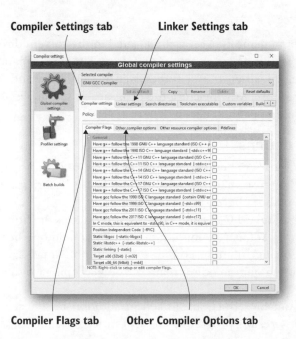

Compiler Flags tab   **Other Compiler Options tab**

Figure 1.8   Finding useful stuff in the Code::Blocks' Settings dialog box

Preset options are listed on the Compiler Flags tab, illustrated in figure 1.8. This tab is a subtab of the Compiler Settings tab, also called out in the figure. The command-line switches for each option are shown at the end of the descriptive text.

Use the Other Compiler Options tab to specify any options not found on the Compiler Flags tab. I can't think of any specific options you might consider adding, but this tab is where they go.

Click the Linker Settings tab (refer to figure 1.8) to add libraries. Click the Add button to browse for a library to link in. You must know the folder in which the library file dwells. Unlike command-line compiling, default directories for library files aren't searched automatically. Ditto for header files, which are often included in the same directory tree as the libraries.

To specify command-line arguments for your programs in Code::Blocks, use the Project > Set Programs' Arguments command. The problem here is that the apostrophe is misplaced on the menu; it should read *Program's*. I mention this because my editor will query me otherwise.

After choosing the grammatically incorrect Set Programs' Arguments command, you see the Select Target dialog box. Use the Program Arguments text field to specify required arguments for the programs you run in the IDE. The limitation here is that your command-line program must be built as a project in Code::Blocks. Otherwise, the option to set command-line arguments is unavailable.

Please be aware that the tiny programs presented in this book are designed to run at the command prompt, which makes it weird to set arguments in an IDE. Because the IDE creates a program, you can always navigate to the program folder to run the program directly at a command prompt. If possible, discover whether your IDE allows you quick access to the folder containing the program executable. Or just surrender to the inevitable ease and self-fulfilling joy of programming in a terminal window.

1.4.2 Using command-line compiler options

It's easy and obvious to type compiler options and program arguments at a command prompt in a terminal window: no extra settings, menus, mouse clicks, or other options to hunt for. Again, these are many of the reasons programming at the command prompt makes sense for the programs presented in this book, as well as for lots of tiny C projects.

Of the slate of command-line options, one worthy of note is -l (little L). This switch is used to link in a library. The -l is followed immediately by the library name, as in:

```
clang -Wall weather.c -lcurl
```

Here, the libcurl library, named curl, is linked along with the standard C library to build a program based on the weather.c source code file. (You don't need to specify the standard C library, because it's linked in by default.)

To specify an output filename, use the -o switch as covered earlier in this chapter:

```
clang -Wall weather.c -lcurl -o weather
```

With some compilers, option order is relevant. If you see a slew of linker errors when using the -l switch, change the argument order to specify -l last:

```
clang -Wall weather.c -o weather -lcurl
```

At the command line, the compiler searches default directories for locations of library files as well as header files. In Unix and Linux—but not OS/X—these locations follow:

- Header files: /usr/include
- Library files: /usr/lib

Custom library and header files you install can be found at these locations:

- Header files: /usr/local/include
- Library files: /usr/local/lib

The compiler automatically searches these directories for header files and libraries. If the library file exists elsewhere, you specify its pathname after the -l switch.

No toil is involved in specifying command-line arguments for your programs. Unlike an IDE, the arguments are typed directly after the program name:

```
./weather KSEA
```

Here, the weather program runs in the current directory with a single argument, KSEA. Simple. Easy. I shan't use further superlatives.

1.5   *Quiz*

I decided against adding a quiz.

Daily greetings

Your computer day starts when you sign in. The original term was *log in*, but because trees are so scarce and signs are so plentiful, the term was changed by the Bush administration in 2007. Regardless of such obnoxious federal overreach, your computer day can start with a cheerful greeting after you sign in or open a terminal window, customized by a tiny C program. To make it so, you will:

- Review the Linux startup process.
- Discover where in the shell script to add your greeting.
- Write a simple greetings program.
- Modify your greetings program to add the time of day.
- Update the timestamp with the current moon phase.
- Enhance your greetings message with a *bon mot*.

The programs created and expanded upon in this chapter are specific to Linux, macOS, and the Windows Subsystem for Linux (WSL), where a startup script is available for configuring the terminal window. A later section explains which startup scripts are available for the more popular shells. This chapter doesn't go into creating a daily greeting message when the GUI shell starts.

I suppose you could add a startup message for the Windows terminal screen, the command prompt. It's possible, but the process bores me, and only hardcore Windows nerds would care, so I'm skipping the specifics. The greetings programs still run at the Windows command prompt, if that's your desire. Otherwise, you may lodge your complaints with me personally; my email address is found in this book's introduction. I promise not to answer a single email from a whiny Windows user.

2.1   *The shell starts*

Linux has a long, involved, and thoroughly exciting boot process. I'm certain that you're eager to read all the nitty-gritty details. But this book is about C programming. You must seek out a Linux book to know the complete, torrid steps involved with rousing a Linux computer. The exciting stuff relevant to creating a daily greeting happens later, after the operating system completes its morning routine, when the shell starts.

2.1.1   *Understanding how the shell fits in*

Each user account on a Linux system is assigned a default shell. This shell was once the only interface for Linux. I recall booting into an early version of Red Hat Linux back in the 1990s and the first—and only—thing I saw was a text mode screen. Today things are graphical, and the shell has been shunted off to a terminal window. It's still relevant at this location, which is great for C programming.

The default shell is configured by the something-or-other. I'm too lazy to write about it here. Again, this isn't a Linux book. Suffice it to say that your account most likely uses the *bash* shell—a collision of the words "Bourne again shell," so my writing "*bash* shell" is redundant (like ATM machine), but it looks awkward otherwise.

To determine the default shell, start a terminal window. At the prompt, type the command **echo $SHELL**:

```
$ echo $SHELL
/bin/bash
```

Here, the output confirms that the assigned user shell is *bash*. The $SHELL argument represents the environment variable assigned to the startup shell, which is /bin/bash here. This output may not reflect the current shell—for example, if you've subsequently run the *sh* or *zsh* or similar command to start another shell.

To determine the current shell, type the command **ps -p $$**:

```
$ ps -p $$
  PID TTY          TIME CMD
    7 tty1     00:00:00 bash
```

This output shows the shell command is bash, meaning the current shell is *bash* regardless of the $SHELL variable's assignment.

To change the shell, use the *chsh* command. The command is followed by the new shell name. Changing the shell affects only your account and applies to any new terminal windows you open after issuing the command. That's enough Linux for today.

2.1.2   *Exploring various shell startup scripts*

When a shell starts, it processes commands located in various startup scripts. Some of these scripts may be global, located in system directories. Others are specific to your account, located locally in your home folder.

Startup scripts configure the terminal. They allow you to customize the horrid text-only experience, perhaps adding colors, creating shortcuts, and performing various tasks you may otherwise have to manually perform each time a terminal window opens. Any startup script file located in your home directory is yours to configure.

Given all that, the general advice is not to mess with startup shell scripts. To drive home this point, the shell script files are hidden in your home directory. The filenames are prefixed with a single dot. The dot prefix hides files from appearing in a standard directory listing. This stealth allows the files to be handy yet concealed from a casual user's attempts to meddle with them.

Because you want to meddle with the shell startup script, specifically to add a personalized greeting, it's necessary to know the script names. These names can differ, depending upon the shell, though the preferred startup script to edit appears in table 2.1.

Table 2.1   Tediously dry info regarding Linux shell scripts

Shell	Name	Command	Startup filename
Bash	Bash, "Bourne again shell"	*/bin/bash*	`.bash_profile`
Tsch	Tee C shell	*/bin/tsch*	`.tcshrc`
Csh	C shell	*/bin/csh*	`.cshrc`
Ksh	Korn shell	*/bin/ksh*	`.profile`
Sh	Bourne shell	*/bin/sh*	`.profile`
Zsh	Z shell	*/bin/zsh*	`.zshrc`

For example, for the *bash* shell, I recommend editing the startup script `.bash_profile` to add your greeting. Other startup scripts may run when the shell starts, but this is the script you can modify.

To view your shell's startup script, use the *cat* command in a terminal window. Follow the command with the shell's startup filename. For example:

```
$ cat ~/.bash_profile
```

The ~/ pathname is a shortcut for your home directory. After you issue the preceding command, the contents of the shell startup script vomit all over the text screen. If not, the file may not exist and you need to create it.

When you see the file's contents, somewhere in the morass you can stick your greetings program on a line by itself. The rest of the script shouldn't be meddled with—unless you're adept at coding in the scripting language and crafting brilliant startup scripts, which you probably aren't.

2.1.3 *Editing the shell startup script*

Shell startup scripts are plain text files. They consist of shell commands, program names, and various directives, which makes the script work like a programming language. The script is edited like any text file.

I could wax eloquent for several pages about shell scripting, but I have a dental appointment in an hour and this book is about C programming. Still, you should note two relevant aspects of a startup shell script: the very first line and the file's permissions.

To interpret the lines of text in a startup script, the very first line of the file directs the shell to use a specific program to process the remaining lines in the file. Traditionally, the first line of a Unix shell script is:

```
#!/bin/sh
```

This line starts with the #, which makes it a comment. The exclamation point, which the cool kids tell me is pronounced "bang," directs the shell to use the /bin/sh program (the original Bourne shell) to process the remaining lines of text in the file. The command could be anything, from a shell like *bash* to a utility like *expect*.

All shell scripts have their executable permissions bit set. If the file exists, this setting is already made. Otherwise, if you're creating the shell script, you must bless it with the executable bit after the file is created. Use the *chmod* command with the +x switch, followed by the script filename:

```
chmod +x .bash_profile
```

Issuing this command is required only when you initially create the script.

Within the startup script, my recommendation is to set your greetings program on a line by itself at the end of the script. You can even prefix it with a comment, starting the line before with the # character. The cool kids have informed me that # is pronounced "hash."

For practice, edit the terminal window's startup script: open a terminal window and use your favorite text editor to open the shell's startup script, as noted in table 2.1. For example, on my Linux system, I type:

```
vim ~/.bash_profile
```

Add the following two lines at the bottom of the script, after all the stuff that looks impressive and tempting:

```
# startup greetings
echo "Hello" $LOGNAME
```

The first line is prefixed with a #. (I hope you said "hash" in your head.) This tag marks the line as a comment.

The second line outputs the text "Hello" followed by the contents of environment variable $LOGNAME. This variable represents your login account name.

Here's sample output:

```
Hello dang
```

My account login is *dang*, as shown. This line of text is the final output generated by the shell startup script when the terminal window first opens. The C programs generated for the remainder of this chapter replace this line, outputting their cheerful and interesting messages.

When adding your greetings program to the startup script, it's important that you specify its pathname, lest the shell script interpreter freak out. The path can be full, as in:

```
/home/dang/cprog/greetings
```

Or it can use the ~/ home directory shortcut:

```
~/cprog/greetings
```

In both cases, the program is named `greetings`, and it dwells in the `cprog` directory.

2.2 A simple greeting

All major programming projects start out simple and have a tendency to grow into complex, ugly monsters. I'm certain that Excel began its existence as a quick-and-dirty, text mode calculator—and now look at it. Regardless, it's good programming practice not to begin a project by coding everything you need all at once. No, it's best to grow the project, starting with something simple and stupid, which is the point of this section.

2.2.1 Coding a greeting

The most basic greetings program you can make is a simple regurgitation of the silly *Hello World* program that ushers in the pages of every introductory C programming book since Moses. Listing 2.1 shows the version you could write for your greetings program.

> **Listing 2.1 Source code for** `greet01.c`

```c
#include <stdio.h>

int main()
{
    printf("Hello, Dan!\n");

    return(0);
}
```

Don't build. Don't run. If you do, use this command to build a program named greetings:

```
clang -Wall greet01.c -o greetings
```

You may substitute *clang* with your favorite-yet-inferior compiler. Upon success, the resulting program is named `greetings`. Set this program into your shell's startup script, adding the last line that looks like this:

```
greetings
```

Ensure that you prefix the program name with a pathname—either the full pathname, like this:

```
/home/dang/bin/greetings
```

or a relative pathname:

```
~/bin/greetings
```

The startup script cannot magically locate program files, unless you specify a path, such as my personal `~/bin` directory shown in the examples. (I also use my shell startup script to place my personal `~/bin` directory on the search path—another Linux trick found in another book somewhere.)

After the startup script is updated, the next terminal window you open runs a startup script that outputs the following line, making your day more cheerful:

```
Hello, Dan!
```

And if your name isn't Dan, then the greeting is more puzzling than cheerful.

2.2.2   *Adding a name as an argument*

The initial version of the `greetings` program is inflexible. That's probably why you didn't code it and are instead eager to modify it with some customization.

Consider the modest improvement offered in listing 2.2. This update to the code allows you to present the program with an argument, allowing it to be flexible.

Listing 2.2   Source code for `greet02.c`

```c
#include <stdio.h>

int main(int argc, char *argv[])
{
    if( argc<2)
        puts("Hello, you handsome beast!");
    else
        printf("Hello, %s!\n",argv[1]);

    return(0);
}
```

The argument count is always 1 for the program name; if so, a default message is output.

The first word typed after the program name is represented as `argv[1]` and is output here.

Build this code into a program and thrust it into your shell's startup script as written in the ancient scrolls but also in the preceding section:

```
greetings Danny
```

The program now outputs the following message when you open a new terminal window:

```
Hello, Danny!
```

This new message is far more cheerful than the original but still begging for some improvement.

2.3   The time of day

One of the first programs I wrote for my old DOS computer greeted me every time I turned on the computer. The program was similar to those created in the last two sections, which means it was boring. To spice it up, and inspired by my verbal interactions with humans I encounter in real life, I added code to make the greeting reflect the time of day. You can do so as well with varying degrees of accuracy.

2.3.1   Obtaining the current time

Does anyone really know what time it is? The computer can guess. It keeps semi-accurate time because it touches base with an internet time server every so often. Otherwise, the computer's clock would be off by several minutes every day. Trust me, computers make lousy clocks, but this truth doesn't stop you from plucking the current time from its innards.

The C library is rife with time functions, all defined in the time.h header file. The *time_t* data type is also defined in the header. This positive integer value (*long* data type, *printf()* placeholder %ld) stores the Unix epoch, the number of seconds ticking away since midnight January 1, 1970.

The Unix epoch is a great value to use in your greetings program. For example, imagine your joy at seeing—every day when you start the terminal—the following jolly message:

```
Hello, Danny, it's 1624424373
```

Try to hold back any emotion.

Of course, the *time_t* value must be manipulated into something a bit more useful. Listing 2.3 shows some sample code. Be aware that many time functions, such as *time()* and *ctime()* used in the code for time01.c, require the address of the *time_t* variable. Yup, they're pointers.

Listing 2.3   Source code for time01.c

```
#include <stdio.h>
#include <time.h>        ◁─┐   The time.h header file is
                            │   required, lest the compiler
int main()                  │   become cross with you.
{
    time_t now;
```

```
    time(&now);
    printf("The computer thinks it's %ld\n",now);
    printf("%s",ctime(&now));

    return(0);
}
```

The *time()* function requires the *time_t* variable's address, prefixed here with the & address-of operator.

The *ctime()* function requires a pointer argument and returns a string appended with a newline.

Here is sample output from the resulting program:

```
The computer thinks it's 1624424373
Tue Jun 22 21:59:33 2021
```

The output shows the number of seconds of tick-tocking since 1970. This same value is swallowed by the *ctime()* function to output a formatted time string. This result may be acceptable in your greetings program, but time data can be customized further. The key to unlocking specific time details is found in the *localtime()* function, as the code in listing 2.4 demonstrates.

Listing 2.4   Source code for `time02.c`

```
#include <stdio.h>
#include <time.h>

int main()
{
    time_t now;
    struct tm *clock;

    time(&now);
    clock = localtime(&now);
    puts("Time details:");
    printf(" Day of the year: %d\n",clock->tm_yday);
    printf(" Day of the week: %d\n",clock->tm_wday);
    printf("            Year: %d\n",clock->tm_year+1900);
    printf("           Month: %d\n",clock->tm_mon+1);
    printf("Day of the month: %d\n",clock->tm_mday);
    printf("            Hour: %d\n",clock->tm_hour);
    printf("          Minute: %d\n",clock->tm_min);
    printf("          Second: %d\n",clock->tm_sec);

    return(0);
}
```

Because *localtime()* returns a pointer, it's best to declare the structure as a pointer.

The first day of the week is 0 for Sunday.

You must add 1900 to the tm_year member to get the current year; you will forget this.

The tm_mon member ranges from 0 to 11.

I formatted the code in listing 2.4 with oodles of spaces so that you could easily identify the `tm` structure's members. These variables represent the time tidbits that the *localtime()* function extracts from a `time_t` value. Ensure that you remember to adjust some values as shown in listing 2.4: the year value `tm_year` must be increased by 1900 to reflect the current, valid year; the month value `tm_mon` starts with zero, not one.

The output is trivial, so I need not show it—unless you send me a check for $5. Still, the point of the code is to show how you can obtain useful time information with which to properly pepper your terminal greetings.

2.3.2 *Mixing in the general time of day*

The program I wrote years ago for my DOS computer was called GREET.COM. It was part of my computer's AUTOEXEC.BAT program, which ran each time I started my trusty ol' IBM PC. Because I'm fond of nostalgia, I've kept a copy of the program. Written in x86 Assembly, it still runs under DOSBox. Ah, the sweet perfume of the digital past. Smells like ozone.

Alas, I no longer have the source code for my GREET.COM program. From memory (and disassembly), I see that the code fetches the current hour of the day and outputs an appropriate time-of-day greeting: good morning, good afternoon, or good evening. You can code the same trick—though in C for your current computer and not in x86 Assembly for an ancient IBM PC.

Pulling together resources from the first chunk of this chapter, listing 2.5 shows a current version of my old greetings program.

Listing 2.5 Source code for `greet03.c`

```c
#include <stdio.h>
#include <time.h>

int main(int argc, char *argv[])
{
    time_t now;
    struct tm *clock;
    int hour;

    time(&now);
    clock = localtime(&now);
    hour = clock->tm_hour;

    printf("Good ");
    if( hour < 12 )
        printf("morning");
    else if( hour < 17 )
        printf("afternoon");
    else
        printf("evening");

    if( argc>1 )
        printf(", %s",argv[1]);

    putchar('\n');

    return(0);
}
```

This statement is a convenience to avoid using `clock->tm_hour` over and over.

Before noon, say "Good morning."

Otherwise, it's evening.

From noon to 5:00 P.M., say "Good afternoon."

Check for and output the first command-line argument.

Assuming that the built program is named `greetings`, that the user types in **Danny** as the command-line argument, and that it's 4 o'clock in the afternoon, here is the code's output:

```
Good afternoon, Danny
```

This code effectively replicates what I wrote decades ago as my `GREET.COM` program. The output is a cheery, time-relevant greeting given the current time of day.

For extra humor, you can add a test for early hours, such as midnight to 4:00 AM. Output some whimsical text such as "Working late?" or "Are you still up?" Oh, the jocularity! I hope your sides don't hurt.

2.3.3 *Adding specific time info*

Another way to treat yourself when you open a terminal window is to output a detailed time string. The simple way to accomplish this task is to output the greeting followed by a time string generated by the *ctime()* function. Here are the two relevant lines of code:

```
printf("Good day, %s\n",argv[1]);
printf("It's %s",ctime(&now));
```

These two statements reflect code presented earlier in this chapter, so you get the idea. Still, the program is lazy. Better to incorporate the *strftime()* function, which formats a timestamp string according to your specifications.

The *strftime()* function works like *printf()*, with a special string that formats time information. The function's output is saved in a buffer, which your code can use later. The code shown in listing 2.6 demonstrates.

Listing 2.6   Source code for `greet04.c`

```
#include <stdio.h>
#include <time.h>

int main(int argc, char *argv[])
{
    time_t now;
    struct tm *clock;
    char time_string[64];          ← Storage for the
                                     string filled by the
                                     strftime() function
    time(&now);
    clock = localtime(&now);       ← You must fill a localtime()
                                     tm structure to make the
                                     strftime() function work.
    strftime(time_string,64,"Today is %A, %B %d, %Y%nIt is %r%n",clock);

    printf("Greetings");
    if( argc>1 )
        printf(", %s",argv[1]);
    printf("!\n%s",time_string);
```

```
        return(0);
}
```

You can review the *man* page for *strftime()* to discover all the fun placeholders and what they do. Like the *printf()* function, the placeholders are prefixed by a % character. Any other text in the formatting string is output as is. Here are the highlights from the *strftime()* statement in listing 2.6:

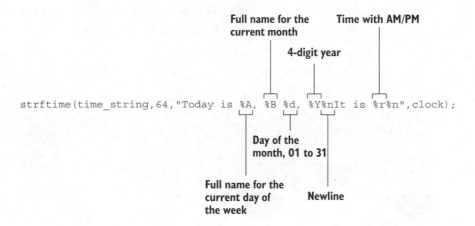

The output reflects the time string generated and stored in the time_string[] buffer. The time string appears after the general greeting as covered earlier in this chapter:

```
Greetings, Danny!
Today is Wednesday, June 23, 2021
It is 04:24:47 PM
```

At this point, some neckbeard might say that all this output can easily be accomplished by using a shell scripting language, which is the native tongue of the shell startup and configuration file anyway. Yes, such people exist. Still, as a C programmer, your job is to offer more insight and power to the greeting. Such additions aren't possible when using a sad little shell scripting language. So there.

2.4   *The current moon phase*

My sense is that most programmers operate best at night. So why bother programming a moon phase greeting when you can just pop your head out a window and look up?

You're correct: the effort is too much trouble, especially when you can write a C program to get a good approximation of the moon phase while remaining safely indoors. You can even delight yourself with this interesting tidbit every time you start a terminal window. Outside? It's overrated.

2.4.1   *Observing moon phases*

The ancient Mayans wrote the first moon phase algorithm, probably in COBOL. I'd print a copy of the code here, but it's just easier to express the pictogram: it's a little guy squatting on a rock, extending a long tongue, wearing a festive hat, and wearing an angry expression on his face. Programmers know this stance well.

The moon goes through phases as it orbits the Earth. The phases are based on how much of the moon is exposed to sunlight as seen from Earth. Figure 2.1 illustrates the moon's orbit. The sunny side always faces the sun, though from the Earth we see different portions of the moon illuminated. These are the moon's phases.

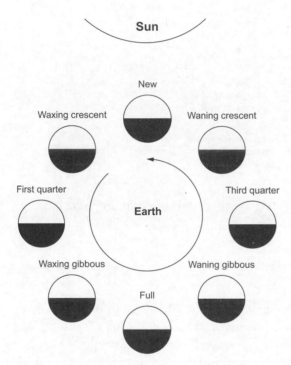

Figure 2.1   **The moon's orbit affects how much of the illuminated side is visible from Earth.**

The phases as they appear from an earthling's perspective are named and illustrated in figure 2.2. During its 28-day journey, the moon's phase changes from new (no illumination) to full and back to new again. Further, half the time, the moon is visible (often barely) during daylight hours.

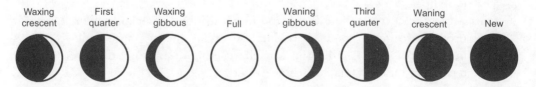

Figure 2.2   **Moon phases as seen from Earth**

The phases shown in figure 2.2 follow the moon's progress from new to full and back again. The latter waning phases happen in the morning, which is why they're only popular with men named Wayne.

2.4.2 Writing the moon phase algorithm

Without looking outside right now, can you tell the moon phase?

Yes, I assume that you're reading this book at night. Programmers are predictable. Congratulations if you're reading this book during the day—outside, even. Regardless of the time, the moon has a current phase. Not a moody teenager phase, but one of the moon how-much-is-illuminated thingies covered in the preceding section.

To determine the moon phase without looking outside or in a reference, you use an algorithm. These are abundant and available on the internet as well as carved into Mayan tablets. The key is the moon's predictable cycle, which can be mapped to days, months, and years. The degree of accuracy of the algorithm depends on a lot of things, such as your location and the time of day. And if you want to be exact, you must use complex geometry and messy stuff I don't even want to look at through one eye half-shut.

Listing 2.7 shows the *moon_phase()* function. It contains an algorithm I found years ago, probably on the old ARPANET. My point is: I don't know where it came from. It's mostly accurate, which is what I find of typical moon phase algorithms that don't use complex and frightening math functions.

Listing 2.7 The *moon_phase()* function

```
int moon_phase(int year,int month,int day)
{
    int d,g,e;

    d = day;
    if(month == 2)
        d += 31;
    else if(month > 2)
        d += 59+(month-3)*30.6+0.5;
    g = (year-1900)%19;
    e = (11*g + 29) % 30;
    if(e == 25 || e == 24)
        ++e;
    return ((((e + d)*6+5)%177)/22 & 7);
}
```

The algorithm presented in listing 2.7 requires three arguments: the integers `year`, `month`, and `day`. These are the same as values found in the members of a *localtime()* tm structure: `tm_year+1900` for the year, `tm_mon` for the month (which starts with 0 for January), and `tm_day` for the day of the month, starting with 1.

Here's how I'm going to explain how the algorithm works: I'm not. Seriously, I have no clue what's going on. I just copied down the formula from somewhere and—by golly—it mostly works. Mostly.

Insert the code from listing 2.7 into your favorite greetings program. If you paste it in above the *main()* function, it won't require a prototype. Otherwise, prototype it as:

```
int moon_phase(int year,int month,int day);
```

The function returns an integer in the range of 0 to 7 representing the eight moon phases shown earlier in figure 2.2, and in that order. An array of strings representing these phases, matching up to the value returned by the *moon_phase()* function, looks like this:

```
char *phase[8] = {
        "waxing crescent", "at first quarter",
        "waxing gibbous", "full", "waning gibbous",
        "at last quarter", "waning crescent", "new"
};
```

You can craft the rest of the code yourself. I've included it as moon.c in this book's code repository as described in the introduction, which you haven't read.

With this knowledge in hand, you can easily add the moon phase as output to your terminal program's initial greeting. One thing you don't want to do, however, is use this moon phase algorithm to accurately predict the moon phase. Seriously, it's for fun only. Don't use this algorithm to launch a manned rocket to the moon. I'm looking at you, Italy.

2.4.3 *Adding the moon phase to your greeting*

You can add the *moon_phase()* function to any of the source code samples for the greetings series of programs listed in this chapter. You need to fetch time-based data, which the *moon_phase()* function requires to make its calculation. You also need an array of strings to output the current moon phase text based on the value the function returns.

Listing 2.6, showing the greet04.c source code, is the best candidate for modification. Make the following changes:

Add a declaration in the *main()* function for integer variable mp to hold the value returned from the *moon_phase()* function:

```
int mp;
```

Add the following two statements after the last *printf()* statement in the existing code, just before the *return*:

```
mp = moon_phase(clock->tm_year+1900,clock->tm_mon,clock->tm_mday);
printf("The moon is %s\n",phase[mp]);
```

You could combine these statements into a single *printf()* statement, eliminating the need for the mp variable: Insert the *moon_phase()* function call (the first line) into the brackets in the *printf()* statement. The result is a painfully long line of code, which is why I split it up. I'd choose readability over a long line of code any day.

A final copy of `greet05.c` can be found in this book's GitHub repository. Here is sample output:

```
$ greetings Danny
Greetings, Danny!
Today is Thursday, June 24, 2021
It is 10:02:33 PM
The moon is full
```

Imagine the delight your users will have, seeing such a meaty message at the start of their terminal window day. They'll lean back and smile, giving a thankful nod as they say, "I appreciate the scintillating details, my programmer friend. Glad I don't have to venture outside tonight. Thank you."

2.5 A pithy saying

The `fortune` program has been a staple of shell startup scripts since the old days, back when some Unix terminals were treadle powered. It remains available today, easily installed from your distro's package manager; search for "fortune."

The name "fortune" comes from the fortune cookie. The idea is to generate a pithy saying, or *bon mot*, which you can use as fresh motivation to start your day. These are inspired by the desserts provided at some Chinese restaurants, which serve the purpose of holding down the paper ticket more than they provide any nutritional value.

Here is an example of a digital fortune cookie, output from the `fortune` program:

```
$ fortune
There is no logic in the computer industry.
        --Dan Gookin
```

It's possible to replicate the `fortune` program output, providing you have a database of pithy sayings and a program eager to pluck out a random one.

2.5.1 Creating a pithy phrase repository

The `fortune` program comes with one or more databases of witticisms. It's from this database that the fortune cookie message is retrieved and output on the screen. You could borrow from this list, but that's cheating. It's also silly, because the `fortune` program is already written. You'd learn nothing. For shame!

Your goal is to write your own version of the pithy phrase database. It need not be quotes or humor, either. The list could contain tips about using the computer, reminders about IT security, and other important information, like the current, trendy hairstyles.

I can imagine several ways to configure the list. This planning is vital to writing good code: a well-organized list means you have less coding to do. The goal is to pluck a random phrase from the repository, which means an organized file is a must. Figure 2.3 outlines the process for writing code to pluck a random, pithy phrase from a list or database.

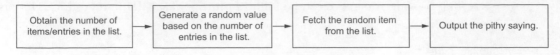

Figure 2.3   The process for reading a random, pithy quote from a file

I can imagine several approaches to formatting the file, as covered in table 2.2.

Table 2.2   Approaches to storing sayings for easy access

File format/data	Pros	Cons
Basic text file	Simple to maintain using existing tools	The file must be read and indexed every time the program runs.
Formatted file with an initial item count reflecting the number of entries	Item count can be read instantly	The item count must be updated as the list is modified.
Hash table with indexed entries	Easy to read and access each record	You will most likely need a separate program to maintain the list, which is more coding to do.

I prefer the basic text file for my list, which means more overhead is required in order to fetch a random entry. It also means that I don't need to write a list maintenance program. Another benefit is that anyone can edit the sayings file, adding and removing entries at their whim.

Eschewing all other options, my approach is to read the file a line at a time, storing and indexing each line in memory. The file needs to be read only once with this method, so it's what I choose to do. The downside? I must manage memory locations, also known as *pointers*.

Fret not, gentle reader.

The bonus of my approach (forgetting pointers for the moment) is that you can use any text file for your list. Files with short lines of text work best; otherwise, you must wrap the text on the terminal screen, which is more work. The file `pithy.txt` can be found in this book's GitHub repository.

2.5.2   *Randomly reading a pithy phrase*

My pithy-phrase greetings program reads lines of text from the repository file, allocating storage space for each string read. As the lines are read and stored, an index is created. This index is a pointer array, but one created dynamically by allocating storage as the file is read. This approach is complex in that it involves those horrifying pointer-pointer things (two-asterisk notation) and liberal use of the *malloc()* and *realloc()* function. I find such activity enjoyable, but I also enjoy natto. So there.

As with any complex topic in programming, the best way to tackle the project is to code it one step at a time. The first step is to read a text file and output its contents.

The code in listing 2.8 accomplishes this first task by reading lines of text from the file
`pithy.txt`. Remember, this code is just the start. The pointer insanity is added later.

Listing 2.8   Source code for `pithy01.c`

```
#include <stdio.h>
#include <stdlib.h>

#define BSIZE 256

int main()
{
    const char filename[] = "pithy.txt";
    FILE *fp;
    char buffer[BSIZE];
    char *r;

    fp = fopen(filename,"r");
    if( fp==NULL )
    {
        fprintf(stderr,"Unable to open file %s\n",filename);
        exit(1);
    }

    while( !feof(fp) )
    {
        r = fgets(buffer,BSIZE,fp);
        if( r==NULL )
            break;
        printf("%s",buffer);
    }

    fclose(fp);

    return(0);
}
```

The file `pithy.txt` is assumed to be in the same directory as the program.

The buffer is used to read text from the file; the size is a guess, set as defined constant `BSIZE` (line 4).

Loops as long as the file isn't empty

The variable `r` ensures that *fgets()* doesn't mess up and read beyond the end of the file; if so, the loop stops.

Outputs all the lines in the file

The purpose of `pithy01.c` is to read all the lines from the file. That's it. Each line is
stored in *char* array `buffer[]` and then output. The same buffer is used over and over.

The program's output is a dump of the contents of file `pithy.txt`. For a release
program, your code must ensure that the proper path to `pithy.txt` (or whatever file
you choose) is confirmed and made available.

Build and run to prove it works. Fix any problems. When it's just right, move on to
the next step: use a pointer and allocate memory to store the strings read. Remember,
the final program stores all the file's strings in memory. Because the number of strings
is unknown, this allocation method works better than guessing an array size.

To proceed with the next improvement, a new variable *entry* is introduced. It's a
char pointer, which must be allocated based on the size of the line read from the file.
Once allocated, the contents of `buffer[]` are copied into the memory chunk referenced by pointer entry. It's this string that's output, not the contents of `buffer[]`.

Another improvement is to count the number of items read from the file. For this task, the *int* variable `items` is added, initialized, and incremented within the *while* loop.

Here are the updates to the code: Add a line to include the `string.h` header file, required for the *strcpy()* function:

```
#include <string.h>
```

In the variable declarations part of the code, add *char* pointer `entry` and *int* variable `items`:

```
char *r,*entry;
int items;
```

Before the *while* loop, initialize variable `items` to zero:

```
items = 0;
```

Within the *while* loop, memory is allocated for variable `entry`. The pointer must be tested to ensure memory is available. Then the contents of `buffer[]` are copied to `entry`, the contents of `entry` output, and the `items` variable incremented. Here is the chunk of code to replace the existing *printf()* statement in the original program:

```
entry = (char *)malloc(sizeof(char) * strlen(buffer)+1);    ◁─────  Enough storage
if( entry==NULL )                                                   for the string,
{                                                                   plus one for the
    fprintf(stderr,"Unable to allocate memory\n");                 null character
    exit(1);
}
strcpy(entry,buffer);
printf("%d: %s",items,entry);
items++;
```

These updates, found in the online repository in `pithy02.c`, only change the output by prefixing each line read with its item number, starting with zero for the first line read from the file. While this update may seem tiny, it's necessary to continue with the next step, which is dynamically storing all the strings read from the file into memory.

As the program sits now, it allocates a series of buffers to store the strings read. Yet the addresses for these buffers are lost in memory. To resolve this issue, a pointer-pointer is required. The pointer-pointer, or address of a pointer, keeps track of all the string's memory locations. This improvement is where the code earns its NC-17 rating.

To track the strings stored in memory, make these improvements to `pithy02.c`, which now becomes `pithy03.c`:

Add a second *int* variable, x, used in a later *for* loop. Also add the pointer-pointer variable `list_base`:

```
int items,x;
char **list_base;
```

The `list_base` variable keeps track of the `entry` pointers allocated later in the code. But first, the `list_base` pointer must be allocated itself. Insert this code just after the file is opened and before the *while* loop:

```
list_base = (char **)malloc(sizeof(char *) * 100);
if( list_base==NULL )
{
    fprintf(stderr,"Unable to allocate memory\n");
    exit(1);
}
```

The illustration in figure 2.4 shows what's happening with the first statement allocating variable `list_base`. It's a pointer to a pointer, which requires the `**` notation. The items it references are character pointers. The size of the list is 100 entries, which is good enough—for now.

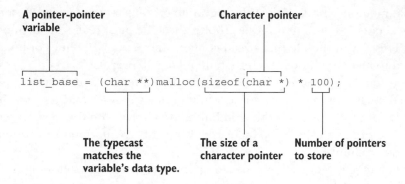

Figure 2.4   How the terrifying pointer-pointer buffer is allocated

Within the *while* loop, remove the *printf()* statement. Outputting statements takes place outside the loop. In place of the *printf()* statement, add this statement below the *strcpy()* statement:

```
*(list_base+items) = entry;
```

Using the offset provided by the `items` count, this statement copies the address stored in pointer variable `entry` into the list maintained at location `list_base`. Only the address is copied, not the entire string. This statement represents crazy pointer stuff—and it works. Figure 2.5 illustrates how the crazy kit 'n' kaboodle looks.

Finally, after the file is closed, output all the items with this *for* loop:

```
for( x=0; x<items; x++ )
    printf("%s",*(list_base+x));
```

In this loop, variable x sets the offset in the list of addresses: `*(list_base+x)` references each line of text read from the file, now stored in memory.

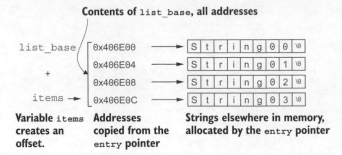

Contents of `list_base`, **all addresses**

Variable `items` creates an offset.

Addresses copied from the `entry` pointer

Strings elsewhere in memory, allocated by the `entry` pointer

Figure 2.5 The `list_base` and `items` variables help store strings allocated by the `entry` pointer.

At this point, the program effectively reads all the text from the file, stores the text in memory, and keeps track of each string. Before a random string can be plucked out of the lot, care must be taken to consider when more than 100 lines are read from the file.

When memory is allocated for the `list_base` variable, only 100 pointers can be stored in that memory chunk. If the value of variable `items` creeps above 100, a memory overflow occurs. To prevent this catastrophe, the code must reallocate memory for `list_base`. This way, if the file that's read contains more than 100 lines of text, they can be stored in memory without the program puking all over itself.

To reallocate memory, or to increase the size of an already-created buffer, use the *realloc()* function. Its arguments are the existing buffer's pointer and the new buffer size. Upon success, the contents of the old buffer are copied into the new, larger buffer. For the size of `list_base` to be increased, it must be reallocated to another 100 *char* pointer-sized chunks.

Only one change is required in order to update the code. The following lines are inserted at the end of the *while* loop, just after the `items` variable is incremented:

```
if( items%100==0 )          Every time items is
{                           exactly divisible by 100 . . .
    list_base = (char **)realloc(list_base,sizeof(char *)*(items+100));
    if( list_base==NULL )
    {                                        . . . existing storage
        fprintf(stderr,"Unable to reallocate memory\n");   is increased by 100
        exit(1);                             pointer-size chunks.
    }
}
```

This update is saved as `pithy04.c`. The code runs the same as the program generated from `pithy03.c`, though if the file that's read contains more than 100 lines of text, each is properly allocated, stored, and referenced without disaster.

The program is now ready to do its job: to select and output a random item from the file. The final step is to remove the *for* loop at the end of the code; it's no longer needed, as the program is required to output only one random line from the file.

Start by including the `time.h` header file:

```
#include <time.h>
```

Replace the declaration for its *int* variable x with a declaration for new variable `saying`:

```
int items,saying;
```

Three lines are added to the end of the code, just above the *return* statement:

```
srand( (unsigned)time(NULL) );
saying = rand() % (items-1);
printf("%s",*(list_base+saying));
```

This is the final update to the code, available in the online repository as `pithy05.c`. When run, the program extracts a random line from the file, outputting its text.

As I wrote earlier in this section, this approach is only one way to resolve the problem. It's quick and it works, which is good enough to add a pithy saying to your shell startup script.

One final note: the program doesn't release any memory directly. Normally, the end of a function would be dotted with *free()* statements, one for each memory chunk allocated. Because the entire code dwells within the *main()* function, freeing memory isn't necessary. The memory allocated is freed when the program quits. Had the allocation taken place in a function, however, it's necessary to release the allocation or risk losing the memory chunk and potentially causing a memory overflow.

2.5.3 Adding the phrase to your greeting code

If your goal is to modify a single greetings program for the shell's startup script, your next task is to add the code from the *pithy* series of programs into your greetings program. Such a task would keep all your efforts in a single program and all the output on a single line in the shell startup script.

Because the *pithy* program is kinda fun, I'm not incorporating it into my previous greetings program code. Instead, I'll leave it as its own line in the shell startup script. That way, I can also run the program from the command prompt any time I need to be humored or am in need of levity. You can work to incorporate the pithy program into your greetings program on your own.

NATO output 3

Count yourself blessed if you've never had to spell your name over the phone. Or perhaps you're named Mary Smith, but you live on a street or in a city you must constantly spell aloud. If so, you resort to your own spelling alphabet, something like, "N, as in Nancy" or "K, as in knife." As a programmer, you can ease this frustration by reading this chapter, where you

- Understand the NATO phonetic alphabet and why they even bother.
- Translate words into the spelling alphabet.
- Read a file to translate words into the phonetic alphabet.
- Go backward and translate the NATO alphabet into words.
- Read a file to translate the NATO alphabet.
- Learn that natto in Japanese is a delicious, fermented soybean paste.

The last bullet point isn't covered in this chapter. I just enjoy eating natto, and now I can write it off as a business expense.

Anyway.

The glorious conclusion to all this mayhem is to not only learn some new programming tricks but also proudly spell words aloud by saying "November" instead of "Nancy."

3.1 The NATO alphabet

Beyond being a handy nickname for anyone named Nathaniel, NATO stands for the North Atlantic Treaty Organization. It's a group of countries who are members of a mutual defense pact.

Established after World War II, blah-blah-blah. I could wax on, but the point is that NATO requires some commonality between its member states. You know, so that when Hans is short on ammo, Pierre can offer him bullets and they fit into the gun. Stuff like that.

One common item shared between NATO countries is a way to spell things out loud. That way, Hans doesn't need to say, "Bullets! That's B, as in bratwurst; U, as in über; L, as in lederhosen. . . ." And so on. Instead, Hans says, "Bravo, Uniform, Lima, Lima, Echo, Tango." This way, Pierre can understand Hans, even over all the surrounding gunfire.

Table 3.1 lists the NATO phonetic alphabet, describing each letter with its corresponding word. The words are chosen to be unique and not easily misunderstood. Two of the words (Alfa and Juliett) are misspelled on purpose to avoid being confusing—and to be confusing.

Table 3.1 The NATO phonetic alphabet.

Letter	NATO	Letter	NATO
A	Alfa	N	November
B	Bravo	O	Oscar
C	Charlie	P	Papa
D	Delta	Q	Quebec
E	Echo	R	Romeo
F	Foxtrot	S	Sierra
G	Golf	T	Tango
H	Hotel	U	Uniform
I	India	V	Victor
J	Juliett	W	Whiskey
K	Kilo	X	Xray
L	Lima	Y	Yankee
M	Mike	Z	Zulu

NATO isn't the only phonetic alphabet, but it's perhaps the most common. The point is consistency. As programmer, you don't need to memorize any of these words, though as a nerd, you probably will. Still, it's the program that can output NATO code—or translate it back into words, depending on how you write your C code. Oscar Kilo.

3.2   *The NATO translator program*

Any NATO translator program you write must have a string array, like the one shown here:

```
const char *nato[] = {
    "Alfa", "Bravo", "Charlie", "Delta", "Echo", "Foxtrot",
    "Golf", "Hotel", "India", "Juliett", "Kilo", "Lima",
    "Mike", "November", "Oscar", "Papa", "Quebec", "Romeo",
    "Sierra", "Tango", "Uniform", "Victor", "Whiskey",
    "Xray", "Yankee", "Zulu"
};
```

The array's notation, *nato[], implies an array of pointers, which is how the compiler builds this construction in memory. The array's data type is *char*, so the pointers reference character arrays—strings—stored in memory. It's classified as a constant because it's unwise to create an array of strings as pointers and then risk modifying them later. The nato[] array is filled with the memory locations of the strings, as illustrated in figure 3.1.

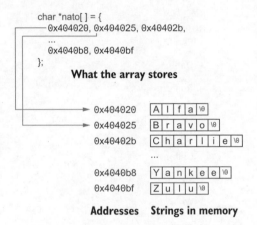

Figure 3.1   How an array of pointers references strings as they sit in memory

For example, in the figure, the string *Alfa* (terminated with a null character, \0) is stored at address 0x404020. This memory location is stored in the nato[] array, not the string itself. Yes, the string appears in the array's declaration, but it's stored elsewhere in memory at runtime. The same structure holds true for all elements in the array: each one corresponds to a string's memory location, from Alfa to Zulu.

The beauty of the nato[] array is that the contents are sequential, matching up to ASCII values 'A' through 'Z' when you subtract the value of 'A'. (See chapter 4 for more details on how this operation works.) This coincidence makes extracting the character corresponding to the NATO word embarrassingly easy.

3.2.1 Writing the NATO translator

A simple NATO translator is shown in listing 3.1. It prompts for input, using the *fgets()* function to gather a word from standard input. A *while* loop churns through the word letter by letter. Along the way, any alphabetic characters are detected by the *isalpha()* function. If found, the letter is used as a reference into the nato[] array. The result is the NATO phonetic alphabet term output.

Listing 3.1   Source code for nato01.c

```
#include <stdio.h>
#include <ctype.h>

int main()
{
    const char *nato[] = {
        "Alfa", "Bravo", "Charlie", "Delta", "Echo", "Foxtrot",
        "Golf", "Hotel", "India", "Juliett", "Kilo", "Lima",
        "Mike", "November", "Oscar", "Papa", "Quebec", "Romeo",
        "Sierra", "Tango", "Uniform", "Victor", "Whiskey",
        "Xray", "Yankee", "Zulu"
    };
    char phrase[64];
    char ch;
    int i;

    printf("Enter a word or phrase: ");
    fgets(phrase,64,stdin);

    i = 0;
    while(phrase[i])
    {
        ch = toupper(phrase[i]);
        if(isalpha(ch))
            printf("%s ",nato[ch-'A']);
        i++;
        if( i==64 )
            break;
    }
    putchar('\n');

    return(0);
}
```

Stores into location phrase 63 characters (plus the null character) from stdin, standard input

Loops until the null character is found in the string

True when character ch is alphabetic

Converts ch to uppercase

ch-'A' transforms the letters to values 0 through 25, matching the corresponding array element.

A long string may not have a null character, so bail when the buffer size is reached.

When built and run, the program prompts for input. Whatever text is typed (up to 63 characters) is translated and output in the phonetic alphabet. For example, "Howdy" becomes:

```
Hotel Oscar Whiskey Delta Yankee
```

Typing a longer phrase such as "Hello, World!" yields:

```
Hotel Echo Lima Lima Oscar Whiskey Oscar Romeo Lima Delta
```

Because nonalpha characters are ignored in the code, no output for them is generated.

Translation into another phonetic alphabet is easy with this code. All you do is replace the `nato[]` array with your own phonetic alphabet. For example, here is the array you can use for the law enforcement phonetic alphabet:

```
const char *fuzz[] = {
    "Adam", "Boy", "Charles", "David", "Edward", "Frank",
    "George", "Henry", "Ida", "John", "King", "Lincoln",
    "Mary", "Nora", "Ocean", "Paul", "Queen", "Robert",
    "Sam", "Tom", "Union", "Victor", "William",
    "X-ray", "Young", "Zebra"
};
```

3.2.2   *Reading and converting a file*

I'm unsure of the need to translate all the text from a file into the NATO phonetic alphabet. It's a C project you can undertake, primarily for practice, but practically speaking, it makes little sense. I mean, it would be tedious to hear three hours of *Antony and Cleopatra* done entirely in the NATO alphabet, though if you're a theater/IT dual major, give it a shot. Still, this is a book and I'm a nerd, so the topic will be explored for your betterment.

Listing 3.2 presents code that devours a file and translates each character into its NATO phonetic alphabet counterpart. The filename is supplied at the command prompt. If not, the program bails with an appropriate error message. Otherwise, similar to the code in `nato01.c`, the code churns though the file one character at a time, spewing out the matching NATO words.

Listing 3.2   Source code for `nato02.c`

```
#include <stdio.h>
#include <stdlib.h>
#include <ctype.h>

int main(int argc, char *argv[])
{
    const char *nato[] = {
        "Alfa", "Bravo", "Charlie", "Delta", "Echo", "Foxtrot",
        "Golf", "Hotel", "India", "Juliett", "Kilo", "Lima",
        "Mike", "November", "Oscar", "Papa", "Quebec", "Romeo",
        "Sierra", "Tango", "Uniform", "Victor", "Whiskey",
        "Xray", "Yankee", "Zulu"
    };
    FILE *n;
    int ch;                      If fewer than two arguments
                                 are present, the filename
    if( argc<2 )      ◁────      option is missing.
    {
        fprintf(stderr,"Please supply a text file argument\n");
        exit(1);
    }
```

```
    n = fopen(argv[1],"r");
    if( n==NULL )
    {
        fprintf(stderr,"Unable to open '%s'\n",argv[1]);
        exit(1);
    }

    while( (ch=fgetc(n))!=EOF )
    {
        if(isalpha(ch))
            printf("%s ",nato[toupper(ch)-'A']);
    }
    putchar('\n');

    fclose(n);

    return(0);
}
```

Opens the filename supplied at the command prompt, referenced as `argv[1]`

Reads one character at a time from the file, storing it in variable `ch`**. The EOF marks the end of the file**

Processes only text characters

Uses the uppercase version of the character, minus the value of `'A'` **to index the** `nato[]` **array**

Remember to use integer variables when processing text from a file. The EOF flag that marks the end of a file is an *int* value, not a *char* value. The *while* statement in the code is careful to extract a character from the file as well as evaluate the character to determine when the operation is over.

To run the program, type a filename argument after the program name. Text files are preferred. The output appears as a single line of text reflecting the phonetic alphabet words for every dang doodle character in the file.

For extra fun on the Macintosh, pipe the program's output through the *say* command:

```
nato02 antony_and_cleopatra.txt | say
```

This way, the phonetic alphabet contents of the file given are read aloud by the Mac, from start to end. Sit back and enjoy.

3.3   *From NATO to English*

Phonetic alphabet translation is supposed to happen in your head. Someone spells their hometown: India, Sierra, Sierra, Alfa, Quebec, Uniform, Alfa, Hotel. And the listener knows how to write down the word, spelling it properly. The word is *Issaquah,* which is a city where I once lived. I had to spell the name frequently. The beauty of this operation is that even a person who doesn't know the NATO alphabet can understand what's being spelled, thanks to the initial letter.

More difficult, however, is to write code that scans for phonetic alphabet words and translates them into the proper single characters. This process involves parsing input and examining it word by word to see whether one of the words matches a term found in the lexicon.

3.3.1 *Converting NATO input to character output*

To determine whether a phonetic alphabet term appears in a chunk of text, you must parse the text. The string is separated into word chunks. Only after you pull out the words can you compare them with the phonetic alphabet terms.

To do the heavy lifting, use the *strtok()* function to parse words in a stream of text. I assume the function name translates as "string tokenizer" or "string to kilograms," which makes no sense.

The *strtok()* function parses a string into chunks based on one or more separator characters. Defined in the `string.h` header file, the *man* page format is:

```
char *strtok(char *str, const char *delim);
```

The first argument, `str`, is the string to scan. The second argument, `delim`, is a string containing the individual characters that can separate, or *delimit,* the character chunks you want to parse. The value returned is a *char* pointer referencing the character chunk found. For example:

```
match = strtok(string," ");
```

This statement scans characters held in buffer `string`, stopping when the space character is encountered. Yes, the second argument is a full string, even when only a single character is required. The *char* pointer `match` holds the address of the word (or text chunk) found, terminated with a null character where the space or another delimiter would otherwise be. The `NULL` constant is returned when nothing is found.

To continue scanning the same string, the first argument is replaced with the `NULL` constant:

```
match = strtok(NULL," ");
```

The `NULL` argument informs the function to use the string passed earlier and continue the tokenizing operation. The code shown in the next listing illustrates how to put the *strtok()* function to work.

Listing 3.3   Source code for `word_parse01.c`

```
#include <stdio.h>
#include <string.h>

int main()
{
    char sometext[64];
    char *match;

    printf("Type some text: ");
    fgets(sometext,64,stdin);

    match = strtok(sometext," ");        ◁──  The initial call to
    while(match)                              strtok(), with the
                                              string to search.

                                         ◁──  Loops as long as
                                              the return value
                                              isn't NULL.
```

```
{
    printf("%s\n",match);
    match = strtok(NULL," ");
}

return(0);
}
```

> In the second call to
> *strtok()*, NULL is used
> to keep searching the
> same string.

In this code, the user is prompted for a string. The *strtok()* function extracts words from the string, using a single space as the separator. Here's a sample run:

```
Type some text: This is some text
This
is
some
text
```

When separators other than the space appear in the string, they're included in the character chunk match:

```
Type some text: Hello, World!
Hello,
World!
```

To avoid capturing the punctuation characters, you can set this delimiter string:

```
match = strtok(sometext," ,.!?:;\"'");
```

Here, the second argument lists common punctuation characters, including the double quote character, which must be escaped (\"). The result is that the delimited words are truncated, as in:

```
Type some text: Hello, World!
Hello
World
```

You may find some trailing blank lines in the program's output. These extra newline characters are fine for matching text, because the blank lines won't match anything anyhow.

To create a phonetic alphabet input translator, you modify this code to perform string comparisons with an array of NATO phonetic alphabet terms. The *strcmp()* function handles this task, but you must consider two factors.

First, *strcmp()* is case-sensitive. Some C libraries feature a *strcasecmp()* function that performs case-insensitive comparisons, though this function isn't part of the C standard. Second, the string length may vary. For example, if you choose not to count the punctuation characters (" ,.!?:;\"'") in the *strtok()* function—or when an unanticipated punctuation character appears—the comparison fails.

Given these two situations, I figure it's best to concoct a unique string comparison function, one designed specifically to check parsed words for a match with a phonetic alphabet term. This function, *isterm()*, is shown next.

Listing 3.4   The *isterm()* function

```c
char isterm(char *term)
{
    const char *nato[] = {
        "Alfa", "Bravo", "Charlie", "Delta", "Echo", "Foxtrot",
        "Golf", "Hotel", "India", "Juliett", "Kilo", "Lima",
        "Mike", "November", "Oscar", "Papa", "Quebec", "Romeo",
        "Sierra", "Tango", "Uniform", "Victor", "Whiskey",
        "Xray", "Yankee", "Zulu"
    };
    int x;
    char *n,*t;

    for( x=0; x<26; x++)
    {
        n = nato[x];
        t = term;
        while( *n!='\0' )
        {
            if( (*n|0x20)!=(*t|0x20) )
                break;
            n++;
            t++;
        }
        if( *n=='\0' )
            return( *nato[x] );
    }
    return('\0');
}
```

Annotations:
- Sets pointer n to the current NATO word
- Pointer t references the term passed.
- Loops until the NATO term ends
- Logically converts each letter to uppercase and compares; refer to chapter 5 for more info on this and other ASCII tricks.
- Increments through each letter
- For no match, the loop breaks and the next term in nato[] is compared.
- When pointer n is the null character, the terms have matched.
- Returns the first letter of the NATO term

The *isterm()* function accepts a word as its argument. The return value is a single character if the word matches a NATO phonetic alphabet term; otherwise, the null character is returned.

To create a new NATO translation program, add the *isterm()* function to your source code file, below any existing code. You must include both the stdio.h and string.h header files. Then add the following *main()* function to build a new program, nato03.c, as shown here.

Listing 3.5   The *main()* function from nato03.c

```c
int main()
{
    char phrase[64];
    char *match;
    char ch;
```

```
    printf("NATO word or phrase: ");
    fgets(phrase,64,stdin);

    match = strtok(phrase," ");
    while(match)
    {
        if( (ch=isterm(match))!='\0' )
            putchar(ch);
        match = strtok(NULL," ");
    }
    putchar('\n');

    return(0);
}
```

The code scans the line input for any matching phonetic alphabet terms. The *isterm()* function handles the job. The matching character is returned and output. Here's a sample run:

```
NATO word or phrase: india tango whiskey oscar romeo kilo sierra
ITWORKS
```

An input sentence with no matching characters outputs a blank line. Mixed characters are output like this:

```
NATO word or phrase: Also starring Zulu as Kono
Z
```

If you want to add in code to translate special characters, such as punctuation characters, you can do so on your own. Keep in mind that the NATO phonetic alphabet lacks terms with punctuation, though if you're creating your own text-translation program, checking for special characters might be required.

3.3.2 *Reading NATO input from a file*

Reading input to detect and translate an alphabetic language is silly but a good exercise. Reading an entire file to detect an alphabetic language is even sillier. I try not to think of it as a necessity but rather as programming practice: can you scan a file for specific words and then report on their presence? Adopt this notion to justify completing such a program.

As with reading a line of text, to process text in a file for signs of NATO alphabet words, you need the *isterm()* function. The file reads a line at a time, and the contents of each line are examined similarly to the code presented in nato03.c. Mixing in the file commands from nato02.c, I've created a child program, nato04.c. It's found in this book's GitHub repository. Assembling such a program in a kind of Frankenstein way appeals to me. It's the philosophy upon which Stack Overflow is successful.

The guts of nato04.c process an open file by using two *while* loops, illustrated in the next listing. If you've been following along with the NATO series of programs in this chapter, many of the statements are familiar to you.

Listing 3.6   Processing words in a file with nested loops

Loops until the end of open file handle n

Grabs a line of text up to 63 characters

Filters out a lot of characters

Loops until all the words in the line are read

Sends the matching word off to the *isterm()* function

```
while( !feof(n) )
{
    fgets(phrase,64,n);
    match = strtok(phrase," ,.!?=()[]{}'\"");
    while(match)
    {
        if( (ch=isterm(match))!='\0' )
            putchar(ch);
        match = strtok(NULL," ,.!?=()[]{}'\"");
    }
}
putchar('\n');
```

The result of all this cobbled code is to pluck out any matching NATO phonetic alphabet terms stored in a file and pop out the corresponding letter for each. As you may guess, few files have a NATO term smuggled inside, so the output is often empty. Still, I ran the code using the nato04.c source code file as input:

```
$ nato04 nato04.c
ABCDEFGHIJKLMNOPQRSTUVWXYZ
```

Much to its delight, the program found the nato[] array's text and gobbled up all the alphabetic terms, in order, to spew out the alphabet itself. Wonderful.

One problem with the code in nato04.c is that the *fgets()* function reads in only a slice of characters per line. In the source code, if a line of text in the file is shorter than the given number of characters (63 plus one for the null character), the line of text is read up to and including the newline character. If the line of text in a file is longer than the quantity specified by the *fgets()* function, it's truncated. Truncating text when you're looking for a word is bad, though not as bad as truncating an elephant.

To better process the file, and ensure that words aren't split by an unforgiving *fgets()* function, I've recajiggered the code to read the file one character at a time. In this approach, the code works more like a program filter. (Filters are covered in chapter 4.) The words in the file are assembled as each character is digested.

Listing 3.7 shows a *while* loop that processes an open file, represented by *FILE* handle n. Characters are stored in *int* variable ch, read one at a time by using the *fgetc()* function. The integer variable offset tracks the characters read as they're stored in a word[] buffer. This buffer is 64 characters long. If a buffer overflow occurs, the program terminates. I mean, show me a word longer than 64 characters. And if you can legitimately find one, increase the buffer size.

Listing 3.7   Processing words in a file one at a time

```
offset = 0;
while( (ch=fgetc(n))!=EOF )
```

Loops as long as the file has bytes to read

```
        {
            if( isalpha(ch)  )                    Words start with a
            {                                     letter of the alphabet.
Checks for         word[offset] = ch;
overflow;          offset++;                      Stores the
bails if so        if( offset>=64 )               character to
                   {                              build the word
                       fprintf(stderr,"Buffer overflow\n");
                       return(1);
                   }                              A nonalphabetic character
            }                                     is found, meaning the
            else                                  end of a word.
            {
Cap your       if( offset > 0 )                   Confirms that the word[]
strings!       {                                  buffer has some text in it
                   word[offset] = '\0';
                   putchar( isterm(word) );                Processes the word,
                   offset=0;                                returning a valid
               }                                            character or the
            }                            Resets the         null character
        }                                offset to          (doesn't print)
        putchar('\n');                   store the
                                         next word
```

The code shown in listing 3.7 is part of the nato05.c source code file, available in this book's GitHub repository. The program works similarly to nato04.c, though a long line of text read from the file isn't split—which could split a valid word. By processing the file's text one character at a time, such a split can't happen (unless the word is ridiculously long).

The program's output is identical to that of nato04.c in the case of processing the source code file's text:

```
$ nato05 nato05.c
ABCDEFGHIJKLMNOPQRSTUVWXYZ
```

Like any program, the code for nato05.c can be improved upon. As it's written, the code relies upon a nonalphabetic character to terminate a word: the *isalpha()* function returns TRUE when the character (*int* value) examined is in the range 'A' to 'Z' or 'a' to 'z'. This rule eliminates contractions (*don't, o'clock*), though it's rare such contractions would be included in a phonetic alphabet.

Beyond peeking into a file for NATO phonetic alphabetic terms, the code provides a practical example of how to scan any file for specific words. Consider it inspiration for other programs you may create. Or just enjoy your newfound knowledge of the NATO phonetic alphabet, so you can beam with pride when asked to spell your city name over the phone.

Caesarean cipher 4

Caesar wrote, "Gallia est omnis divisa in partes tres." If he had wanted the message to be a secret, he would have written, "Tnyyvn rfg bzavf qvivfn va cnegrf gerf." This subtle encryption was easy to concoct, yet even a literate spy would be unable to translate the scrambled Latin without knowing the key. On the receiving end, where the deciphering method is known, the message is quickly decoded and . . . pity poor Gaul. This method of encoding is today known as the Caesarean cipher.

The Caesarean cipher is by no means secure, but it's a fun programming exercise. It also opens the door to the concepts of filters and filter programming in C. This chapter covers the concept of a filter, including stuff like this:

- Dealing with streaming input and output
- Programming a simple input/output (I/O) filter
- Rotating characters 13 places
- Shifting characters in specific increments
- Coding a hex input filter
- Creating a NATO phonetic alphabet filter
- Writing a filter to find words

Filters abide in the command prompt's realm. Special command characters are used to apply the filter at the prompt, redirecting input and output away from the standard I/O devices. Therefore, I strongly suggest you eschew your beloved IDE for this chapter and dive headfirst into the realm of command-line programming. Doing so makes you almost an über nerd, plus it gives you boasting rights at those few parties you're invited to attend.

4.1 I/O filters

Do you remember singing about I/O back at computer camp? The reason for such merriment was to drive home the point that the computer beehive exists for the purpose of absorbing input and creating modified output. The key is what happens between the I and the O, and not just the slash character. No, what's important are the mechanics of modifying input to generate some type of useful output.

An I/O filter is a program that consumes standard input, does something to it, then spews forth the modified output. It's not an interactive program: input flows into the filter like a gentle stream. The filter does something magical, like remove all the bugs and dirt, and then generates output: pure, clean water (though all this action takes place at a digital level, even the bugs).

4.1.1 Understanding stream I/O

To best implement a filter, you must embrace the concept of stream I/O, which is difficult for many C programmers to understand. That's because your experience with computer programs is on an interactive level. Yet in C, input and output work at the stream level.

Stream I/O means that all I/O gurgles through a program without pause, like water from a garden hose. The code doesn't know when you've paused or stopped typing. It only recognizes when the stream ends as identified by the end-of-file (EOF) character.

Thanks to line buffering, the code may pay only casual attention to the appearance of the newline character, \n (when you press the Enter key). Once encountered, the newline may flush an output buffer, but otherwise stream I/O doesn't strut or crow about what text is input or how it was generated; all that's processed is the stream, which you can imagine as one long parade of characters, as illustrated in figure 4.1.

| a | \n | b | \n | a | b | \n | h | u | h | ? |

Figure 4.1   A stream of text—not as jubilant as a parade, but you get the idea.

Stream I/O may frustrate you, but it has its place. To help you accept it, understand that input may not always come from the standard input device (the keyboard). Likewise, output may not always go to the standard output device (the display). The standard input device, stdin, is just one of several sources of input. For example, input can also come from a file, another program, or a specific device, like a modem.

The code in listing 4.1 demonstrates how many C beginners craft a wannabe interactive program. The assumption made is that input is interactive. Instead, input is read from the stream (refer to figure 4.1). Though the code may prompt for a single letter, it's really reading the next character from the input stream. Nothing else matters—no other considerations are made.

Listing 4.1   stream_demo.c

```c
#include <stdio.h>

int main()
{
    int a,b;

    printf("Type a letter:");
    a = getchar();
    printf("Type a letter:");
    b = getchar();

    printf("a='%c', b='%c'\n",a,b);

    return(0);
}
```

Reads a single character from standard input

Reads the next single character from standard input

The programmer's desire is to read two characters, each typed at its own prompt. What happens instead is that the *getchar()* function plucks each character from the input stream, which includes the first letter typed *plus* the Enter key press (newline). Here's a sample run:

```
Type a letter:a
Type a letter:a='a', b='
'
```

The first character is read by *getchar()*, the letter **a**. Then the user presses Enter, which becomes the next character read by the second *getchar()* statement. You see this character in the output for b (split between two lines). Take a gander at figure 4.2, which illustrates what the user typed as the input stream and how the code read it.

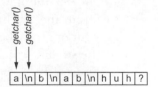

Figure 4.2   The input stream contains two characters read by two *getchar()* functions.

If you type **ab** at the first prompt, you see this output:

```
Type a letter:ab
Type a letter:a='a', b='b'
```

The two *getchar()* functions read characters from the stream, one after the other. If the user types **a** and **b**, these characters are plucked from the stream regardless of the onscreen prompt, lovingly illustrated in figure 4.3. The newline (which appears in the input stream in the figure) isn't read by the code but is used to flush the buffer. It allows the code to process input without the user having to sit and wait for an EOF.

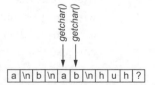

Figure 4.3   Two more characters are read from the input stream.

Understanding stream I/O helps you properly code C programs and also appreciate how an I/O filter works. Even so, you probably remain curious about how interactive programs are constructed. The secret is to avoid stream I/O and access the terminal directly. The Ncurses library is one tool you can use to make programs fully interactive. This library is the foundation upon which full-screen text-mode programs like *vi*, *top*, and others are built. Check out Ncurses if you want to code interactive, full-screen text mode programs for Linux. And, of course, I wrote a book on the topic, which you can order from Amazon: *Dan Gookin's Guide to Ncurses Programming.*

> *Enough self-promotion.—Editor*

Another aspect of stream I/O is buffering. You see a bit of this when you press the Enter key to process input for a wannabe interactive program like `stream_demo.c`. In fact, an aspect of I/O buffering is present when the program's first prompt is output:

```
Type a letter:
```

This text appears and output stops because of buffering. Output to the standard output device (`stdout`) is *line buffered* in C. This configuration means that stream output is stored in a buffer until the buffer gets full or when a newline character is encountered in the stream, after which the text is output. It's the presence of the newline that makes output stop in the `stream_demo.c` program.

Another type of buffer is *block buffering*. When this mode is active, output doesn't appear until the buffer is full—or when the program ends. Even if a newline appears in the stream, block buffering stores the character in the stream, la-di-da.

Buffering for an I/O device is set by using the *setbuf()* function, defined in the `stdio.h` header file. This function overrides the terminal's default line buffering and establishes block buffering using a specific chunk of memory. In effect, it disables line buffering for the given file handle (or standard I/O device) and activates block buffering.

The code in the next listing uses the *setbuf()* function to alter output from line buffering to block buffering. The *setbuf()* statement helps demonstrate how the output stream (`stdout`) is affected.

Listing 4.2 buffering.c

```c
#include <stdio.h>

int main()
{
    char buffer[BUFSIZ];        A holding bin for standard output;
    int a,b;                    BUFSIZ is defined in stdio.h.

    setbuf(stdout,buffer);      Commits standard output
                                to block buffering
    printf("Type a letter:");
    a = getchar();
    printf("Type a letter:");
    b = getchar();
```

```
    printf("a='%c', b='%c'\n",a,b);

    return(0);
}
```

If you build and run `buffering.c`, you see no output. Instead, the *getchar()* function prompts for input, so the program waits. The output is held back, stored in the character array `buffer`, waiting for text to fill the buffer or for the program to end.

Here is a sample run of the code, where no prompt appears. Still, the user is somehow prescient enough to provide input, typing **ab** at the blinking cursor. Only after the Enter key is pressed does the program end and the buffer is flushed, revealing standard output:

```
ab
Type a letter:Type a letter:a='a', b='b'
```

By the way, some C programmers use the *fflush()* function to force output or to clear the input stream. This function, defined in the `stdio.h` header file, dumps the stream for the named file handle, such as `stdin` or `stdout`. I find it unreliable and an awkward method to force stream I/O to somehow feign an interactive C program. Using this technique (which I confess to recommending in some of my other books) is known as a *kludge*. This term implies that using *fflush()* to empty an input or output buffer may be a workable solution but not the best.

4.1.2   *Writing a simple filter*

Filters modify stream input and generate stream output. They manipulate the stream at the character level: a tiny character pops in, it's somehow manipulated, and then something else pops out or not at all. The two functions most commonly used to perform the filter's magic are *getchar()* and *putchar()*, both defined in the `stdio.h` header file.

The *getchar()* function reads a single character from standard input. For most compilers, *getchar()* is a macro, equivalent to the *fgetc()* function:

```
c = fgetc(stdin);
```

The *fgetc()* function reads a single character (byte) from an open file handle. On the preceding line, `stdin` is used as the standard input device. The integer value returned is stored in the *int* variable c. This variable *must* be declared of the integer data type, not character. The reason is that important values, specifically the end-of-file (EOF) marker, are integer values. Assigning the function's return value to a *char* variable means the EOF won't be interpreted properly.

The *putchar()* function sends a single character to standard output. As with *getchar()*, *putchar()* is often defined as a macro that expands to the *fputc()* function:

```
r = fputc(c,stdout);
```

The *fputc()* function sends an integer value c to the open file handle represented by stdout, the standard output device. The return value, r, is the character written or EOF for an error. As with *fgetc()*, both variables r and c must be integers.

A do-nothing filter is presented in listing 4.3. It uses a *while* loop to process input until the EOF (end-of-file) marker is encountered. In this configuration, a character is read from standard input and stored in an *int* variable ch. The value of this character is then compared with the EOF defined constant. Providing that the character read isn't the EOF, the loop spins. Such a loop can be constructed in other ways, but by using this method, you ensure that the EOF isn't output accidentally.

Listing 4.3 io_filter.c

```
#include <stdio.h>

int main()
{                         I/O deals with integers,
    int ch;               not characters.

    while( (ch = getchar()) != EOF)        Reads input until the end
        putchar(ch);                       of file is encountered;
                                           EOF is an integer value.
    return(0);            Spews
}                         output
```

The result of the io_filter.c program is to do nothing. It works just like plumbing: water goes in, water comes out. No modification is made to the characters; the *putchar()* function outputs the character input, ch. Even so, the program demonstrates the basic structure for creating a filter that does something useful.

If you run the filter program by itself, you see input echoed to output: pressing Enter flushes the output buffer, causing the echoed text to appear:

```
hello
hello
```

Press the EOF key to halt the program. In Linux, the EOF key is Ctrl+D. In Windows, press Ctrl+Z for the EOF.

To make the filter do something, build up the *while* loop in the io_filter.c source code. The goal is to modify the characters' input before sending them to output. (Otherwise: plumping.)

As an example, you could modify the input so that all vowels are detected and replaced with an asterisk character. This modification takes place within the *while* loop, as it processes the input stream. Here is one way to accomplish this task:

```
while( (ch = getchar()) != EOF)
{
    switch(ch)
    {
        case 'a':
        case 'A':
```

```
      case 'e':
      case 'E':
      case 'i':
      case 'I':
      case 'o':
      case 'O':
      case 'u':
      case 'U':
          putchar('*');
          break;
      default:
          putchar(ch);
  }
}
```

The full source code for this modification is available in this book's GitHub repository as censored.c. Here's a sample run:

```
hello
h*ll*
```

EXERCISE 4.1

Now that you have the basic filter skeleton in io_filter.c, you can perform your own modifications, testing your filter programming skills. Here is such a challenge you can code on your own: write a filter that converts lowercase characters to uppercase. The effect of such a filter is to generate output in ALL CAPS. My solution to this exercise is found in this book's GitHub repository as allcaps.c.

EXERCISE 4.2

Write a filter that randomizes character text, modifying standard input to generate output in either upper- or lowercase, regardless of the original character's case. I have included my potential solution to this exercise in this book's GitHub repository as ransom.c.

4.1.3   *Working a filter at the command prompt*

You can't test a filter from within an IDE, so banish yourself to the command prompt if you haven't already. The I/O redirection tools you need are shown in table 4.1. These single-character commands modify the stream, altering the flow of input or output—or both!

Table 4.1   I/O redirection characters and their functions

Character	Name	What it does
>	Greater than	Redirects output (not really used for filters)
<	Less than	Redirects input
|	Pipe	Sends output through another program

Assume that you've completed exercise 4.2, where you create a filter to randomize character text. This filter program is named `hostage`. To use this filter, you must specify the program's full pathname. For the following commands, it's assumed that the filter is stored in the same directory where the command is typed; the `./` prefix directs the operating system to find the program in the current directory:

```
echo "Give me all your money" | ./hostage
```

The *echo* command sends a string of text to standard output. However, the pipe character intercepts standard output, sending it away from the standard output device (the terminal window). Instead, the *echo* command's output is provided as input to the named program, ransom. The result is that the filter processes the string of text as its input:

```
gIvE ME AlL yoUR mONey
```

Another way to churn text through a filter is to use input redirection. In this configuration, the filter program name comes first. It's followed by the input redirection character, < (less than), and the source of input, such as a text file:

```
./hostage < file.txt
```

Above, the contents of `file.txt` are redirected as input for the `hostage` program, which outputs the file's text using random upper- and lowercase letters.

The output redirection character doesn't really play a role with a filter. Instead, it takes a program's output and sends it to a file or a device: The program (or construction's) output supplies text for the file. If the file exists, it's overwritten. Otherwise, a new file is created:

```
echo "Give me all your money" | ./hostage > ransom_note.txt
```

Above, the *echo* command's text is processed through the `hostage` filter. The output would normally go to the standard output device, but instead it's redirected and saved into the file `ransom_note.txt`.

Remember that output redirection doesn't supply input for a filter. Use the pipe to send output from one program (or some other source) into the filter.

4.2 On the front lines with Caesar

Julius Caesar didn't invent the cipher that's been given his name. The technique is old but effective with a mostly illiterate population: Caesar could send an encrypted letter and—should it fall into enemy hands—the bad guys would be clueless. Silly Belgae. Yet once received by the right person, the text was instantly deciphered and pity poor Gaul again.

Figure 4.4 illustrates how the cipher works, which is a simple letter shift. It's based upon a starting pair, such as A to D, shown in the figure. This relationship continues throughout the alphabet, shifting letters based on the initial pair: A to D, B to E, C to F, and so on.

| A | B | C | D | E | F | G | ... | W | X | Y | Z |

↓ ↓ ↓ ↓ ↓ ↓ ↓   ↓ ↓ ↓ ↓

| D | E | F | G | H | I | J | ... | Z | A | B | C |

Figure 4.4   The Caesarean cipher is based upon a letter shift.

When you know the initial pair of the cipher, the message is easily decoded. In fact, you may have used this type of cipher if you have ever obtained a secret decoder ring: the initial pair is given and then rest of the message is encoded or decoded, letter by letter:

EH VXUH WR GULQQ BRXU RYDOWLQH.

Surprisingly, the Caesarean cipher, also called a substitution cipher, is still used today. It's admittedly weak, but don't tell the neighbors. The *rot13* filter is perhaps the most common, which you can read about in the next section. Still, it's a fun filter to program, and it has its place in the realm of encryption techniques.

4.2.1   *Rotating 13 characters*

The most common Caesarean cipher known to Unix mavens is the *rot13* filter. Please say "rote 13" and not "rot 13." Thank you.

The *rot13* program works as a filter. If it's not included with your Linux distro, use your package manager to locate it as well as other ancient and nifty command-line tools.

The name *rot13* comes from the character substitution pattern: the Latin alphabet (and ASCII) holds 26 characters, A to Z. If you perform an A-to-N character substitution, the upper half of the alphabet is swapped with the lower, as illustrated in figure 4.5. The program "rotates 13" characters. The beauty of this translation is that running that *rot13* filter twice restores text to the original. This way, the same filter is used to both encrypt and decrypt messages.

Figure 4.5   The *rot13* filter swaps the upper half of the alphabet with the lower half, effectively "rotating" the characters by 13 positions.

Back on the old ARPANET, as well as on early internet, *rot13* was used as a filter in messaging services to hide spoilers, punchlines, and other information people may not want to read right away. Figure 4.6 shows a run of the *rot13* filter on a message. In the original text, the joke appears in standard text with the punchline concealed. After applying the *rot13* filter, the joke text is concealed but the punchline is revealed, for a hearty har-har.

This type of Caesarean cipher is easy to code, because you either add or subtract 13 from a given character's ASCII value, depending on where the character squats in the alphabet: upper or lower half. The addition or subtraction operation works for both upper- and lowercase letters.

Original text:

Knock, knock
Who's there?
Tnvhf Whyvhf Pnrfne naq sbhe Ebzna yrtvbaf!

Rot13 text:

Xabpx, xabpx
Jub'f gurer?
Gaius Julius Caesar and four Roman legions!

Figure 4.6 The effect of applying the *rot13* filter to text, scrambled and unscrambled

In listing 4.4, the code for caesar01.c uses the *isalpha()* function to weed out letters of the alphabet. The *toupper()* function converts the letters to uppercase so that it can test for characters in the range from A through M. If so, these characters are shifted up 13 places: ch+= 13. Otherwise, the *else* statement catches the higher letters of the alphabet, shifting them down.

Listing 4.4   caesar01.c

```c
#include <stdio.h>
#include <ctype.h>

int main()
{
    int ch;

    while( (ch = getchar()) != EOF)
    {
        if( isalpha(ch))
        {
            if( toupper(ch)>='A' && toupper(ch)<='M')
                ch+= 13;
            else
                ch-= 13;
        }
        putchar(ch);
    }

    return(0);
}
```

Only processes alphabet characters

Searches for "A" through "M" or "a" through "m"

Rotates (shift) up for the lower half of the alphabet

Otherwise, rotates (shift) down

As with all filters, you can employ I/O redirection commands (characters) to see it in action at the command prompt. Refer to section 4.1.3 for the specifics. If the program for the caesar01.c source code is named caesar01, here's a sample run:

```
$ echo "Hail, Caesar!" | ./caesar01
Unvy, Pnrfne!
```

When the program is run directly, it processes the text you type as standard input:

```
$ ./caesar01
Unvy, Pnrfne!
Hail, Caesar!
```

Because the *rot13* filter decodes and encodes the same text, you can put the program to the test by running text through it twice. In the command-line construction below, text is echoed through the program once and then again. The result is the original text, thanks to the magic of the *rot13* process:

```
$ echo "Hail, Caesar!" | ./caesar01 | ./caesar01
Hail, Caesar!
```

Remember that the *rot13* filter isn't designed to keep information completely secure. Still, it provides a handy and common way to keep something concealed but not necessarily encrypted beyond reach:

> *Why did Caesar cross the Rubicon?*
> *Gb trg gb gur bgure fvqr.*

4.2.2   *Devising a more Caesarean cipher*

Caesar didn't use the *rot13* filter to encrypt his messages, mostly because he never upgraded to Linux from his trusty Commodore 64. No, he preferred the A-to-D shift. Sometimes it was just an A-to-B shift. Regardless, coding such a beast is a bit more involved than the convenient 13-character shift of the *rot13* filter.

Properly transposing letters based on a value other than 13 means the letters will wrap. For example, an A-to-D translation means that Z would wrap to some character Z+3 in the ASCII table. Therefore, to keep the translation going, the letter shift must wrap from Z back to C (refer to figure 4.4). You must account for such wrapping in your code, confirming that characters are contained within the 26-letter change of the alphabet—both upper- and lowercase.

To account for such wrapping, specifically with an A-to-D translation, your code must construct a complex *if* condition using logical comparisons to account for characters that shift out of range. Figure 4.7 illustrates how such an expression works. It tests for values greater than `'Z'` and less than `'a'`, but also greater than `'z'`. This arrangement exists due to how characters are encoded with the ASCII standard. (See chapter 5 for more details on ASCII.)

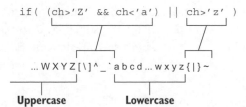

Figure 4.7   Detecting overflow characters when performing an A-to-D shift

When a character is detected as out of range by the *if* statement, its value must be reduced by 26, wrapping it back to `'A'` or `'a'`, depending on the letter's original case.

Due to the proximity of uppercase `'Z'` to lowercase `'a'`, this *if* statement test works because this particular shift is only three characters. From figure 4.7, you see that the ASCII table sets only six characters between uppercase Z and lowercase a. For larger character shifts, more complex testing must be performed.

Listing 4.5 shows how the A-to-D character shift cipher is coded, complete with the complex *if* statement that wraps overflow characters. Otherwise, the character is shifted by the value of variable `shift`, calculated as `'D' - 'A'`. This shift is expressed backward to properly calculate as three. Therefore, three is added to each alphabetic character in the code—unless the character is out of range.

Listing 4.5   caesar02.c

```
#include <stdio.h>
#include <ctype.h>

int main()
{
    int shift,ch;

    shift = 'D' - 'A';          ◁── Shifts from A to D, which
                                     is done backward here
                                     because math
    while( (ch = getchar()) != EOF)
    {                           ◁── Handles letters
        if( isalpha(ch))             specifically
        {
            ch+=shift;          ◁── Shifts the letter
            if( (ch>'Z' && ch<'a') || ch>'z')   ◁── Determines whether
                ch-= 26;        ◁──                  the new character
        }                           If so, adjusts   is out of range
        putchar(ch);                its value back
    }                               within range

    return(0);
}
```

Here is a sample run:

```
Now is the time for all good men...
Qrz lv wkh wlph iru doo jrrg phq...
```

Unlike with a *rot13* filter, you can't run the same program twice to decode the A-to-D shift. Instead, to decode the message, you must shift from D back to A. Two changes are required to make this change. In the code shown in listing 4.5, first alter the shift calculation:

```
shift = 'A' - 'D';
```

Second, the out-of-bounds testing must check the underside of the alphabet, so see whether a character's value has dipped below `'A'` or `'a'`:

```
if( ch<'A' || (ch>'Z' && ch<'a'))
    ch+= 26;
```

If the character wraps on the underside of the alphabet, its value is increased by 26, which wraps it back up to the Z end, correcting the overflow.

The final program is available as `caesar03.c` in this book's GitHub repository. Here is a sample run:

```
Now is the time for all good men
Klt fp qeb qfjb clo xii dlla jbk
Qrz lv wkh wlph iru doo jrrg phq...
Now is the time for all good men...
```

The first two lines show the D-to-A shift of normal text, how the filter encodes plain text. The second two lines show how the D-to-A shift decrypts the original A-to-D shift of the `caesar02.c` code. (Refer to the output shown earlier.)

As with any filter, you can pipe output through both filters to recover the original text:

```
$ echo "Hail, Caesar!" | ./caesar02 | ./caesar03
Hail, Caesar!
```

Of course, the best way to code a more Caesarean cipher is to let the user determine which letters to shift. To make this filter work, command-line arguments are required; filters are not interactive, so the user isn't given the opportunity to provide input otherwise.

The command-line arguments provide the two letters for the shift, from argument 1 to argument 2. The code then works out the process, performing the shift on whatever text is flung into standard input.

Letting the user decide options is always good. Providing this feature means that the bulk of the code is used to interpret the command-line options: you must check to see whether the options are present and then confirm that both are letters of the alphabet. Such code is available in the GitHub repository as `caesar04.c`. The extra step of checking for two command-line arguments in this source code file consumes 16 lines of code.

Once the two shifting characters are set, they're saved in *char* variables a and b. A *while* loop then processes the text based on the shift value of the two characters supplied. Because the shift can be up or down, and to best check for out-of-range values, the loop must separate upper- and lowercase characters. This approach is best to detect shift overflow and deal with it properly. The program's core *while* loop and the various tests from my `caesar04.c` program are shown in the next listing.

Listing 4.6   The *while* loop in caesar04.c that performs the character shift

```
while( (ch = getchar()) != EOF)
{
    if( isupper(ch) )         <───┤  Upper- and lowercase characters
    {                               must be handled differently.
        ch+= shift;
        if( ch>'Z' ) ch-=26;       Adjusts appropriately for
        if( ch<'A' ) ch+=26;       overflow in either direction
        putchar(ch);
    }
```

```
    else if( islower(ch) )
    {
        ch+= shift;
        if( ch>'z' ) ch-=26;          Adjusts appropriately for
        if( ch<'a' ) ch+=26;          overflow in either direction
        putchar(ch);
    }
    else
    {
        putchar(ch);
    }
}
```

Here is a sample run of the *caesar04* program with an A-to-R shift:

```
$ ./caesar04 A R
This is a test
Kyzj zj r kvjk
```

And to reverse, the R-to-A shift is specified as command line arguments:

```
$ ./caesar04 R A
Kyzj zj r kvjk
This is a test
```

As an improvement, it might be better to have a single argument that specifies the character shift, such as **RA** instead of the separate R and A just shown. Then again, as with most programmers, messing with code is an eternal process. I leave this task up to you.

4.3   *Deep into filter madness*

I've created a slew of filters over my programming career. It's amazing to think of the fun things you can accomplish. Well, fun for nerds. Non-nerds are reading a romance novel right now. Let me spoil it: his work is more important to him than she is. There. Saved you 180 dreary pages.

Regardless of what a filter does, the method for composing a filter is always the same: read standard input, modify it, and then generate standard output.

Before the chapter closes (and I must hurry because my work is important), I offer a few different filter ideas to help churn your creative juices. The possibilities are endless.

4.3.1   *Building the hex output filter*

Just because one character flows into a filter doesn't mean another character must always flow out. Some filters may spew out several characters of output for each character input. Other filters may not output any modification of text, such as the *more* filter.

The *more* filter is a handy text-reading utility. It's used to page output. Shoving output through the *more* filter prompts for input after each screen of text:

```
cat long.txt | more
```

Above, the contents of file `long.txt` are output via the *cat* command. The *more* filter pauses the display after every screenful of text. This filter was popular enough in Unix that Microsoft "borrowed" it for inclusion with its text-mode operating system, MS-DOS.

For a filter that generates more output than input, consider the following listing. The code accepts standard input and outputs the hex values for each character. The *printf()* statement generates two-digit hex values.

Listing 4.7   hexfilter01.c

```c
#include <stdio.h>

int main()
{
    int ch;

    while( (ch=getchar()) != EOF )
    {
        printf("%02X ",ch);        ◁──┐  Outputs character
    }                                  │  as two-digit hex byte,
                                       │  with a leading zero
    return(0);
}
```

The code for `hexfilter01.c` works well, but it does have a problem with its output: the two-digit character format appears as a long string of text. Often a text value is split between two lines. A better approach would be to monitor output to avoid splitting a hex value at the end of a line.

EXERCISE 4.3

Assuming that the terminal screen is 80 characters wide, modify the code to `hexfilter01.c` so that output doesn't split a hex value between two lines. Further, when a newline character is encountered, have the line of output terminated with a newline. My solution for this exercise can be found in the GitHub repository as `hexfilter02.c`. Please try this exercise on your own before you peek at my solution.

4.3.2   *Creating a NATO filter*

Chapter 3 covered the NATO phonetic alphabet, which—surprise—can also be applied as a filter. For example, the filter reads standard input, plucking out all the alphabetic characters. For each one, the filter outputs the corresponding NATO term. This program is another example of a filter that does more than a single-character exchange.

To make the phonetic alphabet translation, the code must borrow the `nato[]` array of terms presented in chapter 3. This array is shown in listing 4.8. It's coupled with the standard I/O filter *while* loop. In the loop, the *isalpha()* function detects alphabetic characters. Some math is performed to obtain the proper term offset in the array, which outputs the correct term for each letter processed.

Listing 4.8   nato01.c

```c
#include <stdio.h>
#include <ctype.h>

int main()
{
    char *nato[] = {
        "Alfa", "Bravo", "Charlie", "Delta", "Echo", "Foxtrot",
        "Golf", "Hotel", "India", "Juliett", "Kilo", "Lima",
        "Mike", "November", "Oscar", "Papa", "Quebec", "Romeo",
        "Sierra", "Tango", "Uniform", "Victor", "Whiskey",
        "Xray", "Yankee", "Zulu"
    };
    char ch;

    while( (ch=getchar()) != EOF)
    {
        if(isalpha(ch))
            printf("%s ",nato[toupper(ch)-'A']);
        if( ch=='\n' )
            putchar(ch);
    }
    putchar('\n');

    return(0);
}
```

Translates a character into an offset within the `nato[]` array

Outputs a newline when encountered to keep the output clean

Here's a sample run:

```
$ ./nato
hello
Hotel Echo Lima Lima Oscar
```

It's important to know that any nonalphabetic characters (aside from newline) are ignored by this filter. Ignoring input in a filter is legitimate; a filter need not generate one-to-one output based on input.

4.3.3   *Filtering words*

Filters operate on character I/O, but this limitation doesn't restrict a filter from affecting words, sentences, or other chunks of text. The key is to store input as it arrives. Once the proper text chunks are assembled, such as a word or sentence, the filter can process it.

For example, to slice standard input by word, you write a filter that collects characters until a word boundary—a space, comma, tab, or period, for example—is encountered. The input must be stored, so further testing must be done to ensure that the storage doesn't overflow. Once the buffer contains a word (or whatever size text chunk you need), it can be sent to standard output or manipulated in whatever way the filter needs to massage the data.

In listing 4.9, a 64-character buffer word[] stores words. The *while* loop is split into *if-else* conditions. The *if* test marks the end of a word, capping the word[] buffer with a null character, confirming that a full word is ready to output, and then outputting the word. The *else* test builds the word, ensuring that the buffer doesn't overflow. The result is a filter that pulls out words and sets each one on a line by itself.

Listing 4.9   word_filter.c

The *isspace()* function returns TRUE for whitespace characters, marking the end of a word.

```
#include <stdio.h>
#include <ctype.h>

#define WORDSIZE 64

int main()
{
    char word[WORDSIZE];
    int ch,offset;

    offset = 0;
    while( (ch = getchar()) != EOF)
    {
        if( isspace(ch) )
        {
            word[offset] = '\0';
            if( offset>0 )
                printf("%s\n",word);
            offset = 0;
        }
        else
        {
            word[offset] = ch;
            offset++;
            if( offset==WORDSIZE-1 )
            {
                word[offset] = '\0';
                printf("%s\n",word);
                offset = 0;
            }
        }
    }

    return(0);
}
```

The word size is set here; this way, you can update the buffer size in a single spot, and various other parts of the code are updated to reflect the change.

Initializes the offset value

Always cap your strings!

Ensures that the buffer has text in it to print

Outputs the buffer's contents (a word, hopefully) on a line by itself

Resets the offset

Printable characters are handled here, filling the buffer.

Stores the character

Increments the offset

Checks for potential overflow, a full buffer

Cap the string!

Outputs the word, dumping the buffer

Resets the offset

To build words, the code in word_filter.c replies upon the *isspace()* function, defined in the ctype.h header file. This function returns TRUE when a whitespace character is encountered on input. These characters include space, tab, and newline. These whitespace characters trigger a word boundary, though the code could be modified to account for other characters as well.

Here's a sample run:

```
$ ./word_filter
Is this still the Caesarean Cipher chapter?
Is
this
still
the
Caesarean
Cipher
chapter?
```

Twice in the code you see statements that cap the word[] buffer with a null character:

```
word[offset] = '\0';
```

It's vital that all strings in C end with the null character, \0. Especially when you build your own strings, as is done in the word_filter.c code, confirm that the string that's created is capped. If not, you get an overflow and all kinds of ugly output—and potential bad things happening.

Encoding and decoding

It's easy to confuse the topic of encoding and decoding with encryption. These are similar procedures, but the purpose of encryption is to conceal and safeguard information. Encoding is done for transportation of information that may be too complex for the medium or to translate between different systems or for other innocuous purposes. Regardless, the process of encoding and decoding has the potential to be action packed and full of intrigue.

Well, perhaps not.

Still, back in the early days of computer telecommunications, encoding and decoding were regular occurrences. I remember transferring my first program over a modem: 16 kilobytes that took 16 minutes to transfer. That program consisted of binary data, but it was transported as plain text. It required encoding on the sending end and decoding on the receiving end. Such magic happens today as well, though probably much faster.

To explore the concept of encoding and decoding, regardless of the thrills and dangers, you must:

- Appreciate how characters are represented on computers
- Learn various ASCII encoding tricks
- Play with character representation
- Translate plain text into hex bytes for data transfer
- Reverse translate hex bytes back into text (or data)
- Improve encoding techniques by adding checksums
- Explore the URL encoding method

None of these items is dreary, not like that book on 100 fun and legal home projects you can do with an ironing board. But if you want to know more about encryption, refer to chapter 4.

5.1 The concept of plain text

The computer doesn't know text. The *char* data type is merely a tiny integer, ranging in value from 0 through 255 (*unsigned*) or –128 to 127 (*signed*). It's only the presentation of the *char* data type that makes it look like a character.

In C, the *putchar()* function outputs a value as a character. The function's *man* page declares the function's argument as an integer, though it appears on the standard output device as a character.

The *printf()* function is a bit more understanding of characters. It outputs a *char* data type as a character but only when the %c placeholder is used in the format string. If you substitute %d, the decimal integer output placeholder, the data is output as a number.

But what thing is output? How does the computer know to match a specific value with a given character? The answer comes in the form of the venerable digital acronym, ASCII.

5.1.1 Understanding ASCII

It's important to note that ASCII is pronounced "ass-key." That's right: ass and key. Titter all you like, but if you say, "ask two," everyone will know you're a dork.

It's unimportant to note that ASCII stands for the American Standard Code for Information Interchange. Yes, it's a standard devised by people who sit around all day having fun creating standards. And though the standard was developed in the early 1960s, it wasn't until the mid-1980s that pretty much every computer on the planet began using ASCII codes consistently.

By adopting the ASCII standard for assigning codes to characters, computers can exchange basic information without requiring any translation. Before it was widely adopted in the late 1970s, computers had to run translation programs to get even a text file to read properly from one system to the next. But today, a text file on your overpriced Macintosh is easily readable on my cheap-o Linux box that my friend Don built in the back of his shop for $499.

The way ASCII works is to assign codes, integer values, to common characters and symbols. This translation originated from the telegraph era, where the codes had to be consistent for a message to be translated—encoded and decoded—lest the Hole-in-the-Wall Gang rob the 12:10 yet again because old Hamer McCleary was taking a nap at the Belle Fourche station.

ASCII codes are devised in a clever pattern, which is amazing for any group of humans to produce. The pattern allows for all sorts of fun and creative things to happen, as covered in section 5.1.4. Figure 5.1 lists the ASCII code table in its common, four "stick" presentation. See whether you can spy any of the patterns.

Dec	Oct	Hex	C	Dec	Oct	Hex	C	Dec	Oct	Hex	C	Dec	Oct	Hex	C
0	0	0	–	32	40	20		64	100	40	@	96	140	60	`
1	1	1	–	33	41	21	!	65	101	41	A	97	141	61	a
2	2	2	–	34	42	22	"	66	102	42	B	98	142	62	b
3	3	3	–	35	43	23	#	67	103	43	C	99	143	63	c
4	4	4	–	36	44	24	$	68	104	44	D	100	144	64	d
5	5	5	–	37	45	25	%	69	105	45	E	101	145	65	e
6	6	6	–	38	46	26	&	70	106	46	F	102	146	66	f
7	7	7	–	39	47	27	'	71	107	47	G	103	147	67	g
8	10	8	–	40	50	28	(	72	110	48	H	104	150	68	h
9	11	9	–	41	51	29	)	73	111	49	I	105	151	69	i
10	12	a	–	42	52	2a	*	74	112	4a	J	106	152	6a	j
11	13	b	–	43	53	2b	+	75	113	4b	K	107	153	6b	k
12	14	c	–	44	54	2c	,	76	114	4c	L	108	154	6c	l
13	15	d	–	45	55	2d	–	77	115	4d	M	109	155	6d	m
14	16	e	–	46	56	2e	.	78	116	4e	N	110	156	6e	n
15	17	f	–	47	57	2f	/	79	117	4f	O	111	157	6f	o
16	20	10	–	48	60	30	0	80	120	50	P	112	160	70	p
17	21	11	–	49	61	31	1	81	121	51	Q	113	161	71	q
18	22	12	–	50	62	32	2	82	122	52	R	114	162	72	r
19	23	13	–	51	63	33	3	83	123	53	S	115	163	73	s
20	24	14	–	52	64	34	4	84	124	54	T	116	164	74	t
21	25	15	–	53	65	35	5	85	125	55	U	117	165	75	u
22	26	16	–	54	66	36	6	86	126	56	V	118	166	76	v
23	27	17	–	55	67	37	7	87	127	57	W	119	167	77	w
24	30	18	–	56	70	38	8	88	130	58	X	120	170	78	x
25	31	19	–	57	71	39	9	89	131	59	Y	121	171	79	y
26	32	1a	–	58	72	3a	:	90	132	5a	Z	122	172	7a	z
27	33	1b	–	59	73	3b	;	91	133	5b	[	123	173	7b	{
28	34	1c	–	60	74	3c	<	92	134	5c	\	124	174	7c		
29	35	1d	–	61	75	3d	=	93	135	5d	]	125	175	7d	}
30	36	1e	–	62	76	3e	>	94	136	5e	^	126	176	7e	~
31	37	1f	–	63	77	3f	?	95	137	5f	_	127	177	7f	

Figure 5.1   The ASCII table showing decimal, octal, hexadecimal, and character values

From figure 5.1, you see that ASCII codes range from 0 through 127. These are binary values 000–0000 through 111–1111. For the C language *char* data type, these values are all positive whether the variable is *signed* or *unsigned*.

Each of the four columns, or "sticks," in the ASCII table (refer to figure 5.1) represents a different category of character types. Again, the codes are organized, probably due to some education from earlier abominable computer character codes that have since been taken out, placed in a dumpster, and set on fire with a jet engine.

The first stick consists of nonprinting control codes, which is why its output looks so dull in figure 5.1. Read more about the control codes in section 5.1.2.

Characters in the second stick in the ASCII table were selected for sorting purposes. The first few characters echo those on a teletype machine, the shifted number keys. These still hold true today for the most part: Shift+1 is the ! (exclamation point), Shift+3 is the # (hash), and so on.

The third stick contains uppercase letters, plus a few symbols.

The fourth stick contains lowercase letters, plus the rest of the symbols.

Miracles and magic surrounding the ASCII table and these codes are covered in the next few sections.

EXERCISE 5.1

Having an ASCII table handy is vital to any programmer. Rather than sell you my handsome ASCII wall chart on Etsy, I decided that you must code your own ASCII table. Make the output appear exactly as shown in figure 5.1—which happens to be the output from my own ASCII program and looks like the wall chart. I often run my ASCII program as a reference because such information is useful and a program is a quick way to keep it handy, though I'm not making any money on Etsy.

The source code for my solution to this exercise is found in this book's online repository as `asciitable01.c`. But please try creating your own before you just ape everything that I did.

5.1.2 Exploring the control codes

I find the first stick of ASCII codes to be the most interesting, from both a historical and hilarious perspective. The control code names are adorable! "End of Text"? Try using that one in a meeting sometime, but just say "Control C" instead. Some people might get it.

"End of Text" is the official name of the Ctrl+C control code, ASCII code 3. Table 5.1 lists the details. Some of the codes or their keyboard equivalents might be familiar to you.

Table 5.1 ASCII control codes

Decimal	Octal	Hex	Name	Ctrl	Esc	Definition
0	0	00	NULL	^@	\0	Null character
1	1	01	SOH	^A		Start of heading
2	2	02	STX	^B		Start of text
3	3	03	ETX	^C		End of text
4	4	04	EOT	^D		End of transmission
5	5	05	ENQ	^E		Enquiry, "Who is?"
6	6	06	ACK	^F		Acknowledgment
7	7	07	BEL	^G	\a	Bell
8	10	08	BS	^H	\b	Backspace
9	11	09	HT	^I	\t	Horizontal tab
10	12	0A	LF	^J	\n	Line feed
11	13	0B	VT	^K	\v	Vertical tab

Table 5.1   **ASCII control codes** *(continued)*

Decimal	Octal	Hex	Name	Ctrl	Esc	Definition
12	14	0C	FF	^L	\f	Form feed
13	15	0D	CR	^M	\r	Carriage return
14	16	0E	SO	^N		Shift out
15	17	0F	SI	^O		Shift in
16	20	10	DLE	^P		Data link escape
17	21	11	DC1	^Q		Device control one, XON
18	22	12	DC2	^R		Device control two
19	23	13	DC3	^S		Device control three, XOFF
20	24	14	DC4	^T		Device control four
21	25	15	NAK	^U		Negative acknowledgment
22	26	16	SYN	^V		Synchronous idle
23	27	17	ETB	^W		End transmission block
24	30	18	CAN	^X		Cancel
25	31	19	EM	^Y		End of medium
26	32	1A	SUB	^Z		Substitute
27	33	1B	ESC	^[	\e	Escape
28	34	1C	FS	^\		File separator
29	35	1D	GS	^]		Group separator
30	36	1E	RS	^^		Record separator
31	37	1F	US	^_		Unit separator

Table 5.1 lists decimal, octal (base 8), and hexadecimal values for each ASCII code. The Name column shows the ancient teletype name, the code's original and forgotten purpose. Still, some of these control codes are used today: the computer's beep remains control code 7, the "bell," keyboard equivalent Ctrl+G and escape sequence \a (for alert or alarm).

The Ctrl column shows the control key combinations used in the terminal window. Modern descriptions use the word *Ctrl* for control, though the grizzled, sandal-wearing Unix coders of yore prefer the caret character, ^. This expression explains why pressing Ctrl+D as the Linux EOF character outputs ^D in a terminal window. And this character's original name is "End of Transmission," which makes sense. (Don't press Ctrl+D just to see the ^D character appear; doing so closes the terminal window.)

Some of the control key shortcuts map directly to other keys on the keyboard, primarily for use in a terminal window. For example, Ctrl+M is the Enter/Return key: pressing Ctrl+M is the same as pressing the Enter key. Other control keys mapped include:

- Ctrl+I to Tab
- Ctrl+H to Backspace
- Ctrl+[to Esc

These shortcuts may not work in all circumstances, but table 5.1 shows how they're mapped.

The Esc column in table 5.1 lists the C escape character equivalent for some of the common control codes. Remember, any code can be specified as an escape character sequence in C if you use the format \x*nn* where *nn* is the character's ASCII code in hexadecimal.

Many of the control keys have lost their purpose in a modern computer. Back in the teletype days—from which the current terminal window in Linux has its roots—they were significant. In fact, the Ctrl+S/Ctrl+Q (XON, XOFF) keys still work to pause and resume a scrolling display of text. It's just that modern terminals display text so rapidly that using these keys today is pointless.

Be careful when outputting a control character in your code. Some of them have predictable functions, specifically those in the Esc column in table 5.1. These escape sequences are useful in C. But sending a weirdo control code to standard output can potentially mess up the display. For example, on some terminals, outputting ^L (code 12, Form Feed) clears the display. When sent to a printer—even a modern printer—^L ejects a sheet of paper.

As a tip—because I know someday you're going to try outputting a control code on purpose or perhaps accidentally—if a control code whacks out the terminal display, issue the *reset* command. Type **reset** and press Enter, and the terminal attempts to recover itself from however you messed it up.

The final control code doesn't appear in the last stick of the ASCII table (refer to table 5.1). This is character code 127, often called Del (Delete) or Rub Out. Like codes 0 through 31, it's nonprintable, but its output doesn't mess up the display. This character is a holdover from the teletype era, where it was used as a backup-and-erase character; the Backspace code (8 or ^H) merely moves the cursor and is a nondestructive backup.

What of the other 128 character codes in a byte?

Even back in the microcomputer era, a byte of data consisted of 256 possible codes, 0 through 255. ASCII characters defined the standard for codes 0 through 127. The other codes were nonstandard—not defined by ASCII, though many early computer users would mislabel them as such.

(continued)

On the IBM PC, codes 128 through 255 were referred to as Extended ASCII. These codes output consistent characters for all PC compatibles (more or less), but not for an Apple II, Commodore 64, or any other popular and wimpy systems of the era. Even then, it was possible to change the Extended ASCII codes by swapping in a new code page on the PC. This diversity of characters caused massive confusion. Fortunately, the state of the computer industry back then was consistent massive confusion, so few people noticed.

Today, any character code above 127 is standardized according to Unicode. These codes define just about every character you've never seen nor heard of. Refer to chapter 8 for additional and scintillating details.

5.1.3 *Generating noncharacter output*

When output as a character, *char* variables appear as a character. And thank goodness: the days of computers showing raw data are over—except for the movies, where computers still feature blinking lights and displays that output row upon row of numbers. Then again, monitors in movies make noise when displaying text and "hackers" type endlessly at a computer where they should be using a mouse. Silly Hollywood.

Using conversion characters other than %c, you can write code that outputs *char* data as decimal or hexadecimal values—even using the same variable:

```
printf("%c = %d = %x\n",ch,ch,ch);
```

In this statement, variable ch is output thrice: once as its character value, once as a decimal integer, and again as a hexadecimal integer. If you're into octal, you can use %o to output the value in base 8 as well. In fact, if you wrote code for exercise 5.1, you probably used a *printf()* statement along these lines.

But what about binary?

The standard C library lacks a binary output function. Therefore, it's your job to write one. Or you can just rely upon what I use, my *binString()* function.

Listing 5.1 shows the 8-bit version of my *binString()* function, concocted to output values stored in the *char* data type. The function uses the bitwise & operator to determine whether the far left bit in the character byte is on (1). If so, the character '1' is placed into the b[] buffer; otherwise, '0' is set. The value in variable a is then shifted one bit position to the left, and the operation repeats. As the bits are checked, string b[] is filled with ones and zeros. This string is declared *static*, so its value can be returned and the binary string used by whatever statement calls the *binString()* function.

Listing 5.1   The 8-bit *binString()* function

```
char *binString(char a)
{
    static char b[9];         ◄─   The string is static so that its value is retained; nine
    int i;                         characters allow for an 8-bit byte, plus another
                                   element for the terminating null character.
```

Initializes the index variable →
```
    i = 0;
    while( i<8 )
    {
        b[i] = a&0x80 ? '1' : '0';
        a <<= 1;
        i++;
    }
    b[i] = '\0';

    return(b);
}
```

← **Loops for each bit in the 8-bit byte**

← **The ternary operator sets a 1 or 0 into the string, depending on the value of the far left bit in variable a.**

← **Variable a's value is shifted one bit position to the left.**

← **At this point, i is equal to 8, so the string is capped.**

The 8-bit *binString()* function can be woven into code to output values in the ASCII table in binary, which is yet another way to generate noncharacter output—more interesting than dull decimal, sexy hex, or outdated octal.

To see *binString()* function in action, refer to the source code file `binascii01.c` included in this book's online repository. Its program outputs an ASCII table with binary data.

As a nerd, I enjoy the patterns created by binary values and how they relate to hexadecimal. In fact, I find it easy to convert between hex and binary, often doing so in my head. This relationship is illustrated in table 5.2, which makes it easy to understand some common ASCII conversion tricks revealed in the next section.

Table 5.2   Binary to hexadecimal conversions

Binary	Hex	Binary	Hex
0000	0	1000	8
0001	1	1001	9
0010	2	1010	A
0011	3	1011	B
0100	4	1100	C
0101	5	1101	D
0110	6	1110	E
0111	7	1111	F

Figure 5.2 illustrates binary bit positions, which help continue my nerd-gushing adoration of the binary-hexadecimal affair. For example, note that even numbers have zero set as the first binary digit. (Like decimal, binary digits are ordered from right to left, lowest to highest.) Odd values have the 1 digit in the first position.

Other things I find cool: binary 1010 is hex A, which is 10 decimal. The double "10" digits is a nice clue. Binary 1011 is hex B, or 11 decimal. Other patterns are obvious if you examine table 5.2 and figure 5.2—but be wary of becoming a nerd, too, if you overly enjoy such things.

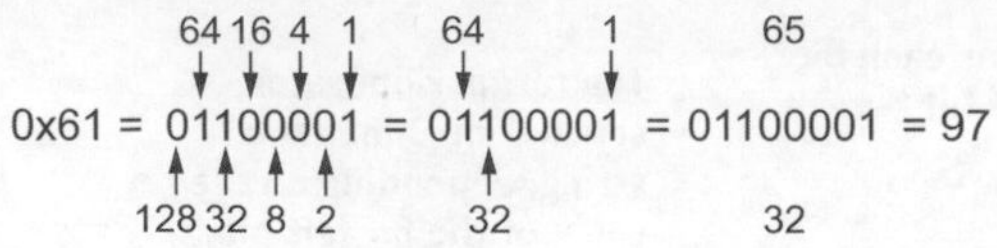

Figure 5.2   Bit positions in a byte and how they factor out into a value

5.1.4   *Playing with ASCII conversion tricks*

The folks who laid out the ASCII table, assigning codes to characters, were clever—for humans. Either they were towering geniuses who appreciated knowledge as they coordinated values and characters, or they just hit the luck jackpot. I don't care either way. But I will take advantage of the serendipity.

Oh, and I loathe the word *serendipity.*

One of the tricks I take advantage of is the way digits 0 through 9 are mapped to hex values 0x30 through 0x39. This arrangement makes it easy to perform simple math on the character values to translate them into numeric values. For example:

```
printf("%d\n",'9' - '0');
```

This *printf()* statement subtracts '0' from '9', which look like character values but are seen by the compiler as 0x39 – 0x30. The result is output as decimal value nine, which is what '9' represents.

If *char* variable a contains a digit character, you can extract its integer value with:

```
b = a - '0';
```

You can pull a similar trick with letters of the alphabet to get them in the range of 0 though 25, though the hexadecimal value of A or a isn't as sexy. For example, assume an uppercase letter is in *char* variable ch:

```
offset = ch - 'A';
```

Here, the value of offset is equal to the number of the uppercase letter in ch, zero through 25 for A through Z. An example of this operation at work appears in chapter 3, where the nato[] array is referenced by using a letter of the alphabet. See nato01.c and nato02.c in this book's online repository for chapter 3.

ASCII table sticks one and three (refer to table 5.1) show the same characters for a different run of numbers. The control codes in the first stick use characters ^@ through ^_ (underscore) and the third stick uses character @ through _ (underscore). So, one way to express a control code is to add hex value 0x40 to the character's value for output. In the following *printf()* statement, *char* variable cc holds a control code value (0x00 through 0x1F), which is output as ^@ through ^_:

```
printf("Control code: ^%c\n",cc+0x40);
```

The following statement reflects another way to express the statement with the same output:

```
printf("Control code: ^%c\n",cc+'@');
```

If you compare the ASCII table's third and fourth sticks (again in figure 5.1), you see that the upper- and lowercase characters differ by exactly 32 or 0x20. This arrangement allows for some interesting character manipulations to switch between upper- and lowercase letters:

- To convert an uppercase letter to lowercase, you reset the sixth bit in the byte.
- To convert a lowercase letter to uppercase, you set the sixth bit in the byte.

Figure 5.3 illustrates the bit setting and resetting process with the letters A and a. The same relationship holds for all letters of the Latin alphabet: setting or resetting the sixth bit changes a character between upper- and lowercase.

```
A   65   0x41   0010-0001
                   ↑
                   ↓                Figure 5.3   How the sixth bit in
a   97   0x61   0110-0001           a byte affects letter case
```

To magically manipulate the sixth bit in a byte, you use a bitwise logical operator, & (AND) or | (OR). You most likely skipped over these operators when you first learned C. For shame.

To convert uppercase to lowercase, you must set the sixth bit. This operation is handled by the | (OR) operator on the byte's sixth bit. The expression is:

```
c = c | 0x20;
```

Above, the uppercase letter in *char* variable c is converted to its lowercase equivalent. The code can also be abbreviated as:

```
c |= 0x20;
```

To convert a lowercase letter to uppercase, you must reset (change to zero) the sixth bit in the byte. To handle this operation, use the & bitwise operator, which masks out bits:

```
c = c & 0xdf;
```

Also:

```
c &= 0xdf;
```

The binary representation of 0x20 is `01000000`. The binary representation of 0xdf is `10111111`.

The source code shown in listing 5.2 demonstrates these techniques. The sample string in `sentence[]` is processed twice. The first time, a *while* loop plucks uppercase characters from the string, converting them to lowercase by the bitwise `| 0x20` operation. The second *while* loop targets lowercase letters, converting them to uppercase with the `& 0xdf` operation. Pointer `s` is used to work through the `sentence[]` array one character at a time.

Listing 5.2   Source code for `casetricks01.c`

```
#include <stdio.h>

int main()
{
    char sentence[] = "ASCII makes my heart beat faster\n";
    char *s;

    s = sentence;
    while(*s)
    {
        if( *s>='A' && *s<='Z' )          Filters out
            putchar( *s | 0x20 );         uppercase text
        else
            putchar(*s);                  Outputs the
        s++;                              lowercase
    }                                     character

    s = sentence;
    while(*s)
    {
        if( *s>='a' && *s<='z' )          Filters out
            putchar( *s & 0xdf );         lowercase text
        else
            putchar(*s);                  Outputs the
        s++;                              uppercase
    }                                     character

    return(0);
}
```

Here is sample output:

```
ascii makes my heart beat faster
ASCII MAKES MY HEART BEAT FASTER
```

In my code, I often revert to using the ctype functions *tolower()* or *toupper()* to make the conversion. But these bitwise operations perform the trick just as well, with the bonus that they make your code look super cryptic.

5.2   The hex encoder/decoder

My first telecommunications file transfer took 16 minutes. It was between a friend's TRS-80 computer and mine, using an analog modem over standard phone lines. The transfer speed was 300 BPS, if you want to feign an appalled expression.

The data transferred was plain text. It could have been binary because, quite honestly, the phone line doesn't care which bits in a byte represent characters. Still, I sat for 15 minutes watching jibber jabber flow down my screen and magically transform into a program: the original binary was encoded as two-digit hexadecimal values, transmitted, and then another program on my computer digested the hex bytes, converting them back into binary data.

Another example of this hexadecimal encoding was found in the computer magazines of the era. Articles showcased amazing programs that you could type in; the hex bytes were listed on the pages. Hobbyists eagerly typed byte after byte into their keyboards, a hex decoder program gobbling up all the digits and creating a binary program that—fingers crossed—ran the first time and performed some wondrous task. Those were the days.

By the way, hex encoding isn't encryption nor is it compression. It's merely a way to express binary data in a printable manner.

5.2.1   Writing a simple hex encoder/decoder

The most important part about converting ASCII—and binary—to hex is doing so in a format that's reliably converted back. After all, some type of verification is required to ensure that the data was successfully backed out of the encoding garage.

One way to translate any information into hex is to write a filter, such as the one shown in the next listing. (Refer to chapter 4 if you need brushing up on filters.) The filter processes each byte (*int* ch) input. The *printf()* statement's conversion character %02X outputs the byte as a 2-digit hex value with a leading zero, if necessary. The code outputs a newline only after all input is processed, which means the translation is one long string of hex bytes.

Listing 5.3   Source code for `hexenfilter01.c`

```
#include <stdio.h>

int main()
{
    int ch;

    while( (ch=getchar()) != EOF )
    {
        printf("%02X",ch);
    }
    putchar('\n');

    return(0);
}
```

Here's a sample run at the command prompt, using standard input (the keyboard), assuming that the program name is *hexe* and it exists in the current directory:

```
$ ./hexe
Hello there, hex!
48656C6C6F2074686572652C20686578210A
```

Figure 5.4 illustrates what's going on with the output, how each character of input is translated into the hex bytes.

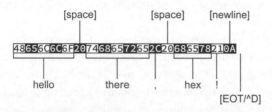

Figure 5.4   What's going on with the output of a simple hex encoder

This filter can process more than plain text. You can redirect input from any file type, including a binary executable:

```
$ ./hexe < hexe
```

The problem with this serial hex digit approach is that the output is useful only to the decoder program. I wouldn't expect a user to type in a long string of hex digits. Such a chore would be a nightmare.

To decode the long-string-of-text hex filter, you must write a program that properly translates 2-digit hex values into their byte-value equivalent. The assumption made in such a program is that it's receiving the exact type of information that the encoder generates—which is a huge assumption, and one I'd never make in any program I planned on releasing as a practical utility.

A big part of the translation is identifying and converting hexadecimal digits into their integer values. To accomplish this task, I present the *tohex()* function, shown in the following listing. It hunts down ASCII characters 0 through 9 and A through F, translating them into their integer equivalents. Anything out of range generates a return value of −1. (The function doesn't convert lowercase hex digits, which isn't necessary for decoding in this example.)

Listing 5.4   The *tohex()* function.

```
int tohex(c)
{
    if( c>='0' && c<='9' )
        return(c-'0');
    if( c>='A' && c<='F' )
        return(c-'A'+0xA);
    return(-1);
}
```

Eliminates the digits 0 through 9

Returns the digit's integer value

Eliminates the letters *A* through *F*

Returns the character's hex value: 'A'==0x0A

All other characters return −1.

The *tohex()* function fights only part of the battle. The rest of the job is to read standard input, assembling every two hex digits into a byte. To accomplish this task, I wrote an endless *while* loop, shown next. It fetches the two characters, sticks them together, and then outputs the resulting value, which can be binary or plain text.

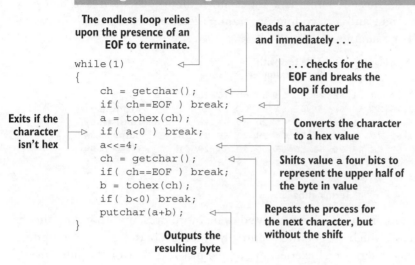

Listing 5.5   Decoding the endless line of a hex filter

The endless loop relies upon the presence of an EOF to terminate.

Reads a character and immediately . . .

```
while(1)
{
    ch = getchar();
    if( ch==EOF ) break;
    a = tohex(ch);
    if( a<0 ) break;
    a<<=4;
    ch = getchar();
    if( ch==EOF ) break;
    b = tohex(ch);
    if( b<0) break;
    putchar(a+b);
}
```

. . . checks for the EOF and breaks the loop if found

Exits if the character isn't hex

Converts the character to a hex value

Shifts value a four bits to represent the upper half of the byte in value

Repeats the process for the next character, but without the shift

Outputs the resulting byte

The entire batch of code is available in this book's online repository as `hexdefilter01.c`. It can be run straight-up, assuming you know a smattering of hex values to type in:

```
$ ./hexd
48656C6C6F2C20776F726C64210A
Hello, world!
```

The program stops when it encounters a nonhex digit or when the EOF is encountered, which helps match it up perfectly with the output from the `hexenfilter01.c` program. In fact—the true test of encoding and decoding—you can pump output through both filters and end up with the original data:

```
$ echo "This proves whether it works!" | ./hexe | ./hexd
This proves whether it works!
```

Text is echoed to standard input but first piped through the *hexe* (`hexenfilter01.c`) program, assumed to be in the current directory. This encoded output is then piped through the *hexd* (`hexdefilter01.c`) program. The output is the original text.

These simple filters process information, whipping it into one long string of hexadecimal characters. This type of hex encoding may work for transferring a silly game on a 300 BPS modem in the last century, but good luck getting a user to type in all those bytes without crossing their eyes. No, additional formatting is necessary for a better hex encoder/decoder.

5.2.2 *Coding a better hex encoder/decoder*

I prefer a hex encoding method that shows its details in a neat, orderly manner. Especially back in the old days, if you were typing in row upon row of hex bytes published in a computer magazine to input a program, you didn't need to see the Great Wall of Hex.

A good approach to hex-encoding data, especially if the information is to be presented both for a human and a decoding program, is to format the output in neat rows and columns. For example:

```
                              Title text with
                              version number
HEX ENCODE v1.0         ⊲
 54 68 69 73 20 69 73 20 61 6E 20 65 78 61 6D 70 6C 65
 20 6F 66 20 68 65 78 20 65 6E 63 6F 64 69 6E 67 20 69    Neatly and
 6E 20 61 20 66 6F 72 6D 61 74 74 65 64 20 6D 61 6E 6E    consistently
 65 72 2E 20 49 20 61 70 70 6C 61 75 64 20 79 6F 75 20    outputs rows
 66 6F 72 20 62 65 69 6E 67 20 61 20 6E 65 72 64 20 61    of hex values
 6E 64 20 64 65 63 6F 64 69 6E 67 20 74 68 69 73 20 65
 78 61 6D 70 6C 65 2E 0A
HEX ENCODE END     ⊲    Terminating line
```

This output is from a filter, though it's formatted to be more presentable and predictable. It still has its flaws, which I'll get into eventually, but it's a better encoder despite the data output being a series of hexadecimal digits, just like that of the filter presented in the preceding section.

Listing 5.6 shows the source code for the *Hex Encode 1.0* program. It's based on a typical I/O filter, though it formats output based on a certain number of hex digits per line, shown in the code as defined constant BYTES_PER_LINE. Variable bytes tracks the digits output, ensuring that the hex digit pairs stay consistent line by line. This value is reset when the number of digits output equals the defined constant BYTES_PER_LINE, and a new line of hex digits is output. The final line output marks the end of encoding.

Listing 5.6 Source code for `hexencode01.c`

```c
#include <stdio.h>              Set this value as a
                                defined constant so that
#define BYTES_PER_LINE 18   ⊲   it can be updated easily.

int main()
{
    int ch,bytes;          Initializes the
                           byte counter
    bytes = 0;        ⊲                     Outputs the header
    printf("HEX ENCODE v1.0\n");        ⊲  line before processing
    while( (ch=getchar()) != EOF )         standard input
    {
        printf(" %02X",ch);
        bytes++;                            Checks for the
        if( bytes == BYTES_PER_LINE)   ⊲    end of the line
```

```
            {
                putchar('\n');          ◁───── If so, outputs a newline . . .
                bytes = 0;              ◁──┐
            }                             └──┘ . . . and resets the byte counter
        }
        printf("\nHEX ENCODE END\n");    ◁──┐
                                            │ After processing standard
        return(0);                          │ input (including the EOF),
}                                           │ outputs the tail line
```

The hex-encoding code works like any filter, waiting for the EOF or, when using standard input, a press of the Ctrl+D key to terminate. Here is sample output:

```
$ echo "Hello, World!" | ./hexencode
HEX ENCODE v1.0
 48 65 6C 6C 6F 2C 20 57 6F 72 6C 64 21 0A
HEX ENCODE END
```

Writing the encoding program is the easy part. More difficult is decoding, where you must properly interpret the format to convert the hex digits back into bytes. As with any complex coding contraption, I accomplish such a task one step at a time.

The first step to writing the hex decoder is to write a filter that processes a line of input at a time. This proto-program is shown in the next listing. It's incomplete as far as decoding is concerned. It extracts a line of text from standard input and stores it in the line[] buffer. The buffer is output once it's filled, which is dull. Still, future versions of the program will use the line[] buffer to process the encoded values.

Listing 5.7 Source code for `hexdecode01.c`

```
#include <stdio.h>
                                          Calculates the buffer size for the number
                                          of bytes times the number of spaces
#define BYTES_PER_LINE 18                 used, plus one for the null character
#define LENGTH (BYTES_PER_LINE*3+1)   ◁──┘

int main()
{
    char line[LENGTH];
    int x,ch;

    x = 0;
    while( (ch=getchar()) != EOF )   ┌─ Stores incoming
    {                                │  characters in the
        line[x] = ch;        ◁───────┘  buffer
Increments  x++;
the offset └─▷ if( ch=='\n' || x==LENGTH)   ◁──┐ Checks for newline (as the decoded
        {                                      │ file is formatted) or a full buffer
            if( line[x-1]=='\n')      ◁──┐
                line[x-1] = '\0';        │ Replaces the newline with a
            else                         │ null character; otherwise,
                line[x] = '\0';          │ caps the string
```

```
        printf("%s\n",line);
        x = 0;
    }
  }

  return(0);
}
```

◁——┐ **Outputs the line,
     unmodified**

As written, the source code for hexdecode01.c processes any input line by line. The lines are truncated at LENGTH number of characters, which is calculated as the exact length of lines output by the *hexencode* program shown earlier. No other processing is done on the incoming data, so the program's output looks exactly like whatever is input. Here, you see the file sample.txt, created by the *hexencode* program, which is output as is by the *hexdecode* program:

```
$ ./hexdecode < sample.txt
HEX ENCODE v1.0
 54 68 69 73 20 69 73 20 61 6E 20 65 78 61 6D 70 6C 65
 20 6F 66 20 68 65 78 20 65 6E 63 6F 64 69 6E 67 20 69
 6E 20 61 20 66 6F 72 6D 61 74 74 65 64 20 6D 61 6E 6E
 65 72 2E 20 49 20 61 70 70 6C 61 75 64 20 79 6F 75 20
 66 6F 72 20 62 65 69 6E 67 20 61 20 6E 65 72 64 20 61
 6E 64 20 64 65 63 6F 64 69 6E 67 20 74 68 69 73 20 65
 78 61 6D 70 6C 65 2E 0A
HEX ENCODE END
```

The program works, so the code accomplished the first step in the process. To improve the code, the next change confirms that the input data is formatted properly. After all, this is a decoding program for a specific encoded data format. This improvement takes advantage of the *hexencode* program's first and last lines of output (shown in the sample output): the initial line HEX ENCODE 1.0 must be detected or else the file is improperly formatted and no further processing is necessary. Also, the final line, HEX ENCODE END, is tested to determine when line processing is over.

Several small chunks of code must be added to hexdecode01.c to make these improvements. First, the new code uses the *exit()* and *strncmp()* functions, which require the inclusion of two header files:

```
#include <stdlib.h>
#include <string.h>
```

A new variable declaration is required, pointer r. This pointer holds the return value from the *fgets()* function, which is used to determine whether input is valid:

```
char *r
```

The variable declarations are followed by a chunk of code designed to read the initial line of text. The *fgets()* function reads the line from standard input (stdin), which is then tested with an *if* statement. If the return value from *fgets()* is NULL or the string doesn't compare with the required hex-encoding header, an error message is output and the program terminates:

The first line of input is gobbled up.   **fgets() returns NULL on invalid input; otherwise, the strncmp() function performs an exact comparison on the first line of text versus the required text.**

```
r = fgets(line,LENGTH,stdin);
if( r==NULL || strncmp(line,"HEX ENCODE",10)!=0 )
{
    fprintf(stderr,"Invalid HEX ENCODE data\n");
    exit(1);
}
```

An error message is sent to the standard error device to avoid output confusion.

I omitted version testing on the first line of text, which I'm saving for a later improvement to the code, covered in the next section.

The final chunk of text is added in the *while* loop, just before the *printf()* statement that outputs the value of line[]. The statements test for the terminating line in the formatted hex encoding. If found, the loop is broken without outputting the final line:

```
if( strncmp(line,"HEX ENCODE END",13)==0 )
    break;
```

All these modifications are included in the source code file hexdecode02.c, available in this book's online repository.

When compiled and run, the output is similar to the earlier program, but an improperly formatted hex encode file is identified right away. So, if you run the program on its own source code file, you see this output:

```
$ ./hexdecode < hexdecode02.c
Invalid HEX ENCODE data
```

Otherwise, the output looks the same as the first version. The hex byte lines are read and output with no further processing:

```
$ ./hexdecode < sample.txt
 54 68 69 73 20 69 73 20 61 6E 20 65 78 61 6D 70 6C 65
 20 6F 66 20 68 65 78 20 65 6E 63 6F 64 69 6E 67 20 69
 6E 20 61 20 66 6F 72 6D 61 74 74 65 64 20 6D 61 6E 6E
 65 72 2E 20 49 20 61 70 70 6C 61 75 64 20 79 6F 75 20
 66 6F 72 20 62 65 69 6E 67 20 61 20 6E 65 72 64 20 61
 6E 64 20 64 65 63 6F 64 69 6E 67 20 74 68 69 73 20 65
 78 61 6D 70 6C 65 2E 0A
```

The final improvement is to process the hex digits, translating them into values. This change requires only one new variable and one additional chunk of statements. The new variable is integer hex, which can be added to the existing *int* variable declarations:

```
int x,ch,hex;
```

To translate the hexadecimal character pairs into bytes, the *while* loop's *printf()* statement is replaced with a nested *while* loop. This inner loop processes the line[] buffer, parsing out the hex digit pairs. I use the *strtok()* function to handle the parsing or "tokenizing," if that's what the *tok* stands for. Using this function saves a lot of overhead, reducing the code by several statements.

Within the nested *while* loop, a *sscanf()* function translates the parsed hex digits, which are now considered a 2-character string, into an integer value. The value generated is sent to standard output. The process repeats until the entire line is processed, which is the beauty of the *strtok()* function:

Parses the string (input line of text), separating its content by spaces

As long as the *strtok()* function returns a non-NULL value, loops

```
r = strtok(line," ");
while(r)
{
    sscanf(r,"%02X",&hex);
    printf("%c",hex);
    r = strtok(NULL," ");
}
```

Translates the 2-character hex string into an integer value

Outputs the integer value (which can be non-ASCII)

Keeps scanning the same string

This final modification to the code is available in the repository as hexdecode03.c. It completes the project. The resulting program, which I've named *hexdecode*, can properly decode the data encoded by the *hexencode* program.

To put the program to the test, I encoded and then decoded the program file itself. The first step is to encode the program file, saving the output for use later:

```
$ ./hexencode < hexdecode > hexdecode.hex
```

This command processes the binary data in the *hexdecode* program file. The output is redirected to a new file named hexdecode.hex. This file is plain text but formatted as shown throughout this section: with a header, rows of hex digits, and a tail.

To decode the file and translate it back into binary data, use this command:

```
cat hexdecode.hex | ./hexdecode > hexdecode.bin
```

The *cat* command outputs the encoded file, hexdecode.hex, created earlier. This output (which is plain text) is piped through the *hexdecode* program. The result—now binary data, so standard output looks ugly—is redirected into a new file, hexdecode.bin.

To ensure that both the original hexdecode program file and the encoded/decoded data file hexdecode.bin are identical, I use the *diff* command:

```
diff hexdecode hexdecode.bin
```

Because the *diff* program generates no output, it's confirmed that the original binary file was encoded into a text file of hexadecimal character pairs *and* successfully decoded back into its original binary format. The *hexencode/hexdecode* filters work. Then again, I wouldn't have written all this stuff if they didn't. No spoilers.

5.2.3   *Adding a wee bit of error-checking*

I was delighted with my original efforts for the hexencode/hexdecode series of filters. That's until I started looking at the encoded information and trying to figure out how it could be messed up. After all, upon successful creation of any program, you as a C coder must immediately figure out how to break it.

Consider that you're a teen with a computer (and no social life, natch), and you're eager to type in the new *Laser Blaster* game fresh from the pages of *Compute!* magazine. You type line after line, hex digit after digit. Did you screw up? If so, at what point did the mistake happen?

To help track entry errors, early hex dumps in magazines offered a checksum digit at the end of each row. This checksum is merely the total of all the byte values in the row, sometimes modulo 0x100 to make it look like another two digit hex value. When the user typed in the code, they could run the checksum (or their hex decoder program would) to determine whether a mistake was made and which line had to be reread and whether the entire operation had to start all over again. Yes, this is one reason Jolt Cola came in 12-packs.

The source code for checksum01.c is shown in the next listing. It demonstrates how to perform a simple type of checksum. Each successive value from array hexbytes[] is accumulated in *int* variable checksum. This result is output modulo 0x100, which keeps it byte-size for consistency.

Listing 5.8   Source code for checksum01.c

```c
#include <stdio.h>

int main()
{
    int hexbytes[] = {
        0x41, 0x42, 0x43, 0x44, 0x45,        Just a random assortment
        0x46, 0x47, 0x48, 0x49, 0x4A         of hex values; 10 total
    };
    int x,checksum;                   Initializes the checksum
                                      variable here
    checksum = 0;
    for( x=0; x<10; x++ )                      Accumulates
    {                                          the totals
        checksum += hexbytes[x];
        printf(" %02X",hexbytes[x]);
    }
    printf("\nChecksum = %02X\n",checksum%0x100);      Outputs the checksum,
                                                       but limited to a char-
    return(0);                                         size value
}
```

Writing a program like checksum01.c is an approach I often take to solving a larger programming project. Whenever I add a new feature to any program, I want to ensure that it works. If instead I add the feature to existing code, the process may introduce other problems that complicate bug hunting.

Here's sample output from the `checksum01.c` program:

```
41 42 43 44 45 46 47 48 49 4A
Checksum = B7
```

More complex methods exist to calculate a checksum, including some clever variations that can even tell you which specific value is incorrect. But never mind!

Adding a checksum to the *hexencode/hexdecode* programs requires that both source code files are modified. Yes, it's version 2.0, now featuring (modest) error checking. So, not only must both programs calculate and output a checksum byte, but the version number must also be updated and verified. If you want to go further, you can have the *hexdecode* program still decode version 1.0 files without applying the checksum. More work to do!

EXERCISE 5.2

Update the source code to `hexencode01.c` to add a checksum hex value to be output at the end of each row. Don't forget the final row's checksum (hint, hint). Oh, and update the version number to 2.0. My solution is found in this book's online repository as `hexencode02.c`.

The code for your solution to exercise 5.2 may not look exactly as mine does, but the output should resemble something like this:

```
HEX ENCODE v2.0
 54 68 69 73 20 69 73 20 61 6E 20 65 78 61 6D 70 6C 65 8F
 20 6F 66 20 68 65 78 20 65 6E 63 6F 64 69 6E 67 20 69 4A
 6E 20 61 20 66 6F 72 6D 61 74 74 65 64 20 6D 61 6E 6E 9F
 65 72 2E 20 49 20 61 70 70 6C 61 75 64 20 79 6F 75 20 12
 66 6F 72 20 62 65 69 6E 67 20 61 20 6E 65 72 64 20 61 37
 6E 64 20 64 65 63 6F 64 69 6E 67 20 74 68 69 73 20 65 8C
 78 61 6D 70 6C 65 2E 0A BF
HEX ENCODE END
```

This output is like the program's first (1.0) version's output, but an extra hex value appears at the end of each row. This value is the checksum.

Decoding this data, turning it back into binary, requires an update to the *hexdecode* program, obviously: first, it must check the version number. If the encoded data shows "v2.0," the decoder must examine the byte value and confirm that the line was properly decoded. If not, decoding stops and the information is flagged as invalid. And, yes, I'm making you perform this change on your own as the next exercise.

EXERCISE 5.3

Convert the source code for `hexdecode03.c` to handle the extra checksum byte set there by the program created from `hexencode01.c` (exercise 5.2). You must properly account for and use the checksum byte to ensure that each line of the encoded text file is read properly. My solution is named `hexdecode04.c`, which is available in the online repository. Please attempt this exercise on your own before you cheat and see how I did it. Comments in my code explain what's going on—and a particularly lucky turn of events that surprised even me.

Alas, my solution isn't perfect, as you can read in my code comments. Further modification may help send the code in the right direction. This is a topic I may explore on my blog in the future, especially after I've eaten lots of cake.

5.3   *URL encoding*

Another type of text encoding, one that you've probably seen before and become frightened over, is URL encoding. Also known as percent encoding, this encoding format preserves web page address and online form content by using printable characters and a smattering of percent signs. This encoding avoids some characters appearing in a URL that may offend our internet overlords.

Specifically, for a web page address, URL encoding is used when referencing something that may otherwise be misinterpreted by the web server, such as a binary value, embedded web page, spaces, or other sneaky data. URL encoding allows this information to be sent as plain text and properly decoded later.

As with any other encoding, you can write a URL-encoding translation program in C. All you need to know are all the URL encoding rules.

5.3.1   *Knowing all the URL encoding rules*

To help you make the connection between what you may have seen and how URL encoding looks, here's an example:

```
https%3A%2F%2Fc-for-dummies.com%2Fblog%2F
```

All the encoding is plain text; URL-encoded is human-readable. Although every character could be encoded, only special characters are presented as a 2-digit hex value prefixed with a percent sign—for example, %24 for the dollar sign character, ASCII code 0x24.

Though various rules exist regarding this encoding method, the HTML 5 standard defines it as follows:

- Alphanumeric characters are not translated (0 to 9, A to Z, upper- and lowercase).
- The characters – (dash), . (period), _ (underscore), and * (asterisk) are retained.
- Spaces are converted into the + (plus) character, though the %20 code is also used.
- All other characters are represented as their hexadecimal ASCII value, prefixed with a percent sign.
- If the data to encode is wider than a byte, such as a Unicode character, it's divided into byte-size values, each a 2-digit hex number prefixed with a percent sign. This final point may not be consistent for all wide-character values.

Subtle variations on these rules exist, but you get the gist of it. This information is adequate for you to experience the joy of writing your own URL encoding and decoding programs.

5.3.2   *Writing a URL encoder*

The key to success with writing a URL-encoding program, a filter in this incarnation, is to catch the exceptions first. Output whatever characters need no translation just as they are. Once these items are eliminated, all other characters the program outputs must obey the percent-hexadecimal encoding method.

The source code for `urlencoder01.c` appears in the following listing. It's a standard filter that processes input one character at a time. The four URL encoding exceptions are handled first (– . _ *) followed by the space. The *isalnum()* function weeds out all alphanumeric characters. Anything remaining is output using the %-hexadecimal format, as shown in the code's *printf()* statement.

Listing 5.9   Source code for `urlencoder01.c`

```
#include <stdio.h>
#include <ctype.h>

int main()
{
    int ch;

    while( (ch=getchar()) != EOF )
    {
        if( ch=='-' || ch=='.' || ch=='_' || ch=='*' )      ◁  These characters
            putchar(ch);                                        are okay; output
        else if( ch==' ' )          ◁  The space is output     as-is.
            putchar('+');               as a + character.
        else if( isalnum(ch) )      ◁
            putchar(ch);               Alphanumeric characters
        else                           are output as-is.
            printf("%%%02X",ch);    ◁
    }                                  The %% is required to output a
    return(0);                         percent sign, followed by a 2-digit
}                                      hexadecimal value, prefixed by a
                                       leading zero if necessary.
```

Here is a sample run of the program, which I've named *urlencoder*:

```
$ ./urlencoder
https://c-for-dummies.com/blog/
https%3A%2F%2Fc-for-dummies.com%2Fblog%2F%0A^D$
```

Here, the filter is run at the prompt, so all keyboard input appears in the output. This approach explains why you see the `%0A` character for the newline at the end of the final line, followed by the Ctrl+D key (`^D`) to terminate input. The command prompt, $, appears immediately after.

If you're used to seeing URL encoding, and understand the basic parts of a URL, you may recognize a few common codes:

- `%3A` for the colon, :
- `%2F` for the forward slash, /

Other codes I see often are:

- %3F for the question mark, ?
- %26 for an ampersand, &

Of course, beyond being a nerd, you need not memorize these common URL encodings. Instead, you can write your own URL decoder, which is also a sign of being a nerd but with a potential to garner an income.

5.3.3   *Creating a URL decoder*

I hope you won't find creating a URL decoder too difficult. Unlike the encoder, the only incoming character the filter should care about is the percent sign. Oh, sure, you could test for "illegal" characters such as those out of range; I'll leave the extra coding up to you.

The key to weeding out the hex digits is to scan for the % character. Once it's encountered, you can use a function like *tohex()*, covered way back in section 5.2.1, to translate the next two incoming hex digits. Again, more testing can be done to determine whether the characters were legitimate hexadecimal digits—but you get the idea.

Presented in the next listing is my quick-and-dirty solution to the URL decoder. It uses a modified version of the *tohex()* function shown earlier; this one also checks for lowercase hexadecimal digits. Otherwise, the only "bad" incoming character this code scans for is the EOF.

Listing 5.10   Source code for `urldecoder01.c`

```c
#include <stdio.h>

int tohex(int c)
{
    if( c>='0' && c<='9' )
        return(c-'0');
    if( c>='A' && c<='F' )
        return(c-'A'+0xA);            ◁— Modified to add lowercase
    if( c>='a' && c<='f' )
        return(c-'a'+0xA);
    return(-1);
}

int main()
{
    int ch,a,b;

    while( (ch=getchar()) != EOF )    Checks for the % sign and grabs the next two characters
    {
        if( ch=='%' )                 ◁—
        {
            ch = getchar();           Bails on EOF
            if( ch==EOF ) break;
            a = tohex(ch);            ◁— Converts the hex digit to an integer
```

```
        ch = getchar();          ←——  Grabs the next
        if( ch==EOF ) break;           character
        b = tohex(ch);
        putchar( (a<<4)+b );     ←——  Outputs the proper
    }                                  character value
    else
        putchar(ch);
}

return(0);
}
```

The program created from the url_decoder01.c source code translates URL encoding, dealing with the % values as they're encountered. Its major problem, however, is that it doesn't know how to deal with improperly formed URL-encoded text. Some error checking is in order . . . but I've reached my assigned page count for this chapter—plus, it's almost midnight and I'm out of Ritalin.

EXERCISE 5.4

Your task is to improve the URL decoder shown in listing 5.10. To do so, ensure that an unwanted character doesn't filter in. When such an offense occurs, exit the program with an appropriate error message. Further, check the return value from the *tohex()* function to ensure that it properly reads hexadecimal values.

You can find my solution in this book's online source code repository. The file is named urldecoder02.c. Please try this exercise on your own. Don't cheat. You know the drill.

Password generators 6

Are you weary of the prompts? You know when some website asks you to apply a password to your account? "Ensure that it has at least one uppercase letter, one number, a symbol, and some hieroglyphics." Or, "Here's a suggested password that you're incapable of typing, let alone committing to memory." It's exasperating.

I hope you recognize the importance of applying a password to a digital account. And I trust that you're familiar with the common rules: don't use easily guessed passwords. Don't use any words or terms easily associated with you. Don't set the same password for every account. These admonishments are tedious but important.

Setting a solid password is a must these days. As a C programmer, you can bolster your weary password arsenal by:

- Understanding password strategy
- Creating basic, jumble passwords
- Ensuring the password has the required characters
- Taking a detour in the world of Mad Libs
- Using random words to build passwords

At its core, of course, a password is nothing more than a string. Authentication is a case-sensitive, character-by-character comparison of the input password with a password stored in an encrypted database. True, the process is more complex than this; I assume at some point the process involves a squirrel on a treadmill. Still, once decrypted, it's that good old comparison that unlocks the digital door. The point of setting a good password is to create a key no one else knows about or can even guess.

6.1   *Password strategies*

Unix systems have always had password requirements for accounts. I mean, look at Unix nerds! Do you trust them? Better question: did they trust each other? Probably not, because the Unix logon has always prompted for a username and password.

Despite knowing about computer security for decades, Microsoft didn't require a password for Windows until Windows 95 escaped the castle laboratory in 1996. Even then, one of the most common emails I received from users at the time would ask how to avoid typing in the Windows password. Unlike Unix and other multiuser systems, PC users were unaccustomed to security. Proof of their ignorance is the proliferation of viruses in the 1990s, but I digress. Windows users just wanted to access the computer. Many of them avoided passwords on purpose.

Enter the internet.

As more of our lives are absorbed by the digital realm, creating and using passwords—serious passwords—becomes a must. Yes, at first, these were silly passwords just to meet the minimum requirement. But as the Bad Guys grew more sophisticated, passwords required more complexity.

6.1.1   *Avoiding basic and useless passwords*

Lazy Windows 95 users must still be with us. Inept passwords are used every day. Silly humans. You'll find a list of the top 10 most common passwords in table 6.1. These aren't even the silly or weak passwords—just the most common. Dwell on that thought for a moment.

Table 6.1   Stupid passwords

Rank	Password	Comment
1.	123456	The bare minimum for a "must be six characters long" password.
2.	123456789	A "more than six characters long" password.
3.	qwerty	Keyboard, top row, left.
4.	password	An all-time classic. No one would guess!
5.	12345	Some people are just lazy.
6.	qwert123	Must have letters and numbers.
7.	1q2w3e	Keyboard, numbers and characters, top left.
8.	12345678	More unclever numbers.
9.	111111	Repetitive unclever numbers.
10.	1234567890	Probably using the numeric keypad for this baby.

The reason using these passwords is useless is that every Bad Guy knows them and tries them first. And you know what? Sometimes they work! Lots of cases documented every day show some high-and-mighty official whose online security is compromised because the bozo was lazy and used a convenient password. It seems like such a person deserves to be hacked.

Not listed in table 6.1, but still incredibly stupid, are using the following personal information tidbits foolishly in or as a password:

- Your birth year
- The current year
- Your first name
- Your favorite sports team's name
- A curse word
- The word *sex*
- Your city or street name or street number

The list goes on. These items are important to avoid—and why those quizzes on social media ask you such silly questions. Trust me—confessing who your best friend was in high school doesn't tell Facebook which *Star Wars* character you are any more than rolling dice does. The Bad Guys are smart. Humans are dumb. The common answers people provide are used later to crack their passwords.

Knowing these tricks is important when crafting a better password. After all, it's easy for someone to take a stab at what might be your password than to brute-force combinations of letters, numbers, and symbols to try to guess a password. Be smart.

EXERCISE 6.1

Write a program that brute-force guesses the password *password*. Have your code spin through all the letter combinations *aaaaaaaa* through *zzzzzzzz* until it matches *password*. Eventually it will, of course, but the purpose of this exercise is to see how long the process takes. The solution I coded takes about 8 minutes to crack the password on my fastest computer (generating no output).

My solution is titled `brutepass01.c`, and it's available in this book's online repository. It uses recursion to spin through letters of the alphabet like miles turning on an odometer. Comments in the code explain my madness.

6.1.2 Adding password complexity

To help you be smart when it comes to passwords, your kind and loving system administrators have devised a few rules. These started simple:

Have a password. Please.

Then complexity was added:

Your password must contain both letters and numbers.

As the Bad Guys grew more adept at guessing passwords, or applying brute-force methods, more details were added:

Your password must contain at least one uppercase letter.
Your password must be at least eight (or more) characters long.
Your password must contain a symbol.

These suggestions add complexity, making it difficult to guess or brute-force the password. Even then, some websites offer even more annoying specifics. For example, figure 6.1 shows the rules for creating a new password at my bank. These rules are about as complex as they can get.

Password Rules

- Must contain at least one letter
- Must contain a least one number
- May contain the following special characters: +_%@!$*~
- Must be between 8 and 25 characters in length
- Must not match or contain your ID
- Must not match one of the previous four passwords

Figure 6.1   Bank password restrictions are about as obnoxious as you can get.

To add even more security, many services employ two-factor authentication. This technique involves a confirmation code sent to your cell phone or a code value generated by an app or special device. This extra level of security ensures that even if your password is compromised, the second-factor security key keeps your information safe.

6.1.3   *Applying the word strategy*

Studies have shown that your typical jumbled password is no better at thwarting the Bad Guys than a password consisting of several words slung together and separated by numbers or symbols. For example, this password:

```
fbjKehL@g4jm7Vy$Glup
```

offers no added security over this one:

```
Bob3monkeys*spittoon
```

The second password has the advantage of being easier to remember and type. Yet when put to the test, password-cracking software takes the same if not longer amount of time to break the second, more readable password than the useless jumble.

This better approach to password creation is what I call the *word strategy*: string together three or more words, mix in some upper- and lowercase letters, add numbers and symbols. In fact, the password requirements shown in figure 6.1 allow both password types shown in this section, but the word strategy is better.

The word strategy also has the advantage of hashing. For example, you can key specific passwords to the sites and services you frequent. Should a password become compromised, you would immediately identify the source. Such a thing happened to me, when I received an email saying that "I know your password." The Bad Guy listed the password—which was one I've used. I recognized it as my old Yahoo! password, which

I changed after hackers stole the Yahoo! user database. I knew the password was compromised, and, based on the words used in the password, I knew the source. I wasn't surprised or concerned by this revelation.

6.2 The complex password jumble

You may think it's relatively easy to write code that outputs your typical, jumbled text password. It is. You may have written such a program in your digital youth: a silly random-character generator. But like all things easy, it's not a really good way to code a password program. Don't let the silliness of the exercise dissuade you.

6.2.1 Building a silly random password program

Listing 6.1 shows my random password generator, a silly version titled `randomp01.c` because the filename `silly.c` is already taken on my computer. It slices off the printable character ASCII spectrum from the exclamation point to the tilde, codes 33 through 126. (Refer to chapter 5 for fun details on ASCII.) This value sets the random number range. The character value output is added to the exclamation point character, which brings it back into printable range.

Listing 6.1 Source code for `randomp01.c`

```c
#include <stdio.h>
#include <stdlib.h>
#include <time.h>

int main()
{
    int x;
    char ch;
    const int length = 10;          ◁— Makes the password 10 characters long

    srand( (unsigned)time(NULL) );

    for( x=0; x<length; x++ )        ◁— Sets the range of random values to printable characters
    {
        ch = rand() % ('~' - '!' + 1);
        putchar( ch+'!' );           ◁— Outputs the printable character
    }
    putchar('\n');

    return(0);
}
```

The program's output is delightfully random but practically useless as a password:

```
aVd["o_rG2
```

First, good luck memorizing that. Second, better luck typing it. Third, hope that the website allows all the characters' output; the double-quote is suspect. Obviously, some conditions must be applied to the output.

6.2.2   *Adding conditions to the password program*

Most of those random password generator routines on the internet produce a jumble of letters, numbers, and symbols, like a festive salad of nonsense but—like real salad—supposedly healthy for you. Obviously, some sort of intelligent programming is going on, as opposed to silly random character generation shown in the preceding section.

A generated password's characters can still be random, but they must be typed: uppercase, lowercase, numbers, symbols. The quantity of each depends on the password length, and the ratio of character types varies.

To improve the silly password program and make it smarter, consider limiting the password's contents to the following:

- One uppercase letter
- Six lowercase letters
- One number
- Two symbols

The total number of characters is 10, which is good for a password.

Random letters and numbers are easy to generate, but to avoid running afoul of any character restrictions, I would offer that these symbols are safe, though you're always free to create your own list:

```
! @ # $ % * _ -
```

The task now is to limit the password to the restrictions given.

EXERCISE 6.2

Write code that generates a random password limited to the characters listed in this section (10 total). Name the code `randomp02.c`. Include in your solution these four functions: *uppercase()*, *lowercase()*, *number()*, and *symbol()*. The *uppercase()* function returns a random character in the range from A to Z. The *lowercase()* function returns a lowercase character, A to Z. The *number()* function returns a character 0 through 9. And the *symbol()* function plucks a random character from an array of safe symbols and returns it. The password is output in the *main()* function, which uses this pattern: one uppercase letter, six lowercase letters, one number, two symbols.

As a tip, I use defined constants to create the pattern:

```
#define UPPER 1
#define LOWER 6
#define NUM 1
#define SYM 2
```

These defined constants save time later, as the code is updated.

6.2.3   *Improving upon the password*

My solution to exercise 6.2 generates output like this:

```
Tmxlqeg8#@
Gdnqgrs2@%
Whizxxb9-*
```

These valiant attempts at generating a random, jumbled password are successful but uninspired. Further, they might be easily compromised in that their pattern is predictable: they all start with an uppercase letter, six lowercase letters, a number, and finally two symbols. Writing a password-cracking program would be easier knowing this pattern.

A better way to output the random characters is to scramble them. For this improvement, the password must be stored in an array as opposed to output directly (which is what I did for my solution to exercise 6.2). So, the first step in making the conversion from `randomp02.c` to `randomp03.c` is to store the generated password—still using the same functions and pattern as before.

Listing 6.2 shows the *main()* function from my updated code `randomp03.c`. The `password[]` buffer is created, equal to the number of characters stored—all defined constants created earlier in the code—plus one for the terminating null character. I replaced the *for* loops in my version of `randomp02.c` with *while* loops, which pack the array with the necessary characters. The string is terminated and then output.

Listing 6.2   Improvements to the *main()* function for `randomp03.c`

```
int main()
{
    char password[ UPPER+LOWER+NUM+SYM+1 ];        ◁─  Necessary storage for
                                                        the password, plus one
                                                        for the null character
    int x;
                                                   ◁─  Seeds the
    srand( (unsigned)time(NULL) );                     randomizer

    x = 0;                                         ◁─  Fetches the uppercase letters and
    while( x<UPPER )                                   puts them in the password[] array
        password[x++] = uppercase();
    while( x<UPPER+LOWER )                         ◁─  Fetches the
        password[x++] = lowercase();                   lowercase letters
    while( x<UPPER+LOWER+NUM )                     ◁─
        password[x++] = number();                      Fetches the
    while( x<UPPER+LOWER+NUM+SYM )                      numbers
        password[x++] = symbol();
    password[x] = '\0';                            ◁─  Caps the string with
                                                        a null character
    printf("%s\n",password);                       ◁─  Outputs the
                                                        password
    return(0);
}
```

Initializes the index variable x → `x = 0;`

Fetches the symbols → `while( x<UPPER+LOWER+NUM+SYM )`

The program's output is unchanged, but this incremental step stores the password. With the password stored in a buffer, it can be passed to a new function, *scramble()*, which randomizes the characters in the buffer.

My *scramble()* function is shown in listing 6.3. It uses a temporary buffer key[] to determine which characters need to be randomized. This array is initialized with null characters. A *while* loop spins, generating random values in the range of 0 through 9—the same as the number of elements in both the passed array p[] and local array key[]. If a random element contains the null character, a character from the passed array is stored in that position. The *while* loop repeats until all characters from the passed array are copied. A final *for* loop updates the passed array.

Listing 6.3   The *scramble()* function to randomize characters in an array

```
void scramble(char p[])
{
    const int size = UPPER+LOWER+NUM+SYM+1;      Calculates the
    char key[size];                              buffer size
    int x,r;

    for( x=0; x<size; x++ )       Initializes the array
        key[x] = '\0';            with null characters

    x = 0;           The index into
    while(x<size-1)  the passed array
    {                             Loops until the passed array
        r = rand() % (size-1);    has been fully processed (minus
        if( !key[r] )             one for the null character)
        {
            key[r] = p[x];        Generates a random value, 0
            x++;                  through the buffer size (minus
        }                         one for the null character)
    }
                                  If the random value at element
    for( x=0; x<size; x++ )       r is a null character...
        p[x] = key[x];
}                                 ... it copies the original character
                                  to its new, random position.
```

Updates the index

Copies the randomized array into the passed array

To call the *scramble()* function, update the code from randomp03.c. First add the *scramble()* function somewhere before the *main()* function. This position negates the need to prototype the function earlier in the source code file. Then insert the following line before the *printf()* statement in the *main()* function:

```
scramble(password);
```

The full source code is available as randomp04.c in the book's online repository. Here is sample output:

```
z%Wea#zhuX
```

Yay! It's still a horrible password to memorize or type, but it's blessedly randomized.

Further modification to the code can be made to adjust the password length and the specific number of the different type of characters. I had originally thought of presenting command-line switches to set the number of options and overall password length. For example:

```
pass_random -u1 -l6 -n1 -s2
```

These arguments set one uppercase letter, six lowercase letters, one number, and two symbols. These options allow for more flexibility in creating the password. You could take the idea further and specify which symbols to include in the random password. Oh! I could go nuts coding this thing, but personally I prefer to use words in my passwords, so I'm moving on to the next section.

6.3   Words in passwords

I gave up on jumbled passwords years ago. My preferred approach is to string a few random words together, along with the requisite capital letter and symbol, and at the desired length. This approach is far easier to remember and type. In fact, I still remember my old CompuServe password, with was just two words separated by a number. A password generator that spews forth words and the proper quantities of symbols and such is far more useful and interesting to code than the random password generator.

6.3.1   Generating random words, Mad Libs style

To build a random word password generator, you need a routine that spits out random words. If they're to be legitimate words, you most likely need some type of list from which to extract the words. Writing a word-generating function is a good approach, plus it gives you an opportunity to create a list of words you like, silly words, or words you frequently say in Walmart.

Listing 6.4 highlights my *add_word()* function as it appears in the source code file randwords01.c. The function contains a dozen words (actually pointers to strings) in array vocabulary[]. Variable r holds a random value in the range of zero to the number of elements in the array: sizeof(vocabulary) returns the number of bytes occupied by the array. This value is divided by sizeof(char *), which is the size of each element in the array—a *char* pointer. The result is 12, which means r holds a random number from 0 through 11. This expression ensures that no matter how many words are in the array, the random number calculated is in the proper range. The function returns the random array element, a pointer to a string.

> **Listing 6.4   The *add_word()* function in** randwords01.c

```
#include <stdio.h>
#include <stdlib.h>
#include <time.h>

#define repeat(a) for(int x=0;x<a;x++)
```

This macro makes the
for loop more readable
in the *main()* function.

```
const char *add_word(void)
{
    const char *vocabulary[] = {
        "orange", "grape", "apple", "banana",
        "coffee", "tea", "juice", "beverage",
        "happy", "grumpy", "bashful", "sleepy"
    };
    int r;

    r = rand() % (sizeof(vocabulary)/sizeof(char *));
    return( vocabulary[r] );
}

int main()
{
    srand( (unsigned)time(NULL) );

    repeat(3)
        printf("%s ", add_word() );
    putchar('\n');

    return(0);
}
```

Generates a random value, zero through the number of elements in the array (minus one)

Returns the random element—the word

Outputs three random words

The code calls the *add_word()* function thrice, though no guarantee is provided to prevent the same word from repeating, as shown in this sample output:

```
banana grape grape
```

As a C programmer, you could add code to prevent duplicates from appearing in the output, but I would offer that a repeated word is also random. Still, this code is merely one step in a longer process.

After writing the `randwords01.c` code, I felt inspired to ape the famous Mad Libs word game. Mad Libs is a registered trademark of Penguin Random House LLC and is fairly used here for educational purposes. Please don't sue me.

The first step in coding a Mad Libs program, all while avoiding a lawsuit, is crafting several functions along the lines of *add_word()* used in the `randwords01.c` code. You must write one function for each word category as found in a Mad Libs: *add_noun()*, *add_verb()*, and *add_adjective()*, for example. Each function is populated with its own `vocabulary[]` array, packed with the corresponding word types: nouns, verbs, and adjectives. The *main()* function calls each function as required to fill in the blanks for a Mad Libs–like sentence, carefully crafted to avoid legal peril, such as the deliberately weak and unfunny example shown here.

Listing 6.5   The *main()* function from `madlib01.c`

```
int main()
{
    srand( (unsigned)time(NULL) );
```

Seeds the randomizer

```
            printf("Will you please take the %s %s ",    ◄─         Outputs the
                    add_adjective(),            ◄─                   first part of
   Fills in         add_noun()          ◄─         Fills in the     the sentence
   a noun     ├─▷  );                             adjective
   blank                                          blank
            printf("and %s the %s?\n",  ◄─
                    add_verb(),   ◄─
                    add_noun()    ◄─         Outputs the last
                    );                       part of the sentence
                                Fills in
            return(0);          another      Fills in the
                                noun blank    verb blank
   }
```

Yes, my Mad Libs prototype is embarrassing. If you really want to treat yourself to a good Mad Libs, obtain one of the books from Leonard Stern and Roger Price because they won't sic their lawyers on me. Still, the code works, fetching a random word from each of the functions. The output is less than hilarious, which, like any Mad Libs game, depends on good word choices:

```
Will you please take the ripe dog and slice the necklace?
```

One way to add a richer variety of words to the various functions is to take the code a step further and read words from a vocabulary text file. For example, a `noun.txt` file contains dozens or hundreds of nouns, each on a line by itself. This format keeps the list accessible, easy to view and edit. Similar files could be created for other word types: `verb.txt`, `adjective.txt`, and so on.

To read through the files and pluck out a random word, you can borrow a technique presented in chapter 2: the "pithy saying" series of programs ended with code that read from a text file, stored all the lines from the file, and then selected a random line of text for output. This approach can be used in an update to the Mad Libs program, where three separate files are scanned for random words. The code from chapter 2 is incorporated into the *build_vocabulary()* function found in my updated Mad Libs program.

In the next listing, you see the *main()* function from my updated Mad Libs program, `madlib02.c`. To handle numerous problems, and effectively shunt a lot of the work to the *build_vocabulary()* function, I chose to use structures to hold information about the various types of words. The output is lamentably the same pathetic text generated by the `madlib01.c` program.

Listing 6.6   The *main()* function from `madlib02.c`

```
int main()
{                                                          Structures are
                                                           declared and defined,
    struct term noun = {"noun.txt",NULL,0,NULL};     ◄─    saving lotsa code.
    struct term verb = {"verb.txt",NULL,0, NULL};
    struct term adjective = {"adjective.txt",NULL,0, NULL};
```

```
build_vocabulary(&noun);
build_vocabulary(&verb);
build_vocabulary(&adjective);

srand( (unsigned)time(NULL) );

printf("Will you please take the %s %s ",
        add_word(adjective),
        add_word(noun)
      );
printf("and %s the %s?\n",
        add_word(verb),
        add_word(noun)
      );

return(0);
}
```

The **build_vocabulary()** function reads words from a file and creates a list in memory with each word indexed. This information is saved in the `term` structure specific to each word type.

The **add_word()** function reads well in English, making the code understandable.

The *main()* function begins by defining three `term` structures to hold and reference the types of words to fill in the Mad Libs. Each member in the structure is defined, with `NULL` constants set for the two pointer items.

Here is the unfunny output:

```
Will you please take the pretty car and yell the motorcycle?
```

You can view the entire source code file found in this book's online repository. It's named `madlib02.c`. It helps if you have this code visible in your editor as I discuss the details over the next few pages.

The workhorse in the `madlib02.c` code is the *build_vocabulary()* function. It relies upon the `term` structure, which is defined externally so that it's visible to all the functions in the source code file:

A string representing the filename to open

A `FILE` pointer referencing the open file listed in the filename member

```
struct term {
    char filename[16];
    FILE *fp;
    int items;
    char **list_base;
};
```

The total number of words extracted from the file

A block of memory containing pointers referencing each word extracted from the file

By throwing these items in a structure, each call to the *build_vocabulary()* function needs only one argument. The *build_vocabulary()* function is based on the source code for `pithy05.c` (covered in chapter 2). Major retooling is done to use the passed structure members instead of local variables, but most of the code remains the same. Here is the prototype:

```
void build_vocabulary(struct term *t);
```

The structure is passed as a pointer, struct term *t, which allows the function to modify the structure's members and have the updated data retained. Otherwise, when the structure is passed directly (not as a pointer), any changes are abandoned when the function terminates. Because a pointer is passed, structure pointer notation (->) is used within the function.

The *build_vocabulary()* function performs these tasks:

1 Open the t->filename member, saving the FILE pointer in variable t->fp upon success.
2 Allocate storage for the t->list_base member, which eventually references all strings read from the file.

A *while* loop reads each string (word) from the file. It performs these tasks:

1 Fetches the string and double-checks to confirm the EOF isn't encountered.
2 Allocates memory for the string.
3 Copies the string into allocated memory.
4 Removes the newline (\n) from the string. This step isn't found in the original pithy05.c code. It's required to ensure that the word returned doesn't contain a newline.
5 Confirms that the t->list_base buffer isn't full. If so, reallocates the buffer to a larger size.

The last step takes place after the *while* loop is done:

6 Closes the open file.

At the end of the function, the items member of the structure contains a count of all the words read from the file. The list_base member contains the addresses for each string stored in memory.

The *main()* function in listing 6.6 also references the *add_word()* function. This function doesn't require a pointer as an argument because it doesn't modify the structure's contents. Here is the *add_word()* function:

```
char *add_word(struct term t)          ←——— The function returns a
{                                            char pointer, a string.
    int word;

    word = rand() % t.items;           ←———  Generates a random
    return( *(t.list_base+word) );     ←———   value ranging from zero
}            References a random word stored at   to the number of items
        t.list_base, and returns its address
```

Most of the *add_word()* function exists in the original pithy05.c code. It was set into a function here because it's called with different structures, each one representing a grammatical word category.

These programs can be used in any application where words stored in a file must be fetched and referenced as a program runs. By keeping the words stored in memory, the list can be accessed multiple times without having to reread the file.

6.3.2   *Building a random word password generator*

You can craft two different types of random word password programs based on the two versions of the Mad Libs programs shown in the preceding section. The first program (madlib01.c) uses arrays to store a series of random words. For more variety, however, you can use the second (madlib02.c) code to take advantage of files that store your favorite password words.

The easy version of the random word password generator works like the earlier *randomp* series of programs, specifically from the source code for randomp04.c. The goal is to create functions that return specific password pieces: a random word, a random number, and a random symbol. The words should already be mixed case. My version is named passwords01.c, and it's found in this book's online repository. Open it in an editor window so that you can follow along in the text.

The *number()* and *symbol()* functions are retained from the earlier code, though each now returns a string as opposed to a single character. A *static char* array holds the character to return as two-character string: The random character is saved in the first element, and a null character is saved in the second, making the array a string. Here are both functions:

```
char *number(void)
{
    static char n[2];                  ◁          The static array's
                                                   contents are retained
    n[0] = rand() % 10 + '0';   ◁                  when the function
    n[1] = '\0';                                   terminates.
                        Generates a random
    return(n);          character, 0 through 9,
}                       storing it as the first
                        element of array n[]
char *symbol(void)
{
    char sym[8] = "!@#$%*_-";
    static char s[2];              ◁

    s[0] = sym[rand() % 8];    ◁       Plucks a random character
    s[1] = '\0';                       from the sym[] array and
                                       sets it as the first element
    return( s );                       of array n[]
}
```

Caps the string with a null character

To generate words for the password, I borrowed the *add_noun()* function from madlib01.c, changing it to reflect a series of random words with a few uppercase letters thrown in:

```
char *add_word(void)
{
    char *vocabulary[] = {
        "Orange", "Grape", "Apple", "Banana",
        "coffee", "tea", "juice", "beverage",
        "happY", "grumpY", "bashfuL", "sleepY"
    };
    int r;

    r = rand() % 12;
    return( vocabulary[r] );
}
```

What I didn't need from the `randomp04.c` code were the functions *scramble(), uppercase(),* and *lowercase().* The *main()* function, shown here, assembles everything into the final password string.

Listing 6.7   The *main()* function from `passwords01.c`

```
int main()                                      Storage where
{                                               the password
    char password[32];            ◁──           is built

    srand( (unsigned)time(NULL) );          Initializes the string
                                            so that the strcpy()
    password[0] = '\0';           ◁──       function doesn't puke

    strcpy(password,add_word());      ◁──       Copies the first word
    strcat(password,number());        ──▷       generated into the
    strcat(password,add_word());      ──▷       password[] array
    strcat(password,symbol());        ◁──
    strcat(password,add_word());      ◁──   Appends a
                                            symbol
    printf("%s\n",password);
                                        Appends the
    return(0);                          final word
}
```

Appends a number — `strcat(password,number());`
Appends the second word — `strcat(password,add_word());`

Here is a sample run:

```
juice9grumpY%Grape
```

Nothing is done in the code to prevent a word from being repeated, and the output might be missing an uppercase letter. But if you don't like the words, add more by expanding the `vocabulary[]` array in the *add_word()* function. Or, better, devise a system where you have files containing words you like to use in a password, like the way the second Mad Libs program works. In fact, you can use the same word files, `noun.txt`, `verb.txt`, and `adjective.txt`.

My source code for `passwords02.c` pulls in elements from both `passwords01.c` and `madlib02.c`—specifically, the *build_vocabulary()* function that reads words from a file and stores them in memory.

You can see how both source code files are merged by examining the *main()* function from `passwords02.c` in the following listing. Yes, I'm being lazy with this code, where the first part of the *main()* function pulled from the *Mad Libs* program and the second part from `passwords02.c`. The output is a string containing three random words, a random number, and a random symbol.

Listing 6.8   The *main()* function from `passwords02.c`

```
int main()
{
    char password[32];              ◄——  Stolen from the first
    struct term noun = {"noun.txt",NULL,0,NULL};       passwords code
    struct term verb = {"verb.txt",NULL,0,NULL};            Stolen from
    struct term adjective = {"adjective.txt",NULL,0,NULL};  ◄——  madlib02.c

    build_vocabulary(&noun);
    build_vocabulary(&verb);
    build_vocabulary(&adjective);

    srand( (unsigned)time(NULL) );
                                        Always cap a
    password[0] = '\0';          ◄——   string you build!
    strcpy(password,add_word(noun));
    strcat(password,number());
    strcat(password,add_word(verb));
    strcat(password,symbol());
    strcat(password,add_word(adjective));

    printf("%s\n",password);

    return(0);
}
```

Here is a sample run, which isn't any different from the `passwords01.c` code's program output:

```
eyeball9yell!ripe
```

On a positive note, this password output is far more hilarious than the output from any of my Mad Libs programs. Still, it has a password problem: where is the uppercase letter?

EXERCISE 6.3

Add another function to the source code from `passwords02.c` to create a new source code file, `passwords03.c`. This new function, *check_caps()*, examines a string for an uppercase letter. If no uppercase letter is found, the function converts a lowercase letter to uppercase at some random position within the string. My solution is available online as `passwords03.c`, but try this exercise on your own before you sneak off to see how I did it.

String utilities 7

It's often said, and rightly so, that the C programming language lacks a string data type. Such a thing would be nice. It would be easier to guarantee that every string in a program is bona fide and that all string functions work cleanly without flaw. But such claims are untrue. A string in C is a character array, weakly typed, and easy for any C programmer to screw up.

Yes, handy string functions exist in C. A crafty coder can easily cobble together any string function, imitating what's available in some other, loftier programming language but lacking in C. Still, any creative approach to handling an absent string function in C still must deal with the language's myopic perception of the string concept. Therefore, some extra training is required, which includes:

- Reviewing what's so terrible about strings in C
- Understanding how string length is measured
- Creating interesting and useful string functions
- Building your own string function library
- Exploring make-believe object-oriented programming

Despite what you can do with strings in C, the grousing and disdain remains—and it's legitimate. C strings are squishy things. It's easy to mess up when you create or manipulate a string, even for experienced programmers. Still, strings exist as a valid form of data and are necessary for communications. So, prepare to bolster your string knowledge and build up your programming arsenal.

7.1   Strings in C

That which you call a string doesn't exist in C as its own data type, like an *int* or a *double*. No programmer worries about malforming an integer or incorrectly encoding the binary format of a real number. These data types—*int*, *double*, and even *char*—are atoms. A string is a molecule. It must be constructed specifically.

Technically, a string is a special type of character array. It has a beginning character, located at some address in memory. Every following character in memory is part of the string, up until the null character, \0, is encountered. This ad hoc structure is used as a string in C—though it remains squishy. If you require further understanding of the squishy concept, table 7.1 provides a comparative review.

Table 7.1   Squishy things

Thing	Why it's squishy
Street intersection limit line	Because few cars stop at the limit line. Most just roll through.
Grandpa saying "No"	Just give it time. Making a cute face helps.
Building permits	Different wait times apply, depending on how friendly you are with the mayor.
Food	Doesn't mean the same thing on an airplane.
Personality	Good to have yourself; bad for a blind date.
Obese	Actuarial tables haven't been updated since the 1940s.
Fame on social media	Wait a few hours.
Sponge cake	By design.

7.1.1   Understanding the string

It's important to separate what you believe to be a string from a character array. Though all strings are character arrays, not all character arrays are strings. For example:

```
char a[3] = { 'c', 'a', 't' };
```

This statement creates a *char* array a[]. It contains three characters: c-a-t. This array is not a string. The following *char* array, however, is a string:

```
char b[4] = { 'c', 'a', 't', '\0'};
```

Array b[] contains four characters: c-a-t plus the null character. This terminating null character makes the array a string. It can be processed by any C language string function or output as a string.

To save you time, and to keep the keyboard's apostrophe key from wearing out, the C compiler lets you craft strings by enclosing characters in double quotes:

```
char c[4] = "cat";
```

Array c[] is a string. It consists of four characters, c-a-t, plus the null character added automatically by the compiler. Though this character doesn't appear in the statement, you must account for it when allocating storage for the string—always! If you declare a string like this:

```
char d[3] = "cat";
```

the compiler allocates three characters for c-a-t, but none for the null character. This declaration might be flagged by the compiler—or it might not. Either way, the string is malformed, and, minus the terminating null character, manipulating or outputting the string yields unpredictable and potentially wacky results.

Because the compiler automatically allocates storage for a string, the following declaration format is used most often:

```
char e[] = "cat";
```

With empty brackets, the compiler calculates the string's storage and assigns the proper number of elements to the array, including the null character.

Especially when building your own strings, you must take care to account for the terminating null character: storage must be allocated for it, and your code must ensure that the final character in the string is the \0.

Here are some string considerations:

- When allocating string storage, always add one for the null character. Strings are allocated directly as a *char* array declaration or via a memory-allocation function such as *malloc()*.

- When using string storage, remember that the final character in storage must be the null character, whether or not the buffer is full.

- The *fgets()* function, often used to read string input, automatically accounts for the null character in its second argument, size. So, if you use the value 32 as the size argument in an *fgets()* statement, the function stores up to 31 characters before it automatically adds the null character to terminate the input string.

- Without the terminating null character, string functions continuing processing bytes until the next random null character is encountered. The effect could be garbage output or—worse—a segmentation fault.

- One problem with forgetting the null is that often memory is already packed with null characters. A buffer can overflow, but the random null characters already in memory prevent output from looking bad—and from your mistake being detected. Never rely upon null characters sitting in memory.

- The null character is necessary to terminate a string but not required. The compiler doesn't check for it—how could it? This lack of confirmation, of string containment, is what makes strings squishy in C.

7.1.2   *Measuring a string*

The title of this section has a completely different definition for my grandmother. No, she doesn't code, but she crochets. The strings are longer in crocheting, but in programming you don't use the word *skein*. Instead, you fuss over character count.

As stored in memory, a string is one character longer than its text, this extra character being the null character terminating the string. It's part of the string but not "in" the string.

According to the *strlen()* function, the string is only as long as its number of characters, minus one for the nonprinting null character.

So, how long is the string?

The *man* page for the *strlen()* describes its purpose:

```
The strlen() function calculates the length of the string . . .
excluding the terminating null byte ('\0').
```

The *strlen()* counts the number of characters in the string, with escaped characters counted as a single character. For example, the newline \n is a single character, though it occupies two character positions. The tab \t is also a single character, though the terminal may translate it into multiple spaces when output.

Regardless of the nits I pick, the value returned by *strlen()* can be used elsewhere in the code to manipulate all characters in the string without violating the terminating null character or double-counting escaped characters. If you want to include the null character in the string's size, you can use the *sizeof* operator, but be aware that this trick works only on statically allocated strings (otherwise, the pointer size is returned).

In the following listing, a comparison is made between values returned by *strlen()* and *sizeof*. A string s[] is declared at line 6, which contains 10 characters. The *printf()* statement at line 8 outputs the string's *strlen()* value. The *printf()* statement at line 9 outputs the string's *sizeof* value.

Listing 7.1   Source code for `string_size.c`

```c
#include <stdio.h>
#include <string.h>

int main()
{
    char s[] = "0123456789";        ◁──┘  10 characters

    printf("%s is %lu characters long\n",s,strlen(s));
    printf("%s occupies %zu bytes of storage\n",s,sizeof(s));

    return(0);
}
```

Here's the output:

```
0123456789 is 10 characters long
0123456789 occupies 11 bytes of storage
```

The *strlen()* function returns the number of characters in the string; *sizeof* returns the amount of storage the string occupies—essentially `strlen()+1`, though, if the string is smaller than its allocated buffer size, *sizeof* returns the buffer size and not `strlen()+1`. If you make this change to line 6 in the code:

```
char s[20] = "0123456789";                    Now 20 characters
                                               of storage
```

Here is the updated output:

```
0123456789 is 10 characters long
0123456789 occupies 20 bytes of storage
```

Despite the larger buffer size, the null character still sits at element 10 (the 11th character) in the s[] array. The remainder of the buffer is considered garbage but is still reported as the string's "size" by the *sizeof* operator.

Measuring a string also comes into play with the grand philosophical debate over what is a null string and what is an empty string. The difference is relevant in other programming languages, where a string can be explicitly defined as being either null or empty. In C, with its weak data types and squishy strings, the difference is less obvious. Consider the following:

```
char a[5] = { '\0' };
char b[5];
```

Of the two arrays, a[] and b[], which is the null string and which is the empty string?

You may think that C doesn't care about which string is which. Obviously, array a[] is initialized and b[] is not. The rest of the discussion is semantics, but according to computer science, a[] is the empty string and b[] is the null string.

In the next listing, I perform a test comparing the two strings, empty a[] and null b[], to see whether the compiler notices the difference between a null string or an empty string. The *strcmp()* function is used, which returns zero when both strings are identical.

Listing 7.2   Source code for `empty-null.c`

```
#include <stdio.h>
#include <string.h>                           The empty
                                               string
int main()
{                                             The null string
                                              (uninitialized)
    char a[5] = { '\0' };
    char b[5];
                                              If both strings
                                              are identical
    if( strcmp(a,b)==0 )
        puts("Strings are the same");                              Size according
    else                                                           to strlen()
        puts("Strings are not the same");
    printf("Length: a=%lu b=%lu\n",strlen(a),strlen(b));
```

```
    printf("Storage: a=%zu b=%zu\n",sizeof(a), ),<linearrow /sizeof(b));    <─┐

    return(0);                                                          Size according
}                                                                           to sizeof
```

The program's output describes how the strings are seen internally:

```
Strings are not the same
Length: a=0  b=4
Storage: a=5 b=5
```

Of course, there's always a random chance that the garbage in memory for string b[] may match up with the contents of string a[]. Therefore, even this output can't truly be trusted. I mean, why does strlen(b) return the value 4?

As far as strings in C are concerned, I prefer to think of a null string as uninitialized. An empty string is an easier concept to understand. After all, it's completely legitimate in C to have a string that contains only the terminating null character: such a string's length is zero. It can be manipulated by all string functions. Beyond these curiosities, however, you can leave the debate over "empty string" and "null string" to the grand viziers of other, trendier programming languages.

7.1.3   *Reviewing C string functions*

Many C language functions understand and process strings. The assumption is that the string is a *char* array that properly terminates. This format is how functions such as *printf()*, *puts()*, *fgets()*, and others deal with strings.

String functions are prototyped in the string.h header file. Standard C library string manipulation functions are listed in table 7.2.

Table 7.2   Common C library string functions

Function	Description
strcat()	Appends one string to another, sticking both together
strncat()	Sticks two strings together, but limited to a certain number of characters
strchr()	Returns a pointer to the location of a specific character within a string
strcmp()	Compares two strings, returning zero for a match
strncmp()	Compares two strings up to a given length
strcoll()	Compares two strings using locale information
strcpy()	Copies characters from one string into another or into a buffer
strncpy()	Copies a given number of characters from one string to another
strlen()	Returns the number of characters in a string
strpbrk()	Locates the first instance of a character from one string found in another

Table 7.2 Common C library string functions *(continued)*

Function	Description
strrchr()	Returns a pointer to character within a string, measured from the end of the string
strspn()	Returns the position of specified characters in one string found in another
strcspn()	Returns the position of specified characters in one string not found in another
strstr()	Returns the position of one string found within another
strtok()	Parses a string based on separator characters (called repeatedly)
strxfrm()	Transforms one string into another based on locale information

Many string functions feature an "n" companion, such as *strcat()* and *strncat()*. The *n* indicates that the function counts characters or otherwise tries to avoid an overflow by setting a string size value.

Though table 7.2 lists only common C library string functions, your compiler's library may feature more. For example, the *strcasecmp()* function works like *strcmp()*, but it ignores letter case when making the comparison. (See chapter 11.) Also, the *strfry()* function is available specifically with GNU C libraries. It randomly swaps characters in a string, similar to the *scramble()* function discussed in chapter 6.

Just to ensure that you're always alarmed or confused, some compilers may also feature a `strings.h` header file. This header defines a few additional string functions, such as *strcasecmp()*, with some C libraries. I don't cover these functions in this chapter.

7.1.4 *Returning versus modifying directly*

Functions that manipulate strings in C have two ways they can make their changes. The first is to return a modified version of the string. The second is to manipulate the passed string directly. Choosing an approach really depends on the function's purpose.

For example, the *strcat()* function appends one string to another. Here is the *man* page format:

```
char *strcat(char *dest, const char *src);
```

String `src` (source) is appended to the end of string `dest` (destination). The function assumes enough room is available in the `dest` buffer to successfully append the string. Upon success, string `dest` contains both `dest` plus `src`. The function returns a pointer to `dest`. The *strcat()* function is an example of manipulating a passed string directly.

In the next listing, two strings are present in the *main()* function, `s1[]` and `s2[]`. It's the job of the *strappend()* function to stick both strings together, returning a pointer to the new, longer string. The secret is that within the *strappend()* function is the *strcat()* function, and its value (the address of `dest`) is returned.

Listing 7.3 Source code for `strcat.c`

```
#include <stdio.h>
#include <stdlib.h>
#include <string.h>

char *strappend(char *dest, char *src)
{
    return( strcat(dest,src) );
}

int main()
{
    char s1[32] = "This is another ";
    char s2[] = "fine mess!";
    char *s3;

    s3 = strappend(s1,s2);
    printf("%s\n",s3);

    return(0);
}
```

The *strcat()* function returns pointer `dest`, the newly combined string.

Array `s1[]` contains enough storage for both strings.

The program's output shows the concatenated string:

```
This is another fine mess!
```

In this example, the function doesn't really create a new string. It merely returns a pointer to the first string passed, which now contains both strings.

EXERCISE 7.1

Modify the source code for `strcat.c`. Remove the *strcat()* function from the code, replacing it with your own code that sticks the contents of argument `src` to the end of argument `dest`. Do not use the *strcat()* function to accomplish this task! Instead, determine the size of the resulting string and allocate storage for it. The *strappend()* function returns the address of the created string.

You can further modify the code so that string `s1[]` holds only the text shown; it doesn't need to allocate storage for the new string. Proper allocation is instead made within the *strappend()* function.

My solution to this exercise is available in the online repository as `strappend.c`. Comments in the code explain my approach. Remember, this code demonstrates how a string function can create a new string as opposed to modifying a string passed as an argument.

7.2   *String functions galore*

C has plenty of string functions, but apparently not enough for the grand poohbahs of those other programming languages. They disparage C as being weak on string manipulation. Of course, any function you feel is missing from the C library—one that happily dwells in some other, trendier programming language—can easily be coded.

All you must do is remember to include the all-important terminating null character, and anything string-related is possible in C.

In this section, I present a smattering of string functions, some of which exist in other programming languages, others of which I felt compelled to create because of some personal brain defect. Regardless, these functions prove that anything you can do with a string in those Johnny-come-lately programming languages is just as doable in C.

Oh! One point to make: the functions found in other languages are sometimes called *methods* because they pertain to object-oriented programming. Well, *la-di-da.* I can call my car the Batmobile, but it's still a Hyundai.

7.2.1   *Changing case*

Functions that change text case in a string are common in other languages. In C, the ctype functions *toupper()* and *tolower()* convert single characters, letters of the alphabet to upper- or lowercase, respectively. These functions can easily be applied to an entire string. All you need to do is write a function that handles the task.

The following listing shows the source code for `strupper.c`, which converts a string's lowercase letters to uppercase. The string is modified within the function, where a *while* loop processes each character. If the character is in the range of `'a'` to `'z'`, its sixth bit is reset (changed to zero), which converts it to lowercase. (This bit-wise manipulation is discussed in chapter 5.) The *strupper()* function avoids using any ctype functions.

Listing 7.4   Source code for `strupper.c`

```c
#include <stdio.h>

void strupper(char *s)              Loops until *s references
{                                   the null character (end
    while(*s)                       of the string)
    {
        if( *s>='a' && *s<='z' )              Changes only
        {                                     lowercase letters
            *s &= 0xdf;
        }                           Resets the sixth
        s++;                        bit to convert to
    }                               uppercase
}

int main()
{
    char string[] = "Random STRING sample 123@#$";

    printf("Original string: %s\n",string);
    strupper(string);
    printf("Uppercase string: %s\n",string);

    return(0);
}
```

Here is the program's output:

```
Original string: Random STRING sample 123@#$
Uppercase string: RANDOM STRING SAMPLE 123@#$
```

The *strupper()* function could also convert characters to uppercase by performing basic math. Due to the layout of the ASCII table, the following statement also works:

```
*s -= 32;
```

Subtracting 32 from each character's ASCII value also converts it to lowercase.

It's easy to modify the *strupper()* function to create a function that converts characters to lowercase. Here is how a *strlower()* function may look:

```
void strlower(char *s)
{
    while(*s)
    {
        if( *s>='A' && *s<='Z' )        ◁─── Converts only
        {                                      uppercase
            *s += 32;        ◁──┐              letters
        }                       │  Adds 32 to
        s++;                    │  make the
    }                           │  conversion
}
```

The complete source code showing the *strlower()* function is found in this book's online repository as `strlower.c`.

EXERCISE 7.2

Write a function, *strcaps()*, that capitalizes the first letter of every word in a string. Process the text "This is a sample string" or a similar string that contains several words written in lowercase, including at least one one-letter word. The function modifies the string directly as opposed to generating a new string.

My solution is found in the online repository as `strcaps.c`. It contains comments that explain my approach.

7.2.2   *Reversing a string*

The key to changing the order of characters in a string is knowing the string's length—where it starts and where it ends.

For the string's start, the string's variable name is used, which holds the base address. The string's ending address isn't stored anywhere; the code must find the string's terminating null character and then use math to calculate the string's size. This math isn't required in other programming languages, where every aspect of the string is fully known. Further, in C the string can be malformed, which would make the process impossible.

Figure 7.1 illustrates a string lounging in memory, with both array and pointer notation calling out some of its parts. The terminating null character marks the end of the string, wherever its location may be, measured as offset *n* from the string's start.

Figure 7.1   Measuring a string in memory

The easiest way to locate the end of a string is to use the *strlen()* function. Add the function's return value to the string's starting location in memory to find the string's end.

For the do-it-yourself crowd, you can craft your own string-end function or loop to locate the string's caboose. Assume that *char* pointer s references the string's start and that *int* variable len is initialized to zero. If so, this *while* loop locates the string's end, where the null character dwells:

```
while(*s++)
    len++;
```

After this loop is complete, pointer *s references the string's terminating null character, and the value of len is equal to the string's length (minus the null character). Here is a more readable version of the loop:

```
while( *s != '\0' )
{
    len++;
    s++;
}
```

The stupidest way to find the end of a string is to use the *sizeof* operator. The operator isn't dumb, but when used on a *char* pointer argument, *sizeof* returns the number of bytes the pointer (memory address variable) occupies, not the size of the buffer the pointer references. For example, on my computer, a pointer is 4 bytes wide, so no matter what size buffer *s refers to, sizeof(s) always returns 4.

After obtaining the string's length, the reversing process works backgrounds through the string, copying each character into another buffer, front to back. The result is a new string containing the reverse character order of the original.

The *strrev()* function shown in the next listing creates a new string, reversed. First, a *while* loop calculates the string's size (argument *s). Second, storage is allocated for the new string based on the original string's size. I don't need to +1 in the *malloc()* statement to make room for the null character, because variable len already references the null character's offset. Finally, a *while* loop processes string s backward as it fills string reversed with characters.

Listing 7.5   The *strrev()* function

```
char *strrev(char *s)
{
    int len,i;
    char *reversed;              Variable len contains the
                                 offset of the null character
                                 and also the string's length.
    len = 0;
    while( *s )                  Loops until *s references the
    {                            null character terminating
        len++;                   the passed string
        s++;
    }
                                                    Allocates storage for
                                                    the reversed string; same
                                                    length as the passed string
    reversed = malloc( sizeof(char) * len );
    if( reversed==NULL )
    {
        fprintf(stderr,"Unable to allocate memory\n");
        exit(1);
    }                            Backs up s over the terminating
                                 null character; it now points to the
                                 last character in the passed string
    s--;
    i = 0;
    while(len)                   Copies the number of characters
    {                            in the original string
        *(reversed+i) = *s;
        i++;                         Increments the offset
        len--;                       for the reversed string
        s--;
    }                            Decrements the offset
    *(reversed+i) = '\0';        for the original string

    return(reversed);            Always cap a newly
}                                constructed string with
                                 the null character!
         Don't free the pointer here!
         Its data must be retained.
```

Indexes into the new string, reversed

Copies the characters

Backs up the pointer

This function is included with the source code for strrev.c, found in the book's online repository. In the *main()* function a sample string is output, and then the reversed string is output for comparison. Here's a sample run:

```
Before: A string dwelling in memory
After: yromem ni gnillewd gnirts A
```

This code shows only one way to create a string reversal function, though the general approach is the same for all variations: work the original string backward to create the new string.

7.2.3 *Trimming a string*

String-truncating functions are popular in other programming languages. For example, I remember the LEFT$, RIGHT$, and MID$ commands from my days of programming in BASIC. These commands lack similar functions in C, but they're easy enough to craft. Figure 7.2 gives you an idea of what each one does.

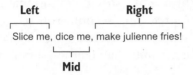

Figure 7.2   Extracting portions of a string: left, middle, and right

Each function requires at least two arguments: a string to slice and a character count. The middle extraction function also requires an offset. For my approach, I decided to return a new string containing the desired chunk, which leaves the original string intact.

The next listing shows my concoction of a *left()* function, which extracts len characters from the passed string s. As with each of these trimming functions, storage is allocated for a new string. The *left()* function is the easiest to code because it copies the first len characters of the passed string s into the target string buf. The address of buf is returned.

Listing 7.6   The *left()* function

```
char *left(char *s,int len)
{
    char *buf;              ⟵  Storage for the
    int x;                      new string

    buf = malloc(sizeof(char)*len+1);   ⟵  Allocates storage for the
    if( buf==NULL )                         new string, plus one for
    {                                       the null character
        fprintf(stderr,"Memory allocation error\n");
        exit(1);
    }                       ⟵  Copies the len
                                characters
    for(x=0;x<len;x++)     ⟵
    {
        if( *(s+x)=='\0' )     ⟵  Checks for an unexpected null
            break;                 character and terminates the
        *(buf+x) = *(s+x);     ⟵  loop if found
    }                             Copies
    *(buf+x) = '\0';       ⟵     characters

    return(buf);            ⟵  Caps the newly
}                              created string
```

Figure 7.3 illustrates the guts of the *left()* function.

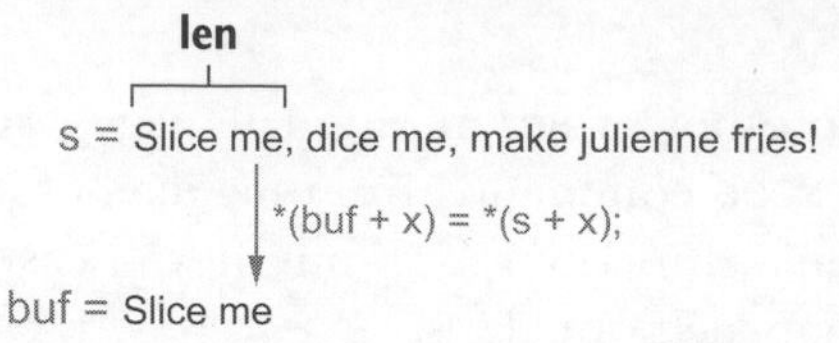

len

s = Slice me, dice me, make julienne fries!

*(buf + x) = *(s + x);

buf = Slice me

Figure 7.3   The way the *left()* function slices a string

Unlike the *left()* function, chopping off the right side of a string requires that the program knows where the string ends. From the preceding section, you recall that C doesn't track a string's tail. Your code must hunt down that terminating null character. For the *right()* function, I count backward from the null character to lop off the right side of the string.

My *right()* function is shown in the following listing. It borrows its allocation routine from the *left()* function shown in listing 7.6. After the buffer is created, the code hunts for the end of the string, moving the pointer start to this location. Then the value of len is subtracted from start to reposition the pointer to the beginning of the right-end string chunk desired. Then len number of characters are copied into the new string.

Listing 7.7   The *right()* function

```c
char *right(char *s,int len)
{
    char *buf;
    char *start;
    int x;

    buf = (char *)malloc(sizeof(char)*len+1);
    if( buf==NULL )
    {
        fprintf(stderr,"Memory allocation error\n");
        exit(1);
    }

    start = s;                    ← Uses the pointer start as
                                    the offset to retain for later
                                    the address in variable s
    while(*start!='\0')           ← Searches for the
        start++;                    end of the string
    start -= len;                 ← Adjusts the pointer start to reference
    if( start < s )                 where the right end of the string starts
        exit(1);

    for(x=0;x<len;x++)            ← Copies the rightmost portion of
        *(buf+x) = *(start+x);      the string into the new buffer
    *(buf+x) = '\0';             ← Caps the newly
                                    created string
    return(buf);
}
```

Checks for underflow and exits if true

The *right()* function's operation is illustrated in figure 7.4.

The final string-trimming function is really the only one you need: when given the proper arguments, the *mid()* function can easily substitute for the *left()* or *right()*

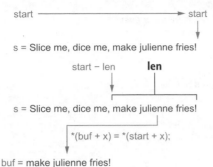

Figure 7.4 **The calculations made to extract the right side of a string**

functions. In fact, these two functions could be macros based on *mid()*. I blab more on this topic in a few paragraphs.

My *mid()* function has three arguments:

```
char *mid(char *s, int offset, int len);
```

Pointer s references the string to slice. Integer offset is the character position to start extraction. And integer len is the number of characters to extract.

The full *mid()* function is shown in listing 7.8. It performs a straight character-by-character copy from the passed string s into the new string buffer buf. The key, however, is adding the offset value when passing the characters:

```
*(buf+x) = *(s+offset-1+x)
```

The offset value must be reduced by 1 to account for the fact that characters in the string start at offset 0, not offset 1. If I were to write documentation for the function, I'd need to explain that valid values for argument offset are in the range of 1 through the string's length. Unlike in C coding, you don't want to start with zero—though you could. Again, state so in the function's documentation.

Listing 7.8 The *mid()* function

```
char *mid(char *s, int offset, int len)
{
    char *buf;
    int x;

    buf = (char *)malloc(sizeof(char)*len+1);
    if( buf==NULL )
    {
        fprintf(stderr,"Memory allocation error\n");
        exit(1);
    }

    for(x=0;x<len;x++)          ◁────  Copies len number of characters
    {
        *(buf+x) = *(s+offset-1+x);   ◁──── The offset value is decreased by 1 because the first character is offset 0, not offset 1.
```

```
        if( *(buf+x)=='\0')          ◁─┐   Catches any overflow
            break;                       │   and stops
    }
    *(buf+x) = '\0';          ◁──┐   Always cap a
                                  │   string you've
    return(buf);                  │   created yourself.
}
```

Figure 7.5 illustrates how the *mid()* function operates.

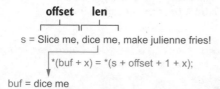

buf = dice me   **Figure 7.5   The operations of the *mid()* function**

As I wrote earlier, the *left()* and *right()* functions are easily reproduced by using specific formats for the *mid()* function. If you were to write a macro for the *left()* function, you could use this format:

```
#define left(s,n) mid(s,1,n)
```

With an offset of 1, this *mid()* function returns the leftmost `len` characters of string s. (Remember, the `offset` value is reduced by 1 in the *mid()* function.)

Crafting the *right()* function equivalent of *mid()* requires that the string's length be obtained in the call:

```
#define right(s,n) mid(s,strlen(s)-n,n)
```

The second argument is the string's length (obtained by the *strlen()* function), minus the number of characters desired. It bothers me to call the *strlen()* function in a macro, but my point is more to show that the true power function for string slicing is the *mid()* function.

You can find all these string-trimming functions—*left()*, *right()*, and *mid()*—in the source code file `trimming.c`, found in this book's online repository.

7.2.4   Splitting a string

I wrote my string-splitting function out of spite. Another programmer, a disciple of one of those fancy new languages, scoffed, "You can't even split a string in C with fewer than 20 lines of code."

Challenge accepted.

Though I can easily code a string-splitting function in C with fewer than 20 lines of code, one point I must concede is that such a function requires at least four arguments:

```
int strsplit(char *org,int offset,char **s1,char **s2)
```

Pointer `org` references the string to split. Integer `offset` is the location of the split. And the last two pointers, `s1` and `s2`, contain the two sides of the split. These pointers are passed by reference, which allows the function to access and modify their contents.

The next listing shows my *strsplit()* function, with its cozy 15 lines of code—and no obfuscation. I used white space and indents as I normally do. The size of the original string is obtained and used to allocate storage for `s1` and `s2`. Then the *strncpy()* function copies the separate portions of the original string into the separate strings. The function returns 1 upon success, and 0 when things foul up.

Listing 7.9   The *strsplit()* function

Obtains the original string's length

```
int strsplit(char *org,int offset,char **s1,char **s2)
{
    int len;

    len = strlen(org);
    if(offset > len)
        return(0);
    *s1 = malloc(sizeof(char) * offset+1);
    *s2 = malloc(sizeof(char) * len-offset+1);
    if( s1==NULL || s2==NULL )
        return(0);
    strncpy(*s1,org,offset);
    strncpy(*s2,org+offset,len-offset);
    return(1);
}
```

If the `offset` argument is out of range, return zero—error.

Allocates storage for split string 1, argument `s1` dereferenced

Allocates storage for split string 2, calculating the proper size

Copies the proper number of characters into the new strings

Returns an error if either allocation fails

The *strsplit()* function you see in listing 7.9 is my first version, where my goal was to see how few lines of code I could use. It calls C library string functions to perform some of the basic operations, which means this version of the *strsplit()* function relies upon the `string.h` header file. I wrote another version that avoids using the string library functions, though its code is obviously much longer.

The *strsplit()* function shown in listing 7.9 is found in the online repository in the `strsplit.c` source code file.

7.2.5   Inserting one string into another

When I originally thought of writing a string insertion function, I figured I'd use two C library string functions to accomplish the task: *strcpy()* and *strcat()*. These functions can build the string one step at a time: the *strcpy()* function copies one string to another, duplicating a string in another array or chunk of memory. The *strcat()* function sticks one string onto the end of another, creating a larger string. The inserted string is pieced together: original string, plus insert, plus the rest of the original string.

The function would have this declaration:

```
int strinsert(char *org, char *ins, int offset);
```

Pointer `org` is the original string, which must be large enough to accommodate the inserted text. Pointer `ins` is the string to insert; integer `offset` is the location (starting with 1) at which string `ins` is inserted into string `org`.

My *strinsert()* function returns 1 upon success, 0 on error.

It didn't work.

The problem with using *strcpy()* and *strcat()* is that I must split the original string, save the remainder, and then build final string. This step requires a temporary buffer for the remainder of string `org` at position `offset`, as illustrated in figure 7.6. Then string `ins` is concatenated to the new end of string `org`, then the original end of string `org` is concatenated to the result. Messy.

Offset 23

org = Well, this is another mess!

ins = fine

Split off into a buffer

org = Well, this is another mess!

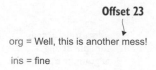

Well, this is another   fine   mess!

Figure 7.6   **The process of using string library functions makes inserting a string overly complex.**

Further, as shown in figure 7.6, the hope is that the user has allocated enough storage for the original string `org` to accommodate the inserted text. To me, this hope is too risky, so I changed my approach. Here is the function's updated declaration:

```
char *strinsert(char *org, char *ins, int offset);
```

The function's return value is a newly created string, which avoids the necessity that string `org` be large enough to also accommodate inserting string `ins`. Returning the string, that is, creating it within the function, also avoids having to temporarily store the remainder of string `org` for concatenation later.

In this new approach, I build the new string character by character, inserting string `ins` at `offset` characters as the new string is built. Figure 7.7 illustrates how the improved version of the function operates.

Rather than use the *strcat()* and *strcpy()* functions, my improved version of the *strinsert()* function copies characters sequentially from string `org` into a newly created

Offset 23

```
org = Well, this is another mess!
ins = fine
```

```
org = Well, this is another mess!
new = Well, this is another
```

```
ins =                fine
new = Well, this is another fine
```

```
org =     Well, this is another mess!
new = Well, this is another fine mess!
```

Figure 7.7 The improved technique for inserting one string into another

buffer, new. Once the character count is equal to offset, characters are copied from string ins into the newly created buffer. After that, the count continues from string org.

You find the full *strinsert()* function in the following listing. It builds the string new character by character from arguments org and ins. The C library's *strlen()* function is used; otherwise, the string is built using statements within the function.

Listing 7.10 The *strinsert()* function

```c
char *strinsert(char *org, char *ins, int offset)
{
    char *new;
    int size,index,append;

    size = strlen(org)+strlen(ins);
    if( offset<0 )
        return(NULL);

    new = malloc(sizeof(char) * size+1);
    if( new==NULL )
    {
        fprintf(stderr,"Memory allocation error\n");
        exit(1);
    }
    offset -= 1;
    index = 0;
    append = 0;
    while( *org )
    {
        if( index==offset )
        {
            while( *ins )
            {
```

Obtains the size of the new string

Returns an empty string if the offset is a silly value

Allocates storage for the new string

Indexes to track progress through new string

Reduces the offset value to account for strings starting at 0, not 1

Status variable to track whether ins string has been inserted

Loops through the original string

Immediately checks for the offset value to account for offset = 0

Inserts ins string, adding it to string new

```
                *(new+index) = *ins;
                index++;
                ins++;                    Marks that the
            }                             string has been
            append = 1;          ◁        inserted
        }
        *(new+index) = *org;     ◁       Continues building
        index++;                          the new string from
        org++;                            the original string
    }
    if( !append )                ◁       Confirms that a string
    {                                     was inserted; if not,
        while( *ins )                     string ins is appended
        {
            *(new+index) = *ins;
            index++;
            ins++;
        }
    }
    *(new+index) = '\0';         ◁       Always cap
                                          a string you
    return(new);                          create yourself!
}
```

In the function, I tried to handle a condition when the `offset` argument is larger than the length of string `org`. I couldn't quite get it to work, so I decided to use the out-of-range value as a feature: if the value of `offset` is longer than string `org`, string `ins` is appended to string `org` regardless of the `offset` value.

You can find the *strinsert()* function inside the source code file `strinsert.c` in this book's online repository. Here is the program's output, where the string "fine" (plus a space) is inserted into the string "Well, this is another mess!" at offset 23:

```
Before: Well, this is another mess!
After: Well, this is another fine mess!
```

7.2.6   *Counting words in a string*

To solve the puzzle of counting words in a string, you must write code that recognizes when a word starts. You've already written such code if you completed exercise 7.2, which capitalizes the first character of words in a string. The *strcaps()* function can be modified to count words rather than convert characters to uppercase.

The next listing shows an update to my solution for exercise 7.2 (do you regret reading this chapter front-to-back?), where the *strwords()* function consumes a string's characters in sequence, one after the other. The variable `inword` determines whether the current character is inside a word. Each time a new word starts, variable `count` is incremented.

Listing 7.11   The *strwords()* function inside source code `strwords.c`

```
#include <stdio.h>
#include <ctype.h>

int strwords(char *s)
{
    enum { FALSE, TRUE };
    int inword = FALSE;
    int count;

    count = 0;
    while(*s)
    {
        if( isalpha(*s) )
        {
            if( !inword )
            {
                count++;
                inword = TRUE;
            }
        }
        else
        {
            inword = FALSE;
        }
        s++;
    }

    return(count);
}

int main()
{
    char string[] = "This is a sample string";

    printf("The string '%s' contains %d words\n",
            string,
            strwords(string)
          );

    return(0);
}
```

Annotations:

- Creates the constants `FALSE=0` and `TRUE=1`
- Starts out assuming the code isn't reading inside of a word
- Word count initialized
- Loops through string `s`
- Is the current letter alphabetic?
- Confirms that a word isn't being processed
- Inside the word, increments the count
- Resets the `inword` variable
- For nonalpha characters, `inword` is **FALSE**

Here is a sample run of the `strwords.c` program:

```
The string 'This is a sample string' contains 5 words
```

If you change the word *is* to *isn't* in the string, here is the modified output:

```
The string 'This isn't a sample string' contains 6 words
```

Hmmm.

EXERCISE 7.3

Modify the *strwords()* function shown in listing 7.11 so that it accounts for contractions. This task has a simple solution, one that's presented in the first C language programming book, *The C Programming Language*, by Brian Kernighan and Dennis Ritchie (Pearson, 1988). Without cheating, see if you can accomplish the same task.

My solution is titled `strwords2.c`, and it's available in this book's online repository.

7.2.7 Converting tabs to spaces

The terminal you use in Linux is smart enough to output tab characters to the next virtual tab stop on the display. These tab stops are set at 8 characters by default. Some shells, such as *bash* and *zsh*, feature the *tabs* command, which can set the tab stops to a different character interval: for example, **tabs 4** sets a terminal tab stop that is 4 characters wide.

The following *printf()* statement outputs a string with two tab characters:

```
printf("Hello\tHi\tHowdy\n");
```

Here is the output:

```
Hello   Hi      Howdy
```

The tab character didn't expand to a constant number of characters. Instead, it's interpreted by the shell and expanded to the next virtual tab stop at 8-character intervals across the display. This effect ensures that columns line up perfectly as you use tabs to line up text or create tables.

Obviously, you don't need to convert tabs into spaces for output on the terminal. But one function you can write is one that sets variable-width tab stops in a program's output. The width for these tab stops is created by outputting spaces; this book doesn't go into terminal hardware programming.

To set a tab stop, you must know where text output is going across the screen—the current column value. This value is compared with the tab stop width desired, using the following equation:

```
spaces = tab - (column % tab)
```

Here is how this statement works out:

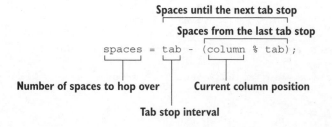

The (column % tab) expression returns the number of spaces since the last tab stop interval (tab) based on the cursor's current column offset (column). To obtain the number of spaces until the *next* tab stop, this value is subtracted from the tab stop width. The result is the number of spaces required to line up the next character output with a tab stop.

The tab calculation equation exists as a statement in the *strtabs()* function, shown in the next listing. The function outputs a string, carefully checking each character for the tab, \t. When encountered, the next tab stop offset is calculated, and the given number of spaces are output.

Listing 7.12   The *strtabs()* function inside source code file strtabs.c

```c
#include <stdio.h>

void strtabs(const char *s, int tab)
{
    int column,x,spaces;          The column variable
                                  tracks the current
    column = 0;                   column position.
    while(*s)
    {                                    Catches the          Calculates the
        if( *s == '\t')                  tab character        number of spaces to
        {                                                     output to line up at
            spaces = tab - (column % tab);                    the next tab stop
            for( x=0; x<spaces; x++ )
                putchar(' ');            Outputs the
            column += spaces;           required spaces
        }
        else                            Updates the
        {                               column offset
            putchar(*s);
            if( *s=='\n' )              If a newline is
                column = 0;             output, resets the
            else                        column value
                column++;
        }
        s++;
    }
}

/* calculate and display a tab */
int main()
{
    const char *text[3] = {
      "Hello\tHi\tHowdy\n",
      "\tLa\tLa\n",
      "Constantinople\tConstantinople\n"
    };
    int x,y;                      Nested loop to output the three
                                  sample strings at three different
    for(y=4;y<32;y*=2)            tab stops: 4, 8, and 16 spaces
    {
        printf("Tab width: %d\n",y);
```

Loops through the string

Handles other characters here

```
            for(x=0;x<3;x++)
            {
                strtabs(text[x],y);
            }
        }

    return(0);
}
```

The program's output generates three strings, with different tab patterns using three different tab stop settings. Here's the output:

```
Tab width: 4
Hello   Hi  Howdy
    La  La
Constantinople  Constantinople
Tab width: 8
Hello   Hi      Howdy
        La      La
Constantinople  Constantinople
Tab width: 16
Hello           Hi              Howdy
                La              La
Constantinople  Constantinople
```

When the terminal window encounters a tab, it doesn't convert the tab into multiple spaces like the `strtabs.c` program does. For the terminal window, the cursor itself moves the required number of character positions across the screen; spaces aren't output. To prove so, take the standard output of some program that generates tabs and look at the raw data. You see tab characters (ASCII 9) instead of a series of spaces.

7.3   *A string library*

One of the best ways to put all string-manipulation functions to work, or to deal with any targeted collection of functions, is to create your own custom library. It's a way to share the functions with others or have them ready for yourself in a practical way.

You know about other libraries and have probably used them, such as the math library. Creating these tools isn't that difficult, nor is knowing how to create them a secret: if you know how to compile code, you can create a library.

All C libraries are created by someone—some clever coder who cobbles together functions and other elements required to let you share in their genius. Even the C standard library is written and maintained by C coders, the high lords of the programming realm.

Using your string library is as easy as using another library; your string library is linked into the object code file at build time. The functions are prototyped and supported by a custom header file. Everything works for your library just as it does for other libraries.

For the string library, I'll include many of the functions demonstrated in this chapter. If you have additional, favorite string functions, feel free to add them as well.

Directions throughout this section explain the details and offer tips for creating your own custom library.

7.3.1 Writing the library source and header file

Creating a library starts with a source code editor. Your goal is to create two files at minimum:

- A source code file
- A header file containing the functions' prototypes

The source code is one or more files (depending on how you work) containing all the functions for the library—just the functions. You don't need a *main()* function, because you're building a library, not a program. This file is compiled just like any other source code file, but it's not linked. You need only the object code file, .o, to create the library.

The library also requires a header file, which contains the function prototypes's defined constants, necessary includes, and other goodies that assist the functions. For example, if a function uses a structure, it must be declared in the source code file as well as in the header file. Programmers who use your library need the structure definition to make the function work. The header file is where you put these things, and it's where they're referenced when programmers use your library.

In listing 7.13, you see the first part of the mystring.c source code file, which contains many of the string functions demonstrated in this chapter. The file has descriptive comments, which can be expanded to show version history, offer tips, and provide examples. The #include directives in the source code file are required for the functions, just as they would be in any source code file. Further, see how I've feebly attempted to document each function, showing the arguments and return value? Yes, this information can be expanded upon; documentation is good.

Listing 7.13 The first part of the mystring.c library source code file

```
/* mystring library */              Comments introducing
/* 10 September 2021 */             the library file
/* Dan Gookin, dan@gookin.com */

#include <stdio.h>                  Headers required
#include <stdlib.h>                 for the functions
#include <string.h>                 in this file
#include <ctype.h>

/* Return the left portion of a string      Comments introducing
   s = string                               and describing each
   len = length to cut from the left        function
   return value: new string
 */
char *left(char *s,int len)         ◄────  The function
{                                          itself (continues)
```

The order of the functions inside the source code file doesn't matter—unless one function references another. In such a situation, ensure that the referenced function appears before (above) the function it's referenced in.

The companion header file for your library isn't listed in the library's source code file (refer to listing 7.13). The header file is necessary to provide support for programmers who use your library; only if items in the header file are referenced in the code (defined constants, for example) do you need to include the library's header file in the source code file. Key to the header file are the function prototypes, structures, global/external variable definitions, macros, and defined constants.

As with the library's source code file, I recommend commenting the header file to document its parts. Be helpful to your programmer pals. Further, I add version number defined constants to my header files, as shown here.

> **Listing 7.14   The `mystring.h` header file to support the mystring library**

```
/* mystring library header file */        Details about your
/* 10 September 2021 */                    library header file
/* Dan Gookin, dan@gookin.com */           in the comments

#define mystring_version "1.0"             Version number
#define mystring_version_major 1           defined constants
#define mystring_version_minor 0

char *left(char *s,int len);
char *mid(char *s, int offset, int len);
char *right(char *s,int len);
void strcaps(char *s);
char *strinsert(char *org, char *ins, int offset);
void strlower(char *s);                    Function
char *strrev(char *s);                     prototypes
int strsplit(char *org,int offset,char **s1,char **s2);
void strtabs(const char *s, int tab);
void strupper(char *s);
int strwords(char *s);
```

Both files, the source code and header file, are necessary to use the library.

7.3.2   Creating a library

Libraries are created from object code files. The *ar* (archive) utility is what transforms the object code file into a library. Therefore, the first step to creating a library is to compile—but not link—your library's source code file. Once you have the compiled object code, you use the *ar* utility to create the library.

For this example, I'm using the `mystring.c` source code file, which is available from this book's online code repository. To compile the source code into object code, the `-c` switch is specified. This switch is available to all C compilers. Here is the command format for *clang*:

```
clang -Wall -c mystring.c
```

The -c switch directs *clang* to "compile only." The source code file is compiled into object code, mystring.o, but it's not linked to create a program. This step is repeated for all source code files, though you can specify the lot in a single command:

```
clang -Wall -c first.c second.c third.c
```

For this command, three object code files are created: first.o, second.o, and third.o.

The next step is to use the archive utility *ar* to build the library. This command is followed by three arguments: command switches, the name of the library file, and finally the object code files required to build the library. For example:

```
ar -rcs libmystring.a mystring.o
```

Here are what the switches do:

- -c—Creates the archive
- -s—Indexes the archive
- -r—Inserts file(s) into the archive

You can specify them as *-rcs* or *-r -c -s*—either way.

The name of the library file will be libmystring.a. The *ar* utility uses the object code file mystring.o to create the library. If multiple object code files were required, specify them after mystring.o.

Upon success, the *ar* utility creates the library named libmystring.a. This naming format follows the convention used in Linux: libname.a. The library starts with lib, and then name, which is the library name. The filename extension is dot-a.

The .a extension, as well as the process outlined in this section for creating a library, is designed for static library, as opposed to a dynamic library. The static model works best for this type of library, which is used only by command-line programs and doesn't require the capabilities of a dynamic library. I do not cover dynamic libraries in this book.

7.3.3 *Using the string library*

To use a library other than the standard C library, its name must be specified at build time. The -l (little L) switch is immediately followed by the library name. The name is the only part of the library filename used, not the first three letters (lib) or the .a extension.

If you've copied the library into the /usr/local/lib folder, the linker searches for it there. Otherwise, the -L (big L) switch directs the linker to look in a specific directory for library files. For a library you create in the same folder as your program, such as when working the examples in this book, specify the -L. (dash-big L-period) switch to direct the linker to look in the current directory. For example:

```
clang -Wall -L. libsample.c -lmystring
```

When *clang* builds the source code from `libsample.c` into a program, it directs the linker to look in the current directory (`-L.`) for the library file `libmystring.h` (`-lmystring`). The format for this command is important; the `-l` switch must be specified last or else you see linker errors. (Some compilers may be smart enough to discover the library switch as any command-line argument, though my experience leads me to recommend putting the `-l` switch last.)

The next listing shows the source code found in `libsample.c`, available in this book's online repository. The *strcaps()* function at line 8 is part of the mystring library. Its prototype is found in the `mystring.h` header file (also included in the repository), though it's the library that contains the function's code. Line 2 shows the header file in double quotes, which directs the compiler to locate it in the current directory.

Listing 7.15   Source code for `libsample.c`

```
#include <stdio.h>
#include "mystring.h"            ◁——┐  Looks in the current directory for
                                       this header file, which contains the
int main()                             prototype for the strcaps() function
{
    char string[] = "the great american novel";

    strcaps(string);           ◁——┐  This function is found in the
    printf("%s\n",string);             libmystring.a library,
                                       linked in at build time.
    return(0);
}
```

Here is the program's output when built and linked using the command shown earlier:

```
The Great American Novel
```

Just as you can place a copy of your personal library in the `/usr/local/lib` folder, you can place a copy of the library's header file into the `/usr/local/include` folder. This step avoids having to use the double quotes to set the header file's location; as with `/usr/local/lib`, the compiler scans the `/usr/local/include` folder for header files.

7.4   *A kinda OOP approach*

C is a procedural programming language. Inelegantly put, this description means that C code runs from top to bottom, with one thing happening after another. Older programming languages like C are also procedural. The list includes BASIC, Fortran, COBOL, and other relics. But don't let the antiquity fool you! COBOL programmers made bank during the Y2K crisis.

Newer programming languages are object-oriented. They approach the programming task differently, something you can read about in wonderful books about these popular and trendy digital dialects. Without getting too far into the weeds, and keeping this discussion vague to avoid the nitpickers, object-oriented programming (OOP) involves methods instead of functions. *Methods* work like functions, though they're often a part of the data type they manipulate.

For example, if you want to obtain the length of a string in the Java programming language, you use this construction:

```
Len = Str.length()
```

The string variable is named `Str`. The dot operator accesses the *length()* method, which is attached to all string objects. (Get it?) The result returned is the number of characters in string `Str`. The equivalent C language statement is:

```
len = strlen(str);
```

The dot operator is also used in C, specifically in a structure. And one of the members of a string can be . . . a function. Surprise.

7.4.1   Adding a function to a structure

A structure contains members of specific data types: *int, float, char,* and so on. As it turns out, a function is also a data type, and it can serve as a member of a structure.

For comparison, if you've been around the C language a while, you know that many functions can accept another function as an argument; the *qsort()* function uses another function (its name as an address) as one of its arguments. As with functions as arguments, specifying a function as a structure member involves using a specific format:

```
type (*name)(arguments)
```

The `type` is a data type, the value returned from the function or *void* for nothing returned.

The `name` is the function's name, which is secretly a pointer. In this format, the function's name isn't followed by parentheses. Instead, the `arguments` item lists any arguments passed to the function.

To form a clear picture, here is a structure definition that has a function as one of its members:

```
struct str {
    char *string;
    unsigned long (*length)(const char *);
};
```

The `str` structure's function member is referenced as the `length`. It takes a *const char* pointer—a string—as its argument. And it returns an *unsigned long* value. This declaration merely creates a function as a member of the `str` structure, which also contains a string member. To make the function member work, it must be assigned to a specific function. In this case, the function I have in mind is *strlen()*, which takes a *const char* pointer as an argument and returns an *unsigned long* value.

Creating a structure merely defines its members. To use the structure, a variable of the structure type is created. Here, structure `str` variable `str1` is created:

```
struct str str1;
```

And its members must be assigned values. Here is how the `length` member is assigned:

```
str1.length = &strlen;
```

The `length` member's function is *strlen()*. It's specified without the parentheses, prefixed by the ampersand to obtain its address. Once assigned, the function member can be called like any function. For example:

```
len = str1.length(str1.string);
```

Member `str1.length` is a function (secretly *strlen()*). It operates on the `string` member of the same structure, `str1.string`. The value returned, the length of the string, is stored in variable `len`.

The following listing demonstrates all these crazy steps in the source code for `struct_funct.c`. This file is available in this book's online repository.

Listing 7.16   Source code for `struct_funct.c`

```
#include <stdio.h>
#include <string.h>          ◁——  Must include the string.h
                                   header for the definition of
                                   the strlen() function
int main()
{
    struct str {
        char *string;
        unsigned long (*length)(const char *);   ◁——  The function
    };                                                 member of
    struct str str1;        ◁——  Variable str1 is created of      structure str
    char s[] = "Heresy";          the str structure type.

    str1.string = s;
    str1.length = &strlen;  ◁——  The function is assigned, no
                                  parentheses, and prefixed by
                                  the address-of operator.
    printf("The string '%s' is %lu characters long\n",
            str1.string,
            str1.length(str1.string)    ◁——  The function is
        );                                    called in the printf()
                                              statement.
    return(0);
}
```

The **string** member is assigned.

Here is the program's output:

```
The string 'Heresy' is 6 characters long
```

I confess that the expression `str1.length(str1.string)` doesn't magically transform C into an object-oriented programming language. Yet for those intrepid coders who strive to make C more OOP-like, this is the approach they take. They may even cobble together macros to make the contraption look cleaner, such as `str.length()`, which is what I'd be pleased with. Still, C wasn't created to offer such constructions. Most coders who want to use OOP drift to languages such as C++, C#, and Python.

7.4.2 *Creating a string "object"*

I'm risking certain heresy charges and banishment from the C programming world, but it's possible to further expand upon the idea of making C more OOP-like. Consider that you could create a string structure "object." The problem with C is that the implementation must be done through functions.

For example, you could write a function to create the pseudo string object. The function would require a string structure to be passed. Such a structure might look like this:

```
struct string {
  char *value;
  int length;
};
```

This example is brief. You could add other string descriptors as structure members and perhaps a smattering of functions as well. But, for a pseudo string object demonstration, this construction is sufficient.

To create the phony string object, a *string_create()* function is needed. This function is passed a pointer to a `string` structure along with the string's contents (text):

```
int string_create(struct string *s, char *v)
```

The pointer is necessary to allow the function to modify the structure directly. Without the pointer, any changes made to the passed structure within the function are discarded. The string passed, `v`, is eventually incorporated into the structure along with other informative goodies.

The next listing illustrates the *string_create()* function. It returns TRUE or FALSE values depending on whether the object is successfully created: the string's length is obtained and stored in the structure's `length` member. This value is used to allocate storage for the string. I feel that allocating storage specifically for the string is better than duplicating the passed string's pointer, which could change in the future.

> **Listing 7.17   The *string_create()* function**

```
int string_create(struct string *s, char *v)
{
    if( s==NULL )
        return(FALSE);
```

Confirms that a string is
available; if not, returns **FALSE**

Assigns the string's length →
```
s->length = strlen(v);

s->value = malloc( sizeof(char) * s->length +1 );          ←  **Allocates storage for the string**
if( s->value==NULL )
    return(FALSE);                      **Copies the original string to newly allocated storage**
strcpy(s->value,v);           ←

return(TRUE);          ←    **Returns TRUE upon success**
}
```

Just as an object is created, a companion *string_destroy()* function must exist. This function removes the object, which means deallocating the string's storage and zeroing out any other structure members.

The next listing shows the *string_destroy()* function, called with the sole argument as the `string` structure to clear. The function does three things: frees the allocated memory, assigns the value pointer to NULL (which confirms that the memory is deallocated), and sets the string's length to zero. This function doesn't obliterate the structure variable, unlike OOP languages that may also remove the variable that's created.

> **Listing 7.18   The *string_destroy()* function**

```
void string_destroy(struct string *s)
{
    free(s->value);                **Assigns the pointer to NULL,**
    s->value = NULL;           ←    **which can be used later to test**
    s->length = 0;         ←        **for a valid string structure**
}
```
Free string storage memory   **Resets the string length to zero**

Of course, after destroying a string structure variable, it can be reused or reassigned. The point is to have both a create function and a destroy function for the "object," which mimics how some object-oriented programming languages work with objects.

The source code file `string_object.c`, available on this book's online repository, showcases both functions. In the code, you see that the `string` structure is declared externally, which allows all functions to access its definition.

It's possible to expand upon the `string` structure, adding more members that describe the string—including function members. I leave this topic to you for further exploration, though keep in mind that object-oriented programming languages are available for you to learn and play. Forcing C into this mold is a consideration, but I would recommend focusing on the language's strengths as opposed to pretending it's something else.

Unicode and wide characters

In the beginning was Morse code, a simple method of translating electrical pulses—long and short—into a string of characters and readable text. Morse wasn't the first electronic encoding method, but it's perhaps the best known. Developed in 1840, it's named after Samuel Morse, who helped invent the telegraph and who also bears an uncanny resemblance to *Lost in Space*'s Dr. Smith.

Some 30 years after Morse code came the Baudot code. Also used in telegraph communications, *Baudot* (baw-DOH) represents letters of the alphabet using a 5-bit sequence. This code was later modified into Murray code for use on teletype machines with keyboards, as well as early computers. Then came IBM's Binary Coded Decimal (BCD) for use on their mainframe computers. Eventually, the ASCII encoding standard ruled the computer roost until Unicode solved everyone's text encoding problems in the late 20th century.

This chapter's topic is character *encoding*, the art of taking an alphabet soup of characters and assigning them a code value for digital representation in a computer. The culmination of this effort is Unicode, which slaps a value to almost every imaginable written scribble in the history of mankind. To help explore Unicode in the C language, in this chapter you will:

- Review various computer encoding systems
- Study ASCII text, code pages, and Unicode
- Set the locale details for your programs
- Understand different character types, such as UTF-8
- Work with wide characters and strings
- Perform wide character file I/O

I really don't see any new text-encoding format taking over from Unicode. It's a solid system, with new characters assigned every year. Its only limitation seems to be its spotty implementation in various typefaces. Therefore, although you can program Unicode in a Linux terminal window, text output may not appear accurately. To best resolve this issue, ensure that your terminal program window lets you change fonts so that you can witness the interesting, weird, and impressive text Unicode can produce.

8.1 *Text representation in computers*

Computers understand numbers, bits organized into bytes dwelling in memory, manipulated by the processor, and stored long-term on media. The system really doesn't care about text, and it's totally ignorant of spelling. Still, to communicate with humans, many of these byte values correspond to printed characters. It's the consistency of this character encoding that allows computers to communicate with humans and exchange information, despite their innate reluctance to do so.

8.1.1 *Reviewing early text formats*

The only time you hear about Morse code these days is in the movies. Something important must happen, and communications takes place only via tapping on a pipe or something equally desperate and silly. One of the characters responds with the cliché that their knowledge of Morse code is "rusty," but the message is decoded, the audience impressed, and the day saved.

Morse code is composed of a series of dashes and dots, long or short pulses, to encode letters and numbers. No distinction is necessary between upper- and lowercase. Some common codes are known among nerds, such as S-O-S, though I can't readily remember which triplex series of dots and dashes belongs to the S or O. I suppose I can look at table 8.1 to determine which is which.

Table 8.1   Morse code

Character	Code	Character	Code	Character	Code
A	. -	M	- -	Y	- . - -
B	- . . .	N	- .	Z	- - . .
C	- . - .	O	- - -	1	. - - - - -
D	- . .	P	. - - .	2	. . - - -
E	.	Q	- - . -	3	. . . - -
F	. . - .	R	. - .	4	. . . . -
G	- - .	S	. . .	5	. . . . .
H	. . . .	T	-	6	- . . . .
I	. .	U	. . -	7	- - . . .

Table 8.1 Morse code *(continued)*

Character	Code	Character	Code	Character	Code
J	.---	V	...-	8	---..
K	-.-	W	.--	9	----.
L	.-..	X	-..-	0	-----

I'll avoid getting into the weeds with technical details about the length of a dash or dot and spaces and such. Though, one nerdy point I can bring up is that the encoding is designed so that frequently used letters have fewer units, such as E, T, I, A, N, and so on.

The next listing shows the *toMorse()* function, which outputs a Morse code character string based on an input character. The character strings are stored in two *const char* arrays, matching the sequences A to Z for morse_alpha[] and 0 to 9 for morse_digit[]. An *if-else* structure uses ctype functions to pull out alpha and numeric characters; all other characters are ignored.

Listing 8.1 The *toMorse()* function

```
void toMorse(char c)
{
    const char *morse_alpha[] = {
        ".-", "-...", "-.-.", "-..", ".", "..-.",
        "--.", "....", "..", ".---", "-.-", ".-..",
        "--", "-.", "---", ".--.", "--.-", ".-.",
        "...", "-", "..-", "...-", ".--", "-..-",
        "-.--", "--.."
    };
    const char *morse_digit[] = {
        "-----", ".----", "..---", "...--", "....-",
        ".....", "-....", "--...", "---..", "----."
    };
    if( isalpha(c) )
    {
        c = toupper(c);
        printf("%s ",morse_alpha[c-'A']);
    }
    else if( isdigit(c) )
    {
        printf("%s ",morse_digit[c-'0']);
    }
    else if( c==' ' || c=='\n' )
    {
        putchar('\n');
    }
    else
        return;
}
```

Arrays declared as **const char** *to keep the code from otherwise messing with them; this type of construction dislikes being manipulated.*

Pulls out alphabetic characters

Converts to uppercase; Morse is case-insensitive.

Subtracts the character from 'A' to obtain the proper array element offset

Checks for digits 0 through 9

Subtracts the digit from '0' to obtain the proper array element offset

For spaces and newlines, outputs a newline

Ignores non-Morse characters; no output is generated.

The *toMorse()* function is easily set into a filter, which translates text input into Morse code strings for output. Such a filter is found in the source code file `morse_code_filter.c`, available in this book's online repository.

Another text encoding scheme is Baudot. This term may be strange to you—unless you're an old timer who once referred to your dial-up modem's speed in "baud." A 300-baud modem crept along at 300 characters per second. Because baud isn't exactly a representation of characters per second, faster modems (and today's broadband) are measured in bits per second (BPS) and not baud.

Anyway.

The Baudot scheme encodes text in 5-bit chunks. This code was adapted by engineer and inventor Donald Murray into Murray code for use on teletype machines. These machines featured a QWERTY keyboard and were often used as input devices for early computer systems. Specifically, Murray developed paper tape to store and read keystrokes. Holes punched in the paper tape represented characters, as illustrated in figure 8.1.

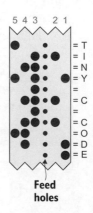

Figure 8.1   Paper tape with holes punched representing Baudot–Murray code

The International Telegraph Alphabet No. 2 (ITA2) standard for Baudot–Murray code was introduced in 1928. In the United States, the standard is named US-TTY (TTY for teletype). Because it's 5 bits wide, not enough values are available to handle the full character set. Therefore, the code requires a shift character to switch between the alpha and symbol sets.

Table 8.2 lists the Baudot–Murray hexadecimal codes for alphanumeric characters, the letter set. The code 0x1B switches to the figure set characters, shown in table 8.3. Code 0x1B or code 0x1F switches back.

Table 8.2   Baudot–Murray codes for ITA2 and US-TTY, letter set

Code	Character	Code	Character	Code	Character	Code	Character
0x00	\0	0x08	\r	0x10	T	0x18	O
0x01	E	0x09	D	0x11	Z	0x19	B
0x02	\n	0x0A	R	0x12	L	0x1A	G
0x03	A	0x0B	J	0x13	W	0x1B	shift
0x04	space	0x0C	N	0x14	H	0x1C	M
0x05	S	0x0D	F	0x15	Y	0x1D	X
0x06	I	0x0E	C	0x16	P	0x1E	V
0x07	U	0x0F	K	0x17	Q	0x1F	del

Table 8.3   Baudot–Murray codes for ITA2 and US-TTY, figure set

Code	Character	Code	Character	Code	Character	Code	Character
0x00	\0	0x08	/r	0x10	5	0x18	9
0x01	3	0x09	$	0x11	"	0x19	?
0x02	\n	0x0A	4	0x12	)	0x1A	&
0x03	-	0x0B	'	0x13	2	0x1B	shift
0x04	space	0x0C	,	0x14	#	0x1C	.
0x05	\a	0x0D	!	0x15	6	0x1D	/
0x06	8	0x0E	:	0x16	0	0x1E	;
0x07	7	0x0F	(	0x17	1	0x1F	letters

Don't try to make sense of the character mapping used in Baudot–Murray. If you're pleased with the way ASCII codes are organized (refer to chapter 5), the text encoding shown in tables 8.2 and 8.3 is particularly baffling. Keep in mind that these codes were created for consistency with earlier systems. Perhaps some sense is to be found in the encoding. Who knows?

I was all excited to write a program that translates between ASCII and Baudot–Murray encoding. The problem with such translation is that the resulting code is pretty much brute force, a character-to-character swap. Mix in the shifting character sets, and such a programming chore becomes a nightmare with no practical purpose.

8.1.2   Evolving into ASCII text and code pages

Beyond the Baudot–Murray code used on teletype machines, IBM invented a text-encoding standard for its mainframes: Extended Binary Coded Decimal Interchange Code (EBCDIC). This scheme was one of the first 8-bit character encoding standards, though it was used primarily with IBM mainframes.

For input, IBM systems used punch cards. Therefore, the EBCDIC encoding scheme was designed to allocate codes for characters with the goal of keeping the punched holes in the card from collecting in clusters. This approach was necessary to prevent the cards from tearing or the holes from connecting with each other. To meet this goal, the EBCDIC codes feature gaps in their sequences; many EBCDIC character codes are blank.

As computing moved away from punch cards, throngs of programmers rejoiced. A new encoding standard—ASCII—was developed by the American Standards Association in 1963. A 7-bit standard, ASCII added logic and—more important—compassion to text encoding.

The 7-bit ASCII code is still in use today, though bytes today are consistently composed of 8 bits. This extra bit means that modern computers can encode 256 characters for a byte of data, only half of which (codes 0 through 127) are standardized by ASCII.

You can read more about having fun with ASCII in chapter 4. My focus in this section is about character codes 128 through 255, the so-called extended ASCII character set.

Extended ASCII was never an official standard, nor was it consistent among all 8-bit computers. These extra 128 characters in a byte were mapped to non-ASCII characters on various microcomputers in the late 1970s and early 1980s. Having the codes available meant that more symbols could be generated on a typical computer, including common characters such as ×, ÷, ±, Greek letters, fractions, accented characters, diglyphs, and so on.

Figure 8.2 lists the extended ASCII character set available on the original IBM PC series of computers back in the early 1980s. Though the variety of characters is rich, these 128 bonus symbols weren't enough to represent every available or desired character—only a tease.

	0	1	2	3	4	5	6	7	8	9	A	B	C	D	E	F
0x80	Ç	ü	é	â	ä	à	å	ç	ê	ë	è	ï	î	ì	Ä	Å
0x90	É	æ	Æ	ô	ö	ò	û	ù	ÿ	Ö	Ü	¢	£	¥	₧	ƒ
0xa0	á	í	ó	ú	ñ	Ñ	ª	º	¿	⌐	¬	½	¼	¡	«	»
0xb0	░	▒	▓	│	┤	╡	╢	╖	╕	╣	║	╗	╝	╜	╛	┐
0xc0	└	┴	┬	├	─	┼	╞	╟	╚	╔	╩	╦	╠	═	╬	╧
0xd0	╨	╤	╥	╙	╘	╒	╓	╫	╪	┘	┌	█	▄	▌	▐	▀
0xe0	α	ß	Γ	π	Σ	σ	µ	τ	Φ	Θ	Ω	δ	∞	φ	ε	∩
0xf0	≡	±	≥	≤	⌠	⌡	÷	≈	°	∙	·	√	ⁿ	²	■	

Figure 8.2   The original IBM PC "extended ASCII" character set

To accommodate more characters, early computers used code pages. A *code page* represents a different collection of characters, for both ASCII (codes 0 through 127) and the 8-bit character codes, 128 to 255.

The characters shown in figure 8.2 for codes 128 through 255 represent IBM PC code page 437. Other code pages use different symbols. Eventually code pages were made available for specific foreign languages and alphabetic. Chinese, Japanese, Arabic, and other character sets are featured on various code pages.

Commands available in the venerable MS-DOS operating system allowed code page character sets to be switched, though the computer was still limited to using only one code page of characters at a time. In the system configuration file (CONFIG.SYS), the COUNTRY command set locale details, including available code pages. At the command prompt, the CHCP command is used to check the current code page as well as change the character set to a new code page.

Linux doesn't use code pages, mostly because it implements Unicode (see the next section). Windows, however, still uses the same extended ASCII code page as the original IBM PC. You can view these legacy characters when a program outputs character code values from 128 through 255.

The source code in the following listing generates the contents of figure 8.2. The core of the program consists of nested *for* loops that output rows and columns representing the traditional extended ASCII character set, or code page 1. Formatting within the *printf()* statements ensure that the output appears in a handy table.

Listing 8.2   Source code for `extended_ascii.c`

```
#include <stdio.h>

int main()
{
    int x,y;

    printf("      ");
    for(x=0; x<16; x++)
        printf(" %X ",x);
    putchar('\n');

    for( x=0x80;x<0x100; x+=0x10 )
    {
        printf(" 0x%2x ",x);
        for( y=0; y<0x10; y++ )
        {
            printf(" %c ",x+y);
        }
        putchar('\n');
    }

    return(0);
}
```

Six spaces to line up output

Output header row

Output left column

Inner loop that outputs characters, x+y, calculating proper offset

The program generated by the `extended_ascii.c` source code works best on Windows computers. If you run it under Linux or on a Mac, the table is empty or populated with question marks. The characters aren't missing; they just aren't generated in the Linux/Unix environment unless a specific locale is set in the code. The topic of setting a locale is covered later in this chapter.

The tasks of swapping code pages and exploring extended ASCII character sets are no longer required to generate fancy text. With the advent of Unicode in the 1990s, all the text encoding inconsistencies since the early telegraph days are finally resolved.

8.1.3   *Diving into Unicode*

Back in the 1980s, those computer scientists who sat around thinking of wonderful new things to do hit the jackpot. They considered the possibilities of creating a consistent way to encode text—not just ASCII or Latin alphabet characters, but every scribble, symbol, and gewgaw known on this planet, both forward and backward in time. The result, unveiled in the 1990s, is Unicode.

The original intention of Unicode was to widen character width from 8 bits to 16 bits. This change doesn't double the number of characters—it increases possible character encodings from 256 to over 65,000. But even this huge quantity wasn't enough.

Today, the Unicode standard encompasses millions of characters, including hieroglyphics and emojis, a sampling of which is shown in figure 8.3. New characters are added all the time, almost every year. For example, in 2021, 838 new characters were added.

U+2318   U+0156   U+16DF   U+1B0D   U+1F970

Figure 8.3   Various Unicode characters

The current code space for Unicode (as of 2022) consists of 1,114,111 code points. *Code space* is the entire spectrum of Unicode. You can think of *code points* as characters. Not every code point has a character assigned, however: many chunks of the code space are empty. Some code points are designed as overlays or macrons to combine with other characters. Of the plethora, the first 128 code points align with the ASCII standard.

Unicode characters are referenced in the format U+*nnnn*, where *nnnn* is the hexadecimal value for the code point. The code space is organized into code panes representing various languages or scripts. Most web pages that reference Unicode characters, such as unicode-table.com, use these code planes or blocks when you browse the collection of characters.

To translate from a Unicode code point—say, U+2665—into a character in C, you must adhere to an encoding format. The most beloved of these encoding formats is the Unicode Transformation Format, UTF. Several flavors of UTF exist:

- UTF-8 uses 8-bit chunks (bytes) to hold character values, with multiple bytes containing the code for some values. The number of bytes varies, but they're all 8-bit chunks.
- UTF-16 uses 16-bit chunks (words) to hold character values. This format isn't as popular as UTF-8.
- UTF-32 uses 32-bit chunks (long words). All characters are represented by 32 bits whether or not they need the storage space. This format isn't that popular because it occupies more space than many code points require.

These encoding formats play a role with setting the locale, which is the key to working with Unicode text in C. More information on the locale is offered in section 8.2.1

The character itself is described as a *wide character*, or a character that may require more than a single byte to generate output. This topic is covered later in section 8.2.2.

Finally, be aware that not every typeface supports the entire Unicode host. Missing characters are output as blanks, question marks, or boxes, depending on the font. You may encounter this problem when running some of the programs later in this chapter. The solution is to set another font for the terminal window or to configure the terminal window so that it's capable of outputting Unicode text.

8.2   *Wide character programming*

Just outputting a wide character to the console doesn't work. You can try. Maybe you'll be lucky, especially in Windows. But to properly output and program Unicode text in your C programs, you must first set the locale. This setting informs the computer that the program is capable of handling wide characters.

After setting the locale, the code must access and use wide characters for its text I/O. This process is how some text mode programs output fancy Unicode characters in a terminal window—and how email messages and even text messages show emojis and other fun characters. Your program can do so as well, once you learn the steps introduced in this section.

8.2.1 Setting the locale

Locale settings in a program establish such details as language, date and time format, currency symbol, and others specific to a language or region. This function and its pals allow you to write programs for different regions while being lazy about researching, for example, the culture's thousands separator or currency symbol.

For wide character output, setting the proper locale allows your code to use wide characters—the Unicode character set. Yes, setting the locale is the secret.

To view the current locale settings in the Linux environment, type the **locale** command in the terminal window. Here is the output I see:

```
LANG=C.UTF-8
LANGUAGE=
LC_CTYPE="C.UTF-8"
LC_NUMERIC="C.UTF-8"
LC_TIME="C.UTF-8"
LC_COLLATE="C.UTF-8"
LC_MONETARY="C.UTF-8"
LC_MESSAGES="C.UTF-8"
LC_PAPER="C.UTF-8"
LC_NAME="C.UTF-8"
LC_ADDRESS="C.UTF-8"
LC_TELEPHONE="C.UTF-8"
LC_MEASUREMENT="C.UTF-8"
LC_IDENTIFICATION="C.UTF-8"
LC_ALL=
```

The UTF-8 character format is what allows Unicode text I/O—though to enable UTF-8 output in your code, you must use the *setlocale()* function, prototyped in the `locale.h` header file. Here is the format:

```
char *setlocale(int category, const char *locale);
```

The first argument, `category`, is a defined constant representing which aspect of the locale you want to set. Use `LC_ALL` to set all categories. The `LC_CTYPE` category is specific to text.

The second argument is a string to set the specific locale details. For example, for text you can specify `"en_US.UTF-8"`, which activates the 8-bit Unicode character set for English. An empty string can also be specified.

The *setlocale()* function returns a string representing the specific information requested. You need not use the string; setting the locale is good enough for wide character I/O.

Be aware that the *setlocale()* function isn't available in some Windows compilers. The method for accessing Unicode characters in Windows is different from what's described in this chapter.

The next listing shows a tiny program that uses the *setlocale()* function to output locale details—specifically, the character set in use. Line 8 uses the *setlocale()* function to return a string describing the current locale, saved in variable `locale`. A *printf()* statement outputs the locale string. Used in this way, the *setlocale()* function doesn't change the locale settings; it only reports information.

Listing 8.3   Source code for `locale_function.c`

```
#include <stdio.h>
#include <locale.h>          ←|  The setlocale() function requires
                                the locale.h header file.
int main()
{                               Pointer to a string to retain
    char *locale;        ←      the function's output
                                                    Synchronizes the
                                                    GPU so that the
    locale = setlocale(LC_ALL,"");          ←       work completes
    printf("The current locale is %s\n",locale);  ←
                                                    Outputs the
    return(0);                                      locale details
}
```

Here is sample output:

```
The current locale is C.UTF-8
```

The C stands for the C language. If it doesn't, it should. UTF-8 is the character encoding.

After setting the locale, the next step to outputting Unicode characters is to understand the concept of wide characters.

8.2.2   *Exploring character types*

To invoke the magic that enables access to Unicode's humongous character set, you must be familiar with the three types of characters used in computerdom:

- Single-byte characters
- Wide characters
- Multibyte characters

Single-byte characters provide the traditional way to generate text. These are 8-bit values, the *char* data type, equal to a single byte of storage. Though *char* values range from 0 through 255 (unsigned), only values 0 through 127 are assigned characters using the ASCII standard.

The wide character data type uses more than 8-bits to encode text. The number of bytes can vary, depending on the character. In C, the *wchar_t* data type handles wide characters, and the wide character (wchar) family of functions manipulates these characters.

A multibyte character requires several bytes to represent the character. This description includes wide characters but also characters that require a prefix byte, or lead unit, and then another sequence of bytes to represent a single character. This type of multibyte character may be used in specific applications and computer platforms. It's not covered in this book.

To represent a single-byte character, you use the *char* data type in C. For example:

```
char hash = '#';
```

The hash character is assigned to *char* variable hash. The character code is 35 decimal, 23 hex.

To represent wide characters, use the *wchar_t* data type. Its definition is found in the wchar.h header file, which must be included in your code. This header file also prototypes the various wide character functions. (See the next section.)

The following statement declares the wide character yen:

```
wchar_t yen = 0xa5;
```

The Yen character ¥ is U+00a5. This value is assigned to *wchar_t* variable yen. The compiler won't let you assign the character directly:

```
wchar_t yen = L'¥';
```

The L prefix defines the character as long (wide). This prefix works like the L suffix applied to *long* integer values: 123L indicates the value 123 specified as a *long int* value. Although this L-prefix trick works with ASCII characters expressed as wide characters, your C compiler most likely chokes on the attempt to compile with such a character in the source code file; the warning I see is "Illegal character encoding." Your editor also may not allow you to type or paste wide characters directly.

The L prefix is also used to declare a wide character string. Here is a wide character string:

```
wchar_t howdy[] = L"Hello, planet Earth!";
```

The string above, "Hello, planet Earth!", is composed of wide characters, thanks to the L prefix. The *wchar_t* data type declares wide string howdy.

As with single characters, you cannot insert special characters into a wide string. The following declaration is flagged as illegal character encoding:

```
wchar_t monetary[] = L"$¥€£";
```

Such a string is instead composed in this manner:

```
wchar_t monetary[] = {
    0x24, 0xa5, 0x20ac, 0xa3, 0x0
};
```

Hex values above represent the characters dollar sign, yen, euro, and British pound, followed by the null character caboose to terminate the string.

To output wide characters and wide strings, use the *wprintf()* function. This function works like the standard library *printf()* function, though it deals with wide strings. Special placeholders are used for wide characters and wide strings:

- The `%lc` placeholder represents a single wide character.
- The `%ls` placeholder represents a wide string.

Lowercase L in the placeholder identifies the target variable as the wide or *wchar_t* data type. This character is analogous to the little L in the `%ld` placeholder for *long* decimal integer values.

8.2.3   *Generating wide character output*

To output wide characters in C, you employ the functions declared in the `wchar.h` header file, which also conveniently defines the *wchar_t* data type. The functions parallel the standard string functions (from `string.h`), with most companion functions prefixed by a w or some other subtle difference. For example, the wide character version of *printf()* is *wprintf()*.

Oh, and you need the `locale.h` header file because the wide character functions must be activated by first setting the locale. Refer to section 8.2.1 for details on using the *setlocale()* function.

The next listing shows source code that uses the *wprintf()* function in the traditional "Hello, world!" type of program, with my own wide twist. The *setlocale()* function isn't required because the output is ASCII, albeit wide ASCII, which is why the *wprintf()* formatting string is prefixed by an L (long, or wide character). The *stdio.h* header isn't required because none of its functions appear in the code.

> **Listing 8.4   Source code for `hello_wworld01.c`**

```
#include <wchar.h>          ◁———  Wide character
                                  definitions and
int main()                        functions
{
    wprintf(L"Hello, wide world!\n");   ◁———  The wprintf() function is analogous
                                              to the printf() function. The L prefix
    return(0);                                is required for a string composed of
}                                             wide characters. Even though the
                                              text here is ASCII, wide characters are
                                              used internally to represent the text.
```

Here is the program's output:

```
Hello, wide world!
```

Nothing surprising, but don't let the lack of suspense lull you into a false sense of familiarity. To help ease you into the wide character functions, you can modify the code in two steps.

First, set the string as its own declaration earlier in the code:

```
wchar_t hello[] = L"Hello, wide world!\n";
```

The *wchar_t* data type defines array hello[] composed of characters present in the wide string. If the L prefix is omitted, the compiler barfs up a data type mismatch error. Yes, it's an error: the code won't compile. To create a wide string, you need both the *wchar_t* data type and the L prefix on the text enclosed in double quotes.

Second, modify the *wprintf()* statement to output the string:

```
wprintf(L"%ls",hello);
```

The L prefix is required for the formatting string, because all wide character functions deal with wide characters. The %ls placeholder represents a string of wide characters. Argument hello references the address of the wide hello[] array.

These two updates to the hello_wworld01.c code are found in the online repository in the source code file hello_wworld02.c. The output is the same as from the first program.

To output a single wide character, use the *putwchar()* function. It works like *putchar()*, and it's one of several wide character functions where the *w* is found in the middle of its name.

The code in the next listing outputs the four playing card suits: spades, hearts, clubs, and diamonds. Their Unicode values are assigned as elements of the suits[] array. The *setlocale()* function is required because these are not ASCII characters. Within the *for* loop, the *putwchar()* function outputs the characters. A final *putwchar()* function outputs a newline—a wide newline.

Listing 8.5   Source code for suits.c

```
#include <wchar.h>
#include <locale.h>

int main()
{
    const int count = 4;
    wchar_t suits[count] = {          Unicode values for the
        0x2660, 0x2665, 0x2663, 0x2666   ◁— four playing card suits
    };
    int x;

    setlocale(LC_CTYPE,"en_US.UTF-8");   ◁— The locale is set
                                             because these are
                                             not ASCII characters.

    for( x=0; x<count; x++ )
        putwchar(suits[x]);              ◁— The putwchar() function
    putwchar('\n');                          outputs each wide
                                             character value.
    return(0);
}
```

Here is the code's output:

♠♥♣♦

On my Linux systems, the output is monochrome. But on my Macintosh, the hearts and diamonds symbols are colored red. This difference is based on the font used. The Mac seems to have a better selection of Unicode characters available in its terminal window than are available in my Linux distro.

The code for `suits.c` illustrates how many Unicode strings are created and then output. The technique for creating the `suits[]` array is how you build a wide character string from scratch, though `suits[]` is a character array and not a string, which must be terminated with the null character.

In the following listing, three Unicode strings are declared in the *main()* function. Each one ends with newline and null characters. The *fputws()* function sends the strings as the output to the *stdout* device (file handle, defined in `stdio.h`). This function is the equivalent of the *fputs()* function.

Listing 8.6   Source code for `wide_hello.c`

```
#include <stdio.h>              ←┐  Required for the
#include <wchar.h>               │  definition of stdout
#include <locale.h>

                                    Each array is created as a
int main()                          string, including the newline
{                                   and null characters.
    wchar_t russian[] = {      ←
        0x41f, 0x440, 0x438, 0x432, 0x435, 0x442, '!' , '\n', '\0'
    };
    wchar_t chinese[] = {
        0x4f31, 0x597d, '\n', '\0'
    };
    wchar_t emoji[] = {
        0x1f44b, '\n', '\0'
    };

    setlocale(LC_ALL,"en_US.UTF-8");
    fputws(russian,stdout);    ←┐
    fputws(chinese,stdout);     │  The fputws() function
    fputws(emoji,stdout);       │  requires a wide string and
                                    file handle as arguments.
    return(0);
}
```

Figure 8.4 shows the output generated by the `wide_hello.c` program. This screenshot is from my Macintosh, where the Terminal app properly generates all the Unicode characters. The output looks similar in Linux, though under Windows 10 Ubuntu Linux, only the Cyrillic text is output; the rest of the text appears as question marks in boxes. These generic characters mean that the Unicode characters shown in figure 8.4 are unavailable in the terminal's assigned typeface.

Figure 8.4   The properly interpreted output of the `wide_hello.c` program

The inability of some typefaces to properly render portions of the Unicode character set is something you should always consider when coding wide text output.

Not every string you output requires all wide text characters, such as those strings shown in listing 8.6. In fact, most often you may find a single character required in a string of otherwise typable, plain ASCII text. One way to sneak such a character into a string is demonstrated next. Here, the Yen character (¥) is declared on its own as *wchar_t* variable yen. This value is output in the *wprintf()* function by using the %lc placeholder.

Listing 8.7   Source code for yen01.c

```
#include <wchar.h>
#include <locale.h>

int main()
{
    wchar_t yen = 0xa5;              ◁─┐  The character is specified by
                                         its Unicode value, U-00A5.

    setlocale(LC_CTYPE,"en_US.UTF-8");

    wprintf(L"That will be %lc500\n",yen);   ◁─  The %lc placeholder
                                                 represents the wide
                                                 character value in yen.
    return(0);
}
```

Here is the code's output:

```
That will be ¥500
```

In the code, I set the locale LC_CTYPE value to en_US.UTF-8, which is proper for the English language as it's abused in the United States. You don't need to set the Japanese locale (ja_JP.UTF-8) to output the character.

Another way to insert a non-ASCII Unicode character in a string is substitution. For example, you can create a wide character string of ASCII text, then plop in a specific character before the string is output.

To modify listing 8.7, first you create a wide character string with a placeholder for the untypable Unicode character:

```
wchar_t s[] = L"That will be $500\n";
```

At element 13 in wide character string s[], I've used a dollar sign instead of the Yen sign I need. The next step is to replace this element with the proper wide character:

```
s[13] = 0xa5;
```

This assignment works because all characters in string s[] are wide. Character code 0xa5 replaces the dollar sign. The string is then output with this statement:

```
wprintf(L"%ls",s);
```

This update to the code is named yen02.c, and it's found in this book's online repository. If you perform a trick like this, ensure that you properly document what value 0xa5 is, so as not to confuse any other programmers who may later examine your code.

EXERCISE 8.1

Using the method described earlier, and available in the source code file yen02.c, substitute a Unicode (untypable) character in a string. Create a program that outputs this text:

```
I ♥ to code.
```

The Unicode value for the heart symbol is U+2665, shown earlier in the suits.c source code.

My solution is available in the online repository as code_love.c.

8.2.4 *Receiving wide character input*

Wide character input functions are prototyped in the wchar.h header file along with their output counterparts, covered in the preceding section. Like the wide character output functions, these input functions parallel those of standard input. For example, the *getwchar()* function receives wide character input just as the *getchar()* function receives normal character input. Or should it be called *thin* character input?

The tricky part about wide character input is how to generate the wide characters. Standard keyboard input works as it always does—the characters interpreted as their wide values. Some keyboards have Unicode character keys, such as the £ or € symbols. Check to see whether your Linux terminal program allows for fancy character input methods, often from a right-click menu. When these tools aren't available to you, the only trick left is to copy and paste Unicode characters from elsewhere, such as a web page or the output of some Unicode-happy application.

The source code for mood.c is shown in the following listing. It uses the *getwchar()* function to process standard input, including wide characters. The single-character input is echoed back in the *wprintf()* statement. The %lc placeholder represents *wchar_t* variable mood.

Listing 8.8 Source code for mood.c

```
#include <locale.h>
#include <wchar.h>

int main()
{
    wchar_t mood;              The single wide character variable mood holds input.

    setlocale(LC_CTYPE,"en_US.UTF-8");

    wprintf(L"What is your mood? ");     This string is ASCII, but the L prefix makes it composed of wide characters.
    mood = getwchar();
    wprintf(L"I feel %lc, too!\n",mood);   Obtains a wide character from standard input and stores it in wchar_t variable mood
```

The %lc placeholder represents wide character mood.

```
        return(0);
}
```

The program created by mood.c reads from standard input, though any text you type is represented internally by using wide characters. Therefore, the program runs whether you type a Unicode character or any other keyboard character, as in this example:

```
What is your mood? 7
I feel 7, too!
```

The true test, however, is to type a Unicode character, specifically an emoji. With some versions of Linux (not the Windows version), you can right-click (or control-click) in the terminal window to access emoji characters for input.

In Windows, press the Windows and period keys on the keyboard to bring up an emoji palette. This trick works in the Ubuntu Linux shell window.

On the Macintosh, press the Ctrl+Command+Space keyboard shortcut to see a pop-up emoji palette, as shown in figure 8.5. From this palette, you can choose an emoji to represent your mood, which then appears in the output string.

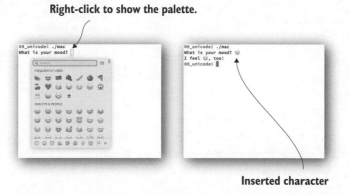

Figure 8.5 **Using the Macintosh emoji input panel in the Terminal app**

As a last resort, you can copy and paste the desired character from another program or website. Providing that the terminal window's typeface has the given character, it appears in the program's output.

The *getwchar()* function deals with stream input the same way that *getchar()* does; it's not an interactive function. Review chapter 4 for information on stream I/O in C. The same rules apply to wide characters as they do to the standard *char* data type.

To read more than a single character, use the *fgetws()* function. This function is the wide character version of *fgets()*, with a similar set of arguments. Here is the *man* page format:

```
wchar_t *fgetws(wchar_t *ws, int n, FILE *stream);
```

The first argument is a *wchar_t* buffer to store input. Then comes the buffer size, which is the input character count minus one for the null character, which is automatically added, and finally, the file stream, such as stdin for standard input.

The *fgetws()* function returns the buffer's address upon success or NULL otherwise.

The source code for wide_string_in.c, illustrated in the next listing, shows how the *fgetws()* function is used. The wide character buffer input stores wide characters read from the standard input device (stdin). A *wprintf()* function outputs the characters stored in the input buffer.

Listing 8.9   Source code for `wide_in.c`

```
#include <stdio.h>        ←──  Required for the
#include <wchar.h>             definition of stdin
#include <locale.h>

int main()                      Uses a constant to
{                               set the buffer size
    const int size = 32;     ←─
    wchar_t input[size];     ←─
                                 Wide character
    setlocale(LC_CTYPE,"UTF-8"); input buffer

                                      Reads the size characters
    wprintf(L"Type some fancy text: ");  into the input buffer from
    fgetws(input,size,stdin);       ←─   standard input
    wprintf(L"You typed: '%ls'\n",input); ←─
                                      Uses the %ls placeholder
    return(0);                        to output the wide
}                                     character string
```

The program created from the wide_in.c source code works like any basic I/O program—something you probably wrote when you first learned to program C. The difference is that wide characters are read, stored, and output. So, you can get fancy with your text, as shown in this sample run:

```
Type some fancy text: 你好，世界
You typed: '你好，世界
'
```

As with standard input and the *fgets()* function, the newline character is retained in the input string. You see its effect on the output where the final single quote appears on the following line.

Another wide input function I reluctantly want to cover is *wscanf()*. This function is based on *scanf()*, which is perhaps my least favorite C language input function, though it does have its purposes. Still, the function is a booger to work with because you must get the input data just right or else the thing collapses like a professional soccer player with a hangnail.

Here is the *man* page for *wscanf()*:

```
int wscanf(const wchar_t *restrict format, …);
```

This format is identical to that of the *scanf()* function, though the formatting string (the first argument) is composed of wide characters. If you use this function, you will probably forget the L prefix on the formatting string at least once or twice.

Listing 8.10 shows a silly I/O program, one that I may use in a beginner's programming book. The only Unicode character involved is the British pound sign (£), which is declared early in the code. Otherwise, pay attention to how the *wscanf()* function uses the L prefix for its formatting string. All the statements output wide characters. Input can be in wide characters as well, though only ASCII digits 0 through 9 hold any meaning to the code.

Listing 8.10   Source code for `wscanf.c`

```c
#include <wchar.h>
#include <locale.h>

int main()
{
    const wchar_t pound = 0xa3;        The pound character is
    int quantity;                      defined as a wchar_t
    float total;                       constant.

    setlocale(LC_CTYPE,"en_US.UTF-8");
                                       Just like a scanf()
    wprintf(L"How many crisps do you want? ");   statement, but with
    wscanf(L"%d",&quantity);                      a wide character
    total = quantity * 1.4;                       formatting string
    wprintf(L"That'll be %lc%.2f\n",
            pound,                     Random math, just
            total                      to have the code do
           );                          something

    return(0);                         The %lc placeholder
}                                      outputs the pound symbol;
                                       %.2f formats the amount to
                                       two decimal places.
```

Here is a sample run:

```
How many crisps do you want? 2
That'll be £2.80
```

They must be very nice crisps.

EXERCISE 8.2

Source code file `wide_in.c` (listing 8.9) processes a string of input. But when the string is shorter than the maximum number of characters allowed, the newline is retained in the string. Your task is to modify the source code so that any newline in the string is removed from output.

One way to accomplish this task is to write your own output function. That's too easy. Instead, you must create a function that removes the newline added by the *fgetws()* function, effectively trimming the string.

My solution is available in this book's online repository as `wide_in_better.c`. Please try this exercise on your own before you sneak a peek at my solution.

8.2.5 *Working with wide characters in files*

The `wchar.h` header file also defines wide character equivalents of file I/O functions available in the standard C library—for example, *fputwc()* to send a wide character to a stream, the equivalent of *fputc()*. These wide character functions are paired with the standard library file I/O functions, such as *fopen()*. This mixture creates an exciting pastiche of wide and nonwide characters, so mind your strings!

As with standard I/O, your wide character file functions must set the locale. The file must be opened for reading, writing, or both. Wide character file I/O functions are used to put and get text from the file. The `WEOF` constant is used to identify the wide end-of-file character, *wint_t* data type. Once the file activity is done, the file is closed. This operation should be familiar to you if you've worked with file I/O in C.

As an example, consider code to output the 24 uppercase letters of the Greek alphabet, alpha to omega, A (U+0391) to Ω (U+03A9), saving the alphabet to a file. The Unicode values increment successively for each letter, though a blank spot exists at code U+03A2. These values parallel the lowercase Greek alphabet, which starts at U+03B1. The uppercase blank spot keeps the upper- and lowercase values parallel, as two lowercase sigma characters are used in Greek. These Unicode values are represented by constants within the code:

```
const wchar_t alpha = 0x391;
const wchar_t omega = 0x3a9;
const wchar_t no_sigma = 0x3a2;
```

After the file is created, the uppercase Greek characters are written to the file one at a time, using a *for* loop as shown in the next listing. Constants `alpha` and `omega` represent the first and last characters' Unicode values. The *wchar_t* constant `no_sigma` is used in an *if* test with the loop so that its character (U+03A2, which is blank) is skipped.

> **Listing 8.11   A loop that writes the uppercase Greek alphabet to a file**

Loops through the Greek alphabet

Lets the user know what's going on

```
wprintf(L"Writing the Greek alphabet...\n");
for( a=alpha; a<=omega; a++ )
{
    if( a==no_sigma )
        continue;
    fputwc(a,fp);
    fputwc(a,stdout);
}
fputwc('\0',fp);
```

Tests for the blank spot and . . .

. . . skips over this noncharacter, continuing the loop

Writes the Greek letter to the file (*FILE* pointer `fp`)

Also sends the character to standard output

Writes a null character to the file so that wide string file input functions can be used to read it in later

The rest of the code, not shown in listing 8.11, is available in this book's online repository in the source code file `greek_write.c`. Missing are the statements to open and close the file, along with various variable declarations. Here is sample output:

```
Writing the Greek alphabet...
ΑΒΓΔΕΖΗΘΙΚΛΜΝΞΟΠΡΣΤΥΦΧΨΩ
Done
```

With the locale set, the file contains the Greek uppercase alphabet and not junk. Because the terminal window is intelligent enough to recognize Unicode, you can use the *cat* command to dump the file:

```
$ cat alphabeta.wtxt
ΑΒΓΔΕΖΗΘΙΚΛΜΝΞΟΠΡΣΤΥΦΧΨΩ $
```

The filename is `alphabeta.wtxt`. I made up the `wtxt` extension for a wide text file. You also see that the file's content lacks a newline, which is why the command prompt ($) appears after the Omega.

Here is output from the *hexdump* utility, to show the file's raw bytes:

```
0000000 91ce 92ce 93ce 94ce 95ce 96ce 97ce 98ce
0000010 99ce 9ace 9bce 9cce 9dce 9ece 9fce a0ce
0000020 a1ce a3ce a4ce a5ce a6ce a7ce a8ce a9ce
0000030 0000
0000031
```

Several approaches are possible for reading wide characters from a file. Because I wrote the null character at the end of the alphabet, you can use the *fgetws()* function to read in the line of text. This function is the wide character sibling of the *fgets()* function.

The following listing shows the file-reading code, found in source code file `greek_read01.c` in this book's online repository. Traditional file I/O commands open the file. The locale is set. Then the *fgetws()* function does its magic to read the uppercase alphabet wide string. The line is output, and the file is closed.

Listing 8.12 Source code for `greek_read01.c`

```c
#include <stdio.h>
#include <stdlib.h>
#include <wchar.h>
#include <locale.h>

int main()
{
    const char *file = "alphabeta.wtxt";    ◁      The file to open
    const int length = 64;                  ◁      Defines a constant
    FILE *fp;                                      for the input buffer
    wchar_t line[length];         ◁─────── The wide character input buffer

    fp = fopen(file,"r");         ◁─────── Opens the file for reading
    if( file==NULL )
```

Handles any errors

```
{
    fprintf(stderr,"Unable to open %s\n",file);
    exit(1);
}

setlocale(LC_CTYPE,"en_US.UTF-8");

wprintf(L"Reading from %s:\n",file);         ◁──────  Lets the user know
fgetws(line,length,fp);          ◁                     what's going on
wprintf(L"%ls\n",line);          ◁──────  Reads a line of text
                                           from the file (up to
fclose(fp);                                the null character)

return(0);
                                  Outputs the line read
}
```

Because the source code for greek_write.c adds a null character to the end of the alphabet, the *fgetws()* function in greek_read01.c reads text from the file in one chunk: like the *fgets()* function, *fgetws()* stops reading when it encounters the null byte, a newline, or the buffer fills. Here is the program's output:

```
Reading from alphabeta.wtxt:
ΑΒΓΔΕΖΗΘΙΚΛΜΝΞΟΠΡΣΤΥΦΧΨΩ
```

To read one wide character at a time from a file, use the *fgetwc()* function, which is the wide character counterpart of *fgetc()*. Like *fgetc()*, the value returned by *fgetwc()* isn't a character or even a wide character. It's a wide integer. Here is the *fgetwc()* function's *man* page format:

```
wint_t fgetwc(FILE *stream);
```

The function's argument is an open file handle, or *stdin* for standard input. The value returned is of the *wint_t* data type. As with *fgetc()*, the reason is that the wide end-of-file marker, *WEOF*, can be encountered, which the *wchar_t* type doesn't interpret properly.

To modify the code from greek_read01.c to read single characters from the file, only a few changes are required:

The line[] buffer is removed, along with the length constant. In its place, a single *wint_t* variable is declared:

```
wint_t ch;
```

To read from the file, the *fgetws()* statement, as well as the *wprintf()* statement, are replaced with these statements:

```
while( (ch=fgetwc(fp)) != WEOF )
    putwchar(ch);
putwchar('\n');
```

The *while* loop's condition both reads a character (a *wint_t* value) from the open file handle fp. This value is compared with *WEOF*, the wide character end-of-file marker. As long as the character isn't the end of file, the loop repeats.

The loop's sole statement is `putwchar(ch)`, which outputs the character read. A final *putwchar()* statement outputs a newline, cleaning up the output.

The complete source code for `greek_read02.c` is available in this book's online repository. The program's output is the same as for the program version that used the *fgetws()* function to read the alphabet:

```
Reading from alphabeta.wtxt:
ΑΒΓΔΕΖΗΘΙΚΛΜΝΞΟΠΡΣΤΥΦΧΨΩ
```

EXERCISE 8.3

Using my Greek alphabet programs as a guide, create code that writes the Cyrillic alphabet to a file. You can optionally write a program that reads in the Cyrillic alphabet from the file you create, though the *cat* command works just as well.

The first letter of the Cyrillic alphabet, А, is U+0410. The last letter is Я, U+042F. These are the uppercase letters. Unlike Greek, no blanks are found in the Unicode sequence.

My solution is called `cyrillic.c`, and it's available in this book's online code repository.

Hex dumper

9

I've looked with my own eyes and I just can't see files stored on media. This task was easier in the old days, when you could pop out a floppy disk and see the actual media. The data on the media, however, remains encoded as teensy electronic particles, invisible to the naked eye—or even to an eye with clothes on. No, the only way to peer into a file's raw contents is to use a utility, something like *hexdump*.

Yes, *hexdump* is a Linux utility, available as part of the default installation. It's quite capable and popular among the nerds. There's no need to re-create it—unless you want to improve upon it. Or perhaps you want to expand your knowledge of programming and learn a few tricks along the way, such as:

- Examining storage at the basic level
- Properly outputting byte-size data
- Reading raw data from a file
- Adjusting and aligning program output
- Adding and processing command-line switches

The goal of this chapter isn't to ape the *hexdump* utility but rather to see how much you can understand what it does and appreciate it more by doing it yourself. Along the way, you'll discover more about writing such utilities and how to hone your own programs to work the way you prefer.

9.1 Bytes and data

Computers know nothing of bytes. Digital information is stored in bits—*bit* is a collision of the words *bi*nary and digi*t*. Binary digits are 1 and 0, and a bit is either 1 or 0. Bytes cluster bits into convenient, happy groups, where they represent larger numbers.

One question raised from the early days of computing is how many bits pack into a byte? If the techies wanted to do so, a computer's entire storage space could be a single byte that is billions of bits long. Such length would be painfully impractical. So, the nerds organized bits into smaller chunks, with byte sizes ranging from a few bits to over a dozen bits per byte.

Today the standard is eight bits per byte. But even then, larger-capacity storage is necessary when dealing with information in a computer.

9.1.1 Reviewing storage units and size mayhem

Way back when computer nerds sported slicked-back hair, skinny black ties, horn-rimmed glasses, and prized pocket protectors—yes, even the women—a byte, or *syllable*, as it was known, was composed of any number of bits, depending on the system hardware. I remember using mainframes with 12-bit bytes. I know of smaller, custom systems that used 6-bit bytes. When the microcomputer craze transformed these machines into the must-have-computers-for-business craze in the early 1980s, the computer world settled on 8-bit bytes.

In C, the 8-bit byte corresponds directly to the *char* data type. Although you won't find any of the C grand poohbahs who openly admit that, yes, "a byte is a *char*," it's pretty much true. (Even so, be aware that data types are implementation-dependent in C.)

Computers deal with larger values than bytes, which requires their organization into chunks called *words* (16-bit), *doublewords* (32-bit), *quadwords* (64-bits), and *double-quad words* (128-bits). This word-jumble-worthy mayhem is summarized in table 9.1, minus the double-quad word because its values can't fit in the table.

Table 9.1 Bit width descriptions and details

Bit width	Description	Data type	Value range (signed)	Value range (unsigned)
8	Byte	*char*	–128 to 127	0 to 255
16	Word	*short*	–32,768 to 32,767	0 to 65,535
32	Doubleword	*Int*	–2,147,483,648 to 2,147,483,647	0 to 4,294,967,295
64	Quadword	*long*	–9,223,372,036,854,775,808 to 9,233,372,036,854,775,807	0 to 18,446,744,073,709,551,615

Values shown in table 9.1 are related to the data chunk's bit width. For example, the range of a doubleword is from -2^{31} to $2^{31} - 1$. If a 128-bit integer were available in C (and some language extensions offer it), its signed value would range from -2^{127} to $2^{127} - 1$. Were this book's margins wide enough, I'd write out the specific values in full. Or—better—if this book had a centerfold, I'm sure that the value $2^{127} - 1$ printed out would be appealing to some programmers.

You can quickly cobble together a C program that reveals the values of the various data types and their bit widths. To do so, you need to know the size of each data type. For example, use this expression to obtain the size of a byte in bits:

```
unsigned long byte = sizeof(char)*8;
```

The *sizeof* operator returns the number of bytes used by a specific C language data type, *char,* described earlier. This value is multiplied by eight to obtain the number of bits. The result is stored in *unsigned long* variable byte; the *sizeof* operator returns an *unsigned long* value. Similar statements are used for word/*short*, doubleword/*int*, and quadword/*long* variables and data types.

Use this *printf()* statement to output the values:

```
printf("%11s %2lu bits %21.f\n",
        "Byte",
        byte,
        pow(2,byte)
    );
```

The *printf()* function's format string ensures that values output are spaced properly, formatted for a table. Several statement output details for each data type, resulting in a table that lists the data size, the number of bits, and then the decimal size value. The *pow()* function raises the power of two to the number of bits pow(2,byte). The *pow()* function requires inclusion of the math.h header file.

The source code file containing all the *printf()* statements to output a data type table is available in this book's online archive as byte_sizes.c. It requires you to link the math library: in Linux, ensure that you specify the -lm switch as the compiler's final command-line option to link in the math (m) library. Here is sample output:

```
      Byte  8 bits                     256
      Word 16 bits                   65536
Doubleword 32 bits              4294967296
  Quadword 64 bits    18446744073709551616
```

You don't need to perform the math and overhead used in the byte_sizes.c code. The reason is that the compiler itself has a limit. Specifically, the limit values are set as defined constants in the appropriately named limits.h header file.

The next listing outputs the popular constants defined in limits.h. Run this code on your system to see what the values and ranges are, though for most programmers these values align with those shown back in table 9.1. The key to the code is identifying the defined constants in limits.h. These defined constants appear here.

Listing 9.1   Source code for limits.c

```
#include <stdio.h>
#include <limits.h>
```

```
int main()
{
    printf("Char:\n");
    printf("\tNumber of bits: %d\n",CHAR_BIT);
    printf("\tSigned minimum: %d\n",SCHAR_MIN);
    printf("\tSigned maximum: %d\n",SCHAR_MAX);
    printf("\tUnsigned max: %d\n",UCHAR_MAX);

    printf("Short:\n");
    printf("\tSigned minimum: %d\n",SHRT_MIN);
    printf("\tSigned maximum: %d\n",SHRT_MAX);
    printf("\tUnsigned max: %d\n",USHRT_MAX);

    printf("Int:\n");
    printf("\tSigned minimum: %d\n",INT_MIN);
    printf("\tSigned maximum: %d\n",INT_MAX);
    printf("\tUnsigned max: %u\n",UINT_MAX);

    printf("Long:\n");
    printf("\tSigned minimum: %ld\n",LONG_MIN);
    printf("\tSigned maximum: %ld\n",LONG_MAX);
    printf("\tUnsigned max: %lu\n",ULONG_MAX);

    printf("Long long:\n");
    printf("\tSigned minimum: %lld\n",LLONG_MIN);
    printf("\tSigned maximum: %lld\n",LLONG_MAX);
    printf("\tUnsigned max: %llu\n",ULLONG_MAX);

    return(0);
}
```

The *char* type is the only one that seems to have the "BIT" defined constant.

Signed *char* maximum

Signed *char* minimum

Unsigned *char* maximum; zero is minimum.

Unsigned integer max uses the %u placeholder.

Long integers require the %ld placeholder.

Unsigned long requires %lu placeholder.

Double-longs require %lld.

The double-unsigned long placeholder is %llu.

The output appears here, though the point of the exercise is that these minimum and maximum values can be obtained from the constants defined in the limits.h header file; your code need not do the math:

```
Char:
    Number of bits: 8
    Signed minimum: -128
    Signed maximum: 127
    Unsigned max: 255
Short:
    Signed minimum: -32768
    Signed maximum: 32767
    Unsigned max: 65535
Int:
    Signed minimum: -2147483648
    Signed maximum: 2147483647
    Unsigned max: 4294967295
Long:
    Signed minimum: -9223372036854775808
    Signed maximum: 9223372036854775807
    Unsigned max: 18446744073709551615
```

```
Long long:
    Signed minimum: -9223372036854775808
    Signed maximum: 9223372036854775807
    Unsigned max: 18446744073709551615
```

When you desire a specific size integer, it's best to use the specific integer type variables. The following types are available:

- *int8_t* for 8-bit integers
- *int16_t* for 16-bit integers
- *int32_t* for 32-bit integers
- *int64_t* for 64-bit integers

Variables declared with these types are always at the specific width indicated. These *typedef* values (which is what the *_t* suffix indicates) are defined in the stdint.h header file, which is automatically included in stdio.h for most C compilers. So, feel free to use these data type definitions to utilize an integer value of a specific width.

The reason for these exact integer width types is historical. When I first learned to program C, the *int* data type was 16 bits wide. Today, it's 32. Yet the *int16_t* and *int32_t* types are always set to the width indicated.

Given the variety of integer widths, a byte is still the basic counting unit in a computer. Memory capacity, media storage, file size—all these quantities are measured in 8-bit bytes, *char* values. This yardstick gives rise to two systems for counting bytes: one based on the powers of two (binary), the other on the powers of 10 (decimal).

The traditional way to count bytes, what I grew up with, is the kilobyte system: when I was a proto-nerd, 1 K was one kilobyte of data, or 1024 bytes. The value 1,024 is 2^{10}, which seemed good enough for computer nerds; 1,024 is close enough to 1,000 for digital accounting purposes, with the extra 24 bytes often taken away by the government in the form of taxes. It was proper in the day to tell beginners that 1 K was "about 1,000 bytes." Alas, this logical, binary definition no longer holds.

Today, 1,024 bytes is known as a *kibibyte*. If you refer to a kilobyte, the experts now claim this value is 1,000 bytes.

- A kilobyte (KB) is 1,000 bytes.
- A kibibyte (KiB) is 1,024 bytes.

The reason for the change is that the terms *kilo, mega, giga,* and so on mean one thousand, one million, and one billion exactly when describing quantities in the noncomputer world: a kilometer is 1,000 meters, not 1,024 meters. For consistency, our digital overlords decreed that the term *kilobyte* must also mean exactly 1,000 bytes. The traditional value of 1,024 bytes, or 2^{10}, is demoted to the silly term *kibibyte,* which sounds like a dog food.

Other values to annoy me include mebibyte (MiB) for 2^{20} or 1,048,576, and gibibyte (GiB) for 2^{30} or 1,073,741,824. To me, these are still megabyte (MB) and gigabyte (GB). Anything else is just foolhardy conformist insanity.

9.1.2 Outputting byte values

Forget those wishy-washy C overlords, and in this section accept that a byte is the same size as a character. When you allocate 1 K of memory, you're setting aside 1,024 (yes) *char*-sized pieces of memory as a single chunk. Output a value in the range from 0 to 255, and you're outputting a byte. To deal with memory, you deal with bytes, *char*-sized chunks. This information is common; nerds everywhere accept it.

EXERCISE 9.1

Write code that outputs *char* values from 0 to 255. Each value is output on a line by itself. This exercise may seem mindlessly simple, but I strongly urge you to try it. Come on! It's just a few lines of code. Save your solution as byte_values01.c.

Here is the output from my solution, minus a long chunk of numbers in the middle:

```
0
1
2
3
...
253
254
255
```

Without peeking ahead at my solution, did you try a *for* loop? Did you first attempt the solution by using a *char* variable and then attempt with *unsigned char*? Did you force the output using a technique that didn't seem obvious at first?

Seriously: if you haven't attempted to code a solution, do so now.

My solution appears in the next listing. It uses an endless *while* loop, carefully constructed so that the loop terminates when the value of variable a is equal to 255.

Listing 9.2 Source code for byte_values01.c

```
#include <stdio.h>

int main()                          The range for
{                                   unsigned char is
    unsigned char a;         ◁───── from 0 to 255.

    a = 0;
Loops ──▷ while( 1 )
endlessly    {
                 printf("%d\n",a);  ◁────  Outputs
                 if( a==255 )  ◁─────────  the value
                     break;
                 a++;  ◁─────────          Once the value
             }                             hits 255, breaks
                                           the loop
    return(0);
}                        Otherwise, increments
                         variable a
```

The solution shown in listing 9.2 isn't my first attempt. No, like you (if you actually completed the exercise), I started with a *for* loop:

```
for( a=0; a<=255; a++ )
    printf("%d\n",a);
```

This *for* loop never terminates. The compiler may warn, but the loop has no end. Even though the maximum value for an *unsigned char* is 255 and it seems like the condition is met, it never will be: The value of variable a wraps from 255 down to 0 again and again.

Further, if you want to examine bytes, output them, or otherwise deal with their values, you must use the *int* data type. All *char* or byte-size values easily fit within an integer-sized chunk. The *int* data type avoids any wrapping that occurs with a *char*, which is probably one reason why functions like *getchar()* and *putchar()* use integers instead of *char* types.

The next listing modifies the source code from listing 9.2 by storing the 256 *char* values in a char array, data[]. Two *for* loops process the array, the first to fill it and the second to output its values. Though the array stores only byte values, *int* variable b is used to store the values.

Listing 9.3   Source code for `byte_values02.c`

```
#include <stdio.h>

int main()
{
    unsigned char data[256];        ◁——  Room for the
    int b;                                full variety of
                                          byte values
    for( b=0; b<256; b++ )          ◁——  Fills the array
        data[b] = b;                      with values 0
                                          through 255
    for( b=0; b<256; b++ )          ◁──
        printf("%d\n",data[b]);           Outputs the array,
                                          with each value on
    return(0);                            a line by itself
}
```

The output from `byte_values02.c` is identical to the first program, but the new format, with an array holding the values, allows for modifications and manipulations to be made to the stored data. The goal is to accurately present the data in a readable format. The inelegant term for doing so is *dump*.

9.1.3   *Dumping data*

Dump is both a noun and a verb, neither of which is flattering. Case in point: no type of food preparation uses the word *dump*. The term is inelegant and crude, and what's being dumped isn't considered useful—unless it's data.

In the digital realm, a *dump* is the movement of data from one place to another. You may be familiar with the notorious term *core dump*, which is what happens when your program horrifically screws up and the operating system barfs memory and processor content in the vain hope that you'll examine the data to determine what's wrong. Don't worry—you won't.

Computer hobbyists from the early days may remember the term *screen dump*. It was a copy of all the text on the screen sent to a printer. IBM curtailed the term's use when they added the Print Screen key to their first PC's keyboard. Suddenly the screen dump became a "print screen," though pressing the key still dumped all text from the screen to the printer.

To dump data in C, you copy it from one location to another. You can dump a chunk of memory, though only the memory the program has access to. More frequently, you dump the contents of a file as hexadecimal output on the screen. A programmer can examine the raw data and hopefully gain insight into what's going on or glean some other useful tidbit of information. I've experienced many "aha!" moments while examining file dumps.

To dump data from memory, you can modify the existing source code file `byte_values01.c`. The first change is to dump the data in hexadecimal. Decimal byte values are familiar to humans, but hex digits for values 0 through 255 all neatly pack into two-digit sequences. Further, most nerds recognize hex values and their binary equivalents. This relationship makes it easy to troubleshoot. For non-nerd reference, table 9.2 lists hex values and their relationship to binary with decimal thrown in just because.

Table 9.2 Decimal, hexadecimal, and binary values

Decimal	Hex	Binary	Decimal	Hex	Binary
0	0	0000	8	8	1000
1	1	0001	9	9	1001
2	2	0010	10	A	1010
3	3	0011	11	B	1011
4	4	0100	12	C	1100
5	5	0101	13	D	1101
6	6	0110	14	E	1110
7	7	0111	15	F	1111

Hex dumps are brief and useful. After all, a nerd who may not understand "01001000 01100101 01101100 01101100 01101111 00101100 00100000 01101110 01100101 01110010 01100100 00100001" certainly understands "48 65 6C 6F 2C 20 6E 65 72 64 21".

To output hex, line 12 in the source code for byte_values02.c is altered: the %d placeholder is replaced by %02X to output a 2-digit uppercase hex value with a leading zero when necessary:

```
printf("%02X\n",data[b]);
```

The updated code's output now ranges from 00 through FF, the full spectrum of byte values. But it's all still output in a single column, which isn't efficient.

The second change pads each byte value output with a leading space and eliminates the newline:

```
printf(" %02X",data[b]);
```

To keep output clean, a *putchar()* statement is added after the second *for* loop:

```
putchar('\n');
```

The code's output now appears all on one screen, but inelegantly:

```
 00 01 02 03 04 05 06 07 08 09 0A 0B 0C 0D 0E 0F 10 11 12 13 14 15 16 17 18 19 1
A 1B 1C 1D 1E 1F 20 21 22 23 24 25 26 27 28 29 2A 2B 2C 2D 2E 2F 30 31 32 33 34
35 36 37 38 39 3A 3B 3C 3D 3E 3F 40 41 42 43 44 45 46 47 48 49 4A 4B 4C 4D 4E 4F
 50 51 52 53 54 55 56 57 58 59 5A 5B 5C 5D 5E 5F 60 61 62 63 64 65 66 67 68 69 6
A 6B 6C 6D 6E 6F 70 71 72 73 74 75 76 77 78 79 7A 7B 7C 7D 7E 7F 80 81 82 83 84
85 86 87 88 89 8A 8B 8C 8D 8E 8F 90 91 92 93 94 95 96 97 98 99 9A 9B 9C 9D 9E 9F
 A0 A1 A2 A3 A4 A5 A6 A7 A8 A9 AA AB AC AD AE AF B0 B1 B2 B3 B4 B5 B6 B7 B8 B9 B
A BB BC BD BE BF C0 C1 C2 C3 C4 C5 C6 C7 C8 C9 CA CB CC CD CE CF D0 D1 D2 D3 D4
D5 D6 D7 D8 D9 DA DB DC DD DE DF E0 E1 E2 E3 E4 E5 E6 E7 E8 E9 EA EB EC ED EE EF
F0 F1 F2 F3 F4 F5 F6 F7 F8 F9 FA FB FC FD FE FF
```

To improve the code further, a newline is output every 16 bytes, because 16 is a happy value for hexadecimal. The following modification to the code's second *for* loop adds the newline, which incorporates the recently added *putchar()* statement:

```
for( b=0; b<256; b++ )
{
    printf(" %02X",data[b]);
    if( (b+1)%16==0 )
        putchar('\n');
}
```

The *if* test uses variable b's value to determine when to add a newline. One is added to the value of b, (b+1), to avoid a newline popping out after the first value (zero). Otherwise, each time the value of b is evenly divisible by 16, a newline is output. Here is the result:

```
 00 01 02 03 04 05 06 07 08 09 0A 0B 0C 0D 0E 0F
 10 11 12 13 14 15 16 17 18 19 1A 1B 1C 1D 1E 1F
 20 21 22 23 24 25 26 27 28 29 2A 2B 2C 2D 2E 2F
 30 31 32 33 34 35 36 37 38 39 3A 3B 3C 3D 3E 3F
```

```
40 41 42 43 44 45 46 47 48 49 4A 4B 4C 4D 4E 4F
50 51 52 53 54 55 56 57 58 59 5A 5B 5C 5D 5E 5F
60 61 62 63 64 65 66 67 68 69 6A 6B 6C 6D 6E 6F
70 71 72 73 74 75 76 77 78 79 7A 7B 7C 7D 7E 7F
80 81 82 83 84 85 86 87 88 89 8A 8B 8C 8D 8E 8F
90 91 92 93 94 95 96 97 98 99 9A 9B 9C 9D 9E 9F
A0 A1 A2 A3 A4 A5 A6 A7 A8 A9 AA AB AC AD AE AF
B0 B1 B2 B3 B4 B5 B6 B7 B8 B9 BA BB BC BD BE BF
C0 C1 C2 C3 C4 C5 C6 C7 C8 C9 CA CB CC CD CE CF
D0 D1 D2 D3 D4 D5 D6 D7 D8 D9 DA DB DC DD DE DF
E0 E1 E2 E3 E4 E5 E6 E7 E8 E9 EA EB EC ED EE EF
F0 F1 F2 F3 F4 F5 F6 F7 F8 F9 FA FB FC FD FE FF
```

The full source code file is available as `byte_values03.c` in the online repository. The output is better, but it could still use some improvement. Because the data dump is sequential, it's easy to see patterns and reference rows and columns. However, data won't always look so pretty.

EXERCISE 9.2

Improve the code in `byte_values03.c` in two stages. First, add an initial column showing the byte values' offset. Output this value as a 5-digit hexadecimal number. Then output the row of 16 bytes.

Second, add an extra space to separate the eighth and ninth byte columns. This space makes the rows and columns more readable.

The output from my solution, `byte_values04.c`, is shown here:

```
00000   00 01 02 03 04 05 06 07   08 09 0A 0B 0C 0D 0E 0F
00010   10 11 12 13 14 15 16 17   18 19 1A 1B 1C 1D 1E 1F
00020   20 21 22 23 24 25 26 27   28 29 2A 2B 2C 2D 2E 2F
00030   30 31 32 33 34 35 36 37   38 39 3A 3B 3C 3D 3E 3F
00040   40 41 42 43 44 45 46 47   48 49 4A 4B 4C 4D 4E 4F
00050   50 51 52 53 54 55 56 57   58 59 5A 5B 5C 5D 5E 5F
00060   60 61 62 63 64 65 66 67   68 69 6A 6B 6C 6D 6E 6F
00070   70 71 72 73 74 75 76 77   78 79 7A 7B 7C 7D 7E 7F
00080   80 81 82 83 84 85 86 87   88 89 8A 8B 8C 8D 8E 8F
00090   90 91 92 93 94 95 96 97   98 99 9A 9B 9C 9D 9E 9F
000A0   A0 A1 A2 A3 A4 A5 A6 A7   A8 A9 AA AB AC AD AE AF
000B0   B0 B1 B2 B3 B4 B5 B6 B7   B8 B9 BA BB BC BD BE BF
000C0   C0 C1 C2 C3 C4 C5 C6 C7   C8 C9 CA CB CC CD CE CF
000D0   D0 D1 D2 D3 D4 D5 D6 D7   D8 D9 DA DB DC DD DE DF
000E0   E0 E1 E2 E3 E4 E5 E6 E7   E8 E9 EA EB EC ED EE EF
000F0   F0 F1 F2 F3 F4 F5 F6 F7   F8 F9 FA FB FC FD FE FF
```

The hex display reads better after you've completed exercise 9.2.

A final improvement is to add a third ASCII column after the byte values. This additional information cross-references the hex bytes of displayable ASCII text, providing a handy way for humans to quickly scan the dump for relevant information.

The ordeal of adding an ASCII column to the output is complicated due to stream output. Each row must be processed sequentially: 16 bytes are output as hex values, and then the same bytes are output as printable ASCII characters. To resolve this issue, I concocted the *line_out()* function, which is found in the source code file `byte_values05.c`, available in the online repository.

The *line_out()* function features three arguments, as shown in the next listing: an offset representing a byte count, the length of the data chunk, and the data itself as an *unsigned char* pointer. Most of the code is yanked from the earlier `byte_values04.c` source code, though variable a tracks progress in the *for* loops, and is used with the data pointer to fetch specific byte values: `*(data+a)`. This function outputs a single row of the dump, so it's called from the *main()* function to output all the data.

Listing 9.4   The *line_out()* function

```
void line_out(int offset, int length, unsigned char *data)
{
    int a;

    printf("%05X ",offset);          ◁── Outputs the
                                          offset value
    for( a=0; a<length; a++ )        ◁── The first loop outputs
    {                                     the hex values.
        printf(" %02X",*(data+a));   ◁── The hex value calculation is
        if( (a+1)%8==0 )                  based on the start of the data
            putchar(' ');                 plus the looping value.
    }

    putchar(' ');                    After the eighth hex byte
    for( a=0; a<length; a++ )        output, adds an extra
    {                                space for readability
        if( *(data+a)>=' ' && *(data+a)<='~' )   ◁── Checks the printable
            putchar( *(data+a) );                     character range
        else                         ◁── Outputs a printable
            putchar(' ');                 character
    }

    putchar('\n');
}
```

Adds another space after the hex columns ▷

The second loop outputs the ASCII values— if any. ▷

Otherwise, outputs a space

The *line_out()* function isn't perfect, which I discuss in a later section, but it works for now. Here is some sample output:

```
00000  00 01 02 03 04 05 06 07  08 09 0A 0B 0C 0D 0E 0F
00010  10 11 12 13 14 15 16 17  18 19 1A 1B 1C 1D 1E 1F
00020  20 21 22 23 24 25 26 27  28 29 2A 2B 2C 2D 2E 2F   !"#$%&'()*+,-./
00030  30 31 32 33 34 35 36 37  38 39 3A 3B 3C 3D 3E 3F  0123456789:;<=>?
00040  40 41 42 43 44 45 46 47  48 49 4A 4B 4C 4D 4E 4F  @ABCDEFGHIJKLMNO
00050  50 51 52 53 54 55 56 57  58 59 5A 5B 5C 5D 5E 5F  PQRSTUVWXYZ[\]^_
00060  60 61 62 63 64 65 66 67  68 69 6A 6B 6C 6D 6E 6F  `abcdefghijklmno
00070  70 71 72 73 74 75 76 77  78 79 7A 7B 7C 7D 7E 7F  pqrstuvwxyz{|}~
00080  80 81 82 83 84 85 86 87  88 89 8A 8B 8C 8D 8E 8F
00090  90 91 92 93 94 95 96 97  98 99 9A 9B 9C 9D 9E 9F
000A0  A0 A1 A2 A3 A4 A5 A6 A7  A8 A9 AA AB AC AD AE AF
000B0  B0 B1 B2 B3 B4 B5 B6 B7  B8 B9 BA BB BC BD BE BF
000C0  C0 C1 C2 C3 C4 C5 C6 C7  C8 C9 CA CB CC CD CE CF
```

```
000D0    D0 D1 D2 D3 D4 D5 D6 D7   D8 D9 DA DB DC DD DE DF
000E0    E0 E1 E2 E3 E4 E5 E6 E7   E8 E9 EA EB EC ED EE EF
000F0    F0 F1 F2 F3 F4 F5 F6 F7   F8 F9 FA FB FC FD FE FF
```

The ASCII column appears on the far right, reflecting the printable character values from the hex bytes shown in the center columns. Nonprintable characters appear as spaces.

EXERCISE 9.3

Sadly, the sample output from the *byte_values* series of programs is predictable—a swath of 256-byte values from 0x00 through 0xFF. Why not spice things up a bit and repopulate the data[] buffer with random values?

Modify the source code for byte_values05.c into a new source code file, byte_values 06.c. Have the *main()* function fill the data[] array with 256 random values, each in the range of 0 through 255. Run the program a few times to confirm that the program properly interprets the hexadecimal and ASCII values of the bytes stored.

9.2 Dump that file!

A dump utility is designed to peer into a file's data. Well, a *file* dump utility. This detail is something that the operating system doesn't supply at a glance. No, you can tell a file's name, size, and date from a directory listing. The file type is based on the filename extension, so it could be misleading. No, the only way to peer into a file and examine its brooding data is to dump.

The Linux *hexdump* utility performs the file dumping task quite well. So, this chapter is over.

Seriously, using the utility doesn't help you learn how to write your own file utilities, customized the way you like. I call this new utility *dumpfile*. It works like *hexdump*, but it works the way I like it to.

9.2.1 Reading file data

A *dumpfile* utility could be written as a filter, just like Linux's *hexdump*. As a filter, *hexdump* chews through all input whether it originates from a file or is the output from some program. If you're interested in such a task, review chapter 4 for information on filters in the Linux environment. You can adapt the *dumpfile* code presented in this chapter as a filter, though I prefer that *dumpfile* work as a traditional command-line utility.

Utilities that read data from a file use two approaches. The first is to specify the filename at the command prompt—usually, as the first (and often only) argument. The second way is to prompt for a filename after the utility starts, or to prompt for the filename if it's missing as a command-line argument. For now, I assume that the filename argument is supplied as a command-line argument. Therefore, the utility must check for such an argument. This confirmation requires that the *main()* function specify and use its arguments:

```
int main(int argc, char *argv[])
```

The value of argc is always at least 1, which is the program's filename. If the user types any arguments, the value of argc is greater than 1. The program first confirms that an argument is present. If not, a warning message is sent to the standard error device (*stderr*) and the program terminates:

```
if( argc<2 )
{
    fprintf(stderr,"Format: dumpfile filename\n");
    exit(1);
}
```

The *exit()* function requires that the stdlib.h header file be included. Otherwise, you could use return(1) to exit the *main()* function at this point in the code. I prefer *exit()* in that it can be used in any function to terminate a program, plus it's tied into other functions such as *atexit()* or *on_exit()*, which gives using *exit()* a strategic advantage over the *return* keyword. Also, it's shorter to type.

After the argument count is confirmed, the string held in argv[1] is used in the *fopen()* function to read the file's data. This step not only opens the file but also, upon success, determines whether the file is present. I use the *char* pointer filename to reference the string in argv[1], which aids readability:

```
filename = argv[1];
fp = fopen(filename,"r");
if( fp==NULL )
{
    fprintf(stderr,"Unable to open file '%s'\n",filename);
    exit(1);
}
```

My first choice for processing a file's data was to use the *fgets()* function to read in 16 bytes at a time; 16 is the number of hex bytes in a row of output. But if I want to use my existing *line_out()* function as is, I can't have the 16th byte in the data be the null character. This byte is what the *fgets()* function adds to the buffer it reads, unless a newline is encountered first.

My second choice was to use *fread()*. Where *fgets()* is a string-reading function, *fread()* consumes data in a given chunk size. It could easily fill a 16-byte buffer with raw data, which is what I want. Even so, I opted instead to use the *fgetc()* function, which reads one character a time. Set in a *while* loop, this function gobbles characters, adding them to a 16-byte buffer and handling the EOF condition when it's encountered.

The following listing shows the core of the *main()* function from the source code file dumpfile01.c. The *while* loop repeats until the end of file (EOF) is found for FILE pointer fp. Byte value ch is fetched from the file and immediately tested for the EOF marker. After the EOF is detected, the value of variable index is tested against zero, meaning the buffer still has data to print. If so, the *line_out()* function is called. Otherwise, the file still has data to read, and character ch is stored in the buffer. Once the buffer is full (`index==length`), the *line_out()* function is called. The full code can be found in the online repository as `dumpfile01.c`.

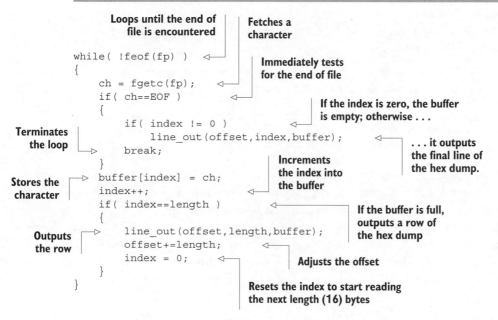

Listing 9.5 The character-reading loop from `dumpfile01.c`

```
while( !feof(fp) )
{
    ch = fgetc(fp);
    if( ch==EOF )
    {
        if( index != 0 )
            line_out(offset,index,buffer);
        break;
    }
    buffer[index] = ch;
    index++;
    if( index==length )
    {
        line_out(offset,length,buffer);
        offset+=length;
        index = 0;
    }
}
```

Loops until the end of file is encountered

Fetches a character

Immediately tests for the end of file

If the index is zero, the buffer is empty; otherwise . . .

Terminates the loop

. . . it outputs the final line of the hex dump.

Increments the index into the buffer

Stores the character

If the buffer is full, outputs a row of the hex dump

Outputs the row

Adjusts the offset

Resets the index to start reading the next length (16) bytes

After reading all bytes from the file, and the *while* loop has terminated, the file is closed and the program finishes.

I've created a test data file to read, `bytes.dat`. It's available in the online repository along with all this chapter's source code files. This file contains sequential byte values from 0x00 through 0xFF, which I used to test and debug the program created from the `dumpfile01.c` source code file. Here is some sample output:

```
00000  00 01 02 03 04 05 06 07  08 09 0A 0B 0C 0D 0E 0F
00010  10 11 12 13 14 15 16 17  18 19 1A 1B 1C 1D 1E 1F
00020  20 21 22 23 24 25 26 27  28 29 2A 2B 2C 2D 2E 2F   !"#$%&'()*+,-./
00030  30 31 32 33 34 35 36 37  38 39 3A 3B 3C 3D 3E 3F  0123456789:;<=>?
00040  40 41 42 43 44 45 46 47  48 49 4A 4B 4C 4D 4E 4F  @ABCDEFGHIJKLMNO
00050  50 51 52 53 54 55 56 57  58 59 5A 5B 5C 5D 5E 5F  PQRSTUVWXYZ[\]^_
00060  60 61 62 63 64 65 66 67  68 69 6A 6B 6C 6D 6E 6F  `abcdefghijklmno
00070  70 71 72 73 74 75 76 77  78 79 7A 7B 7C 7D 7E 7F  pqrstuvwxyz{|}~
00080  80 81 82 83 84 85 86 87  88 89 8A 8B 8C 8D 8E 8F
00090  90 91 92 93 94 95 96 97  98 99 9A 9B 9C 9D 9E 9F
000A0  A0 A1 A2 A3 A4 A5 A6 A7  A8 A9 AA AB AC AD AE AF
000B0  B0 B1 B2 B3 B4 B5 B6 B7  B8 B9 BA BB BC BD BE BF
000C0  C0 C1 C2 C3 C4 C5 C6 C7  C8 C9 CA CB CC CD CE CF
000D0  D0 D1 D2 D3 D4 D5 D6 D7  D8 D9 DA DB DC DD DE DF
000E0  E0 E1 E2 E3 E4 E5 E6 E7  E8 E9 EA EB EC ED EE EF
000F0  F0 F1 F2 F3 F4 F5 F6 F7  F8 F9 FA FB FC FD FE FF
```

9.2.2   *Fixing uneven output*

Only a few files in the digital realm have sizes of a value evenly divided by 16. For these files, the *dumpfile* program works perfectly. True, the program can handle reading bytes from any file size, but when the file size isn't exactly divisible by 16, it has an ugly effect on the output.

Here you see the tail end of the *dumpfile* utility's output applied to the text of Shakespeare's *18th Sonnet*:

```
....
00230   72 65 61 74 68 65 20 6F   72 20 65 79 65 73 20 63   reathe or eyes c
00240   61 6E 20 73 65 65 2C 0A   53 6F 20 6C 6F 6E 67 20   an see, So long
00250   6C 69 76 65 73 20 74 68   69 73 2C 20 61 6E 64 20   lives this, and
00260   74 68 69 73 20 67 69 76   65 73 20 6C 69 66 65 20   this gives life
00270   74 6F 20 74 68 65 65 2E   0A                        to thee.
```

At offset 0x00270 (the last line), you see the file's final byte, 0A, immediately followed by the line's ASCII column. The text "to thee" is several spaces to the left of where it should line up—if the file ended exactly at a 16-byte boundary.

To resolve this problem, the *line_out()* function must be modified. It must know when a line of output doesn't match the default output length of 16 bytes. Speaking of which, in all the code presented so far, the output width is consistently 16 bytes. This specifies this value as a constant in the *main()* function:

```
const int length = 16;
```

Defined here, the constant's value is seen only inside the *main()* function. Because this value is also now relevant to the *line_out()* functions, I've reestablished it as a defined constant. The following preprocessor directive creates it:

```
#define SIZE 16
```

This change is found in the updated source code file, `dumpfile02.c`.

In the next listing, you see how defined constant SIZE is used in the *line_out()* function to help test when the final line of output is shorter than 16 bytes. This change requires the addition of an *if* statement between the two existing *for* loops. The *if* decision helps to balance out the remainder of the last row of output so that the ASCII column lines up.

Listing 9.6   Updating the *line_out()* function to account for a short, final line

```
        If the row has fewer than
           SIZE (16) bytes . . .
                                           Continues the loop
                                           using variable a
if( length<SIZE )     ◄─┐
{                       │
    for( ; a<SIZE; a++ )  ◄────             Outputs three
    {                                       spaces
        printf("   ");   ◄─
```

```
        if( (a+1)%8==0 )
            putchar(' ');           ◁——┐  Adds an extra space
    }                                    │  after the 8th and
}                                        │  16th bytes
```

The *for* loop (refer to listing 9.6) lacks an initializing condition, as it just continues with the current value of variable a as it left the preceding loop. The loop outputs a set of three spaces to balance out any missing hex byte values. The if((a+1)%8==0) test accounts for the extra space added after every eight bytes, which separates the two hex columns.

The full source code is available in the repository as dumpfile02.c. Here is the output using the same file used earlier, but improved now over the first version of the code:

```
...
00230   72 65 61 74 68 65 20 6F   72 20 65 79 65 73 20 63   reathe or eyes c
00240   61 6E 20 73 65 65 2C 0A   53 6F 20 6C 6F 6E 67 20   an see, So long
00250   6C 69 76 65 73 20 74 68   69 73 2C 20 61 6E 64 20   lives this, and
00260   74 68 69 73 20 67 69 76   65 73 20 6C 69 66 65 20   this gives life
00270   74 6F 20 74 68 65 65 2E   0A                        to thee.
```

EXERCISE 9.4

Is programming ever done? To further update the source code for dumpfile02.c, modify the *main()* function so that if the filename argument is missing, the program prompts for it.

It's important that your code identify when the user just presses Enter or otherwise dismisses the filename prompt. There's no point in the program attempting to open a NULL string filename. Beyond this requirement, you don't need to otherwise validate the filename, because the *fopen()* statement does so automatically. My solution is available in the online repository as dumpfile03.c.

9.3   *Command-line options*

What can you add to the *dumpfile* program? For starters, how about abbreviated output, showing only the hex bytes? Or for you old timers, how about adding an option to display the bytes in octal, base 8? You can probably think of more features to add, perhaps color-coded output? Obviously, such complications would require a Help system to provide some documentation. Oh, I could go on!

As a command-line utility, options and features are controlled by *switches*—additional command-line arguments that activate, deactivate, or specify quantities and limits. In Linux, these switches have a format: -a, where a letter is preceded by a dash or hyphen. (Windows uses the slash character (/), which was a dumb decision Microsoft made years ago, before Bill Gates was eligible to vote.)

In Linux, you can specify multiple switches:

```
dumpfile -a -b -c
```

These can be bunched together:

```
dumpfile -abc
```

And some switches can have options:

```
dumpfile -q:5
```

You could toil with tests and loops to examine the switches. Or you can take advantage of a handy C library feature: the *getopt()* function. It helps your program process switches so that you don't have to write the code.

9.3.1   *Using the getopt() function*

The *getopt()* function helps your code process command-line switches. I'm certain it's used by just about every Linux command-line utility in existence, including several from the multiverse. Here is its *man* page format:

```
int getopt(int argc, char * const argv[], const char *optstring);
```

The first two arguments are identical to the *main()* function's argc and *argv[] arguments. The final argument, optstring, is a list of valid switch characters. For example:

```
getopt(argc,argv,"abc");
```

Valid switches here are -a, -b, and -c. The function is called repeatedly, each time returning the ASCII code for a valid character (an *int* value), the character '?' for an unknown option, or –1 when the function has exhausted all command-line options.

The companion *getopt_long()* function handles full word switches, though for this chapter I explore only the *getopt()* function to handle the traditional, single-character switches.

Both *getopt()* and *getopt_long()* require that the unistd.h header file be included in your code.

Listing 9.7 shows code I used as a test before adding the *getopt()* function to my *dumpfile* code. Global variable opterr is set to zero to ensure that *getopt()* doesn't output its own error messages. The *getopt()* function itself resides inside a *while* loop's condition. The function's return value is compared with –1, meaning that all command-line arguments have been examined, which stops the loop. Otherwise, the value returned in variable r is used in a *switch-case* structure to indicate which option is set. This setup is how the *getopt()* function is typically implemented.

Listing 9.7   Source code for `options01.c`

```
#include <stdio.h>
#include <unistd.h>      ⟵───  The unistd.h header file is
                               required for the getopt() function.

int main(int argc, char *argv[])
{
    int r;
```

Suppresses error output from *getopt()*

Examines the character returned

Scans the arguments, repeating the loop until every argument is processed

The *case* statements examine each valid option letter.

A question mark is returned for unknown/ invalid options.

I doubt the *default* condition is ever met.

```
opterr = 0;
while( (r=getopt(argc,argv,"abc")) != -1 )
{
    switch(r)
    {
        case 'a':
            puts("alfa option set");
            break;
        case 'b':
            puts("bravo option set");
            break;
        case 'c':
            puts("charlie option set");
            break;
        case '?':
            printf("Switch '%c' is invalid\n",optopt);
            break;
        default:
            puts("Unknown option");
    }
}

return(0);
}
```

The fun comes when testing the program built from the options01.c source code. First, try no options:

```
$ ./options
```

No output is generated. Good.

All options are specified here:

```
$ ./options -a -b -c
alfa option set
bravo option set
charlie option set
```

And they can be specified in any order:

```
$ ./options -c -a -b
charlie option set
alfa option set
bravo option set
```

Or a single pair, but bunched together:

```
$ ./options -cb
charlie option set
bravo option set
```

The *getopt()* function allows you all the flexibility to read options in this manner without having to code the complex comparisons and processing yourself. Of course, the code so far does nothing with the options. The next step is to add variables that represent on-off switches for what the options attempt to accomplish.

In my update from `options01.c` to `options02.c`, I add three *int* variables: `alfa`, `bravo`, and `charlie`. Each is initialized before the *getopt()* statement in the *while* loop:

```
alfa = 0;
bravo = 0;
charlie = 0;
```

In the *switch-case* structure, remove the *puts()* statements and replace them with statements that set the variables value to 1 (TRUE) for active:

```
alfa = 1;
```

Next, after the *while* loop, add a series of *if* statements to output the results:

```
if( alfa ) puts("alfa option set");
if( bravo ) puts("bravo option set");
if( charlie ) puts("charlie option set");
if( alfa+bravo+charlie==0 ) puts("No options set");
```

The final *if* statement displays a message when no options are set.

The source code for `options02.c` is found in this book's online repository. Here are some sample runs:

```
$ ./options
No options set
```

Because the switches can be examined in this new code, a lack of options is easily identified.

The output for setting all options is the same as with the first version of the code:

```
$ ./options -a -b -c
alfa option set
bravo option set
charlie option set
```

The remaining variations for the switches have the same output as the original program. The difference is that the program is now aware of the settings and can examine the variables to perform whatever magic is requested.

9.3.2   *Updating the dumpfile program code*

To add command-line options to a utility, you must know what the options do. Then you use a function like *getopt()* to scan for and set the options. Finally, the options must be implemented in code.

For the *dumpfile* program, here are options I'm presenting:

- `-a` for abbreviated output
- `-o` for octal output
- `-h` for help

These switches can be processed as shown earlier with the *options* series of source code files. With the *dumpfile* program, however, the first argument is a filename. In fact, it must be a filename: to help process command-line switches, the program can no longer prompt for a filename if one is missing (if you completed exercise 9.4). Further, the filename must always be the first argument, `argv[1]`. (Technically, it's the second argument, because the program filename is first or `argv[0]`.)

The first step to adding and processing arguments is to modify the *main()* function. If a prompt for a missing filename was added in exercise 9.4, it's now removed. The code is honed to assume that the first argument is a filename. The following statements are added before the *while* loop in the *main()* function:

```
if( argc<2 )
{
    puts("Format: dumpfile filename [options]");
    exit(1);
}
```

If the program survives this *if* test, the next new chunk of code checks to see whether the `-h` "help" switch is specified first. If not, the program may attempt to open the file `-h`. So, a quick comparison is made for `-h` as the first argument. If found, the *help()* function is called:

```
filename = argv[1];

if( strcmp(filename,"-h")==0 )
    help();
```

Because the program assumes the first argument is a filename, this step is necessary even if you use the *getopt()* function elsewhere in the code to look for the `-h` switch. In fact, this type of comparison is how I would test for switches if the *getopt()* function were unavailable. If the `-h` switch is the first argument, the *help()* function is called and helpful text is output. The program ends. Otherwise, the program can continue testing options.

To process the rest of the switches, I use a single *int* variable `options`. This variable is declared externally—a global variable, which gives all functions access to its value:

```
int options;
```

As with the *options* series of programs, in the updated code for *dumpfile* each of the three valid switches—`-a`, `-o`, and `-h`—are tested for in a *while* loop, shown in the following listing. I use only one variable, the external integer `options`, to track the settings. It's initialized to zero, along with other variables used elsewhere in the *main()*

function. For two of the switches, a macro alters the value of variable `options`: *set_abbr()* for -a and *set_oct()* for -o. If the help switch is specified, the *help()* function is called where text is output and the program terminates.

Listing 9.8   The *while* loop inside the *main()* function, in `dumpfile04.c`

```
offset = index = options = 0;
while( (r=getopt(argc,argv,"aosh")) != -1 )
{
    switch(r)
    {
        case 'a':
            set_abbr();
            break;
        case 'o':
            set_oct();
            break;
        case 'h':
            help();
        case '?':
            printf("Switch '%c' is invalid\n",optopt);
            break;
        default:
            puts("Unknown option");
    }
}
```

Variables offset and index are used elsewhere in the *main()* function.

Valid switches are a, o, s, and h.

For the -a switch, the *set_abbr()* macro modifies variable `options`.

For the -o switch, the *set_oct()* macro modifies variable `options`.

For -h, the *help()* function is called and the program quits.

By making variable `options` external, the *line_out()* function need not be modified. Otherwise, I'd have to add another argument to the list, one to accept the variable `options` to examine the command-line switches. Having a single variable `options` also avoids adding even more arguments to the *line_out()* function. Its declaration would eventually become a mess. No, this situation is one of those rare times a global variable is an effective solution to a problem.

The macros *set_abbr()* and *set_oct()* allow the code to modify variable `options` by setting specific bits. Each of the *set* macros has a companion *test* macro that can be used in the *line_out()* function. The *test* macro returns TRUE (1) when the option is set, which allows the macro to be used as an *if* condition to activate a feature.

The next listing shows the macros as they're defined at the start of the source code file. First, the `options` variable is declared, and then binary values are assigned for the options, ABBR and OCT. Finally, the *set* and *test* macros are defined, using bitwise logic to set and evaluate the bits in variable `options`.

Listing 9.9   Creating macros to modify and test variable `options`

```
int options;
```

Declares the external variable before it's used

```
#define SIZE 16
#define ABBR 1
```

Size value is used elsewhere in the code, 16 bytes per line.

Abbreviation status is bit 1.

```
#define OCT 2
#define set_abbr() options|=ABBR
#define test_abbr() ((options&ABBR)==ABBR)
#define set_oct() options|=OCT
#define test_oct() ((options&OCT)==OCT)
```

Uses the bitwise logical OR to set bit 1 (ABBR) in variable `options`

Uses the bitwise logical AND to test bit 1 (ABBR) in variable `options`

Octal output status is bit 2.

Uses the bitwise logical AND to test bit 2 (OCT) in variable `options`

Uses the bitwise logical OR to set bit 2 (OCT) in variable `options`

The defined constants ABBR and OCT represent bit positions in the variable `options` that don't overlap. Each bit can be set or examined without changing the other bits. This approach allows for more options to be added in the same manner, on up to the full bit width of an *int* variable.

The macros add to readability, but more important, by creating a macro, I make updating the code easier. For example, changing an option is done in one location as opposed to fishing around the code for everywhere it's referenced.

The full code for the modified *dumpfile* program is available in the online repository as `dumpfile04.c`. The only item I haven't discussed is the *help()* function. It's shown here. The next few sections cover the code required to implement the -a and -o switches.

Listing 9.10   **The *help()* function from** `dumpfile04.c`

```
void help(void)
{
    puts("dumpfile - output a file's raw data");
    puts("Format: dumpfile filename [options]");
    puts("Options:");
    puts("-a abbreviated output ");
    puts("-o output octal instead of hex");
    puts("-h display this text");
    exit(1);
}
```

9.3.3   *Setting abbreviated output*

The *dumpfile* program's current output is good for nerds who want to examine bytes in files. It shows an offset column, hex bytes, and then character representation of ASCII codes. This presentation is what I prefer, though at times all that's needed is just the byte dump. To accomplish this goal, users can specify the -a switch for abbreviated program output.

The mechanics behind the -a switch are already present in the `dumpfile04.c` source code. All that's required is implementing the on-off portions of the code: with abbreviated output active, some items in the *line_out()* function are suppressed. For these items, an *if* statement is added with the *test_abbr()* macro as its condition. The result is a toggle that activates portions of the output only when the -a switch isn't specified.

Modifications must be made at three points in the *line_out()* function. The first is for the initial column, which outputs the offset. The *printf()* statement is executed only when the *test_abbr()* macro returns zero. The not operator (!) is used to negate the macro:

```
if( !test_abbr() )
{
    printf("%05X ",offset);
}
```

If the -a switch is specified, the *printf()* statement is skipped. Otherwise, for normal output, it's executed.

Next, in the *for* loop that outputs the hex bytes, the existing code adds an extra space for readability:

```
if( (a+1)%8==0 )
    putchar(' ');
```

This space isn't needed for a plain hex dump. Again, the *test_abbr()* macro is added to the if condition to disable the space output when the -a switch is specified. Here is the modification:

```
if( (a+1)%8==0 && !test_abbr() )
    putchar(' ');
```

Another space is added when the line length is less than the LENGTH constant. This statement (at line 37 in the dumpfile05.c source code file) need not be modified because the ASCII column is also suppressed.

Finally, the last part of the *line_out()* function to be modified is the *for* loop that outputs the ASCII column. This chunk of code is enclosed in an *if* test like the first column:

```
if( !test_abbr() )
{
    putchar(' ');
    for( a=0; a<length; a++ )
    {
        if( *(data+a)>=' ' && *(data+a)<='~' )
            putchar( *(data+a) );
        else
            putchar(' ');
    }
}
```

Each time the *test_abbr()* macro is used, it's prefixed with the not (!) operator. This may cause you to think about rewriting the macro so that its evaluation is reversed. You could do so, though I chose to be consistent with both macros in that they return 1 when the switch is active.

The full source code for adding the -a switch is available in the online repository as dumpfile05.c. Here is a sample run on the bytes.dat file, which contains sequential value 0 through 255:

```
$ ./dumpfile bytes.dat -a
00 01 02 03 04 05 06 07 08 09 0A 0B 0C 0D 0E 0F
10 11 12 13 14 15 16 17 18 19 1A 1B 1C 1D 1E 1F
20 21 22 23 24 25 26 27 28 29 2A 2B 2C 2D 2E 2F
30 31 32 33 34 35 36 37 38 39 3A 3B 3C 3D 3E 3F
40 41 42 43 44 45 46 47 48 49 4A 4B 4C 4D 4E 4F
50 51 52 53 54 55 56 57 58 59 5A 5B 5C 5D 5E 5F
60 61 62 63 64 65 66 67 68 69 6A 6B 6C 6D 6E 6F
70 71 72 73 74 75 76 77 78 79 7A 7B 7C 7D 7E 7F
80 81 82 83 84 85 86 87 88 89 8A 8B 8C 8D 8E 8F
90 91 92 93 94 95 96 97 98 99 9A 9B 9C 9D 9E 9F
A0 A1 A2 A3 A4 A5 A6 A7 A8 A9 AA AB AC AD AE AF
B0 B1 B2 B3 B4 B5 B6 B7 B8 B9 BA BB BC BD BE BF
C0 C1 C2 C3 C4 C5 C6 C7 C8 C9 CA CB CC CD CE CF
D0 D1 D2 D3 D4 D5 D6 D7 D8 D9 DA DB DC DD DE DF
E0 E1 E2 E3 E4 E5 E6 E7 E8 E9 EA EB EC ED EE EF
F0 F1 F2 F3 F4 F5 F6 F7 F8 F9 FA FB FC FD FE FF
```

9.3.4 *Activating octal output*

Older programmers have more of an attraction to octal than younger coders. I'm on the cusp, at the age where octal was introduced to me as a young coder, but we never got a chance to date.

Octal is the base-8 counting system, which fits in nicely with three bits of data. Before the microcomputer era, this counting base was commonly used on mainframes and in programming. You still see vestiges of octal, primarily in file permission bits in a Linux directory listing. The octal counting base is shown in table 9.3.

Table 9.3 Octal, decimal, and hexadecimal values

Octal	Decimal	Hex	Binary	Octal	Decimal	Hex	Binary
0	0	0	0000	10	8	8	1000
1	1	1	0001	11	9	9	1001
2	2	2	0010	12	10	A	1010
3	3	3	0011	13	11	B	1011
4	4	4	0100	14	12	C	1100
5	5	5	0101	15	13	D	1101
6	6	6	0110	16	14	E	1110
7	7	7	0111	17	15	F	1111

Like many programming languages, C deftly handles octal values. To specify octal, you use the zero prefix: `01` is octal 1, `010` is octal 10 (decimal 8), and so on. Your source code editor may be wise enough to pick up on octal values and highlight them accordingly.

The *printf()* and *scanf()* placeholder for octal values is `%o`. Like other placeholders, it features width values and zero-padding.

For the sake of the old timers, I added an octal output switch to the *dumpfile* program. This switch required several updates to the code, for not only octal output but also spacing and alignment in the program's output.

Three changes are required to activate the `-o` switch, updating the `dumpfile05.c` source code file to its next iteration, `dumpfile06.c`. Each of these changes is found in the *line_out()* function. The *test_oct()* macro is used as an *if* condition, which returns TRUE when the `-o` switch has been specified.

When the octal switch is active, the first column needs to output octal values instead of hex. This decision is in addition to whether the column is output when *test_abbr()* macro is true (or false). An *if-else* structure handles the differing output:

```
if( !test_abbr() )
{
    if( test_oct() )
        printf("%05o ",offset);
    else
        printf("%05X ",offset);
}
```

The `%05o` placeholder outputs the value of variable offset as an octal number five digits wide with zeros padded on the left.

The next change takes place in the *for* loop that outputs the bytes. It's pretty much the same type of decision: when the *test_oct()* macro returns TRUE, octal values are output instead of decimal:

```
if( test_oct() )
    printf(" %03o",*(data+a));
else
    printf(" %02X",*(data+a));
```

The placeholder `%03o` outputs an octal value three digits wide with zeros padded on the left. The effect on the output is that each line of bytes is now wider than a typical 80-column screen. Still, if the user wants octal output, the program provides.

The final change is made when the last line of output is shorter than 16 bytes. Because the octal values are output three characters wide instead of two, four spaces are needed for each missing byte to line up the ASCII column:

```
if( test_oct() )
    printf("    ");
else
    printf("   ");
```

These changes are included in the source code file `dumpfile06.c`, available in this book's online repository. Here is output from the *dumpfile* program on the `bytes.dat` file with both the `-a` and `-o` switches specified:

```
000 001 002 003 004 005 006 007 010 011 012 013 014 015 016 017
020 021 022 023 024 025 026 027 030 031 032 033 034 035 036 037
040 041 042 043 044 045 046 047 050 051 052 053 054 055 056 057
060 061 062 063 064 065 066 067 070 071 072 073 074 075 076 077
100 101 102 103 104 105 106 107 110 111 112 113 114 115 116 117
120 121 122 123 124 125 126 127 130 131 132 133 134 135 136 137
140 141 142 143 144 145 146 147 150 151 152 153 154 155 156 157
160 161 162 163 164 165 166 167 170 171 172 173 174 175 176 177
200 201 202 203 204 205 206 207 210 211 212 213 214 215 216 217
220 221 222 223 224 225 226 227 230 231 232 233 234 235 236 237
240 241 242 243 244 245 246 247 250 251 252 253 254 255 256 257
260 261 262 263 264 265 266 267 270 271 272 273 274 275 276 277
300 301 302 303 304 305 306 307 310 311 312 313 314 315 316 317
320 321 322 323 324 325 326 327 330 331 332 333 334 335 336 337
340 341 342 343 344 345 346 347 350 351 352 353 354 355 356 357
360 361 362 363 364 365 366 367 370 371 372 373 374 375 376 377
```

Output with the `-o` switch alone is too wide to show as text. Figure 9.1 illustrates how the output looks in a terminal window with the dimensions 100 columns by 24 rows.

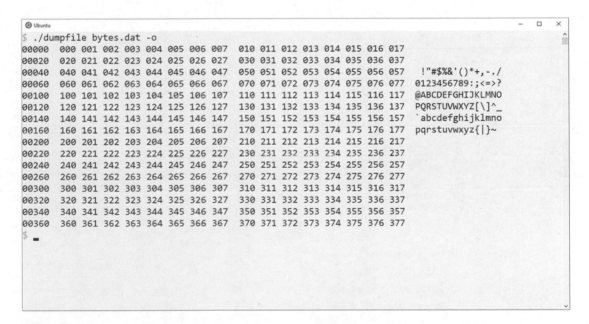

Figure 9.1   Output from the *dumpfile* program with the `-o` switch is kinda wide.

EXERCISE 9.5

How about adding one more switch to the *dumpfile* program? The -v switch is commonly used to output the program's version number. I would recommend setting these values as defined constants: separate major and minor version numbers, or a complete version number string.

Add both the -v switch as well as the code (the *version()* function) to output the version number. The program can quit after performing this task. And remember that some users may use the -v switch as the program's only argument. My solution to this exercise is found in the online repository as `dumpfile07.c`.

Directory tree

10

Of all the programming tasks, I'm embarrassed to admit that I enjoy coding file utilities the most. The casual user is unaware of the mountain of information about files provided by the operating system. It's highly detailed low-hanging fruit, eager for plucking. Plus, exploring files and directories opens your understanding of how computer storage works. Exploring this field may inspire you to write your own interesting file utilities. If it doesn't, you can keep reading this chapter—your introduction to filesystems and storage.

The goal here is to create a directory tree program. The output shows subdirectories as they sit in the hierarchical filesystem. In addition to being exposed to the word *hierarchical* (which I can amazingly both spell and type), in this chapter you learn how to:

- Examine information about a file
- Decipher file modes and permissions
- Read a directory entry
- Use recursion to explore the directory structure
- Extract a directory name from a full pathname
- Output a directory tree
- Avoid confusing the word *hierarchical* with *hieroglyphical*

Before diving into the details, be aware that GUI nomenclature prefers the term *folder* over *directory*. As a C programmer, you must use the term *directory*, not *folder*. All C functions that deal with files and directories use *directory* or contain the abbreviation "dir." Don't wimp out and use the term *folder*.

The point of the directory tree utility is to output a map of the directory structure. The map details which directories are parents and children of each other. Unlike years ago, today's directory structures are busy with lots of organization. Users are more attentive when it comes to saving files. Programs are geared toward this type of organization and provide hints to help users employ the subdirectory concept.

Even if a directory map seems trivial, the process of exploring the directory tree lends itself well to other handy disk utilities. For example, chapter 11 covers a file-finding utility, which relies heavily upon the information presented in this chapter to make the utility truly useful.

10.1   *The filesystem*

At the core of all media storage lies the filesystem. The *filesystem* describes the way data is stored on media, how files are accessed, and various nerdy tidbits about the files themselves.

The only time most users deal with the filesystem concept is when formatting media. Choosing a filesystem is part of the formatting process, because it determines how the media is formatted and which protocols to follow. This step is necessary for compatibility: not every filesystem is compatible with every computer operating system. Therefore, the user is allowed to select a filesystem for the media's format to allow for sharing between operating systems, such as Linux and PC or Macintosh.

The filesystem's duty is to organize storage. It takes a file's data and writes it to one or more locations on the media. This information is recorded along with other file details, such as the file's name, size, dates (created, modified, accessed), permissions, and so on.

Some of the file details are readily obtainable through existing utilities or from various C library functions. But most of the mechanics of the filesystem are geared toward saving, retrieving, and updating the file's data lurking on the media. All this action takes place automatically under the supervision of the operating system.

The good news for most coders is that it isn't necessary to know the minutiae of how files are stored on media. Even if you go full nerd and understand the subtle differences between the various filesystems *and* can tout the benefits of the High Performance File System (HPFS) at nerd cocktail parties, the level of media access required to manipulate a filesystem requires privileges above where typical C programs operate. Functions are available for exploring a file's details. These functions are introduced in the next section.

Aside from knowing the names and perhaps a few details on how filesystems work, if you're curious, you can use common tools on your computer to see which filesystems are in use. In a Linux terminal window, use the **man fs** command to review details on how Linux uses a filesystem and the different filesystems available. The /proc/filesystems directory lists available filesystems for your Linux installation.

Windows keeps its filesystem information tucked away in the Disk Management console. To access this window, follow these steps:

1. Tap the Windows key on the keyboard to open the Start menu.
2. Type **Disk Management**.
3. From the list of search results, choose Create and Format Hard Disk Partitions.

Figure 10.1 shows the Disk Management console from one of my Windows computers. Available media is presented in the table, with the File System column listing the filesystems used; only NTFS is shown in the figure.

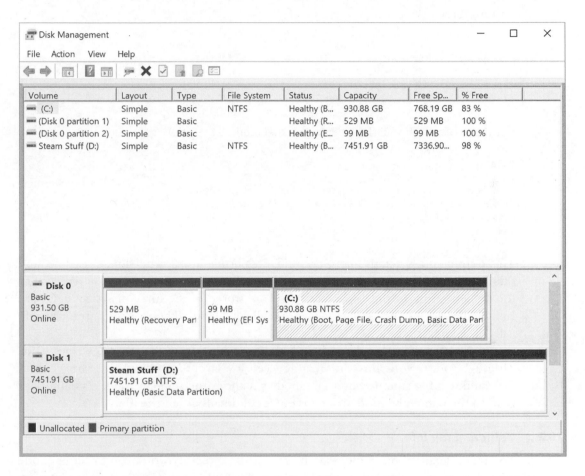

Figure 10.1   The Disk Management console reveals the filesystem used to format media available to the PC.

On the Macintosh, you can use the Disk Utility to browse available media to learn which filesystem is in use. This app is found in the Utilities directory: in the Finder, click Go > Utilities to view the directory and access the Disk Utility app.

If it were easy or necessary to program a filesystem, I'd explore the topic further. For now, understand that the filesystem is the host for data stored on media in a computer. A program such as a directory tree uses the filesystem, but in C, such a utility doesn't need to know details about the filesystem type to do its job.

10.2   *File and directory details*

To gather directory details at the command prompt, use the *ls* command. It's available in all shells, dating back to the first, prehistoric version of Unix used by the ancient Greeks, when the command was known as λσ. The output is a list of filenames in the current directory:

```
$ ls
changecwd.c  dirtree04.c   fileinfo03.c  readdir01.c  subdir01.c  subdir05.c
dirtree01.c  extractor.c   fileinfo04.c  readdir02.c  subdir02.c  subdir06.c
dirtree02.c  fileinfo01.c  fileinfo05.c  readdir03.c  subdir03.c
dirtree03.c  fileinfo02.c  getcwd.c      readdir04.c  subdir04.c
```

For more detail, the -1 (long) switch is specified:

```
$ ls -l
total 68
-rwxrwxrwx 1 dang dang  292 Oct 31 16:26 changecwd.c
-rwxrwxrwx 1 dang dang 1561 Nov  4 21:14 dirtree01.c
-rwxrwxrwx 1 dang dang 1633 Nov  5 10:39 dirtree02.c
...
```

This output shows details about each file, its permissions, ownership, size, date, and other trivia you can use to intimidate your computer illiterate pals. It's not secret stuff; the details output by the ls -1 command are stored in the directory like a database. In fact, directories on storage media are really databases. Their records aren't specifically files, but rather inodes.

An *inode* is not an Apple product. No, it's a collection of data that describes a file. Although your C programs can't readily access low-level filesystem details, you can easily examine a file's inode data. The inode's name is the same as the file's name. But beyond the name, the inode contains oodles of details about the file.

10.2.1   *Gathering file info*

To obtain details about a file, as well as to read a directory, you need to access inode data. The command-line program that does so is called *stat*. Here's some sample output on the *stat* program file fileinfo:

```
  File: fileinfo
  Size: 8464         Blocks: 24        IO Block: 4096    regular file
Device: eh/14d  Inode: 11258999068563657   Links: 1
Access: (0777/-rwxrwxrwx)  Uid: ( 1000/   dang)  Gid: ( 1000/   dang)
Access: 2021-10-23 21:11:17.457919300 -0700
Modify: 2021-10-23 21:11:00.071527400 -0700
Change: 2021-10-23 21:11:00.071527400 -0700
```

These details are stored in the directory database. In fact, part of the output shows the file's inode number: 11258999068563657. Of course, the name `fileinfo` is far easier to use as a reference.

To read this same information in your C programs, you use the *stat()* function. It's prototyped in the sys/stat.h header file. Here is the *man* page format:

```
int stat(const char *pathname, struct stat *statbuf);
```

The `pathname` is a filename or a full pathname. Argument `statbuf` is the address of a `stat` structure. Here's a typical *stat()* function statement, with the `filename` *char* pointer containing the filename, `fs` as a `stat` structure, and *int* variable `r` capturing the return value:

```
r = stat(filename, &fs);
```

Upon failure, value −1 is returned. Otherwise, 0 is returned and the `stat` structure `fs` is joyously filled with details about the file—inode data. Table 10.1 lists the common members of the `stat` structure, though different filesystems and operating systems add or change specific members.

Table 10.1   **Members in the *stat()* function's `statbuf` structure**

Member	Data type (placeholder)	Detail
st_dev	dev_t (%lu)	ID of the media (device) containing the file
st_ino	ino_t (%lu)	Inode number
st_mode	mode_t (%u)	File type, mode, permissions
st_nlink	nlink_t (%lu)	Number of links
st_uid	uid_t (%u)	Owner's user ID
st_gid	gid_t (%u)	Group's user ID
st_rdev	dev_t (%lu)	Special file type's device ID
st_size	off_t (%lu)	File size in bytes
st_blksize	blksize_t (%lu)	Filesystem's block size
st_blocks	blkcnt_t (%lu)	File blocks allocated (512-byte blocks)
st_atime	struct timespec	Time file last accessed
st_mtime	struct timespec	Time file last modified
st_ctime	struct timespec	Time file status last changed

Most of the `stat` structure members are integers; I've specified the *printf()* placeholder type in table 10.1. They're all *unsigned*, though some values are *unsigned long*.

Watch out for the *long unsigned* values because the compiler bemoans using the incorrect placeholder to represent these values.

The `timespec` structure is accessed as a *time_t* pointer. It contains two members: tv_sec and tv_nsec for seconds and nanoseconds, respectively. An example of using the *ctime()* function to access this structure is shown later.

The following listing shows a sample program, `fileinfo01.c`, that outputs file (or inode) details. Each of the `stat` structure members is accessed for a file supplied as a command-line argument. Most of the code consists of error-checking—for example, to confirm that a filename argument is supplied and to check on the return status of the *stat()* function.

Listing 10.1   Source code for `fileinfo01.c`

```
#include <stdio.h>
#include <stdlib.h>
#include <sys/stat.h>
#include <time.h>

int main(int argc, char *argv[])
{
    char *filename;
    struct stat fs;
    int r;

    if( argc<2 )
    {
        fprintf(stderr,"Specify a filename\n");
        exit(1);
    }

    filename = argv[1];
    printf("Info for file '%s'\n",filename);
    r = stat(filename,&fs);
    if( r==-1 )
    {
        fprintf(stderr,"Error reading '%s'\n",filename);
        exit(1);
    }

    printf("Media ID: %lu\n",fs.st_dev);
    printf("Inode #%lu\n",fs.st_ino);
    printf("Type and mode: %u\n",fs.st_mode);
    printf("Hard links = %lu\n",fs.st_nlink);
    printf("Owner ID: %u\n",fs.st_uid);
    printf("Group ID: %u\n",fs.st_gid);
    printf("Device ID: %lu\n",fs.st_rdev);
    printf("File size %lu bytes\n",fs.st_size);
    printf("Block size = %lu\n",fs.st_blksize);
    printf("Allocated blocks = %lu\n",fs.st_blocks);
    printf("Access: %s",ctime(&fs.st_atime));
    printf("Modification: %s",ctime(&fs.st_mtime));
    printf("Changed: %s",ctime(&fs.st_ctime));
```

The filename is supplied as a program argument.

Confirms the first argument

Referring to the argument using char pointer `filename` aids readability.

Calls the *stat()* function

Checks for an error

Outputs the members of the `stat` structure `fs`

The time structures use the *ctime()* function to output their values.

```
        return(0);
}
```

The information output by the `fileinfo01.c` program mirrors what the command-line *stat* utility coughs up. Here's a sample run on the same file, `fileinfo`, this code's program:

```
Info for file 'fileinfo'
Media ID: 14
Inode #7318349394555950
Type and mode: 33279
Hard links = 1
Owner ID: 1000
Group ID: 1000
Device ID: 0
File size 8464 bytes
Block size = 4096
Allocated blocks = 24
Access: Tue Oct 26 15:55:10 2021
Modification: Tue Oct 26 15:55:10 2021
Changed: Tue Oct 26 15:55:10 2021
```

The details are the same as for the *stat* command's output shown earlier in this section. The *stat* command does look up the Device ID, Owner ID, and Group ID details, which your code could do as well. But one curious item is structure member st_mode, the type and mode value. The value shown in the output above is 33279. This integer value contains a lot of details—bit fields—which you see interpreted in the *stat* command's output. Your code can also examine this value to determine the file type and its permissions.

10.2.2   *Exploring file type and permissions*

Examining a file's (or inode's) st_mode value is how you determine whether a file is a regular old file, a directory, or some other special type of file. Remember that in the Linux environment, everything is a file. Using the *stat()* function is how your code can determine which type of file the inode represents.

The bit fields in the st_mode member of the stat structure also describe the file's permissions. Though you could code a series of complex bitwise logical operations to ferret out the specific details contained in the st_mode value's bits, I recommend that you use instead the handy macros available in the sys/stat.h header file.

For example, the S_ISREG() macro returns TRUE for regular files. To update the fileinfo01.c code to test for regular files, add the following statements:

```
printf("Type and mode: %X\n",fs.st_mode);
if( S_ISREG(fs.st_mode) )
    printf("%s is a regular file\n",filename);
else
    printf("%s is not a regular file\n",filename);
```

If the S_ISREG() test on the fs.st_mode variable returns TRUE, the *printf()* statement belonging to the *if* statement outputs text confirming that the file is regular. The *else* condition handles other types of files, such as directories.

In my update to the code, fieinfo02.c (available in the online archive), I removed all the *printf()* statements from the original code. The five statements shown earlier replace the original printf() statements, because the focus of this update is to determine file type. Here's sample output on the fileinfo02.c source code file itself:

```
Info for file 'fileinfo02.c'
Type and mode: 81FF
Fileinfo02.c is a regular file
```

If I instead specify the single dot (.), representing the current directory, I see this output:

```
Info for file '.'
Type and mode: 41FF
. is a directory
```

In the output above, the st_mode value changes as well as the return value from the S_ISREG() macro; a directory isn't a regular file. In fact, you can test for directories specifically by using the S_ISDIR() macro:

```
printf("Type and mode: %X\n",fs.st_mode);
if( S_ISREG(fs.st_mode) )
    printf("%s is a regular file\n",filename);
else if( S_ISDIR(fs.st_mode) )
    printf("%s is a directory\n",filename);
else
    printf("%s is some other type of file\n",filename);
```

I've made these modifications and additions to the code in fileinfo02.c, with the improvements saved in fileinfo03.c, available in this book's online repository.

Further modifications to the code are possible by using the full slate of file mode macros, listed in table 10.2. These are the common macros, though your C compiler and operating system may offer more. Use these macros to identify files by their type.

Table 10.2   Macros defined in sys/stat.h to help determine file type

Macro	True for this type of file
S_ISBLK()	Block special, such as mass storage in the /dev directory
S_ISCHR()	Character special, such as a pipe or the /dev/null device
S_ISDIR()	Directories
S_ISFIFO()	A FIFO (named pipe) or socket
S_ISREG()	Regular files
S_ISLNK()	Symbolic link
S_ISSOCK()	Socket

File type details aren't the only information contained in the st_mode member of the stat structure. This value also reveals the file's permissions. File permissions refer to access bits that determine who-can-do-what to a file. Three access bits, called an *octet*, are available:

- Read (r)
- Write (w)
- Execute (x)

Read permission means that the file is accessed read-only: the file's data can be read but not modified. Write permission allows the file to be read and written to. Execute permission is set for program files, such as your C programs (set automatically by the compiler or linker), shell scripts (set manually), and directories. This is all standard Linux stuff, so if you desire more information, hunt down a grim, poorly written book on Linux for specifics.

In Linux, the *chmod* command sets and resets file permissions. These permissions can be seen in the long listing of a file when using the *ls* command with the -1 (little L) switch:

```
$ ls -l fileinfo
-rwxrwxrwx 1 dang dang 8464 Oct 26 15:55 fileinfo
```

The first chunk of info, -rwxrwxrwx, indicates the file type and permissions, which are detailed in figure 10.2. Next is the number of hard links (1), the owner (dang), and the group (dang). The value 8,464 is the file size in bytes, and then comes the date and time stamp, and finally the filename.

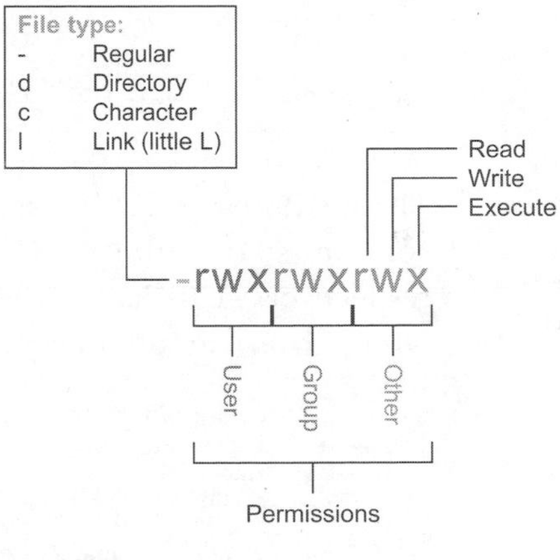

Three sets of file permissions octets are used for a file. These sets are based on user classification:

- Owner
- Group
- Other

Figure 10.2   Deciphering file permission bits in a long directory listing

You are the owner of the files you create. As a user on the computer, you are also a member of a group. Use the *id* command to view your username and ID number, as well as the groups you belong to (names and IDs). View the /etc/group file to see the full list of groups on the system.

File owners grant themselves full access to their files. Setting group permissions is one way to grant access to a bunch of system users at once. The third field, other, applies to anyone who is not the owner or in the named group.

In the long directory listing, a file's owner and group appear as shown earlier. This value is interpreted from the st_mode member of the file's stat structure. As with obtaining the file's type, you can use defined constants and macros available in the sys/stat.h header file to test for the permissions for each user classification.

I count nine permission-defined constants available in sys/stat.h, which accounts for each permission octet (three) and the three permission types: read, write, and execute. These are shown in table 10.3.

Table 10.3   Defined constants used for permissions, available from the sys/stat.h header file

Defined constant	Permission octet
S_IRUSR	Owner read permission
S_IWUSR	Owner write permission
S_IXUSR	Owner execute permission
S_IRGRP	Group read permission
S_IWGRP	Group write permission
S_IXGRP	Group execute permission
S_IROTH	Other read permission
S_IWOTH	Other write permission
S_IXOTH	Other execute permission

The good news is that these defined constants follow a naming pattern: each defined constant starts with S_I. The I is followed by R, W, or X for read, write, or execute, respectively. This letter is followed by USR, GRP, OTH for Owner (user), Group, and Other. This naming convention is summarized in figure 10.3.

Figure 10.3   The naming convention used for permission defined constants in sys/stat.h

For example, if you want to test the read permission for a group user, you use the S_IRGRP defined constant: S_I plus R for read and GRP for group. This defined constant is used in an *if* test with a bitwise AND operator to test the permission bit on the st_mode member:

```
If( fs.st_mode & S_IRGRP )
```

The value in fs_st_mode (the file's mode, including type and permissions) is tested against the bit in the S_IRGRP defined constant. If the test is true, meaning the bit is set, the file has read-only permissions set for the "other" group.

Listing 10.2 puts the testing macros and defined constants to work for a file supplied as a command-line argument. This update to the *fileinfo* series of programs outputs the file type and permissions for the named file. An *if else-if else* structure handles the different file types as listed in table 10.2. Three sets of *if* tests output permissions for the three different groups. You see all the macros and defined constants discussed in this section used in the code. The code appears lengthy, but it contains a lot of copied and pasted information.

Listing 10.2 Source code for `fileinfo04.c`

```c
#include <stdio.h>
#include <stdlib.h>
#include <sys/stat.h>
#include <time.h>

int main(int argc, char *argv[])
{
    char *filename;
    struct stat fs;
    int r;

    if( argc<2 )
    {
        fprintf(stderr,"Specify a filename\n");
        exit(1);
    }

    filename = argv[1];
    r = stat(filename,&fs);
    if( r==-1 )
    {
        fprintf(stderr,"Error reading '%s'\n",filename);
        exit(1);
    }

    printf("File '%s' is a ",filename);
    if( S_ISBLK(fs.st_mode) )            ◁────  Determines the
        printf("block special\n");              file type, a long
    else if( S_ISCHR(fs.st_mode) )              if-else structure
        printf("character special\n");
    else if( S_ISDIR(fs.st_mode) )
        printf("directory\n");
    else if( S_ISFIFO(fs.st_mode) )
        printf("named pipe or socket\n");
    else if( S_ISREG(fs.st_mode) )
        printf("regular file\n");
    else if( S_ISLNK(fs.st_mode) )
        printf("symbolic link\n");
```

New stuff starts here.

```
        else if( S_ISSOCK(fs.st_mode) )
            printf("socket\n");
        else
            printf("type unknown\n");

        printf("Owner permissions: ");        ◁──    Tests owner
        if( fs.st_mode & S_IRUSR )                   permission
            printf("read ");                          bits
        if( fs.st_mode & S_IWUSR )
            printf("write ");
        if( fs.st_mode & S_IXUSR )
            printf("execute");
        putchar('\n');

        printf("Group permissions: ");        ◁──    Tests group
        if( fs.st_mode & S_IRGRP )                   permission
            printf("read ");                          bits
        if( fs.st_mode & S_IWGRP )
            printf("write ");
        if( fs.st_mode & S_IXGRP )
            printf("execute");
        putchar('\n');

        printf("Other permissions: ");        ◁──    Tests other
        if( fs.st_mode & S_IROTH )                   permission
            printf("read ");                          bits
        if( fs.st_mode & S_IWOTH )
            printf("write ");
        if( fs.st_mode & S_IXOTH )
            printf("execute");
        putchar('\n');

        return(0);
}
```

The program I created from the source code shown in listing 10.2 is named a.out, the default. Here is a sample run on the original *fileinfo* program:

```
$ ./a.out fileinfo
File 'fileinfo' is a regular file
Owner permissions: read write execute
Group permissions: read write execute
Other permissions: read write execute
```

The information shown here corresponds to an ls -l listing output of -rwxrwxrwx.
    Here is the output for system directory /etc:

```
$ ./a.out /etc
File '/etc' is a directory
Owner permissions: read write execute
Group permissions: read execute
Other permissions: read execute
```

From this output, the file type is correctly identified as a directory. The owner permissions are rwx (the owner is root). The group and other permissions are r-x, which means anyone on the computer can read and access (execute) the directory.

EXERCISE 10.1

The *if-else* structures in listing 10.2 (fileinfo04.c) contain a lot of repetition. Seeing repetitive statements in code cries out to me for a function. Your task for this exercise is to a write a function that outputs a file's permissions.

Call the function *permissions_out()*. It takes a *mode_t* argument of the st_mode member in a stat structure. Here is the prototype:

```
void permissions_out(mode_t stm);
```

Use the function to output a string of permissions for each of the three access levels: owner, group, other. Use characters r, w, x, for read, write, and execute access if a bit is set; use a dash (-) for unset items. This output is the same as shown in the ls -l listing, but without the leading character identifying the file type.

A simple approach exists for this function, and I hope you find it. If not, you can view my solution in the source code file fileinfo05.c, available in the online repository. Please try this exercise on your own before peeking at my solution; comments in my code explain my philosophy. Use the *fileinfo* series of programs to perform the basic operations for the *stat()* function, if you prefer.

10.2.3 Reading a directory

A directory is a database of files, but call them inodes if you want to have a nerd find you attractive. Just like a file, a directory database is stored on media. But you can't use the *fopen()* function to open and read the contents of a directory. No, instead you use the *opendir()* function. Here is its *man* page format:

```
DIR *opendir(const char *filename);
```

The *opendir()* function accepts a single argument, a string representing the pathname of the directory to examine. Specifying the shortcuts . and .. for the current and parent directory are also valid.

The function returns a pointer to a *DIR* handle, similar to the *FILE* handle used by the *fopen()* command. As the *FILE* handle represents a file stream, the *DIR* handle represents a directory stream.

Upon an error, the NULL pointer is returned. The global errno value is set, indicating the specific booboo the function encountered.

The *opendir()* function features a companion *closedir()* function, similar to the *fclose()* function as a companion to *fopen()*. The *closedir()* function requires a single argument, the *DIR* handle of an open directory stream, humorously called "dirp" in the *man* page format example:

```
int closedir(DIR *dirp);
```

Yes, I know that the internet spells it "derp."

Upon success, the *closedir()* function returns 0. Otherwise, the value −1 is returned and the global `errno` variable is set, yadda-yadda.

Both the *opendir()* and *closedir()* functions are prototyped in the `dirent.h` header file.

In the following listing, you see both the *opendir()* and *closedir()* functions put to work. The current directory "." is opened because it's always valid.

Listing 10.3   Source code for `readdir01.c`

```c
#include <stdio.h>
#include <stdlib.h>
#include <dirent.h>

int main()                          Directory
{                                   handle
    DIR *dp;        ←─────────┐
                              Opens the current
                              directory, whatever
    dp = opendir(".");    ←   it may be
    if(dp == NULL)        ←
    {                                   Exits the
        puts("Unable to read directory");   program upon
        exit(1);                        failure to open
    }

    puts("Directory is opened!");

    closedir(dp);        ←   And just closes
    puts("Directory is closed!");   it back up

    return(0);
}
```

The code in listing 10.3 merely opens and closes the current directory. Boring! To access the files stored in the directory, you use another function, *readdir()*. This function is also prototyped in the `dirent.h` header file. Here is the *man* page format:

```c
struct dirent *readdir(DIR *dirp);
```

The function consumes an open *DIR* handle as its only argument. The return value is the address of a `dirent` structure, which contains details about a directory entry. This function is called repeatedly to read file entries (inodes) from the directory stream. The value NULL is returned after the final entry in the directory has been read.

Sadly, the `dirent` structure isn't as rich as I'd like it to be. Table 10.4 lists the two consistent structure members, though some C libraries offer more members. Any extra members are specific to the compiler or operating system and shouldn't be relied on for code you plan to release into the wild. The only two required members for the POSIX.1 standard are `d_ino` for the entry's inode and `d_name` for the entry's filename.

Table 10.4 Common members of the `dirent` structure

Member	Data type (placeholder)	Description
`d_ino`	*ino_t* (%lu)	Inode number
`d_reclen`	*unsigned short* (%u)	Record length

The best structure member to use, and one that's consistently available across all compilers and platforms, is d_name. This member is used in the source code for readdir02.c, shown in the next listing. This update to readdir01.c removes two silly *puts()* statements. Added is a *readdir()* statement, along with a *printf()* function to output the name of the first file found in the current directory.

Listing 10.4 Source code for `readdir02.c`

```c
#include <stdio.h>
#include <stdlib.h>
#include <dirent.h>

int main()
{
    DIR *dp;
    struct dirent *entry;          ◁—  The dirent structure
                                        is created as a pointer,
                                        a memory address.

    dp = opendir(".");
    if(dp == NULL)
    {
        puts("Unable to read directory");
        exit(1);
    }                                   The entry is read and
                                        stored in the dirent
    entry = readdir(dp);           ◁—  structure entry.

    printf("File %s\n",entry->d_name);   ◁—  The d_name
                                              member is
    closedir(dp);                             output.

    return(0);
}
```

The program generated from the readdir02.c source code outputs only one file—most likely, the entry for the current directory itself, the single dot. Obviously, if you want a real directory-reading program, you must modify the code.

As with using the fread() function to read data from a regular file , the readdir() function is called repeatedly. When the function returns a pointer to a dirent structure, another entry is available in the directory. Only when the function returns NULL has the full directory been read.

To update the code from readdir02.c to readdir03.c, you must change the *read-dir()* statement into a *while* loop condition. The *printf()* statement is then set inside the *while* loop. Here are the changed lines:

```
while( (entry = readdir(dp)) != NULL )
{
    printf("File %s\n",entry->d_name);
}
```

The *while* loop repeats as long as the value returned from *readdir()* isn't NULL. With this update, the program now outputs all files in the current directory.

To gather more information about files in a directory, use the *stat()* function, covered earlier in this chapter. The *readdir()* function's dirent structure contains the file's name in the d_name member. When this detail is known, you use the *stat()* function to gather details on the file's type as well as other information.

The final rendition of the *readdir* series of programs is shown next. It combines code previously covered in this chapter to create a crude directory listing program. Entries are read one at a time, with the *stat()* function returning specific values for file type, size, and access date.

Listing 10.5   Source code for readdir04.c

```
#include <stdio.h>
#include <stdlib.h>
#include <sys/stat.h>
#include <dirent.h>
#include <time.h>

int main()
{
    DIR *dp;
    struct dirent *entry;
    struct stat fs;
    int r;
    char *filename;

    dp = opendir(".");
    if(dp == NULL)
    {
        puts("Unable to read directory");
        exit(1);
    }

    while( (entry = readdir(dp)) != NULL )
    {
        filename = entry->d_name;          ◁——————  Saves the directory
        r = stat( filename,&fs );          ◁——————  entry's name for
        if( r==-1 )                                 readability and
        {                                           easy access
            fprintf(stderr,"Error reading '%s'\n",filename);
                                            Fills the stat structure
            exit(1);                        for the current filename/
        }                                   directory entry
```

```
                    ┌─▷  if( S_ISDIR(fs.st_mode) )
  Calls out    ─────┘         printf(" Dir %-16s ",filename);
 directories            else
 from other                   printf("File %-16s ",filename);
 file types
                            printf("%8lu bytes ",fs.st_size);

                            printf("%s",ctime(&fs.st_atime));
                        }

                        closedir(dp);

                        return(0);
                    }
```

Outputs the directory filename left-justified in a 16-character width

Lines up a standard filename just like the directory filename

Outputs the file size in an 8-character width

Outputs the access time, which automatically adds a newline

This code shows that to truly read a directory, you need both the *readdir()* and *stat()* functions. Together, they pull in details about files in the directory—useful information if you plan on exploring directories or writing similar file utilities, such as a directory tree.

Here is sample output from the program generated by the `readdir04.c` source code:

```
 Dir .                    4096 bytes Sat Oct 30 16:44:34 2021
 Dir ..                   4096 bytes Fri Oct 29 21:55:05 2021
File a.out                8672 bytes Sat Oct 30 16:44:34 2021
File fileinfo             8464 bytes Tue Oct 26 15:55:22 2021
File fileinfo01.c          966 bytes Sat Oct 30 16:24:49 2021
File readdir01.c           268 bytes Fri Oct 29 19:30:10 2021
```

Incidentally, the order in which directory entries appear is dependent on the operating system. Some operating systems sort the entries alphabetically, so the *readdir()* function fetches filenames in that order. This behavior isn't consistent, so don't rely upon it for the output of your directory-reading programs.

10.3   *Subdirectory exploration*

Directories are referenced in three ways:

- As a named path
- As the `..` shortcut to the parent directory
- As a directory entry in the current directory, a subdirectory

Whatever the approach, pathnames are either direct or relative. A direct path is a fully named path, starting at the root directory, your home directory, or the current directory. A relative pathname uses the `..` shortcut for the parent directory—sometimes, a lot of them.

As an example, a full pathname could be:

```
/home/dang/documents/finances/bank/statements
```

This direct pathname shows the directories as they branch from the root, through my home directory, down to the `statements` directory.

If I have another directory, `/home/dang/documents/vacations`, but I'm using the `statements` directory (shown earlier), the relative path from `statements` to `vacations` is:

```
../../../vacations
```

The first `..` represents the `bank` directory. The second `..` represents the `finances` directory. The third `..` represents the `documents` directory, where `vacations` exists as a subdirectory. This construction demonstrates a relative path.

These details about the path are a basic part of using Linux at the command prompt. Understanding these items is vital when it comes to your C programs and how they explore and access directories.

10.3.1 *Using directory exploration tools*

Along with using the *opendir()* function to read a directory and *readdir()* to examine directory entries, your code may need to change directories. Further, the program may want to know in which directory it's currently running. Two C library functions exist to sate these desires: *chdir()* and *getcwd()*. I cover *getcwd()* first because it can be used to confirm that the *chdir()* function did its job.

The *getcwd()* function obtains the directory in which the program is operating. Think of the name as Get the Current Working Directory. It works like the *pwd* command in the terminal window. This function is prototyped in the `unistd.h` header file. Here is the *man* page format:

```
char *getcwd(char *buf, size_t size);
```

Buffer `buf` is a character array or buffer of `size` characters. It's where the current directory string is saved, an absolute path from the root. Here's a tip: you can use the `BUFSIZ` defined constant for the size of the buffer as well as the second argument to *getcwd()*. Some C libraries have a `PATH_MAX` defined constant, which is available from the `limits.h` header file. Because its availability is inconsistent, I recommend using `BUFSIZ` instead. (The `PATH_MAX` defined constant is covered in chapter 11.)

The return value from `getcwd()` is the same character string saved in `buf`, or NULL upon an error. For the specific error, check the global `errno` variable.

The following listing shows a tiny demo program, `getcwd.c`, that outputs the current working directory. I use the `BUFSIZ` defined constant to set the size for *char* array `cwd[]`. The function is called and then the string output.

Listing 10.6   Source code for `getcwd.c`

```
#include <stdio.h>
#include <unistd.h>

int main()                          The defined constant
{                                   BUFSIZ is defined in the
    char cwd[BUFSIZ];       ◁───    stdio.h header file.
```

```
getcwd(cwd,BUFSIZ);
printf("The current working directory is %s\n",cwd);      ◁————┐  **Outputs the**
                                                                 **current working**
return(0);                                                       **directory**
}
```

When run, the program outputs the current working directory as a full pathname. The buffer is filled with the same text you'd see output from the *pwd* command.

The second useful directory function is *chdir()*. This function works like the *cd* command in Linux. If you pay the senior price to see a movie, you may have used the *chdir* command in MS-DOS, though *cd* was also available and quicker to type.

Like *getcwd()*, the *chdir()* function is prototyped in the unistd.h header file. Here is the *man* page format:

```
int chdir(const char *path);
```

The sole argument is a string representing the directory (path) to change to. The return value is 0 upon success, with –1 indicating an error. As you may suspect by now, the global variable errno is set to indicate exactly what went afoul.

I use both directory exploration functions in the changecwd.c source code shown in the next listing. The *chdir()* function changes to the parent directory, indicated by the double dots. The *getcwd()* function obtains the full pathname to the new directory, outputting the results.

Listing 10.7 Source code for `changecwd.c`

```
#include <stdio.h>
#include <stdlib.h>
#include <unistd.h>

int main()
{
    char cwd[BUFSIZ];
    int r;                          │  **Changes to**
                                    │  **the parent**
    r = chdir("..");        ◁——————┘  **directory**
    if( r==-1 )
    {
        fprintf(stderr,"Unable to change directories\n");
        exit(1);                    │  **Obtains**
    }                               │  **the parent**
                                    │  **directory's path**
    getcwd(cwd,BUFSIZ);     ◁——————┘
    printf("The current working directory is %s\n",cwd);    ◁————┐  **Outputs**
                                                                   **the parent**
    return(0);                                                     **directory's path**
}
```

The resulting program outputs the pathname to the parent directory of the directory in which the program is run.

You notice in the source code for changecwd.c that I don't bother returning to the original directory. Such coding isn't necessary. An important thing to remember about using the *chdir()* function is that the directory change happens only in the program's environment. The program may change to directories all over the media, but when it's done, the directory is the same as where the program started.

10.3.2 *Diving into a subdirectory*

It's easy to change to a subdirectory when you know its full path. An absolute path can be supplied by the user or it can be hardcoded into the program. But what happens when the program isn't aware of its directory's location?

The parent directory is always known; you can use the double-dot abbreviation (..) to access the parent of every directory except the top level. Going up is easy. Going down requires a bit more work.

Subdirectories are found by using the tools presented so far in this chapter: scan the current directory for subdirectory entries. Once known, plug the subdirectory name into the *chdir()* function to visit that subdirectory.

The code for subdir01.c in the next listing builds a program that lists potential subdirectories in a named directory. Portions of the code are pulled from other examples listed earlier in this chapter: a directory argument is required and tested for. The named directory is then opened and its entries read. If any subdirectories are found, they're listed.

Listing 10.8   Source code for subdir01.c

```
#include <stdio.h>
#include <stdlib.h>
#include <sys/stat.h>
#include <dirent.h>

int main(int argc, char *argv[])
{
    DIR *dp;
    struct dirent *entry;
    struct stat fs;
    int r;
    char *dirname,*filename;          Confirms that a command-
                                      line argument (directory
    if( argc<2 )        ◄──┘          name) is available
    {
        fprintf(stderr,"Missing directory name\n");
        exit(1);
                                      Assigns a pointer dirname to the
    }                                 first argument for readability
    dirname = argv[1];  ◄──┘

    dp = opendir(dirname);    ◄──┐
    if(dp == NULL)                  Opens the directory
    {                               and tests for an error
        fprintf(stderr,"Unable to read directory '%s'\n",
                dirname
                );
```

```
                exit(1);
        }
                                                            ┌── Reads entries in
        while( (entry = readdir(dp)) != NULL )      ←───┘     the directory
Obtains │ {
 inode  │       filename = entry->d_name;          ←──┐
details └─▷     r = stat( filename,&fs );               │  Assigns a pointer
Tests for ─▷    if( r==-1 )                             │  filename to each
an error │      {                                          entry for readability
         │          fprintf(stderr,"Error on '%s'\n",filename);
                    exit(1);
                }                                       ┌── Tests to see whether
                                                        │   the file is a directory
                if( S_ISDIR(fs.st_mode) )       ←────┘   (subdirectory)
                    printf("Found directory: %s\n",filename);   ←──┐ Outputs the
        }                                                          │ directory's name

        closedir(dp);

        return(0);
}
```

The program generated from the source code subdir01.c reads the directory sup-plied as a command-line argument and then outputs any subdirectories found in that directory. Here is output from a sample run, using my home directory:

```
$ ./subdir /home/dang
Found directory: .
Found directory: ..
Error on '.bash_history'
```

Here is output from the root directory:

```
$ ./subdir /home/dang
Found directory: .
Found directory: ..
Error on 'bin'
```

In both examples, the *stat()* function fails. Your code could examine the errno vari-able, set when the function returns −1, but I can tell you right away what the error is: the first argument passed to the *stat()* function must be a pathname. In the program, only the directory's name is supplied, not a pathname. For example, the .bash_history subdirectory found in the first sample run shown earlier, and the bin directory found in the second don't exist in the current directory.

The solution is for the program to change to the named directory. Only when you change to a directory can the code properly read the files—unless you make the effort to build full pathnames. I'm too lazy to do that, so to modify the code, I add the fol-lowing statements after the statement dirname = argv[1]:

```
r = chdir(dirname);
if( r==-1 )
```

```
{
    fprintf(stderr,"Unable to change to %s\n",dirname);
    exit(1);
}
```

Further, you must include the `unistd.h` header file so that the compiler doesn't complain about the *chdir()* function.

With these updates to the code, available in the online repository as `subdir02.c`, the program now runs properly:

```
$ ./subdir /home/dang
Found directory: .
Found directory: ..
Found directory: .cache
Found directory: .config
Found directory: .ddd
Found directory: .lldb
Found directory: .ssh
Found directory: Dan
Found directory: bin
Found directory: prog
Found directory: sto
```

Remember: to read files from a directory, you must either change to the directory (easy) or manually construct full pathnames for the files (not so easy).

EXERCISE 10.2

Every directory has the dot and dot-dot entries. Plus, many directories host hidden subdirectories. All hidden files in Linux start with a single dot. Your task for this exercise is to modify the source code from `subdir02.c` to have the program not output any file that starts with a single dot. My solution is available in the online repository as `subdir03.c`.

10.3.3 *Mining deeper with recursion*

It wasn't until I wrote my first directory tree exploration program that I fully understood and appreciated the concept of recursion. In fact, directory spelunking is a great way to teach any coder the mechanics behind recursion and how it can be beneficial.

As a review, *recursion* is the amazing capability of a function to call itself. It seems dumb, like an endless loop. Yet within the function exists an escape hatch, which allows the recursive function to unwind. Providing that the unwinding mechanism works, recursion is used in programming to solve all sorts of wonderful problems beyond just confusing beginners.

When the *subdir* program encounters a subdirectory, it can change to that directory to continue mining for even more directories. To do so, the same function that read the current directory is called again but with the subdirectory's path. The process is illustrated in figure 10.4. Once the number of entries in a directory is exhausted, the process ends with a return to the parent directory. Eventually the functions return, backtracking to the original directory, and the program is done.

My issue with recursion is always how to unwind it. Plumbing the depths of subdirectories showed me that once all the directories are processed, control returns to the parent directory. Even then, as a seasoned Assembly language programmer accustomed to working where memory is tight, I fear blowing up the stack. It hasn't happened yet—well, not when I code things properly.

To modify the *subdir* series of programs into a recursive directory spelunker, you must remove the program's core, which explores subdirectories, and set it into a function. I call such a function *dir()*. Its argument is a directory name:

```
void dir(const char *dirname);
```

The *dir()* function uses a *while* loop to process directory entries, looking for subdirectories. When found, the function is called again (within itself) to continue processing directory entries, looking for another subdirectory. When the entries are exhausted, the function returns, eventually ending in the original directory.

The following listing implements the program flow from figure 10.4, as well as earlier versions of the *subdir* programs, to create a separate *dir()* function. It's called recursively (within the function's *while* loop) when a subdirectory is found. The *main()* function is also modified so that the current directory (".") is assumed when a command line argument isn't supplied.

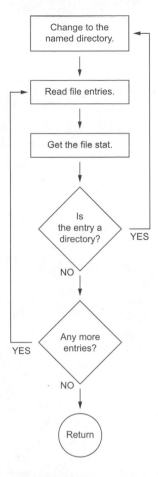

Figure 10.4   The process of recursively discovering directories

---

Listing 10.9   Source code for `subdir04.c`

```
#include <stdio.h>
#include <stdlib.h>
#include <sys/stat.h>
#include <dirent.h>
#include <unistd.h>
#include <string.h>

void dir(const char *dirname)
{
    DIR *dp;
    struct dirent *entry;
    struct stat fs;
    char *filename;
    char directory[BUFSIZ];
```

The function's sole argument is a directory name, `dirname`.

```
if( chdir(dirname)==-1 )        ⟵    Confirms that the program can
{                                      change to the name directory
    fprintf(stderr,"Unable to change to %s\n",dirname);
    exit(1);
}                                Gets the full
                                 pathname
getcwd(directory,BUFSIZ);   ⟵

dp = opendir(directory);    ⟵
if( dp==NULL )                   Confirms that the directory
{                                can be opened
    fprintf(stderr,"Unable to read directory '%s'\n",
            directory
            );
    exit(1);                 Outputs the
}                            directory's        Loops through the
printf("%s\n",directory);    name               directory's entries,
                         ⟵                      looking for subdirectories
while( (entry=readdir(dp)) != NULL )   ⟵
{
    filename = entry->d_name;       ⟵       Saves the found
    if( strncmp( filename,".",1)==0 )  ⟵    filename for readability
        continue;
                                        Ignores the dot and dot-dot
                                        entries as well as hidden files
    stat(filename,&fs);         ⟵
    if( S_ISDIR(fs.st_mode) )
        dir(filename);      ⟵
}                                   Obtains details on the found
                                    directory entry (inode)

closedir(dp);                   Recursively calls the
}                               dir() function again

int main(int argc, char *argv[])
{
    if( argc<2 )        If no argument is
    {                   supplied, assumes the
        dir(".");   ⟵   current directory
    }
    else
        dir(argv[1]);   ⟵   Uses the argument
                            as the named
    return(0);              directory
}
```

Checks for a subdirectory (annotation pointing to `stat(filename,&fs);`)

Don't bother typing in the code for subdir04.c. (Does anyone type in code from a book anymore?) Don't even bother obtaining the source code from the online repository. The program won't blow up your computer, but it contains several flaws.

For example, here is a sample run on my home directory:

```
$ ./subdir ~
/home/dang
/mnt/c/Users/Dan
/mnt/c/Users/Dan/3D Objects
Unable to change to AppData
```

You see the starting directory output correctly, /home/dang. Next, the program jumps on a symbolic link to my user profile directory in Windows (from the Linux command line). So far, so good; it followed the symbolic link to /mnt/c/Users/Dan. It successfully goes to the 3D Objects directory, but then it gets lost. The directory AppData exists, but it's not the next proper subdirectory to which the code should branch.

What's wrong?

The flaw is present in figure 10.4 as well as in the source code shown in listing 10.9: when the *dir()* function starts, it issues the *chdir()* function to change to the named directory, dirname. But the *dir()* function doesn't change back to the parent/original directory when it has finished processing a subdirectory.

To update the code and make the program return to the parent directory, add the following statements at the end of the *dir()* function:

```
if( chdir("..")==-1 )
{
    fprintf(stderr,"Parent directory lost\n");
    exit(1);
}
```

The updated code is found in the online repository as subdir05.c. A sample run on my home directory outputs pages and pages of directories, almost properly.

Almost.

Turns out, the program created from subdir05.c can get lost, specifically with symbolic links. The code follows the symbolic link, but when it tries to return to the parent, it either loses its location or goes to the wrong parent. The problem lies with the *chdir()* chunk of statements just added to the code at the end of the *dir()* function. The parent directory isn't specific:

```
chdir("..");
```

This statement changes to the parent directory, but it's far better to use the parent directory's full path. In fact, as I was playing with the code, I discovered that it's just best to work with full pathnames throughout the *dir()* function. Some changes are required.

My final update redefines the *dir()* function as follows:

```
void dir(const char *dirpath, const char *parentpath);
```

For readability, I changed the arguments name to reflect that both are full pathnames. The first is the full pathname to the directory to scan. The second is the full pathname to the parent directory. Both are *const char* types because neither string is modified within the function.

Listing 10.10 shows the updated *dir()* function. Most of the changes involve removing *char* variable directory and replacing it with argument dirpath. It's also no longer necessary to change to the named directory in the function, which now assumes that the dirpath argument represents the current directory. Further comments are found in the code.

Listing 10.10   The updated *dir()* function from `subdir06.c`

```
void dir(const char *dirpath,const char *parentpath)
{
    DIR *dp;
    struct dirent *entry;
    struct stat fs;
    char subdirpath[BUFSIZ];

    dp = opendir(dirpath);
    if( dp==NULL )
    {
        fprintf(stderr,"Unable to read directory '%s'\n",
                dirpath
                );
        exit(1);
    }

    printf("%s\n",dirpath);
    while( (entry=readdir(dp)) != NULL )
    {
        if( strncmp( entry->d_name,".",1)==0 )
            continue;

        stat(entry->d_name,&fs);
        if( S_ISDIR(fs.st_mode) )
        {
            if( chdir(entry->d_name)==-1 )
            {
                fprintf(stderr,"Unable to change to %s\n",
                        entry->d_name
                        );
                exit(1);
            }

            getcwd(subdirpath,BUFSIZ);
            dir(subdirpath,dirpath);
        }
    }
    closedir(dp);

    if( chdir(parentpath)==-1 )
    {
        if( parentpath==NULL )
            return;
        fprintf(stderr,"Parent directory lost\n");
        exit(1);
    }
}
```

Annotations:

- **Storage for the new directory to change to, storing the full pathname** → `char subdirpath[BUFSIZ];`
- **The program is already in the desired directory, so rather than change to it, the code attempts to open the directory and read entries.** → `dp = opendir(dirpath);`
- **Outputs the current directory path** → `printf("%s\n",dirpath);`
- **Reads all entries in the directory** → `while( (entry=readdir(dp)) != NULL )`
- **Avoids any dot entries** → `if( strncmp( entry->d_name,".",1)==0 )`
- **Checks for a subdirectory entry** → `if( S_ISDIR(fs.st_mode) )`
- **Gets info for each directory entry (inode)** → `stat(entry->d_name,&fs);`
- **Changes to the subdirectory** → `if( chdir(entry->d_name)==-1 )`
- **Gets the subdirectory's full pathname for the recursive call** → `getcwd(subdirpath,BUFSIZ);`
- **Recursively calls the function with the subdirectory and current directory as arguments** → `dir(subdirpath,dirpath);`
- **Closes the current directory after all entries are read** → `closedir(dp);`
- **Changes back to the parent directory—full pathname** → `if( chdir(parentpath)==-1 )`
- **Checks for NULL, in which case, just returns** → `if( parentpath==NULL )`

Updating the *dir()* function requires that the *main()* function be updated as well. It has more work to do: the *main()* function must obtain the full pathname to the current directory or the `argv[1]` value, as well as the directory's parent. This update to the *main()* function is shown here.

Listing 10.11 The updated *main()* function for `subdir06.c`

```
int main(int argc, char *argv[])
{
    char current[BUFSIZ];

    if( argc<2 )                                    For no arguments, obtains
    {                                               and stores the full path to
        getcwd(current,BUFSIZ);                     the current directory
    }
    else                                            Copies the first argument;
    {                                               hopefully, a directory
        strcpy(current,argv[1]);
        if( chdir(current)==-1 )                    Changes to the directory
        {                                           and checks for errors
            fprintf(stderr,"Unable to access directory %s\n",
                    current
                   );
            exit(1);
        }                                           Gets the directory's
        getcwd(current,BUFSIZ);                     full pathname
    }
    dir(current,NULL);                              Calls the function;
                                                    NULL is checked
    return(0);                                      in dir().
}
```

The full source code file is available in the online repository as `subdir06.c`. It accepts a directory argument or no argument, in which case the current directory is plumbed.

Even though the program uses full pathnames, it may still get lost. Specifically, for symbolic links, the code may wander away from where you intend. Some types of links, such as aliases in Mac OS X, aren't recognized as directories, so they're skipped. And when processing system directories, specifically those that contain block or character files, the program's stack may overflow and generate a segmentation fault.

10.4 A directory tree

The ancient MS-DOS operating system featured the TREE utility. It dumped a map of the current directory structure in a festive, graphical (for a text screen) manner. This command is still available in Windows. In the CMD (command prompt) program in Windows, type **TREE** and you see output like that shown in figure 10.5: directories appear in a hierarchical structure, with lines connecting parent directories and subdirectories in a festive manner, along with indentation showing directory depth.

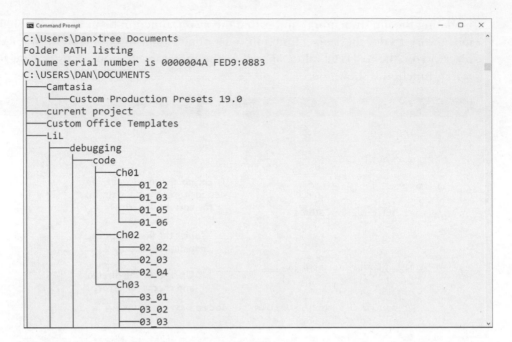

Figure 10.5   Output from the TREE command

The mechanics behind creating a directory tree program are already known to you. The source code for subdir06.c processes directories and subdirectories in the same manner as the output shown in figure 10.5. What's missing are the shortened directory names, text mode graphics, and indentation. You can add these items, creating your own directory tree utility.

10.4.1   *Pulling out the directory name*

To mimic the old TREE utility, the *dir()* function must extract the directory name from the full pathname. Because full pathnames are used, and the string doesn't end with a trailing slash, everything from the last slash in the string to the null character qualifies as the directory's name.

The easy way to extract the current directory name from a full pathname is to save the name when it's found in the parent directory: the entry->d_name structure member contains the directory's name as it appears in the parent's directory listing. To make this modification, the *dir()* function requires another argument, the short directory name. This modification is simple to code, which is why this approach is the easy way.

The problem with the easy way is that the *main()* function obtains a full directory path when the program is started without an argument. So, even if you choose the easy way, you still must extract the directory name from the full pathname in the *main()* function. Therefore, my approach is to code a new function that pulls a directory name (or filename) from the end of a path.

When I add new features to a program, such as when extracting a directory name from the butt end of a pathname, I write test code. In the next listing, you see the test code for the *extract()* function. Its job is to plow through a pathname to pull out the last part—assuming the last part of the string (after the final/separator character) is a directory name. Oh, and the function also assumes the environment is Linux; if you're using Windows, you specify the backslash (two of them: \\) as the path separator, though Windows 10 may also recognize the forward slash.

Listing 10.12 Source code for `extractor.c`

```
#include <stdio.h>
#include <string.h>

const char *extract(char *path)
{
    const char *p;
    int len;

    len = strlen(path);                    If the string is empty, returns NULL
    if( len==0 )
        return(NULL);
    if( len==1 & *(path+0)=='/' )          Performs a special test for the root directory
        return(path);

    p = path+len;                          Positions pointer p at the end of string path
    while( *p != '/' )                     Backs up p to find the separator; for Windows, uses \\ as the separator
    {
        p--;
        if( p==path )                      If p backs up too far, returns NULL
            return(NULL);
    }
    p++;                                   Increments p over the separator character

    if( *p == '\0' )                       Tests to see if the string is empty or malformed and returns NULL
        return(NULL);
    else
        return(p);                         Returns the address where the final directory name starts
}

int main()
{
    const int count=4;
    const char *pathname[count] = {        Tests strings for a variety of configurations
        "/home/dang",
        "/usr/local/this/that",
        "/",
        "nothing here"
    };
    int x;

    for(x=0; x<count; x++)
    {
        printf("%s -> %s\n",
```

```
                        pathname[x],
                        extract(pathname[x])
                    );
        }

    return(0);
}
```

The *extract()* function backs up through the pathname string passed. Pointer p scans for the / separator. It leaves the function referencing the position in the string path where the final directory name starts. Upon an error, NULL is returned. A series of test strings in the *main()* function puts the *extract()* function to work. Here is the output:

```
/home/dang -> dang
/usr/local/this/that -> that
/ -> /
nothing here -> (null)
```

The *extract()* function successfully processes each string, returning the last part, the directory name. It even catches the malformed string, properly returning NULL.

For my first rendition of the directory tree program, I added the *extract()* function to the final update to the *subdir* series of programs, subdir06.c. The *extract()* function is called from within the *dir()* function, just before the main *while* loop that reads directory entries, replacing the existing *printf()* statement at that line:

```
printf("%s\n",extract(dirpath));
```

This update is saved as dirtree01.c. The resulting program, *dirtree*, outputs the directories but only their names and not the full pathnames. The output is almost a directory tree program, but without proper indenting for each subdirectory level.

10.4.2 *Monitoring directory depth*

Programming the fancy output from the old TREE command, shown in figure 10.5, is more complicated than it looks. Emulating it exactly requires that the code use wide character output (covered in chapter 8). Further, the directory's depth must be monitored as well as when the last subdirectory in a directory is output. Indeed, to fully emulate the TREE command requires massively restructuring the *dirtree* program, primarily to save directory entries for output later.

Yeah, so I'm not going there—not all the way.

Rather than restructure the entire code, I thought I'd add some indentation to make the directory output of my *dirtree* series a bit more "tree"-like. This addition requires that the directory depth be monitored so that each subdirectory is indented a notch. To monitor the directory depth, the definition of the *dir()* function is updated:

```
void dir(const char *dirpath,const char *parentpath, int depth);
```

I consider three arguments to be the maximum for a function. Any more arguments, and it becomes obvious to me that what should really be passed to the function is a structure. In fact, I wrote a version of the *dirtree* program that held directory entries in an array of structures. That code became overly complex, however, so I decided to just modify the *dir()* function as shown earlier.

To complete the modification in the code, three more changes are required. First, in the *main()* function, the *dir()* function is originally called with zero as its third argument:

```
dir(current,NULL,0);
```

The zero sets the indent depth as the program starts; the first directory is the top level.

Second, the recursive call within the *dir()* function must be modified, adding the third argument depth:

```
dir(subdirpath,dirpath,depth+1);
```

For the recursive call, which means the program is diving down one directory level, the indent level depth is increased by one.

Finally, something must be done with the depth variable within the *dir()* function. I opted to add a loop that outputs a chunk of three spaces for every depth level. This loop requires a new variable to be declared for function *dir()*, integer i (for indent):

```
for( i=0; i<depth; i++ )
    printf("   ");
```

This loop appears before the *printf()* statement that outputs the directory's name, just before the *while* loop. The result is that each subdirectory is indented three spaces as the directory tree is output.

The source code for dirtree02.c is available in the online repository. Here is the program's output for my prog (programming) directory:

```
prog
   asm
   c
      blog
      clock
      debug
      jpeg
      opengl
      wchar
      xmljson
      zlib
   python
```

Each subdirectory is indented three spaces. The sub-subdirectories of the c directory are further indented.

EXERCISE 10.3

Modify the source code for dirtree02.c so that instead of indenting with blanks, the subdirectories appear with text mode graphics. For example:

```
prog
+--asm
+--c
|   +--blog
|   +--clock
|   +--debug
|   +--jpeg
|   +--opengl
|   +--wchar
|   +--xmljson
|   +--zlib
+--python
```

These graphics aren't as fancy (or precise) as those from the MS-DOS TREE command, but they are an improvement. This modification requires only a few lines of code. My solution is available in the online repository as dirtree03.c.

File finder

11

Back in ancient times, one of the most popular MS-DOS utilities I wrote was the Fast File Finder. It wasn't particularly fast, of course. But it did the job of finding a file anywhere on the PC's hard drive when given a filename. This program was included on the companion floppy diskettes provided with many of my early computing books. Yes, floppy diskettes.

In today's operating systems, finding files is a big deal. Both Windows and Mac OS X feature powerful file-finding tools, locating files by not only name but also date, size, and content. The Linux command prompt offers its own slate of file-finding tools, just as powerful (if not more so) as their graphical counterparts. For a budding C programmer, or anyone desiring to build their C kung fu, using these tools is useful, but you can't improve your programming skills by just using the tools.

Hunting for files, and potentially doing something with them, relies upon the directory-spelunking tools covered in chapter 10. From this base, you can expand your knowledge of C by:

- Reviewing other file-finding utilities
- Exploring methods for finding text
- Locating files in a directory tree
- Using wildcards to match files
- Finding filename duplicates

When I program a utility, especially one that's similar to one that's already available, I look for improvements. Many command-line tools feature a parade of options and features. These switches make the command powerful but beyond what I need. I find the abundance of options overwhelming. Better for me is to build a more specific version of the utility. Although such a program may not have the muscle of something coded by expert C programmers of yore, it's specific to my needs. By writing your own file tools, you learn more about programming in C, plus you get a tool you can use—and customize to your workflow.

11.1 *The great file hunt*

My personal-file finding utilities are based on frustration with the existing crop of Linux file finding tools—specifically, *find* and *grep*.

Nothing is wrong with these commands that some well-chosen curse words can't address. Still, I find myself unable to commit the command formats and options to memory. I constantly refer to the documentation when it comes to using these file-finding tools. I understand that this admission could get me kicked out of the neighborhood computer club.

The *find* command is powerful. In Linux, such power implies options galore, often more command-line switches available than letters of the alphabet—upper- and lowercase. This complexity explains why many nerds resort instead to using GUI file-search tools instead of a terminal window to locate lost files.

Here is the deceptively simple format for the *find* command:

```
find path way-too-many-options
```

Yep. Easy.

Suppose you want to locate a file named `budget.csv`, located somewhere in your home directory tree. Here is the command to use:

```
find ~ -name budget.csv -print
```

The pathname is `~`, shortcut for your home directory. The `-name` switch identifies the file to locate, `budget.csv`. The final switch, `-print` (the one everyone forgets), directs the *find* command to send the results to standard output. You may think something like output would be the necessary default, but the *find* command can do more with found files than send their names to standard output.

The *find* command's desired output may appear on a line by itself, which is fortunate. More common is that you must sift through a long series of errors and duplicate matches. Eventually the desired file is found, and its path revealed:

```
/home/dang/documents/financial/budget.csv
```

Yes, you can create an alias to the specific *find* utility format you use often. No, I'm not going to get into a debate about how powerful and useful the *find* command is or why I'm a dweeb for not comparing it with a sunshine lollypop for delicious goodness.

The other file-finding command is *grep*, which I use specifically to locate files containing a specific tidbit of text. In fact, I've used `grep` many times when writing this book to locate defined constants in header files. From the /usr/include directory, here is the command to locate the time_t defined constant in various header files:

```
grep -r "time_t" *
```

The -r switch directs *grep* to recursively look through directories. The string to find is time_t and the * wildcard directs the program to search all filenames.

Many lines of text spew forth when issuing this command, because the time_t defined constant is referenced in multiple header files. Even this trick didn't locate the specific definition I wanted, though it pointed me in the right direction.

These utilities—*find* and *grep* (and its better cousin, *egrep*)—are wonderful and powerful. Yet I want something friendly and usable without the requirement of chronically checking *man* pages or referring to hefty command-line reference books. This is why I code my own versions, covered in this chapter.

With your knowledge of C, you can easily code your own file-finding utilities specific to your needs, as complex or as simple as you desire. Then, if you forget any of the options, you have only yourself to blame.

11.2   A file finder

My goal for finding files is to type a command like this:

```
find thisfile.txt
```

The utility digs deep through the current directory tree, scouring subdirectory after subdirectory, hunting for the specific file. If found, the full pathname is output—useful information to me. Add in the capability of using wildcards to locate files, and I'll never need the *find* command again—in the specific format to locate a file.

Oh, yeah—I suppose my own utility must be named something other than *find*, already used in Linux. How about *ff* for *Find File*?

11.2.1   Coding the Find File utility

Chapter 10 covers the process of directory exploration, using the recursive *dir()* function to plumb subdirectory depths. Building upon this function is perfect for creating a file-finding utility. The goal is to scan directories and compare those files found with a matching filename supplied by the user.

The *Find File* utility presented in this chapter doesn't use the same *dir()* function from chapter 10. No, the recursive directory-finding function requires modification to locate specific files, not all files. I've renamed the function *find()* because I know the name would infuriate the *find* utility.

My *find()* function features the same first two arguments as *dir()* from chapter 10. But as shown in the next listing, this updated function adds a third argument, match, to help hunt for the named file. Other differences between *dir()* and *find()* are commented in the listing.

Listing 11.1   The recursive *find()* function

```
void find(char *dirpath,char *parentpath,char *match)
{
    DIR *dp;
    struct dirent *entry;
    struct stat fs;
    char subdirpath[PATH_MAX];


    dp = opendir(dirpath);
    if( dp==NULL )
    {
        fprintf(stderr,"Unable to read directory '%s'\n",
            dirpath
                );
        exit(1);
    }

    while( (entry=readdir(dp)) != NULL )
    {
        if( strcmp(entry->d_name,match)==0 )
        {
            printf("%s/%s\n",dirpath,match);
            count++;
        }
        stat(entry->d_name,&fs);
        if( S_ISDIR(fs.st_mode) )
        {
            if( strncmp( entry->d_name,".",1)==0 )
                continue;
            if( chdir(entry->d_name)==-1 )
            {
                fprintf(stderr,"Unable to change to %s\n",
                    entry->d_name
                        );
                exit(1);
            }


            getcwd(subdirpath,BUFSIZ);
            find(subdirpath,dirpath,match);
        }
    }

    closedir(dp);

    if( chdir(parentpath)==-1 )
    {
        if( parentpath==NULL )
            return;
        fprintf(stderr,"Parent directory lost\n");
        exit(1);
    }
}
```

Annotations:

Use the `limits.h` value for the maximum path size (see the discussion in the text).

Performs a comparison for the filename found with the passed filename

Outputs any matching filename

Increments the external `count` variable

Avoids checking the hidden files

The recursive call, again with the passed filename to match as the third argument

Beyond the additions noted in listing 11.1, I use the PATH_MAX defined constant, which requires including the limits.h header file. Because not every C library implements PATH_MAX, some preprocessor directives are required:

```
#ifndef PATH_MAX
#define PATH_MAX 256
#endif
```

The value of PATH_MAX differs depending on the operating system. For example, in Windows it could be 260 bytes, but in my version of Ubuntu Linux, it's 1024. I've seen it as high as 4096 bytes, so 256 seems like a good value that won't blow up anything. If you want to define a higher value, feel free to do so.

My *Find File* utility also counts matched files. To keep track, I use the variable count, which is defined externally. I am loath to use global variables, but in this situation having count be external is an effective way to keep track of files found. Otherwise, I could include count as a fourth argument to the *find()* function, but as a recursive function, maintaining its value consistently introduces all kinds of chaos.

The source code that includes the *find()* function is named findfile01.c, where the *main()* function is shown in the following listing. The *main()* function's job is to fetch the filename from the command line, retrieve the current path, make the call to the *find()* function, and then report the results. The *main()* function is shown here.

Listing 11.2 The *main()* function from `findfile01.c`

```
int main(int argc, char *argv[])
{
    char current[PATH_MAX];          ┐ A command-
                                     │ line argument
    if( argc<2 )          ◄──────────┘ is required.
    {
        fprintf(stderr,"Format: ff filename\n");
        exit(1);
    }

    getcwd(current,PATH_MAX);
    if( chdir(current)==-1 )
    {
        fprintf(stderr,"Unable to access directory %s\n",
                current
                );
            exit(1);
    }                          ┐ Initializes the
                               │ external int variable
    count = 0;    ◄────────────┘ count, keeping track
    printf("Searching for '%s'\n",argv[1]);   of the files found
    find(current,NULL,argv[1]);   ◄──  Calls the function, with
    printf(" Found %d match",count);   the filename argument
    if( count!=1 )          ◄───┐       specified third
        printf("es");           │ Magically adds "es"
    putchar('\n');              │ for any count value
                                │ other than 1
```

Reports the results ──┐
                      └─►

```
        return(0);
}
```

Both *find()* and *main()* are included in the source code file findfile01.c, available in this book's online repository. I've built the source code into the program file named *ff*. Here are a few sample runs:

```
$ ff a.out
Searching for 'a.out'
/Users/Dan/code/a.out
/Users/Dan/code/communications/a.out
/Users/Dan/code/communications/networking/a.out
/Users/Dan/Tiny C Projects/code/08_unicode/a.out
/Users/Dan/Tiny C Projects/code/11_filefind/a.out
 Found 5 matches
```

The *Find File* utility locates all the a.out files in my home directory tree:

```
$ ff hello
Searching for 'hello'
 Found 0 matches
```

In the previous example, the utility doesn't find any files named hello:

```
$ ff *.c
Searching for 'finddupe01.c'
/Users/Dan/Tiny C Projects/code/11_filefind/finddupe01.c
 Found 1 match
```

The utility attempts to locate all files with the .c extension in the current directory. Rather than return them all, you see only the first match reported: finddupe01.c. The problem here is that the code doesn't recognize wildcards; it finds only specific filenames.

To match files with wildcards, you must understand something known as the glob. Unlike The Blob, star of the eponymous 1958 horror film, knowing the glob won't get you killed.

11.2.2 *Understanding the glob*

A glob can be an insidious lump of goo from outer space, but in the computer world, it's short for *glob*al. Specifically, *glob* is a way to use wildcards to specify or match filenames. Most humans I know prefer to say "wildcard" as opposed to "glob." But in the programming realm, the term is *glob,* the process is *globbing,* and people who glob are globbers. The C library function worthy of attention is *glob()*.

As a review, the filename wildcards are:

- ? to match a single character
- * to match a group of more than one character

In Windows, globbing takes place automatically. But in the Linux environment, the glob feature must be activated for wildcards to expand. If not, the * and ? wildcards are interpreted literally, which isn't what most users expect.

To ensure that globbing is active, type the **set -o** command. In the output, the *noglob* option should be set to *off*:

```
noglob    off
```

If you see that the option is on, use this command:

```
set +o noglob
```

When globbing is active, the shell expands the ? and * wildcards to match files. In the preceding section, the input provided is *.c. Yet the program processed only one file named finddupe01.c. The filename is a match, but it's not the only *.c filename in the directory. What gives?

The code in the next listing helps you understand how globbing works when wildcards are typed at the command prompt. The program generated from glob01.c loops through all command-line options typed, minus the first item, which is the program filename.

Listing 11.3   Source code for glob01.c

```
#include <stdio.h>

int main(int argc, char *argv[])
{
    int x;                      Don't bother if only the
                                program name is typed
    if( argc>1 )         ◁──── at the prompt.
    {
        for( x=1; x<argc; x++ )   ◁──── Loops through all
            printf("%s\n",argv[x]);       the arguments
    }

    return(0);
}
```

Here is a sample run of the program created from glob01.c, which is named a.out:

```
$ ./a.out this that the other
this
that
the
other
```

The program dutifully echoes all command-line options. Now try running the same program, but with a wildcard specified:

```
$ ./a.out *.c
finddupe01.c
finddupe02.c
finddupe03.c
finddupe04.c
finddupe05.c
findfile01.c

findfile02.c
glob01.c
glob02.c
```

The *.c wildcard (globby thing) is expanded by the shell, which feeds each matching filename from the current directory to the program as a command-line argument. Instead of a single argument, *.c, multiple arguments are supplied.

The problem with globbing is that your program really doesn't know whether multiple command-line arguments are supplied or a single wildcard is typed and expanded. Further, because the wildcard argument is translated into multiple matching files, you have no way of knowing which wildcard was specified. Perhaps some way exists, because I know utilities that can perform wildcard matching in amazing ways, but I've yet to discover what this magic is.

Rather than be flustered, you can rely upon the *glob()* function to do the pattern matching for you. Here is the *man* page format:

```
int glob(const char *pattern, int flags, int (*errfunc) (const char *epath,
    int eerrno), glob_t *pglob);
```

The function has four arguments:

- const char *pattern is a pathname wildcard pattern to match.
- int flags are options to customize the function's behavior, usually a series of defined constants logically OR'd together.
- int (*errfunc) is the name of an error-handling function (along with its two arguments), which is necessary because the *glob()* function can be quirky. Specify NULL to use the default error handler.
- glob_t *pglob is a structure containing details about the matching files. Two useful members are gl_pathc, which lists the number of matching files, and gl_pathv, which serves as the base of a pointer list referencing matching filenames in the current directory.

The *glob()* function returns zero on success. Other return values include defined constants you can test to determine whether the function screwed up or failed to find any matching files.

More scintillating details are available about the *glob()* function in the *man* pages. Pay special attention to the flags argument because it's easy for various issues to arise.

You must include the glob.h header file in your source code to keep the compiler content with the *glob()* function.

In the next listing, the source code for glob02.c uses the *glob()* function to scan for matching files in the current directory. The user is prompted for input. The input string is scrubbed of any newlines. The *glob()* function is called to process input, searching for filenames that match any wildcards specified. Finally, a *while* loop outputs the matching filenames.

Listing 11.4   Source code for glob02.c

```
#include <stdio.h>
#include <stdlib.h>                        For the definition
#include <glob.h>                          of PATH_MAX—if
#include <limits.h>                        available

#ifndef PATH_MAX                    If PATH_MAX isn't
#define PATH_MAX 256                defined, creates it
#endif

int main()                            The return
{                                     value of glob()
    char filename[PATH_MAX];
    char *r;                          The structure specified
    int g;                            in the glob() function
    glob_t gstruct;
    char **found;                     A double-pointer to the
                                      list of matching filenames

    printf("Filename or wildcard: ");         Prompts for the filename
    r = fgets(filename,PATH_MAX,stdin);       wildcard; this chunk of code
    if( r==NULL )                             is to verify the input and
        exit(1);                              remove the newline.
    while( *r!='\0' )
    {
        if( *r=='\n' )
        {
            *r = '\0';
            break;
        }                          The call to the glob()
    }                              function, mostly
    r++;                           defaults except for
}                                  the GLOB_ERR flag
                                                               Checks for errors,
    g = glob(filename, GLOB_ERR , NULL, &gstruct);             specifically no
    if( g!=0 )                                                 matching filename
    {
        if( g==GLOB_NOMATCH )
            fprintf(stderr,"No matches for '%s'\n",filename);
        else
            fprintf(stderr,"Some kinda glob error\n");
        exit(1);
    }

    printf("Found %zu filename matches\n",[CA]gstruct.gl_pathc);
    found = gstruct.gl_pathv;
                                          Outputs the matches using structure
The gl_pathv member is the base of a pointer     member gl_pathc; the placeholder
list, assigned to double pointer found.          %zu is used for a size_t value.
```

```
        while(*found)
        {
            printf("%s\n",*found);
            found++;
        }
        return(0);
}
```

Outputs the matching filename → *(points to the `printf` line)*

Loops as long as the string referenced by `*found` isn't NULL → *(points to the `while(*found)` line)*

Increments the `found` pointer to reference the next item in the list → *(points to the `found++;` line)*

Remember, the wildcard input must be supplied by the user because the program doesn't interpret wildcard input as a command-line argument. Here is a sample run:

```
Filename or wildcard: find*
Found 7 filename matches
finddupe01.c
finddupe02.c
finddupe03.c
finddupe04.c
finddupe05.c
findfile01.c
findfile02.c
```

The program successfully found all files starting with find. The techniques used in the source code can now be incorporated into the *Find File* utility to use wildcards in its search.

11.2.3   *Using wildcards to find files*

Some modifications are necessary for the Find File utility to take advantage of wildcards. To assist the *glob()* function, the matching filename must now be entered at a prompt, similar to the glob02.c program in the preceding section. Then the *glob()* function must be integrated into the *find()* function to help scour subdirectories for matching filenames.

Modifications to the *main()* function can be found in the source code file, findfile02.c, available in the online repository. These updates reflect added statements from the glob02.c source code file, mostly to accept and confirm input regarding wildcards. The rest of the modifications are shown in the following listing, where the *glob()* function is integrated into the *find()* function. In this version of the code, the string argument match can be a specific filename or a filename including wildcards.

Listing 11.5   The *find()* function from source code file `findfile02.c`

```
void find(char *dirpath,char *parentpath,char *match)
{
    DIR *dp;
    struct dirent *entry;
    struct stat fs;
    char subdirpath[PATH_MAX];
    int g;
    glob_t gstruct;
    char **found;
```

```
dp = opendir(dirpath);
if( dp==NULL )
{
    fprintf(stderr,"Unable to read directory '%s'\n",
            dirpath
           );
    exit(1);
}

g = glob(match, GLOB_ERR, NULL, &gstruct);
if( g==0 )
{
    found = gstruct.gl_pathv;
    while(*found)
    {
        printf("%s/%s\n",dirpath,*found);
        found++;
        count++;
    }
}

while( (entry=readdir(dp)) != NULL )
{
    stat(entry->d_name,&fs);
    if( S_ISDIR(fs.st_mode) )
    {
        if( strncmp( entry->d_name,".",1)==0 )
            continue;
        if( chdir(entry->d_name)==-1 )
        {
            fprintf(stderr,"Unable to change to %s\n",
                    entry->d_name
                   );
            exit(1);
        }

        getcwd(subdirpath,BUFSIZ);
        find(subdirpath,dirpath,match);
    }
}

closedir(dp);

if( chdir(parentpath)==-1 )
{
    if( parentpath==NULL )
        return;
    fprintf(stderr,"Parent directory lost\n");
    exit(1);
}
}
```

Uses *glob()* to find matching files in the directory

Upon success, outputs the found files (here instead of below)

This loop is still necessary to find and explore subdirectories.

Just look for directory files here; matching files already output.

In its final incarnation, the *Find File* utility (source code file findfile02.c) prompts for input, which can be a specific file or a wildcard. All files in the current directory and in all subdirectories are searched with the results reported:

```
$ ff
Filename or wildcard: *.c
Searching for '*.c'
/Users/Dan/code/0424a.c
/Users/Dan/code/0424b.c
...
/Users/Dan/Tiny C Projects/code/11_filefind/sto/unique04.c
/Users/Dan/Tiny C Projects/code/11_filefind/sto/unique05.c
/Users/Dan/Tiny C Projects/code/11_filefind/sto/unique06.c
 Found 192 matches
```

Here, the *Find File* utility located 192 C source code files in my home folder.

```
$ ff
Filename or wildcard: *deposit*
Searching for '*deposit*'
/Users/Dan/Documents/bank deposit.docx
 Found 1 match
```

In the sample run shown here, the *Find File* utility located my bank deposit document. Having the *glob()* function in the program allows wildcards to be used effectively. Though the program can still locate specific files when the full name is input:

```
$ ff
Filename or wildcard: ch03.docx
Searching for 'ch03.docx'
/Users/Dan/Documents/Word/text/ch03.docx
 Found 1 match
```

As I wrote earlier, I use this utility often because it's simple and it generates the results I want. What I don't want is to keep working on the utility, which may eventually lead me to reinvent the *find* program. No, instead, the concept of finding a file can be taken further to locating duplicate files.

11.3   *The duplicate file finder*

One my favorite shareware utilities for MS-DOS is *finddupe*. I've found nothing like it for Windows (not that I've aggressively looked). A version of the utility is still available for the command shell in Windows. It finds duplicate files, not just by name but also by contents. *finddupe* is a handy tool for cleaning up and organizing files on a mass storage device.

I never bothered coding my own *finddupe* utility, mostly because the existing tool is spiffy. Even so, I often thought of the process: the program must not only scan all directories but also must record filenames. From the list of recorded filenames, each must be compared with others in the list to see whether the same name exists. I tremble at the thought of the added process of comparing file contents.

Still, the topic intrigued me: How would you scan files in subdirectories and then check to see whether any duplicate names are found?

The process of creating a *Find Dupe* utility borrows heavily from the subdirectory scanning tools presented in chapter 10 and used earlier in this chapter. But the rest of the code—recording and scanning the list of saved files—is new territory: a list of files must be created. The list must be scanned for duplicates and then the duplicates output, along with their pathnames.

11.3.1   Building a file list

As with any programming projects, I made several attempts to successfully build a list of files found in subdirectories. It was obvious that I'd need some kind of structure to hold the file information: name, path, and so on. But do I create a dynamic array (allocated pointers) of structures, use a linked list, make the structure array external, or just give up and become a dairy farmer?

To me, making any variable external is a last choice. Sometimes it's the only choice, but never should it be a choice because it's easy to do. As shown earlier in this chapter with the count variable, sometimes it's necessary because the other ways to implement the variable are awkward. Especially with recursion, having an external variable untangles some knots that are otherwise at the Christmas-tree-light level.

The two options remaining are to pass a dynamically allocated list or use a linked list. I wrote several iterations of the code where a dynamically allocated list of structures was passed to the recursive function. It failed, which is easy because pointers can get lost in recursion. Therefore, my only remaining option is to create a linked list.

A linked list structure must have as a member a pointer to the next item, or *node*, in the list. This member becomes part of the structure that stores found filenames and their paths. Here is its definition:

```
struct finfo {
  int index;
  char name[BUFSIZ];
  char path[PATH_MAX];
  struct finfo *next;
};
```

I originally named the structure fileinfo. I would have kept the name, but this book's margins are only so wide and I don't like wrapping source code. So, I settled on finfo. This structure contains four members:

- index, which keeps a count of the files found (avoiding an external variable)
- name, which contains the name of the found file
- path, which contains the full path to the file
- next, which references the next node in the linked list, or NULL for the end of the list

This structure must be declared externally so that all functions in the code understand its definition.

My first build of the program is simply to see whether the thing works: that the linked list is properly allocated, filled, and returned from the recursive function. In the next listing, you see the *main()* function. It allocates the first node in the linked list. This structure must be empty; it's the recursive function *find()* that builds the linked list. The *main()* function fetches the starting directory for a call to the recursive function. Upon completion, a *while* loop outputs the names of the files referenced by the linked list.

Listing 11.6   The *main()* function from `finddupe01.c`

```
int main()
{
    char startdir[PATH_MAX];
    struct finfo *first,*current;

    first = malloc( sizeof(struct finfo) * 1 );
    if( first==NULL )
    {
        fprintf(stderr,"Unable to allocate memory\n");
        exit(1);
    }

    first->index = 0;
    strcpy(first->name,"");
    strcpy(first->path,"");
    first->next = NULL;

    getcwd(startdir,PATH_MAX);
    if( chdir(startdir)==-1 )
    {
        fprintf(stderr,"Unable to access directory %s\n",
            startdir
            );
            exit(1);
    }
    find(startdir,NULL,first);

    current = first;
    while( current )
    {
        if( current->index > 0 )
            printf("%d:%s/%s\n",
                    current->index,
                    current->path,
                    current->name
                    );
        current = current->next;
    }
    return(0);
}
```

Annotations:
- **A pointer is needed for the base (`first`) and for examining the items in the list (`current`).**
- **Confirms the pointer is allocated**
- **Allocates the base pointer**
- **Fills the first node with empty values**
- **Obtains the current directory for the *find()* function call**
- **Sets the `current` pointer to the start of the list**
- **Calls the recursive function**
- **Loops as long as the `current` pointer isn't NULL**
- **Skips over the first item in the list, zero**
- **Outputs the index value, pathname, and filename**
- **References the next item in the list**

The *while* loop skips the first node in the linked list, the empty item. I could avoid the
if(current->index > 0) text (shown earlier) by replacing the initialization statement
for current with:

```
current = first->next;
```

I only just thought of this change now, so you won't find it in the source code files.
Either way, the first node in the linked list is skipped over.

The *find()* function for my *Find Dupe* code is based upon the *find()* function in the
Find File utility presented earlier in this chapter. The third argument of the *find()* function is replaced by a pointer to the current node in the linked list. The function's job
is to create new nodes, filling their structures as it finds files in the current directory.

The next listing shows the *find()* function for the *Find Dupe* utility, which is called
from the *main()* function shown in listing 11.6. This function allocates storage for a
new node in the list upon finding a file in the current directory. This change is the
only addition to the function.

Listing 11.7   The *find()* function from `finddupe01.c`

```
void find( char *dirpath, char *parentpath, struct finfo *f)
{
    DIR *dp;
    struct dirent *entry;
    struct stat fs;
    char subdirpath[PATH_MAX];
    int i;
                                              Obtains the current
                                              directory—unchanged
    dp = opendir(dirpath);          ⊲┘
    if( dp==NULL )
    {
        fprintf(stderr,"Unable to read directory '%s'\n",
                dirpath
                );
        exit(1);
        /* will free memory as it exits */
    }

    while( (entry=readdir(dp)) != NULL )
    {                                       Tests for a
        stat(entry->d_name,&fs);            subdirectory
        if( S_ISDIR(fs.st_mode) )     ⊲┘   and recursion
        {
            if( strncmp( entry->d_name,".",1)==0 )
                continue;
            if( chdir(entry->d_name)==-1 )
            {
                fprintf(stderr,"Unable to change to %s\n",
                        entry->d_name
                        );
                exit(1);
            }
```

```
                        getcwd(subdirpath,BUFSIZ);
                        find(subdirpath,dirpath,f);
                }
                else
                {
                        f->next = malloc( sizeof(struct finfo) * 1);
                        if( f->next == NULL )
                        {
                                fprintf(stderr,
                                        "Unable to allocate new structure\n");
                                exit(1);
                        }
                        i = f->index;
                        f = f->next;
                        f->index = i+1;
                        strcpy(f->name,entry->d_name);
                        strcpy(f->path,dirpath);
                        f->next = NULL;
                }
        }

        closedir(dp);

        if( chdir(parentpath)==-1 )
        {
                if( parentpath==NULL )
                        return;
                fprintf(stderr,"Parent directory lost\n");
                exit(1);
        }
}
```

If not a subdirectory, saves the file information

Allocates the next node in the linked list (and does error checking)

References the freshly allocated node

Saves the current index value

Updates the index value

Saves the filename

Saves the pathname

Initializes the next pointer; the rest of the function is the same as the preceding examples.

The *find()* function makes a simple decision based on whether a directory entry is a subdirectory or a file. When a subdirectory is found, the function is recursively called. Otherwise, a new node in the linked list is allocated and the file entry information is recorded.

The full source code for finddupe01.c can be found in the online repository. Here is output from sample run in my working directory:

```
1:/Users/Dan/code/11_filefind/.finddupe01.c.swp
2:/Users/Dan/code/11_filefind/a.out
3:/Users/Dan/code/11_filefind/finddupe01.c
4:/Users/Dan/code/11_filefind/finddupe02.c
5:/Users/Dan/code/11_filefind/finddupe03.c
6:/Users/Dan/code/11_filefind/finddupe04.c
7:/Users/Dan/code/11_filefind/finddupe05.c
8:/Users/Dan/code/11_filefind/findfile01.c
9:/Users/Dan/code/11_filefind/findfile02.c
10:/Users/Dan/code/11_filefind/glob01.c
11:/Users/Dan/code/11_filefind/glob02.c
12:/Users/Dan/code/11_filefind/sto/findword01.c
13:/Users/Dan/code/11_filefind/sto/findword02.c
```

The output was able to record files from the current directory as well as the `sto` subdirectory. However, when I changed to the parent directory (`code`) and ran the program again, the output didn't change. It should: my `code` directory has over 100 files in various subdirectories. So why was the output unchanged?

I puzzled over the bug with the assistance of my cat, trying to discover the solution. After a few purrs, it occurred to me: the problem is the recursive function, which should have been my first clue.

When the *find()* function returns, or "unwinds," the previous value of pointer `f` is used—not the newly allocated value in the recursive call. Each time the function changes to the parent directory, the structures created in the linked list are lost because pointer `f` is reset to the original value passed to the function. Ugh.

Fortunately, the solution is simple: return pointer `f`.

Updating the code requires only three changes and one addition. First, the *find()* function's data type must be changed from *void* to `struct finfo*`:

```
struct finfo *find( char *dirpath, char *parentpath, struct finfo *f)
```

Second, the recursive call must capture the function's return value:

```
f = find(subdirpath,dirpath,f);
```

Effectively, this change updates pointer `f` to reflect its new value after the recursive call.

Third, the *return* statement in the error check for the *chdir()* function must specify the value of variable `f`:

```
return(f);
```

And finally, the *find()* function must have a statement at the end to return the value of pointer `f`:

```
return(f);
```

These updates are found in the source code file `finddupe02.c` in the online repository.

Upon building the code, the program accurately scans subdirectories—and retains the linked list when it changes back to the parent directory. The output is complete and accurate: a record is made via a linked list of all files found in the current directory as well as its subdirectories.

11.3.2 *Locating the duplicates*

The purpose of creating a linked list in the *Find Dupe* program is to find duplicates. At some point, the list must be scanned and a determination made as to which filenames are repeated and in which directories the duplicates are found.

I thought of several ways to accomplish this task. Most of them involved creating a second list of filenames. But I didn't want to build list after list. Instead, I added a new member to the `finfo` structure, `repeat`, as shown in this updated structure definition:

```
struct finfo {
  int index;
  int repeat;
  char name[BUFSIZ];
  char path[PATH_MAX];
  struct finfo *next;
};
```

New member to track repeated filenames

The repeat member tracks how many times a name repeats. Its value is initialized to one in the *find()* function as each node is created. After all, every filename found exists at least once.

To track repeated filenames, the repeat member is incremented as the list is scanned after its creation. In the *main()* function, a nested loop works like a bubble sort. It compares each node in the list sequentially with the rest of the nodes.

To perform the second scan, I need another *struct* finfo variable declared in the *main()* function. This variable, *scan, is used in addition to *first and *current to scan the linked list:

```
struct finfo *first,*current,*scan;
```

The nested *while* loop is added just before the *while* loop that outputs the list. This nested loop uses the *current pointer to process the entire linked list. The *scan pointer is used in an inner *while* loop to compare the current->name member with subsequent name members. When a match is found, the current->repeat structure member for the file with the repeated name is incremented, as shown here.

Listing 11.8   **The nested *while* loops added to the *main()* function in** `finddupe03.c`

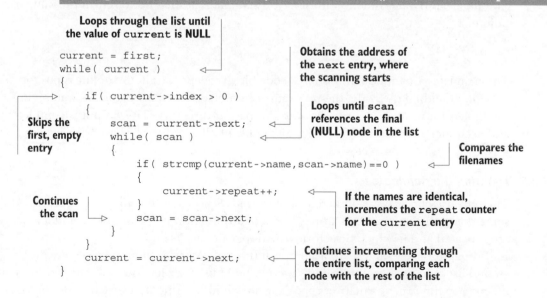

These nested loops update the `repeat` member of structures containing identical file-names. They're followed by the existing *while* loop that outputs the list. The *printf()* statement in that second loop is updated to output the `repeat` value:

```
printf("%d:%s/%s (%d)\n",
        current->index,
        current->path,
        current->name,
        current->repeat
    );
```

All these changes are found in the `finddupe03.c` source code file, available in the online repository. The output doesn't yet show duplicate files. This incremental improvement to the *Find Dupe* series of source code files merely outputs the same, full file list, but with the number of repeats shown at the end of the file pathname string:

```
163:/Users/Dan/code/sto/secret01.c (1)
```

The next update to the *Find Dupe* program is found in source code file `finddupe04.c`. Obtain this source code file from the online repository, and display it in an editor. Follow along with the text to review the two improvements I'll make.

First, a new *int* variable `found` is declared in the *main()* function, up top where I prefer to set my variable declarations:

```
int found = 0;
```

When a repeating filename is discovered in the nested *while* loops, the value of `found` is reset to 1:

```
if( strcmp(current->name,scan->name)==0 )
{
    current->repeat++;
    found = 1;
}
```

The value of `found` need not accumulate; it's effectively a Boolean variable. When it stays at 0, no duplicate filenames are found and the following statements are executed:

```
if( !found )
{
    puts("No duplicates found");
    return(1);
}
```

The "No duplicates found" message is output, then the program exits with a return value of 1.

When the value of found has been reset to 1, duplicate filenames are detected. The second *while* loop in the *main()* function proceeds to process the list. This loop is updated to catch and output the repeats, as illustrated in the following listing. Again, the *scan variable is used in a nested *while* loop, but this time to output duplicate filenames and their pathnames.

Listing 11.9   A second nested *while* loop in the *main()* function in `finddupe04.c`

```
current = first;           ◄──── Churns through the entire
while( current )                  list of files just as before
{
    if( current->index > 0 )
    {
        if( current->repeat > 1 )    ◄──── Looks for items with a repeat
        {                                  count higher than 1
            printf("%d duplicates found of %s:\n",    ◄──── Outputs the number
                current->repeat,                             of duplicates for the
                current->name                               given filename
                );
            printf(" %s/%s\n",
                current->path,
                current->name
                );
            scan = current->next;    ◄──── Starts the nested loop to
            while( scan )                   output the names and paths
            {                               of matching filenames
                if( strcmp(scan->name,current->name)==0 )
                {
                    printf(" %s/%s\n",
                        scan->path,
                        scan->name
                        );
                }
                scan = scan->next;
            }
        }
    }
    current = current->next;
}
```

Outputs the current filename and its path → (annotation pointing to second printf)

This update to the code in `finddupe04.c` outputs a shorter list, showing only those repeated filenames, plus listing all the duplicate names and their paths.

For example, in my programming tree, I see five duplicates of the `a.out` file in the program's output:

```
5 duplicates found of a.out:
 /Users/Dan/code/a.out
 /Users/Dan/code/communications/a.out
 /Users/Dan/code/communications/networking/a.out
 /Users/Dan/Tiny C Projects/code/08_unicode/a.out
 /Users/Dan/Tiny C Projects/code/11_filefind/a.out
```

The problem is that the duplicates also show duplicates. So, the output continues for the same filename as follows for multiple occurrences of the a.out file:

```
4 duplicates found of a.out:
 /Users/Dan/code/communications/a.out
 /Users/Dan/code/communications/networking/a.out
 /Users/Dan/Tiny C Projects/code/08_unicode/a.out
 /Users/Dan/Tiny C Projects/code/11_filefind/a.out
3 duplicates found of a.out:
 /Users/Dan/code/communications/networking/a.out
 /Users/Dan/Tiny C Projects/code/08_unicode/a.out
 /Users/Dan/Tiny C Projects/code/11_filefind/a.out
```

This output is inefficient because it repeatedly lists the duplicates. The reason is that the repeat member for repeated filename structures in the linked list is greater than 1. Because this value doesn't change when the first repeated filename is output, the code catches all the duplicates.

This problem frustrated me because I didn't want to create yet another structure member nor did I want to return to rehab. My goal is to avoid exceptions in an already complex, nested *while* loop.

I stewed over this problem for a while, but eventually inspiration hit me, and a one-line solution presented itself:

```
scan->repeat = 0;
```

This single statement is added to the second nested *while* loop, shown in listing 11.9. It appears after the matching filename is detected:

```
while( scan )
{
    if( strcmp(scan->name,current->name)==0 )
    {
        printf(" %s/%s\n",
                scan->path,
                scan->name
              );
        scan->repeat = 0;
    }
    scan = scan->next;
}
```

In the nested *while* loop, after the repeated filename is output, its repeat value is reset to 0. This change prevents a repeated filename from appearing later in the output. This change is available in the source code file finddupe05.c.

The *Find Dupe* program is complete: it scans the current directory structure and lists matching filenames, showing the full pathname for all duplicates.

Like all code, the *Find Dupe* series can be improved upon. For example, the file's size could be added to the finfo structure. Filename matches and file size matches could be output. And you could go whole hog and try to match file contents as well. The basic framework for whatever system you need is provided in the existing code. All that's left is your desire to improve upon it and the time necessary to anticipate all those unexpected things that are bound to happen along the way.

Holiday detector

No matter the time of year, it seems that a holiday looms on the horizon. It could be a religious holiday, a national day, or some other festive event. Many people may get the day off from work to celebrate. For programmers, the holiday is also a celebration but not from work: coders still code, but it's a more enjoyable experience because everyone else is on vacation, which means fewer interruptions.

Your computer doesn't care whether one day is a holiday. It's not being ignorant; it just doesn't know. To help the computer understand which day is a holiday, and to help you complete other programming projects that rely upon knowing which days are holidays, you must:

- Understand how the operating system uses return values
- Work with date programming in C
- Review major holidays
- Calculate regular holidays
- Deal with irregular holidays
- Figure out when Easter occurs
- Put your holiday function to the test

These tasks help build routines that detect and report on holidays given a specific day of the year. Such a utility isn't specifically useful by itself, but it does come into play when programming dates or performing other tasks where knowing when a holiday occurs is important. For example, I wrote a stock tracker where it was useful to know which days *not* to fetch the stock data because the markets are closed. And my trash pickup reminder shell script uses my holiday program to see whether trash day has shifted.

The routines presented in this chapter also play a role in the calendar programs introduced in chapter 13.

12.1   *The operating system wants its vig*

Ever wonder why *main()* is an integer function? Years ago, C programmers freely declared it a *void* function. Scandalous! Old programmers may still pull a void main() in their code. Goodness, even the first edition of the venerable K&R—*The C Programming Language* (Prentice-Hall)—didn't even bother to cast the *main()* function. Try not to work yourself into a tizzy.

The reason the *main()* function is cast as an *int* is that it must return a value to the operating system. Like any loan shark, when the operating system releases some of its resources (memory and processor time) to another program, it wants something in return, such as the interest—vigorish, or "vig." That something is an integer value. This value is often ignored (just don't miss a payment), or it's used in some clever and innovative way. Either way, the value is required.

12.1.1 *Understanding exit status versus the termination status*

More than one way exists to stop a program. The natural way is for the program to end normally, with a *return* statement at the end of the *main()* function passing its value back to the operating system. This value is officially known as the program's exit status.

If the program stops before the *main()* function exits, it has a termination status. For example, an *exit()* statement nestled in a function other than *main()* halts a program. In this case, the value that *exit()* passes to the operating system is known as the termination status.

Termination status. Exit status. Yes, the nerds love to pick nits. The point is that the way the program quits affects how the value returned is interpreted. Many functions that spawn other programs (processes) use a termination status and not an exit status. The termination status is typically 0 for success or –1 otherwise. This value is different from whatever the exit status might be. Be aware of this difference as you code your programs, and especially if you choose to dialogue with nerds.

12.1.2 *Setting a return value*

The *return* statement in the *main()* function is responsible for sending a value back to the operating system. Sending an integer value up to the mothership is vital for the *main()* function: miss it, and the compiler points its bony finger at you and shrieks like Donald Sutherland at the end of *Invasion of the Body Snatchers*.

The next listing shows the source code for return01.c. This program has only one job: to return a value to the operating system. If the value isn't specified as a command-line argument, zero is returned.

Listing 12.1 Source code for `return01.c`

```
#include <stdlib.h>        ◁─────┐  The stdio.h header isn't required because
                                 │  no I/O functions are used in the code.
int main(int argc, char *argv[])
{
    if( argc>1 )          ◁───┐  If a command-line option is present,
    {                         │  tries to convert it into an integer
        return( strtol(argv[1],NULL,10) );   ◁──┐  Returns the conversion
    }                                           │  of string argv[1] into
    else                                        │  an integer (long) value
    {
        return(0);   ◁───┐  When no argument is
    }                    │  present, returns zero
}
```

The *strtol()* function in `return01.c` converts the string held in `argv[1]`, the first argument at the command prompt, into an integer value, base 10. If the string can't be converted (it contains no digits), the value 0 is returned.

The program surrenders its value via the *return* statement. The *exit()* function could also be used, but this value is an exit status, not a termination status. (I wrote that for the nerds; don't worry about the difference here.)

Here is a sample run:

Yes, the code lacks output, even when you specify an argument. And, yes, the value returned is consumed by the operating system. It's available for the shell to interpret. Despite being a loan shark, the operating system rarely if ever does anything with a program's return value. This job can be done by other programs, but specifically the exit status is available for use by shell scripts.

12.1.3 *Interpreting the return value*

The value a program poops out is left on the operating system's doorstep. Though nothing needs to be done with the value, it remains available for the shell to use—until another program deposits another value.

To demonstrate how the return value is accessed from the shell, rerun the program for `return01.c:`, type the program name, assumed to be *return01*, and a value as an argument, such as:

```
$ ./return01 27
```

The program returns the value 27 to the operating system. This value is accessed via the shell scripting variable $?. To see it, type the *echo* command followed by $?:

```
$ echo $?
27
```

Shell scripts can use this value to determine the result of some operation. Alas, in Linux it's difficult for a non-shell script program to read the return value of another program it spawns. Such a task is possible, and I could so easily get sidetracked to describe the thrilling details, but it's beyond the scope of this chapter.

The source code for return02.c in the following listing attempts to capture the value returned from the *return01* program. The *system()* function is used to execute *return01* with a return value of 99. The purpose of the program is to show how the *system()* function doesn't capture a program's return value.

Listing 12.2   Source code for `return02.c`

```
#include <stdio.h>
#include <stdlib.h>

int main()
{
    int r;

    r = system("./return01 99");         ←┐  Runs the return01
    printf("The return value is %d\n",r); ←   program and sets a
                                              return value of 99
    return(r);
}                                             Reports the value
                                              returned by the
                                              system() function
```

The *system()* function's single argument is something you would type at the command prompt. The function can return a variety of values, though if the call is successful, the value returned is the termination status of the shell launched to run the program. The value is not the return value of the program run. Here's a sample run:

```
The return value is 25344
```

After running the *system()* function, the shell returns the value 25344 to the operating system.

In Windows, the *system()* function works differently. Unlike with Linux, it returns the value generated by any program run. Here's sample output of the same code built in Windows, with the option 99 specified:

```
The return value is 99
```

As an old MS-DOS/Windows coder, I remember using this trick with the *system()* function ages ago in various programs. Because *system()* behaves differently in Linux, relying upon the function to report a program's return value isn't anything you should do.

Yes, I know: the *system()* function in Linux does, in fact, return the exit status of the program run—the shell. The point I'm making is that the function can't be used to examine another program's return value.

Other functions that spawn a process—*fork(), popen(),* and so on—behave similarly to *system()*: the program spawned may generate an exit status, but this value isn't reported by the function making the call.

As I wrote earlier, it's possible to spawn a process and capture its return value. If you're curious to know the procedure, visit my blog and search for the *wait()* function: https://c-for-dummies.com/blog.

12.1.4 *Using the preset return values*

The C overlords want you to know that an exit status of 0 indicates success; everything went as planned. An exit status of 1 means something went wrong. I use this consistency in my code, but don't use the defined constants available in the `stdlib.h` header file:

```
EXIT_FAILURE
EXIT_SUCCESS
```

These two values are defined as 1 and 0 for failure and success, respectively. The defined constants are consistent—the same for all compilers and platforms.

The next listing shows the source code for `return03.c`, which generates a random integer, 0 or 1. This value is used to determine which defined constant is returned as an exit status: `EXIT_FAILURE` or `EXIT_SUCCESS`.

Listing 12.3   Source code for `return03.c`

```
#include <stdio.h>
#include <stdlib.h>
#include <time.h>

int main()
{
    int r;                              Seeds the
                                        randomizer
                                                        Generates a random
    srand( (unsigned)time(NULL) );   ◁─┘               value and stores it in r

                                                        Uses r to test success
    r = rand() % 2;              ◁──                    (zero) or failure (one)
    if(r)                        ◁──────────┘
    {
        fprintf(stderr,"Welp, this program screwed [CA]up!\n");   ◁────┐
        return(EXIT_FAILURE);
    }                                               Outputs the error to the
    else                                            standard error device—
    {                                                      out of tradition
        printf("Everything went ducky!\n");   ◁──┐
        return(EXIT_SUCCESS);                     The non-error
    }                                             message is sent to
}                                                 standard output.
```

The program's output depends on the random number generated. To confirm the value, you can use the `$?` variable at the command prompt:

```
$ ./a.out
Welp, this program screwed up!
$ echo $?
1
```

And:

```
$ ./a.out
Everything went ducky!
$ echo $?
0
```

Remember, return values need not be limited to 0 and 1. Many programs and utilities return different values, each of which can be interpreted by a shell script to determine what happened. The interpretation of these values is up to whatever purpose the program has, to help it fulfill its function.

12.2   *All about today*

Ages ago, US national holidays fell on specific days. I remember, when I was young, getting to take off both Lincoln's birthday *and* George Washington's birthday. As a kid, I'd take two days off school in February over a Nintendo Switch in a heartbeat.

Well, maybe not.

Before you can determine which day is a holiday, you need a point of reference. That point is today, the current date obtained from the operating system. Or you can backfill a tm structure with any old date and work from there. Both items are easy to obtain by invoking the proper C language functions.

12.2.1   *Getting today's date*

One of the hallmarks of the early PC era was the prompt:

```
The current date is: Tue 1-01-1980
Enter the new date: (mm-dd-yy)
```

MS-DOS didn't know whether today was a holiday because it didn't even know which day it was! The user had to input the current date. Eventually, technology was added to the motherboard to retain the current date and time. This setup is how modern computers work, but with the bonus of an internet time server to keep the clock accurate. Your C code can use this information to obtain the current date and time—as it's known to the computer.

The following listing shows the typical time code for the C language. The current epoch value—the number of seconds ticked since January 1, 1970—is obtained from the *time()* function and stored in *time_t* variable now. This variable is used in the *localtime()* function to fill a tm structure, today. The tm structure's members contain individual time tidbit values, which are output.

Listing 12.4 Source code for `getdate01.c`

```
#include <stdio.h>
#include <time.h>

int main()
{
    time_t now;
    struct tm *today;
    int month,day,year,weekday;

    now = time(NULL);
    today = localtime(&now);

    month = today->tm_mon+1;
    day = today->tm_mday;
    weekday = today->tm_wday;
    year = today->tm_year+1900;

    printf("Today is %d, %d %d, %d\n",
            weekday,
            month,
            day,
            year
            );

    return(0);
}
```

Obtains the number of seconds elapsed since January 1, 1970—the Unix epoch

Fills the `tm` structure `today` with time tidbits

The `tm_mon` member starts with 0 for January.

The `tm_year` member starts with 1901.

Outputs the values obtained from the `tm` structure

This code's approach should be familiar to you if you've written any time-related programs. The output shows the current date in this format:

```
Today is 1, 12 6, 2021
```

Of course, the output could be made readable by a human. Unless you're a true nerd you may not recognize "1" as the value for Monday.

EXERCISE 12.1

Update the code for `getdate01.c` to output strings for the days of the week and months. This improvement requires adding two string arrays to the code and other updates, including to the *printf()* function.

My solution is available in the online repository as `getdate02.c`. Please try this exercise on your own before you see how I did it. Comments in my code explain what's going on—including an important point you will probably forget.

12.2.2 Obtaining any old date

The *time()* function obtains the current time, a *time_t* value containing the number of seconds elapsed from January 1, 1970. This value is useless by itself, which is why functions like *localtime()* help sort out the details for you. But what about dates other than today?

It's possible to backfill a `tm` structure. You assign values to the various members, then use the *mktime()* function to translate these time tidbits into a *time_t* value. Further, the *mktime()* function fills in unknown details for you, such as the day of the week. This information is vital if you plan to determine upon which date a holiday falls.

Here is the *man* page format for the *mktime()* function:

```
time_t mktime(struct tm *tm);
```

The function is passed the address of a partially filled `tm` structure. A *time_t* value is returned, but more importantly, the rest of the `tm` structure is filled with key details.

The *mktime()* function is prototyped in the `time.h` header file.

As a quick reference, table 12.1 shows the common members of a `tm` structure.

Table 12.1   Members of the `tm` structure

Member	References	Range/Notes
tm_sec	Seconds	0 to 60 (60 allows for a leap second)
tm_min	Minutes	0 to 59
tm_hour	Hours	0 to 23
tm_mday	Day of the month	1 to 31
tm_mon	Month	0 to 11
tm_year	Year	Current year minus 1900
tm_wday	Day of the week	0 to 6, Sunday to Saturday
tm_yday	Day of the year	0 to 365; zero is January 1
tm_isdst	Daylight saving time	Positive values indicate daylight saving time; zero indicates not; negative values indicate that the data is unavailable

Say you want to find out the day of the week for April 12, 2022. The code shown in the next listing attempts to do so by filling in three members of the `tm` structure: tm_mon, tm_day, and tm_year. Adjustments are made for the tm_mon member, which uses zero for January, and the tm_year member, which starts its count at 1900. A *printf()* statement outputs the result in mm/dd/yyyy format, which also accesses the newly filled tm_wday member to output the day of the week string.

Listing 12.5   Source code for `getdate03.c`

```
#include <stdio.h>
#include <time.h>

int main()
{
    struct tm day;
```

```
                const char *days[] = {
                    "Sunday", "Monday", "Tuesday", "Wednesday",
                    "Thursday", "Friday", "Saturday", "Sunday"
                };

                day.tm_mon = 4-1;
                day.tm_mday = 12;
                day.tm_year = 2022-1900;

                mktime(&day);

                printf("%02d/%02d/%04d is on a %s\n",
                        day.tm_mon+1,
                        day.tm_mday,
                        day.tm_year+1900,
                        days[day.tm_wday]
                    );

            return(0);
        }
```

The 12th day of the month ← `day.tm_mday = 12;`

I use this format because 0 is January, so 4 (April) minus 1 prompts me to double-check. → `day.tm_mon = 4-1;`

This format makes the date I want, 2022, readable. → `day.tm_year = 2022-1900;`

Converts the partially filled `tm` structure → `mktime(&day);`

Outputs the results → `printf(...)`

Here is the program's output:

```
09/11/0122 is on a Tuesday
```

Alas, September 11 in the year 122 wasn't expected, whether or not it's a Tuesday. That is the output from my Linux machine. On the Macintosh, I saw this output:

```
08/22/5839 is on a Thursday
```

Curiously, August 22 in the year 5839 is on a Thursday. The computer is amazing, not only to know the exact date, but that our reptilian overlords will continue to use the common calendar. Obviously, something went wrong. These types of bugs are frustrating, especially when the code cleanly compiles.

The issue is that the `tm` structure contains garbage that's misinterpreted or conflicting with the three values preset. My solution is to also set the values for hour, minute, and second members, adding the following three lines to the code just below the statements where the day, month, and year are set:

```
day.tm_hour = 0;
day.tm_min = 0;
day.tm_sec = 0;
```

This change is found in the source code file `getdate04.c`, available in the online repository. When built, here is the output:

```
04/12/2022 is on a Tuesday
```

I used a greasy old garage calendar to confirm that, indeed, April 12, 2022, is a Tuesday.

The lesson learned is that you can obtain details about a date if you know the month, day, and year, by filling the six `tm` structure members, as outlined here, and calling the *mktime()* function. Yet even then, you may get the wrong date.

12.3   *Happy holidays*

It seems like every day is a holiday, a feast day, a saint's day, or a day of proclamation for this or that cause, celebrity, hero, or historic figure. You've seen the hairspray dolls on local TV cheerfully announce, "Well, today is National Hoot Like an Owl Day . . ." or some such nonsense. Such filler is possible because every day is some sort of celebration—and it's a slow news day.

For purposes of this chapter, a holiday must be a big deal, such as a national holiday when everyone gets the day off. My personal indication of a major holiday is when the mail doesn't come. Excluding every Sunday, these holidays are few, typically one a month. This is the type of holiday I want my holiday detector to report, though you're free to modify the code to list any holiday—including every Sunday.

12.3.1   *Reviewing holidays in the United States*

The United States have a smattering of holidays, though not every national holiday is a day off for everyone. Instead, I consider the specific holidays shown in table 12.2. For these holidays, most people have the day off, government offices are closed, banks are closed, school is out, the mail doesn't come, and people don't bother me as much with phone calls and email.

Table 12.2   US national holidays

Holiday	Date	Notes
New Year's Day	January 1	Friday/Monday holiday when this holiday occurs on a weekend.
Martin Luther King Jr. Day	Third Monday of January	
Washington's Birthday	Third Monday of February	Unofficially called Presidents Day.
Easter	Sunday in March or April	Calculation is made on the lunar calendar, so it varies.
Memorial Day	Last Monday of May	
Juneteenth	June 19	Friday/Monday holiday when this holiday occurs on a weekend.
Independence Day	July 4	Friday/Monday holiday when this holiday occurs on a weekend.
Labor Day	First Monday of September	
Columbus Day	Second Monday of October	Also celebrated as Indigenous Peoples' Day. Not every government office is closed.
Veterans Day	November 11	Friday/Monday holiday when this holiday occurs on a weekend.

Table 12.2   US national holidays *(continued)*

Holiday	Date	Notes
Thanksgiving	Fourth Thursday of November	
Christmas	December 25	Friday/Monday holiday when this holiday occurs on a weekend.

Some holidays, such as Independence Day and Christmas, are specific to a day and date, though the holiday is often observed on the Friday or Monday after it falls on a weekend. Other holidays float based on the week of the month or other factors, as noted in table 12.2.

When calculating a holiday, you can set two dates: the holiday's actual date and the date on which the holiday is observed. Most calendars I've seen show both, such as Christmas and Christmas Observed. Adding such programming is shown later in this chapter, such as when a holiday falls on a Sunday and the celebration is on Monday.

12.3.2 *Discovering holidays in the UK*

As one of the rebels, I have no idea which days are celebrated as holidays in the United Kingdom—or any other country, for that matter. From Dickens, I know that Christmas is a thing in England, at least. I doubt the British celebrate George Washington's birthday—well, perhaps not the way we do in the States. The rest of the UK holidays seem to be bank holidays, most likely celebrating the greatest banks in Britain. Even people who don't work in a bank get the day off, supposedly.

Table 12.3 lists UK national holidays as reported by the internet. Only three of them are tied to a specific date: New Year's Day, Christmas, and Boxing Day. If any of these holidays falls on Saturday or Sunday, the day off is the following Monday. If Christmas or Boxing Day takes place on the weekend, it's possible to see both Monday and Tuesday off, frequently with Tuesday as the day off for Christmas, for some reason.

Table 12.3   UK national holidays

Holiday	Date
New Year's Day	January 1
Good Friday	Friday before Easter
Easter Monday	Monday after Easter
Early May Bank Holiday	First Monday of May
Spring Bank Holiday	Last Monday of May
Summer Bank Holiday	Last Monday of August
Christmas Day	December 25
Boxing Day	December 26

The Easter holiday floats depending on when Easter falls. You must use an algorithm to calculate these holidays: Easter and Good Friday. Such code is presented later in this chapter.

Don't worry, my English, Irish, Scottish, and Welsh friends: I shan't be writing any code to detect holidays in the UK. That's your job. Given the information presented in this chapter, the task is quite doable.

12.4   Is today a holiday?

Humans enjoy plenty of clues about impending holidays. For example, every August, shoppers at Costco are thrilled to see Christmas decorations up for sale. And who can forget early March with all the green shamrocks and cheery leprechauns reminding us of Easter? These cultural clues mean nothing to a computer—unless you, the programmer, are willing to help.

For a computer holiday detector, three timely tidbits are necessary:

- The month number
- The day of the month
- The day of the week

With these three items known, it's possible for a computer to identify a date as a holiday.

For the remainder of this chapter, I use holidays in the United States. The same techniques demonstrated can also be used to detect holidays in other countries, providing they follow a consistency on the solar calendar. I don't cover how to map lunar holidays to solar holidays, except for Easter later in this chapter.

12.4.1   Reporting regular date holidays

The easiest holidays to report are the predictable ones—what I call the regular date holidays. Each of these is fixed to a specific month and day:

- New Year's Day, January 1
- Juneteenth, June 19
- Independence Day, July 4
- Veterans Day, November 11
- Christmas Day, December 25

To report these dates, I use the *isholiday()* function. Here's the prototype:

```
int isholiday(struct tm *d)
```

The function's only argument is the address of a `tm` structure, the same structure returned from the *localtime()* function and used by the *mktime()* function. Reusing this structure is convenient for this stage in the *isholiday()* function's evolution.

The *isholiday()* function shown next returns an integer value: 0 for nonholiday days and 1 for a holiday. The function does a straight-up comparison of month-and-day values to report the regular date holidays, as shown in the listing. Please note that the month values used start with zero for January.

Listing 12.6   The *isholiday()* function

```
int isholiday(struct tm *d)
{
    if( d->tm_mon==0 && d->tm_mday==1)        <————— New Year's Day
        return(1);

    if( d->tm_mon==5 && d->tm_mday==19)       <————— Juneteenth
    return(1);

    if( d->tm_mon==6 && d->tm_mday==4)        <————— Independence Day
        return(1);

    if( d->tm_mon==10 && d->tm_mday==11)      <————— Veterans Day
        return(1);

    if( d->tm_mon == 11 && d->tm_mday == 25)  <————— Christmas
        return(1);

    return(0);
}
```

The *main()* function calls the *time()* and *localtime()* functions to obtain the current time info and pack it into the tm structure. This structure is passed to *isholiday()* and the results reported. You can find the full source code at the online repository as isholiday01.c. Here is a sample run:

```
Today is 12/09/2021, not a holiday
```

For my first update to the *isholiday()* function, I'd like the function to report the holiday's name. To make this improvement, the tm structure must be ditched as the *isholiday()* function's argument. Instead, I use a new structure holiday, defined with these members:

```
struct holiday {
    int month;
    int day;
    char *name;
};
```

The month and day members match up to the tm_mon and tm_mday members of the tm structure. The name member is a *char* pointer to hold the holiday's name. The strings assigned to this pointer are declared in the *isholiday()* function, as shown in the following listing. There you also see the updates to each *if* decision, which now assigns the name member of the holiday structure passed.

Listing 12.7   The *isholiday()* function updated to return the holiday name

```
int isholiday(struct holiday *h)          ◁────  The holiday structure must
{                                                be passed as a pointer because
    char *n[] = {              ◁────             the name member is modified
        "New Years Day",                         within this function.
        "Juneteenth",
        "Independence Day",    Strings assigned
        "Veterans Day",        to holidays in
        "Christmas"            chronological order
    };

    if( h->month==0 && h->day==1)
    {                               Assigns the
        h->name = n[0];      ◁──── name member
        return(1);           ◁────
    }                             Returns 1 for a
                                  true holiday

    if( h->month==5 && h->day==19)     ◁──  The pattern is repeated
    {                                       for each of the five
        h->name = n[1];                     holidays.
        return(1);
    }

    if( h->month==6 && h->day==4)
    {
        h->name = n[2];
        return(1);
    }

    if( h->month==10 && h->day==11)
    {
        h->name = n[3];
        return(1);
    }

    if( h->month== 11 && h->day == 25)
    {
        h->name = n[4];
        return(1);
    }                   Returns 0
                        when the date
    return(0);    ◁──── isn't a holiday
}
```

The *main()* function is also updated to assign values to the holiday structure declared there. The output statements are also modified to output the named holiday. For example:

```
Today is 12/25/2021, Christmas
```

The full source code for this update is found in the online repository as isholiday02.c.

The holidays detected so far are absolute. If you were creating a calendar (see chapter 13) and you wanted to color-code the holidays red, the *isholiday()* function properly reports the values. But if you wanted to note when the holiday is observed, more coding is necessary.

Specifically, when one of these holidays falls on a weekend, it's often the Friday before or the Monday after that everyone takes a day off: when Independence Day (July 4) is on a Sunday, the country takes off Monday, July 5. Though when this type of holiday falls on a Tuesday, Wednesday, or Thursday, the day before or after isn't considered a holiday, even though some people, mostly the lazy, take additional days.

To update the code for `isholiday02.c`, and to improve the *isholiday()* function, some changes are in order. These changes account for those times when the holiday falls on a weekend.

First comes an update to the `holiday` structure, which adds a new member, `wday`. This member echoes the `tm_wday` member of the `tm` structure. It indicates a day of the week—0 for Sunday through 6 for Saturday. Here is the updated definition:

```
struct holiday {
    int month;
    int day;
    int wday;
    char *name;
};
```

Because only two days are required for testing, I also added two defined constants:

```
#define FRIDAY 5
#define MONDAY 1
```

When New Year's Day is observed on a Friday, the date is December 31 of the prior year. This difference makes the New Year's Day test a bit more complex than the other Friday/Monday tests. The next listing shows the code necessary to make the New Year's Day test, which isn't as elegant as the other holiday tests due to the year-before overlap.

Listing 12.8 Statements to detect New Year's Day and any Friday/Monday celebrations

```
if( h->month==11 && h->day==31 && h->wday==FRIDAY )     ⟵  Specifically
{                                                            checks for Friday,
    h->name = n[0];                                          December 31
    return(2);      ⟵  Returns 2 for
}                       "celebration"
                        holidays
if( h->month==0 && h->day==1 )      ⟵  Checks for New
{                                       Year's Day
    h->name = n[0];
    return(1);     ⟵  Returns 1 for
}                      the real holiday
```

```
if( h->month==0 && h->day==2 && h->wday==MONDAY )     ◁——┐  Specifically checks
{                                                          for Monday,
    h->name = n[0];                                        January 2
    return(2);    ◁——┐ Returns 2 for
}                      "celebration" holidays
```

The new return code from the *isholiday()* function is 2, as shown in listing 12.8. This value is handled uniquely in the *main()* function, which is found in the complete update source code file, `isholiday03.c`. Here is a sample run for a nonholiday:

```
Today is 12/09/2021, not a holiday
```

And for a holiday:

```
Today is 12/25/2021, Christmas
```

And a Monday holiday:

```
Today is 12/26/2022, Christmas observed
```

In the code, however, I notice something that bothers me: After New Year's Day is determined, the next four holidays all share similar statements. For example, the construction for Juneteenth is shown in the next listing. The structure of this code matches the structure used to test for the next three holidays. All that changes are the specific day values. That's a lot of repetitious code.

Listing 12.9   **Statements to detect Juneteenth and other holidays**

```
                         Juneteenth is
                         always in June.              Focuses on the relevant
if( h->month==5 )    ◁————                            days, before (18), the
{                                                     day (19), and after (20)
    if( h->day>17 && h->day<21 )     ◁————
    {
        if( h->day==18 && h->wday==FRIDAY )     ◁——┐  Checks for the day
        {                                             before celebration
            h->name = n[1];
            return(2);    ◁——┐ Returns 2 for
        }                     celebration days
        if( h->day==20 && h->wday==MONDAY )     ◁——┐  Checks for the day
        {                                             after celebration
            h->name = n[1];
Returns 2 for   ├——▷ return(2);
celebration days │   }
        if( h->day==19 )     ◁——┐ Checks for the
        {                        actual holiday
            h->name = n[1];
            return(1);    ◁——┐ Returns 1 for
        }                     the holiday
    }
}
```

Whenever I see such repetition in my code, it cries out for a function. The function I created is named *weekend()*. Here is its prototype:

```
int weekend(int holiday, int mday, int wday)
```

The function has three arguments. Integer `holiday` is the day of the month on which the holiday occurs. Integers `mday` and `wday` are the day of the month and day of the week values, respectively. These three items represent the different values that change for each holiday test in the *isholiday()* function from source code file `isholiday03.c`.

The following listing shows the *weekend()* function. It contains most of the code shown in listing 12.9, the statements that repeat, but is modified to use variables instead of specific day-of-the-month values. This code evaluates the days before and after the holiday, Friday and Monday, to determine celebration days. The only item not addressed in the function is the string assignment for the holiday name.

Listing 12.10   The *weekend()* function from `isholiday04.c`

```
int weekend(int holiday, int mday, int wday)
{
  if( mday>holiday-2 && mday<holiday+2 )        ◁──── Narrows down the
  {                                                    days to search
    if( mday==holiday-1 && wday==FRIDAY )       ◁──── Tests for the Friday
      return(2);                                       before the holiday
    if( mday==holiday+1 && wday==MONDAY )        ◁──── Tests for the Monday
      return(2);                                       after the holiday
    if( mday==holiday )          ◁──── Tests for the
      return(1);                        holiday date itself
  }
  return(0);        ◁──── Returns zero
}                          for no matches
```

This function's update is found in the online repository as `isholiday04.c`. The *isholiday()* function is also updated to account for passing most of the work to the *weekend()* function. The code reads more cleanly than it did before.

Further improvements could be made to the *isholiday()* function. But first, the irregular holidays must be dealt with.

12.4.2 *Dealing with irregular holidays*

Unlike specific date holidays, irregular holidays occur on specific weeks and days of the month. The day is Monday, save for Thanksgiving, which takes place on a Thursday. These holidays are irregular in that they fall within a range of dates each year, so the program must think harder about when these holidays occur. As a review, here are the irregular holidays in the United States:

- Martin Luther King Jr. Day, third Monday of January
- Presidents Day, third Monday of February
- Memorial Day, last Monday of May

- Labor Day, first Monday of September
- Columbus Day, second Monday of October
- Thanksgiving, fourth Thursday of November

Unlike the regular date holidays, you don't need to worry about a shifting observance day; these are all specific day-of-the-week holidays. This consistency means that it's possible to calculate a day-of-the-month range for each holiday. I've summarized the day ranges in table 12.4 for weeks in a month.

Table 12.4   Day ranges for Monday holidays on a given week

Week of month	Monday range
First	1 to 7
Second	8 to 14
Third	15 to 21
Fourth	22 to 28
Last	25 and higher

The difference between the fourth and last week occurs in those months with five Mondays, such as May, shown in figure 12.1: when the 31st of May falls on a Monday, it's the fifth Monday. The 24th of May is still in the fourth week (refer to table 12.3), but in this month configuration, where the 31st is on a Monday, it's the last day. This reason is why the last week has a different range than the fourth week.

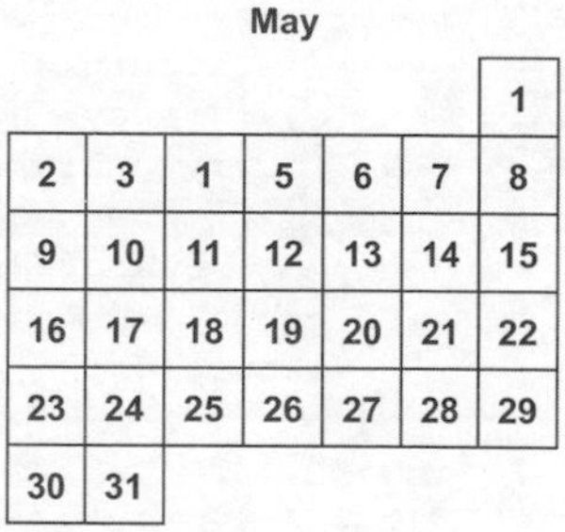

For Thanksgiving, the final Thursday of the month could fall on any day from the 22nd through the 28th. This value is shown in the fourth row in Table 12.3, which also applies to Thursdays.

May

						1
2	3	4	5	6	7	8
9	10	11	12	13	14	15
16	17	18	19	20	21	22
23	24	25	26	27	28	29
30	31					

Figure 12.1   A configuration of May, with five Mondays

The *isholiday()* function is nearly complete when these final, irregular holidays are coded. To help do so, I created a few macros and added the THURSDAY defined constant:

```
#define FRIDAY 5
#define MONDAY 1
#define THURSDAY 4
#define FIRST_WEEK h->day<8
#define SECOND_WEEK h->day>7&&h->day<15
#define THIRD_WEEK h->day>14&&h->day<22
#define FOURTH_WEEK h->day>21&&h->day<29
#define LAST_WEEK h->day>24&&h->day<32
```

The weekday holidays fall on Friday, Monday, or Thursday, so the defined constants add readability to the code.

The macros shown here relate to the date values presented in table 12.3. The variable h->day is used in the *isholiday()* function. These macros add readability to the function. For example, this code doesn't use the macro:

```
if( h->day>14&&h->day<22 )
{
    h->name = n[1];
    return(1);
}
```

But this code, which does the same thing as the previous snippet, is far more readable:

```
if( THIRD_WEEK )
{
    h->name = n[1];
    return(1);
}
```

To avoid any confusion, the entire, updated code for the *isholiday()* function is shown in the next listing. I recognize that it's a bit long, but it shows all the code to capture the 12 annual holidays in the United States, save for Easter, which is covered in the next section. Aside from New Year's Day, pay attention to the patterns used for the regular and irregular holidays. Not shown in the listing are the *weekend()* and *main()* functions.

Listing 12.11   The *isholiday()* function

```
int isholiday(struct holiday *h)
{
    char *n[] = {
        "New Years Day",
        "Martin Luther King Day",
        "Presidents Day",
        "Memorial Day",
        "Juneteenth",
        "Independence Day",
        "Labor Day",
        "Columbus Day",
        "Veterans Day",
        "Thanksgiving",
        "Christmas"
    };
    int r;

    if( h->month==11 && h->day==31 && h->wday==FRIDAY )      ◁─┐ New Year's
    {                                                            Day
        h->name = n[0];
        return(2);
    }
    if( h->month==0 && h->day==1 )
    {
        h->name = n[0];
```

```
        return(1);
    }
    if( h->month==0 && h->day==2 && h->wday==MONDAY )
    {
        h->name = n[0];
        return(2);
    }
    if( h->month==0 && h->wday==MONDAY )        <———  Martin Luther
    {                                                  King Jr. Day
        if( THIRD_WEEK )
        {
            h->name = n[1];
            return(1);
        }
    }

    if( h->month==1 && h->wday==MONDAY )        <———  Presidents Day
    {
        if( THIRD_WEEK )
        {
            h->name = n[2];
            return(1);
        }
    }

    if( h->month==4 && h->wday==MONDAY )        <———  Memorial Day
    {
        if( LAST_WEEK )
        {
            h->name = n[3];
            return(1);
        }
    }

    if( h->month==5 )        <———  Juneteenth
    {
        r = weekend(19,h->day,h->wday);
        h->name = n[4];
        return(r);
    }

    if( h->month==6 )        <———  Independence Day
    {
        r = weekend(4,h->day,h->wday);
        h->name = n[5];
        return(r);
    }

    if( h->month==8 && h->wday==MONDAY )        <———  Labor Day
    {
        if( FIRST_WEEK )
        {
            h->name = n[6];
            return(1);
        }
    }
```

```
    if( h->month==9 && h->wday==MONDAY)        <——— Columbus Day
    {
        if( SECOND_WEEK )
        {
            h->name = n[7];
            return(1);
        }
    }

    if( h->month==10 )        <——— Veterans Day
    {
        r = weekend(11,h->day,h->wday);
        h->name = n[8];
        return(r);
    }

    if( h->month==10 && h->wday==THURSDAY )        <——— Thanksgiving
    {
        if( FOURTH_WEEK )
        {
            h->name = n[9];
            return(1);
        }
    }

    if( h->month==11 )        <——— Christmas
    {
        r = weekend(25,h->day,h->wday);
        h->name = n[10];
        return(r);
    }

    return(0);
}
```

Here is a sample run of the program for a nonholiday:

```
Today is 2/20/2022, not a holiday
```

And for a holiday:

```
Today is 2/21/2022, Presidents Day
```

After testing this code more thoroughly, I discovered a flaw for calculating Veterans Day and Thanksgiving, both of which occur in November. Here is the relevant code chunk:

```
    if( h->month==10 )
    {
        r = weekend(11,h->day,h->wday);
        h->name = n[8];
        return(r);
    }
```

```
if( h->month==10 && h->wday==THURSDAY )
{
    if( FOURTH_WEEK )
    {
        h->name = n[9];
        return(1);
    }
}
```

The first *if* test captures all dates for November and returns. This exit means that the next *if* test for November, h->month==10, never occurs. Oops.

To remedy the situation, a single *if* test must be done for November. Then a test can be made for Thanksgiving and then Veterans Day. Here is the udpated code:

```
if( h->month==10 )
{
    if( h->wday==THURSDAY && FOURTH_WEEK )
    {
        h->name = n[9];
        return(1);
    }
    r = weekend(11,h->day,h->wday);
    h->name = n[8];
    return(r);
}
```

With this change made, the code now faithfully reports both Thanksgiving and Veterans Day. All these updates and additions are found in the full source code listing, isholiday05.c, available in the online repository.

The only holiday left is the most difficult to calculate: Easter.

EXERCISE 12.2

In a major update to the code, add constants for the months of the year. Use these constants in the *isholiday()* function so that this comparison

```
if( h->month==0 && h->wday==MONDAY )
```

now reads like this:

```
if( h->month==JANUARY && h->wday==MONDAY )
```

My solution is available in the online repository as isholiday06.c. For bonus points, see if you can use enumerated constants, which is what I did.

12.4.3 *Calculating Easter*

Easter falls on different dates each year because it's the last holiday remaining in Western culture based on the lunar calendar. On the solar calendar, the date of Easter can be as early as March 22 or as late as April 25. It's always on a Sunday.

For the lunar calendar, Easter is the first Sunday after the first new moon after the vernal equinox. This date is based on the Jewish holiday of Passover. So, first comes the spring equinox, when the sun returns to the northern hemisphere and Hades releases Persephone from the underworld. The next full moon—which could be weeks away—must pass, and then the following Friday is Passover with Easter falling on Sunday.

In my original holiday-detector program, written years ago, I hardcoded the date for Easter. It was easy but not a long-lasting solution.

As with determining the moon phase (refer to chapter 2), the date of Easter is best calculated by using an algorithm. As with the moon algorithm, I have no idea what's going on with my Easter algorithm; I just copied it down. But unlike the moon phase algorithm, the Easter algorithm is extremely accurate.

Just a guess: a lot of what you see in the next listing deals with mapping the moon's cycle to the solar year, as well as accounting for leap years. What a wonder! The value passed to the *easter()* function represents a year. No value is returned, because the function itself outputs the date of Easter. Building this code requires inclusion of the `math.h` header file, which implies that you link in the math library for many platforms: use the `-lm` (little L) switch, specified last when building at the command prompt.

Listing 12.12   The *easter()* function from source code file `easter01.c`

Accepts a year value as the only argument

Lots of `int` variables

Lots of `double` variables

Math goes on for a while.

Obtains the month for Easter, either 3 (March) or 4 (April)

Obtains the day of the month

Outputs results

```c
void easter(int year)
{
    int Y,a,c,e,h,k,L;
    double b,d,f,g,i,m,month,day;

    Y = year;
    a = Y%19;
    b = floor(Y/100);
    c = Y%100;
    d = floor(b/4);
    e = (int)b%4;
    f = floor((b+8)/25);
    g = floor((b-f+1)/3);
    h = (19*a+(int)b-(int)d-(int)g+15)%30;
    i = floor(c/4);
    k = c%4;
    L = (32+2*e+2*(int)i-h-k)%7;
    m = floor((a+11*h+22*L)/451);
    month = floor((h+L-7*m+114)/31);
    day = ((h+L-7*(int)m+114)%31)+1;

    printf("In %d, Easter is ",Y);
    if(month == 3)
        printf("March %d\n",(int)day);
    else
        printf("April %d\n",(int)day);
}
```

The full source code file including the *easter()* function is available in the online repository as `easter01.c`. What's missing from listing 12.13 is the *main()* function. It contains a loop that calls the *easter()* function with year values from 2018 through 2035:

```
In 2018, Easter is April 1
In 2019, Easter is April 21
In 2020, Easter is April 12
In 2021, Easter is April 4
In 2022, Easter is April 17
In 2023, Easter is April 9
In 2024, Easter is March 31
In 2025, Easter is April 20
In 2026, Easter is April 5
In 2027, Easter is March 28
In 2028, Easter is April 16
In 2029, Easter is April 1
In 2030, Easter is April 21
In 2031, Easter is April 13
In 2032, Easter is March 28
In 2033, Easter is April 17
In 2034, Easter is April 9
In 2035, Easter is March 25
```

Merging the *easter()* into the *isholiday()* function requires too much work. Instead, I sought to include *easter()* as a companion function called by *isholiday()*—like the *weekend()* function already in the code.

The *easter()* function must be modified to accept a date value and return 1 or 0 depending on whether the date matches Easter for the given year. To begin this journey, a few changes are required to update the existing *isholiday* code. First, the `holiday` structure must be modified to also include a `year` member:

```
struct holiday {
  int month;
  int day;
  int year;
  int wday;
  char *name;
};
```

Second, the `year` member's value must be assigned in the *main()* function:

```
h.year = today->tm_yeari+1900;
```

Remember to add 1900 to the year value!

Third, a call must be made to *easter()* in the *isholiday()* function. At the start of the function, a string for Easter is added to the `n[]` pointer array. I chose to add the string at the end, which doesn't upset the existing array numbering elsewhere in the function. The `"Easter"` string is last in the array declaration, `n[11]`.

These statements in the *isholiday()* function call the *easter()* function. They are the last few statements in the function, right before the final *return*:

```
r = easter(h);
if( r==1 )
{
    h->name = n[10];
    return(r);
}
```

The next listing shows the updated *easter()* function, changed to accommodate a holiday structure pointer as its argument and to return 1 or 0, whether the current date is or is not Easter, respectively.

Listing 12.13   The updated *easter()* function as it sits in source code `isholiday07.c`

```
int easter(struct holiday *hday)
{
    int Y,a,c,e,h,k,L;
    double b,d,f,g,i,m,month,day;

    Y = hday->year;
    a = Y%19;
    b = floor(Y/100);
    c = Y%100;
    d = floor(b/4);
    e = (int)b%4;
    f = floor((b+8)/25);
    g = floor((b-f+1)/3);
    h = (19*a+(int)b-(int)d-(int)g+15)%30;
    i = floor(c/4);
    k = c%4;
    L = (32+2*e+2*(int)i-h-k)%7;
    m = floor((a+11*h+22*L)/451);
    month = floor((h+L-7*m+114)/31)-1;
    day = ((h+L-7*(int)m+114)%31)+1;

    if( hday->month==month && hday->day==day )
        return(1);
    else
        return(0);
}
```

The function definition is changed, accepting structure pointer `hday` and returning an int value.

I couldn't use variable `h` as the function's argument because it's already used in the algorithm and I don't want to mess with it.

Subtracts one from the final month value because January is zero in this code

Tests to see whether today is Easter

Returns 1 if it is

Returns 0 otherwise

Finally, remember to add the `math.h` header file so that the compiler doesn't barf over the *floor()* function used in the *easter()* function. And ensure that when you build the code, you link in the math library, `-lm` (little L). All these changes and updates are found in the source code file `isholiday07.c`, available from this book's online repository.

The code runs as it did before, but now it recognizes Easter. Here is a sample run for Easter 2022:

```
Today is 4/17/2022, Easter
```

12.4.4 *Running the date gauntlet*

To test the *isholiday()* function, you must run it through the date gauntlet. This test is how I refer to a program that generates dates from January 1 through December 31 for a given year. The goal is to ensure that the *isholiday()* function properly reacts, reporting the national holidays.

The next listing shows the code for gauntlet01.c. It contains two arrays of string constants to represent months and days of the week. The mdays[] array lists the number of days in each month, where it's assumed the year isn't a leap year; February has only 28 days in the code. The dates are output in a nested loop: the outer loop processes months, and the inner loop churns days of the month.

Listing 12.14   Source code for gauntlet01.c

```
#include <stdio.h>

int main()
{
    const char *month[] = {
        "January", "February", "March", "April",
        "May", "June", "July", "August",
        "September", "October", "November", "December"
    };
    const char *weekday[] = {
        "Sunday", "Monday", "Tuesday", "Wednesday",
        "Thursday", "Friday", "Saturday"
    };
    int mdays[] = { 31, 28, 31, 30, 31, 30, 31, 31,
        30, 31, 30, 31 };
    enum { SU, MO, TU, WE, TH, FR, SA };
    int start_day,dom,doy,year,m;

    start_day = SA;
    doy = 1;
    year = 2022;
    for( m=0; m<12; m++ )
    {
        for( dom=1; dom<=mdays[m]; dom++ )
        {
            printf("%s, %s %d, %d\n",
                    weekday[ (doy+start_day-1) % 7],
                    month[m],
                    dom,
                    year
                );
            doy++;
        }
    }

    return(0);
}
```

Determines days of each month, assuming it isn't a leap year

Shortcuts for January 1, starting day of the week

The first day of the year

The year to be output (not a leap year)

Sets the starting day for 2022, Saturday

Loops through 12 months of the year

Loops through each day of the month

Scary math to determine the proper day of the week

Increments the day of the year

The math in the code determines the proper day of the week. This detail is based on the start_day variable set to the proper day of the week for January 1, which is a Saturday—enumerated constant SA in the code. The day-of-the-year variable, doy, is used in this calculation, incremented in the inner loop to keep track of each day of the year.

The source code for gauntlet01.c is available in the online repository. Here is the abbreviated output:

```
Saturday, January 1, 2022
Sunday, January 2, 2022
Monday, January 3, 2022
Tuesday, January 4, 2022
...
Tuesday, December 27, 2022
Wednesday, December 28, 2022
Thursday, December 29, 2022
Friday, December 30, 2022
Saturday, December 31, 2022
```

These days all check out, matching up perfectly with the date and day of the week for the year 2022. I changed some of the variables in the code to test other years as well, and it all works.

The next step is to add the functions *isholiday(), weekend(),* and *easter()* to the code—the entire *isholiday* package—to confirm that all holidays are properly tracked throughout the year. As the gauntlet code churns through days of the year, the *isholiday()* function is called. Only holidays are output. As a review, here are the US national holidays and their days and dates for 2022:

- New Year's Day: Saturday, January 1
- Martin Luther King Jr. Day: Monday, January 17
- Washington's Birthday/Presidents Day: Monday, February 21
- Easter: Sunday, April 17
- Memorial Day: Monday, May 30
- Juneteenth: Sunday, June 19
- Juneteenth observed: Monday, June 20
- Independence Day: Monday, July 4
- Labor Day: Monday, September 5
- Columbus Day: Monday, October 10
- Veterans Day: Friday, November 11
- Thanksgiving: Thursday, November 24
- Christmas: Sunday, December 25
- Christmas Day observed: Monday, December 26

The update to the code is found in the online repository as gauntlet02.c. It features only minor changes to the *main()* function for output formatting. Remember that this code requires linking of the math library, -lm (little L), so that the math functions in Easter all behave well. Here is the output:

```
Saturday, January 1, 2022 is New Years Day
Monday, January 17, 2022 is Martin Luther King Day
Monday, February 21, 2022 is Presidents Day
Sunday, April 17, 2022 is Easter
Monday, May 30, 2022 is Memorial Day
Sunday, June 19, 2022 is Juneteenth
Monday, June 20, 2022 Juneteenth is observed
Monday, July 4, 2022 is Independence Day
Monday, September 5, 2022 is Labor Day
Monday, October 10, 2022 is Columbus Day
Friday, November 11, 2022 is Veterans Day
Thursday, November 24, 2022 is Thanksgiving
Sunday, December 25, 2022 is Christmas
Monday, December 26, 2022 Christmas is observed
```

The *isholiday()* function can be incorporated into a variety of your source code files, or you can make it its own module to be linked in with special programs. This process is reviewed in chapter 13, which covers outputting a colorful calendar.

Calendar

It wasn't just the Mayans who invented their own calendar. Just about every early culture featured some form of classification for the passage of days. The Mayans gained notoriety in 2012 because it was the end of one of their great calendrical cycles—the long count, or *b'ak'tun*. It wasn't the end of the world—more like turning the page on one of those cheap insurance company calendars. Bummer.

Most cultures start with lunar calendars and eventually switch to solar calendars, either fully or reluctantly. Hebrew, Muslim, Eastern Orthodox, and Chinese calendars are still used today, with different year values and lunar features. Julius Caesar took a stab at updating the Roman calendar system—before the Senate took various stabs at him. And Pope Gregory introduced our modern calendar system in the year 1582.

Even with calendar utilities handy, coding your own calendar tools helps hone your time programming skills in C and more. In this chapter, you learn to:

- Appreciate the *cal* program
- Calculate holidays
- Code week, month, and year utilities
- Output color text
- Color-code important dates

Yes, Unix has featured the *cal* program since the steam-powered days. Still, understanding date-and-time programming is important for all C coders. By practicing on these utilities, you can better code your own, custom date programs. You can also use the techniques presented here in any program that relies upon date calculations.

13.1   *The calendar program*

The calendar program developed for AT&T Unix (System V) is called *cal*. Linux inherited this fine tool. The default output, with no options specified, displays the current month in this format:

```
$ cal
    December 2021
Su Mo Tu We Th Fr Sa
          1  2  3  4
 5  6  7  8  9 10 11
12 13 14 15 16 17 18
19 20 21 22 23 24 25
26 27 28 29 30 31
```

The current day is shown inverse, such as the 20th above.

You can follow *cal* with a year argument to obtain the full, 12-month calendar for the given year:

```
$ cal 1993
```

You can add a month argument to see the calendar for a specific month in a specific year:

```
$ cal 10 1960
```

The month can be specified numerically or by name. To see the next three months of output, specify the -A2 argument:

```
$ cal -A2
```

Like many classic Unix utilities, the *cal* program is burdened with a plethora of easily forgettable options and unmemorable switches.

The program's output is consistent: the first row is the full month name and full year. The next row is the weekday header. The program then outputs six rows of text for the calendar. When a month lacks a sixth week, the last row of output is blank.

The only thing the *cal* program doesn't do is output the calendar sideways. This job is handled by the updated version, the *ncal* program:

```
$ ncal
      December 2021
Su      5 12 19 26
Mo      6 13 20 27
Tu      7 14 21 28
We   1  8 15 22 29
Th   2  9 16 23 30
Fr   3 10 17 24 31
Sa   4 11 18 25
```

The advantage of the *ncal* program is that it outputs the entire year in a grid four months wide, which makes it easier to read on a text screen. The *cal* program uses a grid three months wide when it outputs an entire year.

You could just use these utilities and go right along on your merry Linux adventures, but then what do you learn? Further, it's possible to customize calendar output to however you prefer. As with any programming project, the possibilities are endless—providing that the caffeine and chips don't run out.

Calendar trivia

- When Julius Caesar's calendar was adopted in 46 BC, the year became 445 days long. This change was to align the new calendar with the solar year. It became the longest year in history.
- English month names are derived from the old Roman calendar: Ianuarius (January), Februarius (February), Martius (March), Aprilis (April), Maius (May), Iunius (June), Quintilis (July), Sextilis (August), September, October, November, and December.
- Some religious ceremonies continue to be based on Julian calendar dates—specifically, in the Eastern Orthodox Church.
- When Pope Gregory adopted the current, Gregorian calendar in 1582, October 4 was immediately followed by October 15.
- The effect of the Gregorian calendar's adoption by Great Britain is reflected in the *cal* program's output for September 1752. Type **cal 9 1752** to see a shortened month as the old calendar was adjusted to the new.
- Even with the improved Gregorian calendar, leap seconds are added to the year every so often.
- The number of times Friday falls on the 13th in a specific month varies from one to three times a year.
- During nonleap years, February and March share the same date patterns—up until March 29, of course.
- A sidereal year is based on the time it takes Planet Earth to make a lap around the sun. Its value is 365.256363 days.
- A lunar year consists of 12 moon cycles. It's 354.37 days long.
- Intercalary months are added to lunar calendars every few years to resynchronize the moon cycle with the solar calendar.
- A galactic year is 230,000,000 (solar) years long. It's the time it takes the sun to orbit the Milky Way galaxy—or the time it takes a toddler to find a matching pair of socks.

13.2   *Good dates to know*

C programmers familiar with the library's time functions know that date-and-time tidbits can easily be extracted from the current timestamp, available from the operating system: values are available for the year, month, day of the month, and day of the week. These items are all you need to construct a calendar for the current week or month. But what about next month? What about July in 1978? For these details, your code must work harder.

Making date calculations is difficult because some months have 30 days and some have 31. Once every four years, February decides to grow another day—but even this leap day isn't consistent. To help you properly program dates, you must code some tools.

13.2.1 *Creating constants and enumerating dates*

More than most of my programming, it seems like date programming brings in a lot of constants—specifically, string and symbolic constants for weekday and month names. For my date programming, I employ both types of constants and try to do so consistently for all my date-and-time related functions.

For weekday and month names, I use *const char* pointers—string constants. The weekday constants are:

```
const char *weekday[] = {
    "Sunday", "Monday", "Tuesday", "Wednesday",
    "Thursday", "Friday", "Saturday"
};
```

Shorter versions are also used:

```
const char *weekday[] = {
    "Sun", "Mon", "Tue", "Wed",
    "Thu", "Fri", "Sat"
};
```

Here are my favorite month constants:

```
const char *month[] = {
    "January", "February", "March", "April",
    "May", "June", "July", "August",
    "September", "October", "November", "December"
};
```

Each statement creates an array of pointers; storage for each string is allocated by the program at runtime. What remains is an array of addresses. Each array is in a sequence that matches the tm_wday and tm_mon members of the tm structure returned from the *localtime()* function. For example, the tm_mon member for January is numbered 0, and the zeroth element of the month[] array is the string for January.

The *const* classifier declares these arrays as immutable, which prevents them from being accidentally altered elsewhere in the code. The strings can be passed to functions, but don't change them! Doing so leads to unpredictable behavior, but not when they're classified as constants.

Pairing with these two arrays, I also use enumerated constants to represent the weekday and month values. The C language *enum* keyword makes creating these constants easy.

Don't tell me you've avoided the *enum* keyword because it's weird. I did so for too long. Yet *enum* helps you define constants similarly to the way an array defines groups of variables with the same data type. For weekday and month names, *enum* provides a helpful tool to create these constants and make your code more readable.

As a review, the *enum* keyword is followed by a set of braces that contain the enumerated (numbered) constants. Values are assigned sequentially, starting with 0:

```
enum { FALSE, TRUE };
```

Here, constant FALSE is defined as 0; TRUE, as 1.

You can use an assignment operator to alter the number sequencing:

```
enum { ALPHA=1, GAMMA=5, DELTA, EPSILON, THETA };
```

This statement defines constant ALPHA as 1. Constant GAMMA is set equal to 5, with the rest of the constants numbered sequentially: DELTA is 6, EPSILON is 7, and THETA is 8.

The weekday values reported from the *localtime()* function start with 0 for Sunday. Here is the *enum* statement to declare weekday values for use in your code:

```
enum { SUNDAY, MONDAY, TUESDAY, WEDNESDAY, THURSDAY, FRIDAY, SATURDAY };
```

For the 12 months, you can split the *enum* statement across multiple lines, just as you can split any statement in C:

```
enum { JANUARY, FEBRUARY, MARCH, APRIL,
    MAY, JUNE, JULY, AUGUST,
    SEPTEMBER, OCTOBER, NOVEMBER, DECEMBER };
```

As with weekdays, the *localtime()* function uses 0 to represent January. These enumerated constants are ready to use in your code. For example:

```
printf("%s\n",month[JANUARY]);
```

Using the month[] array defined earlier in this section, along with enumerated constant JANUARY, the previous statement outputs the text January. This construction is self-documenting and easier to read than using month[0] or something equally vague without reference to what 0 could mean.

13.2.2 *Finding the day of the week*

After arriving at the destination, the first thing a time traveler asks is, "What year is it?" This question provides a big-picture answer, but it also helps the production design team understand how to visually misinterpret various eras in history. And it allows the locals to predictably respond, "What are you talking about, stranger in the silver pajamas?"

For calendar programming, yes, knowing the current year is important. Also necessary to plotting out a calendar is knowing month, day, and—vitally—the weekday. The day-and-weekday info are key to unlocking the first day of the month. The other time tidbits are easily obtained from the data reported by the *time()* and *localtime()* functions.

In the next listing, the *time()* function obtains the current epoch value, a *time_t* data type. The *localtime()* function uses this value to fill a tm structure, date. The month, month day, year, and weekday values are then interpreted and output, displaying the current day and date.

Listing 13.1   Source code for `weekday01.c`

```
#include <stdio.h>
#include <time.h>

int main()
{
    const char *weekday[] = {                    String constants
        "Sunday", "Monday", "Tuesday", "Wednesday",   for the days of
        "Thursday", "Friday", "Saturday"             the week
    };
    const char *month[] = {                      String constants
        "January", "February", "March", "April",     for months of
        "May", "June", "July", "August",             the year
        "September", "October", "November", "December"
    };
    time_t now;          Variable to store the clock ticks
    struct tm *date;     Variable to store time tidbits

    time(&now);          Obtains the current clock tick value
    date = localtime(&now);    Fills the tm date structure with individual time values

    printf("Today is %s %d, %d, a %s\n",     Outputs the results
            month[ date->tm_mon ],
            date->tm_mday,
            date->tm_year+1900,
            weekday[ date->tm_wday ]
        );

    return(0);
}
```

The string constants declared in `weekday01.c` are used throughout this chapter. Remember to define them as *const char* variables; you don't want to mess with the string's contents, lest all sorts of mayhem ensue.

The program built from the code in listing 13.1 outputs a simple string, reflecting the current date and weekday:

```
Today is May 1, 2022, a Sunday
```

You can use the date info generated in the program to plot out a calendar—for the current month. To figure out how the following July maps out on a calendar, you must apply some math. To help you, and avoid all that boring trial-and-error, you can steal an algorithm from the internet.

Before computers on desktops were a thing, I remember one of my elementary school teachers demonstrating an algorithm to find the weekday for any day, month, and year. It's simple enough that you can perform the math in your head without exploding. I forget what my teacher wrote on the chalkboard, but here's the algorithm, freshly stolen from the internet:

```
int t[] = { 0, 3, 2, 5, 0, 3, 5, 1, 4, 6, 2, 4 };
year -= month<3;
r = ( year + year/4 - year/100 + year/400 + t[month-1] + day) % 7
```

Array t[] holds the algorithm's magic. I'm unsure what the data references, though my guess is that it's probably some sort of month pattern index. The year value is reduced by 1 for the months of January and February. Then variable r captures the day of the week, with Sunday being 0. I assume most of the year manipulation in the expression is to compensate for leap years. Further, this algorithm assumes that the value of January is 1, not 0. These differences can be adjusted as shown in the *dayoftheweek()* function in the following listing.

Listing 13.2   The *dayoftheweek()* function

```
int dayoftheweek(int m,int d,int y)          ◁    The month value, m, ranges from 0 through
{                                                 11 for January through December; d is the
    int t[] = {                      ◁            day of the month, and y is the full year value
        0, 3, 2, 5, 0, 3,            The magic    (tm_year+1900).
        5, 1, 4, 6, 2, 4             array
    };
    int r;                                        The m<2 evaluation is either
                                                  1 or 0, which is added to
    y -= m<2;                                ◁    the year variable.
    r = ( y + y/4 - y/100 + y/400 + t[m] + d) % 7;   ◁
    return(r);                                        The rest of the algorithm,
}                                                     with m used without
                                                      modification as the
                                                      element number
```

I updated the *main()* function from weekday01.c to call the *dayoftheweek()* function. Specific values are set for month, day, and year variables, which are passed to the function. The result is then output. These modifications are found in the online repository as source code file weekday02.c. Here is some sample output:

```
February 3, 1993 is a Wednesday
```

The capability to obtain these four date details—year, month, day, and day of the week—is key to creating a calendar. The next step is to calculate the first day of the month, with the rest of the days flowing after.

EXERCISE 13.1

If you're like me, you probably played with the source code from weekday02.c, typing in your birthday or some other important date out of curiosity. But why keep updating the source code?

Your task for this exercise is to modify the source code from `weekday02.c` so that command-line arguments are interpreted as the month, day, and year for which you want to find the day of the week. And if your locale doesn't like the argument order—you can change it! Here is a sample run of my solution, which I call *weekday*:

```
$ weekday 10 19 1987
October 19, 1987 is a Monday
```

My solution is available in the online repository as `weekday03.c`.

13.2.3   *Calculating the first day of the month*

Today is the 20th day of the month—any month. It's a Monday. On which day of the week did the first day of the month fall?

Uh . . .

Quick! Use the handy illustration in figure 13.1 to help your calculations. If today is Monday the 20th, the first of the month is on a Wednesday, always, for any month where Monday is the 20th.

When given a day of the month and its weekday, the computer can easily calculate upon which day the first of the month falls. Here is the formula I devised to determine the weekday for the first of the month when given the current weekday and day of the month:

Sun	Mon	Tue	Wed	Thu	Fri	Sat
			1	2	3	4
5	6	7	8	9	10	11
12	13	14	15	16	17	18
19	20	21	22	23	24	25
26	27	28	29	30		

Figure 13.1   A month where the 20th is a Monday

```
first = weekday - ( day % 7 ) + 1;
```

To work through the formula with figure 13.1, assume that today is the 23rd—which it is as I write this text. It's a Thursday, numeric value 4:

```
first = 4 - ( 23 % 7 ) + 1
first = 4 - ( 2 ) + 1
first = 3
```

When a month has the 23rd fall on a Thursday, the first is on a Wednesday (value 3). Refer to figure 13.1 to confirm.

To put my first-of-the-month algorithm to the test, the next listing shows code that obtains the current date. It uses the weekday and day of the month values to work the algorithm, outputting on which weekday the first of the month falls.

Listing 13.3   Source code for `thefirst01.c`

```
#include <stdio.h>
#include <time.h>

int main()
{
    const char *weekday[] = {
```

```
         "Sunday", "Monday", "Tuesday", "Wednesday",
         "Thursday", "Friday", "Saturday"
     };
     time_t now;
     struct tm *date;
     int first;                       Obtains the
                                      current clock
                                      tick value
     time(&now);         <───┘                      Fills the tm
     date = localtime(&now);                  <───┘  structure date

                                                              Works the
                                                              algorithm
     first = date->tm_wday - ( date->tm_mday % 7 ) + 1;   <───┘


     printf("The first of this month was on a %s\n",    <───
             weekday[first]                                    Outputs the
           );                                                  results

     return(0);
}
```

The source code for `thefirst01.c` is available in the online repository, but don't get excited about it. If the current weekday value is greater than the weekday value for the first of the month, the program works, as it did on my computer:

```
The first of this month was on a Wednesday
```

If the current weekday value is less than the weekday value of the first of the month, the code fails. For example, if today is Tuesday (2) and the first is on Friday (5), you see something like this delightful output:

```
Segmentation fault (core dumped)
```

The reason for the core dump is that the value stored in `first` drops below 0. This error can be corrected by testing for a negative value of `first`:

```
first = WEDNESDAY - ( 12 % 7 ) + 1;
if( first < 0 )
    first += 7;
```

In this update to the code, I use enumerated constant `WEDNESDAY` as the weekday and 12 as the day of the month. The first of the month is on a Saturday. Here is the code's output:

```
The first of this month was on a Saturday
```

Finding the weekday for the first of the month may seem silly. After all, from the preceding section you find code that locates the day of the week for any day of the month. The issue is that you're often not given the first of the month. Sure, you could write more code that calls the *dayoftheweek()* function after modifying the current day of the month. But I find that using the algorithm works best for me.

EXERCISE 13.2

It's time to write another function! From the source code file `thefirst02.c`, pull out the algorithm portion of the *main()* function and set it into its own function, *thefirst()*. This function is prototyped like this:

```
int thefirst(int wday, int mday)
```

Variable `wday` is the day of the week, `mday` is the day of the month. The value returned is the weekday for the first of the month, range 0 through 6.

My solution is available in the online repository as `thefirst03.c`. I wrote code in the *main()* function to report the first of the month when the current day is the 25th, a Saturday. Comments in the code explain my approach.

13.2.4 *Identifying leap years*

You can't discuss date programming without bringing up the squidgy issue of leap years. The varying number of days in February is yet another example of the universe trying to tell us that nothing would exist if everything were in perfect balance.

When I work with days in the month, I typically write an array like this:

```
int mdays[] = { 31, 28, 31, 30, 31, 30, 31, 31, 30, 31, 30, 31 };
```

This array holds the number of days for January through December. For February, the value is 28. But one out of every four years (on average), February has 29 days—the extra leap day in a leap year.

To determine which years are leap years, and adjust the `mdays[]`, you must do some math. Here are the leap year rules in order of elimination:

- If the year is divisible by both 100 and 400, it's a leap year.
- If the year is divisible only by 100, it's not a leap year.
- If the year is divisible by four, it's a leap year.

Normally, the leap year rules are listed in reverse order: If the year is divisible by four, it's a leap year, unless the year is divisible by 100, in which case it's not a leap year, unless the year is also divisible by 400, in which case it is a leap year.

Got it?

No, it's easier to list the rules upside down, which also helps to write a leap year function, *february()*, shown next. Its purpose is to return the number of days in February, a value then set into an array like `mdays[]` (shown earlier). The rules for calculating a leap year appear in the function as a series of *if* tests based on the `year` value passed.

Listing 13.4   The *february()* function

```
int february(int year)
{
    if( year%400==0 )           ◁─┐  If the year is divisible
        return(29);                │  by 400 (which includes
                                   │  100), it's a leap year.
```

```
if ( year%100==0 )
    return(28);
```
◁— If the year is divisible by 100, it's a leap year.

```
if ( year%4!=0 )
    return(28);
```
◁— If the year is not a multiple of four, it's not a leap year.

```
    return(29);
}
```
◁— Otherwise, it's a leap year.

I use the *february()* function in the source code file `leapyear01.c`, available in the online repository. In the *main()* function, a loop tests the years 1584 through 2101, which span the time from when the Gregorian calendar began to when the lizard people finally invade. If the year is a leap year, meaning the *february()* function returns 29, its value is output. Here is the tail end of a sample run:

```
...
1996
2000
2004
2008
2012
2016
2020
2024
2028
2032
```

The code accurately identifies the year 2000 as a leap year.

The *february()* function is used in programs demonstrated later in this chapter to update the `mdays[]` array to reflect the proper number of days in February for a given year.

13.2.5 *Getting the time zone correct*

One weirdo issue to consider when dealing with dates is the computer's time zone. This value is set according to the system's locale. It reflects the local time of day, which is what's accessed when you program dates and time in C.

Normally, the time zone detail is ignored; what you want to obtain from the *time()* function is the current date and time for the computer or other device's location. However, if your code doesn't account for the difference between GMT, or Greenwich Mean Time, and your local time zone, the time calculation you make could be inaccurate.

For example, my time zone is US Pacific. If I'm not careful, the eight-hour time difference gives me results that are off by eight hours. Believe it or not, this level of chronological accuracy is necessary for a program to spit out an accurate calendar.

To drive home this concern, consider the source code in the next listing. It initializes a *time_t* value to 0, which is the dawn of the Unix epoch, or midnight January 1, 1970. This value is output in a *printf()* statement, which uses the *ctime()* function to convert a *time_t* value into a human-readable string.

Listing 13.5   Source code for `timezone01.c`

```
#include <stdio.h>
#include <time.h>

int main()
{
    time_t epoch = 0;

    printf("Time is %s\n",ctime(&epoch) );

    return(0);
}
```

Presets the *time_t* value to zero, the dawn of the Unix epoch

Outputs the time string for the epoch

When the program is run, I see this text on my computer:

```
Time is Wed Dec 31 16:00:00 1969
```

The output shows eight hours before the epoch began (midnight, January 1) because my computer's time zone is set to GMT-8 (Greenwich Mean Time minus eight hours), or Pacific Standard Time. The output is accurate: when it was midnight on January 1 in the UK, it was 4:00 P.M. the day before here on the West Coast of the United States.

In Linux, you can check the computer's time zone information by examining the `/etc/localtime` symbolic link. Use the **ls -l** (dash-L) command:

```
ls -l /etc/localtime
```

Here is the relevant part of the output I see on my system:

```
/etc/localtime -> /usr/share/zoneinfo/America/Los_Angeles
```

My time zone is set the same as in Los Angeles, though the people are much nicer where I live. The output you see is local to your system, a value set when Linux was first configured.

Your code need not look up the `/etc/localtime` symbolic link to determine the computer's time zone or attempt to change this setting. Instead, you can write code to temporarily set the `TZ` (time zone) environment variable to GMT. To make this update to the source code for `timezone01.c`, you must add two functions: *putenv()* and *tzset()*.

The *putenv()* adds an environment variable to the program's local environment; the change doesn't affect the shell, so it's not something you must undo later in the code. The *man* page format is

```
int putenv(char *string);
```

The `string` is the environment entry to add. In this case, it's `TZ=GMT` for "time zone equals Greenwich Mean Time" exactly, the time zone you want. This function requires the inclusion of the `stdlib.h` library.

The *tzset()* function sets the program's time zone—but only while it runs. The function doesn't otherwise alter the system. Here is the *man* page format:

```
void tzset(void);
```

The *tzset()* function requires no arguments because it uses the TZ environment variable to set the program's time zone. The time.h header file must be included for this function to behave properly.

To update the code for timezone01.c, add the following two statements before the *printf()* statement:

```
putenv("TZ=GMT");
tzset();
```

And don't forget to include the stdlib.h header file for the *putenv()* function. These changes are found in the online repository in the source code file timezone02.c. Here is the program's output:

```
Time is Thu Jan  1 00:00:00 1970
```

The output now reflects the true Unix epoch as the program's time zone is changed to GMT internally.

This code is used later in this chapter, when the full year calendar is generated. Without making the adjustment, the calendar outputs the incorrect year, before or after the desired year based on your local time zone. The time zone adjustment ensures that the calendar is properly aligned. You can also use this trick in other programs that rely upon precise time-and-date calculations.

13.3 Calendar utilities

The Linux *cal* program does more than you can imagine. It's impressive. Given its abundance of options and switches, *cal* can output dates in a given range for a given locale in a specific format. As with other Linux command-line programs I've aped, the goal for my calendar programs is to be specific, as opposed to writing one program that does everything.

I first coded my calendar programs because I wanted to see output for the current month in a wider format than what the *cal* program generates. Also, I just wanted to see whether I could code a calendar for any given month. The result is my *month* program, which I use far more often than *cal*.

One decision to make right away with any calendar utility is whether the week starts on Monday or Sunday. The *cal* program (as you may suspect) has options to set the week's starting day. For my series of calendar programs in this chapter, it's assumed that the week starts on Sunday.

13.3.1 *Generating a week*

I suppose the simplest calendar would output only the current day—something like this:

```
September 2022
Friday
23
```

Most people want more from a calendar. But rather than start with the current month, my first calendar program shows the current week. This code hinges upon knowing the current day of the month and weekday. Here is the output I want to see for the final program:

```
December / January - Week 52
Sun Mon Tue Wed Thu Fri Sat
[26] 27  28   29  30  31   1
```

The current day is December 26. The month (and year) ends on Friday, with Saturday being the first of January and the new year. It's the 52nd week of the year.

Before coding all that output, I want to start small and output only the current week. A loop outputs the days, Sunday through Saturday. No matter which weekday it is currently, the output starts on Sunday. Today's day is highlighted in brackets.

The *localtime()* function reports details about the current day of the week. The formula I use to determine Sunday's date is:

```
sunday = day_of_the_month - weekday;
```

The `day_of_the_month` value is found in the `tm` structure, member `tm_mday`. Today's weekday value is member `tm_wday`. As an example, if today is Thursday the 16th, the formula reads:

```
sunday = 16 - 4;
```

The date for Sunday is the 12th, which checks out on the monthly calendar shown in figure 13.1, earlier in this chapter. The `sunday` value is then used in a loop to output the seven days of the week:

```
for( d=sunday; d<sunday+7; d++ )
```

I output the consecutive days in a space four characters wide. This room allows for today's date to be output embraced by square brackets.

The full code for my `week01.c` program is shown in the next listing. It reads data from the *time()* and *localtime()* functions, outputs the current month (but not the year), and outputs dates for the current week. I use variables `day`, `month`, and `weekday` as readable shortcuts for their related members of the `tm` structure.

Listing 13.6   Source code for `week01.c`

```
#include <stdio.h>
#include <time.h>

int main()
{
    const char *months[] = {
        "January", "February", "March", "April",
        "May", "June", "July", "August",
        "September", "October", "November", "December"
    };
    time_t now;
    struct tm *date;
    int day,weekday,month,sunday,d;

    time(&now);
    date = localtime(&now);

    day = date->tm_mday;
    month = date->tm_mon;
    weekday = date->tm_wday;
    sunday = day - weekday;

    printf("   %s\n",months[month]);
    printf("Sun Mon Tue Wed Thu Fri Sat\n");
    for( d=sunday; d<sunday+7; d++ )
    {
        if( d==day )
            printf("[%2d] ",d);
        else
            printf(" %2d ",d);
    }
    putchar('\n');

    return(0);
}
```

Annotations:
- Obtains the current time in clock ticks → `time(&now);`
- Converts the `time_t` value into `tm` structure members → `date = localtime(&now);`
- Sets the day, `month`, and `weekday` values for convenience and readability → `day = date->tm_mday;` `month = date->tm_mon;` `weekday = date->tm_wday;`
- Calculates the date for Sunday → `sunday = day - weekday;`
- Outputs the first line, the current month → `printf("   %s\n",months[month]);`
- Outputs the day of the week header row → `printf("Sun Mon Tue Wed Thu Fri Sat\n");`
- Loops through days of the week, Sunday through Sunday + 7 → `for( d=sunday; d<sunday+7; d++ )`
- For the current day, outputs its value in brackets → `if( d==day )` `printf("[%2d] ",d);`
- Outputs every other day without brackets → `else` `printf(" %2d ",d);`

The source code from listing 13.6 is available in the online repository as `week01.c`. Its core consists of three lines of output, with the third line generated by a loop. The loop outputs days of the week, starting at Sunday. The current day is highlighted, as shown in the sample output:

```
   September
Sun Mon Tue Wed Thu Fri Sat
 12  13  14  15 [16] 17  18
```

Of course, this code isn't perfect. If the first of the month falls on any day other than Sunday, you see output like this:

```
   September
Sun Mon Tue Wed Thu Fri Sat
 -3  -2  -1   0   1 [ 2]  3
```

Likewise, at the end of the month, you can see output like this:

```
September
Sun Mon Tue Wed Thu Fri Sat
 26  27 [28] 29  30  31  32
```

For my first update to the code, I added another decision in the output: In the *for* loop, if the value of variable d is less than one, spaces are output instead of the day value. Likewise, spaces are output when the day value is greater than the number of days in the current month.

Determining the last day of the month requires more code. Specifically, you must add the mdays[] array that lists days of each month, and also the *february()* function, covered earlier in this chapter. This function is necessary to ensure that the proper number of days in February is known for the current year.

The mdays[] array is added to the code in the variable declaration part of the *main()* function:

```
int mdays[] = { 31, 28, 31, 30, 31, 30, 31, 31, 30, 31, 30, 31 };
```

The *february()* function is also added to the source code. After the *localtime()* function is called, the *february()* function is called to update the mdays[] array, element one:

```
mdays[1] = february(date->tm_year+1900);
```

The following code shows the updated *for* loop in the *main()* function. The first *if* decision outputs spaces for out-of-range dates. The *else* portion consists of the original *if-else* decision from the first version of the code.

Listing 13.7　The updated *for* loop found in week02.c

```
for( d=sunday; d<sunday+7; d++ )
{
    if( d<1 || d>mdays[month] )         ◁── If date d is out of range, less than 1,
        printf("     ");                       or greater than the number of days in
    else                                        the current month, outputs spaces
    {
        if( d==day )           ◁──  Outputs the current
            printf("[%2d]",d);        day with brackets
        else                    ┌── Outputs other days
            printf(" %2d ",d);  ◁──  without brackets
    }
}
```

This update to the source code is found in the online repository as week02.c. It accurately addresses the date overflow issues, as shown in this sample output:

```
September
Sun Mon Tue Wed Thu Fri Sat
                 1 [ 2]  3
```

At the end of the month, the output now looks like this:

```
  September
Sun Mon Tue Wed Thu Fri Sat
 26  27 [28] 29  30
```

Delightfully awkward output happens when today is the first and it's a Saturday:

```
  January
Sun Mon Tue Wed Thu Fri Sat
                        [ 1]
```

I don't want this program to show multiple weeks, which would eventually devolve it into a month program. No, what would be keen is to output those final days from the preceding month, like this:

```
  December / January
Sun Mon Tue Wed Thu Fri Sat
 26  27  28  29  30  31  [ 1]
```

Both months are listed in the header because dates from both months appear in the output. The current date is highlighted so that an astute user (that's you) can tell that the week is the last one of the previous year, but today's date is New Year's Day.

This update to the code from week02.c requires the addition of a new variable, pmonth, which holds the value of the previous month. The pmonth calculation takes place after the current month's value is read and stored in variable month:

```
pmonth = month-1;
if( pmonth<0 )
    pmonth=11;
```

The previous month's value is the current month's value minus one. If it's January (0), the previous month's value is negative. The *if* test catches this condition, in which case the value of pmonth is set to 11, December.

Next, a series of tests are performed to determine which month names to output: a single month, the current and previous months, or the current and next months. These tests are illustrated here.

Listing 13.8 Tests to determine which months to output (from week03.c)

When days from the previous month are calculated, shows the previous and current months

Tests to see whether days from the next month are output

For December, outputs December and January directly

```
if( sunday<1 )
    printf("  %s / %s\n",months[pmonth],months[month]);
else if( sunday+6 > mdays[month] )
{
    if( month==11 )
        printf("  %s / %s\n",months[month],months[0]);
```

```
        else
            printf("  %s / %s\n",months[month],months[month+1]);
}
else
    printf("  %s\n",months[month]);
```

For other months, outputs the current and next month names

No previous or next month dates appear in the output.

To output dates from the previous or next month, the *for* loop in the *main()* function must be modified. Again, an *if else-if else* structure is used, shown in the next listing. Calculations are made to generate the trailing dates from the previous month and the following dates from the next month.

Listing 13.9   The updated *for* loop (from `week03.c`)

The previous month still has days to output.

```
for( d=sunday; d<sunday+7; d++ )
{
    if( d<1 )
        printf(" %2d ",mdays[pmonth]+d);
    else if( d>mdays[month] )
        printf(" %2d ",d-mdays[month]);
    else
    {
        if( d==day )
            printf("[%2d]",d);
        else
            printf(" %2d ",d);
    }
}
```

Outputs the dates using the previous month's number of days minus the value of variable d

If the value of variable d is greater than the number of days in the current month . . .

. . . outputs days from the next month using d minus the number of days in the current month

The final *else* block outputs days from the current month as-is.

These decisions look messy, but they're required to fill in the proper dates for overlapping months. The full source code is available from the online repository as `week03.c`. Here's a sample run:

```
  December / January
Sun Mon Tue Wed Thu Fri Sat
[26] 27  28  29  30  31   1
```

Above, the next month and first day of the month are output for the current week, when today is December 26. Similar output is shown when days from the previous month appear in the week:

```
  November / December
Sun Mon Tue Wed Thu Fri Sat
 28  29 [30]  1   2   3   4
```

And:

```
  November / December
Sun Mon Tue Wed Thu Fri Sat
 28  29  30   1   2 [ 3]  4
```

The program is pretty much complete at this point. Being a nerd, however, I always look for ways to improve upon the code. The only thing I can think to add is to output the current week number as well.

Each year has 52 weeks, though they don't fall in a regular pattern. After all, the first week of the year may have a few lingering days from December. From what I gather, when January 1 falls on a Wednesday or earlier in the week, it's in the first week of the year. Otherwise, January 1 is part of week 52 from the previous year.

An exception occurs during leap years when January 1 falls on a Thursday. Though it could be week 52 of the preceding year, a leap year can have 53 weeks. The next time a year has 53 weeks is in 2032—so hang on to this book!

My first attempt to calculate the current week number resulted in this formula:

```
weekno = (9 + day_of_the_year - weekday) / 7;
```

The day_of_the_year value is kept in the tm structure as member tm_yday. The week-day value is tm structure member tm_wday, where Sunday is zero. The expression is divided by seven, which is rounded as an integer value and stored in variable weekno.

The value of weekno must be tested for the first week of the year—specifically, when the first of January falls late in the week. In this configuration, the weekno value returned by the equation is 0. It should be 52, as it's technically the last week of the previous year. Therefore, some adjustment is necessary before the value is output:

```
if( weekno==0 )
    weekno = 52;
```

To complete the code update from week03.c, you must remove all the newlines from the *printf()* statement that outputs the current month or pair of months. Follow these statements with a new *printf()* statement:

```
printf(" - Week %d\n",weekno);
```

The final program is available in the online repository as week04.c. Here is a sample run:

```
  December / January - Week 52
Sun Mon Tue Wed Thu Fri Sat
[26] 27  28  29  30  31   1
```

Here is the output for January 1 of the same week:

```
December / January - Week 52
Sun Mon Tue Wed Thu Fri Sat
 26  27  28  29  30  31 [ 1]
```

By the way, you can also use the *strftime()* function to obtain the current week number. The placeholder is %W, but it reports the first day of the week as Monday. The week number value is set into a string, which must be converted to an integer to perform any math. Like the formula I chose to use for my update to the code, the *strftime()* function returns 0 for the first week of the year.

13.3.2 *Showing a month*

The month program was the first calendar program I wrote. I used it to help with my C programming blog posts (https://c-for-dummies.com/blog), which I write in advance and schedule for later. Obviously, I could use the *cal* program, which outputs the current month as a default:

```
   December 2021
Su Mo Tu We Th Fr Sa
          1  2  3  4
 5  6  7  8  9 10 11
12 13 14 15 16 17 18
19 20 21 22 23 24 25
26 27 28 29 30 31
```

Oh, and the *cal* program does lots of other things, too. But I didn't let its flexibility stop me. Here is the output from my program, which I call *month*:

```
     December 2021
Sun Mon Tue Wed Thu Fri Sat
              1    2    3    4
  5    6    7    8    9   10   11
 12   13   14   15   16   17   18
 19   20   21   22   23   24   25
 26  [27]  28   29   30   31
```

The output is a bit wider, which I find more readable—even back before I needed reading glasses. After all, my goal is to output the current month. The dimensions of the *cal* program's output are designed so that the entire year can be shown three months wide by three columns deep. My *month* program could output months three wide, but the text won't fit on an 80-column screen. I touch upon this issue later in this chapter.

A month of dates is really a grid: rows for weeks and columns for days of the week. It's not a full grid because the starting point occurs at a specific column; the first row of output is special. The rest of the days of the month flow through the grid until the last day, when output stops.

The following listing shows my test code to ensure that the month program works. It outputs the month of December 2021. The focus is on the nested loop: the *while* loop uses the variable day to churn through days of the month. The inner *for* loop processes weeks. The first week is special, which outputs blanks for days from the previous month.

Listing 13.10   Source code for `month01.c`

```
#include <stdio.h>

int main()
{
    int mdays,today,first,day,d;

    mdays = 31;
    today = 27;
    first = 3;

    printf("December 2021\n");
    printf("Sun Mon Tue Wed Thu Fri Sat\n");

    day = 1;
    while( day<=mdays )
    {
        for( d = 0; d < 7; d++)
        {
            if( d<first && day==1 )
            {
                printf("    ");
            }
            else
            {
                if( day == today )
                    printf("[%2d]",day);
                else
                    printf(" %2d ",day);
                day++;
                if( day>mdays )
                    break;
            }
        }
        putchar('\n');
    }

    return(0);
}
```

Sets today as the 27th

Presets the number of days in the month (for December)

The first day of the month is on Wednesday.

Loops through the days of the month

Starts with the day counter at 1, the first day of the month

Loops through a week, Sunday (0) through Saturday (6)

Checks for the first week of the month

Outputs blanks—and do not increment the day counter!

Outputs days, now that the first week/day has passed

Highlights today

Regular day output

Increments the day counter

Exits the loop after the last day of the month

From listing 13.10, in the *for* loop you can see that the first week of the month is handled differently from the remaining weeks. No output should occur before the first day of the month. Variable `first` holds the weekday value—3 for Wednesday—so the *if* test is TRUE for days before the first of the month:

```
if( d<first && day==1 )
{
    printf("    ");
}
```

Variable d tracks days of the week, Sunday through Saturday (0 through 6). Variable first holds the day of the week on which the first of the month falls. Variable day represents the day of the month.

When the first of the month is encountered, the *else* portion of the *if* decision takes over, outputting the rest of the month grid. Sample output for this version of the month program is shown earlier. The source code file month01.c is available in the online repository.

I messed with variables mdays, today, and first to ensure that the month program output the various month configurations. The next step to improve the code is to use the current month's data. This improvement requires several steps.

First, the code must include the *february()* and *thefirst()* functions, covered earlier in this chapter. You need to add the *february()* function to complete a proper mdays[] array, which contains days of the month for the current year. The other function lets you know upon which weekday the first of the month falls.

Second, the variable declarations are updated to include the month name constants, mdays[] array, and other variables required to report the current month's dates:

```
const char *months[] = {
    "January", "February", "March", "April",
    "May", "June", "July", "August",
    "September", "October", "November", "December"
};
int mdays[] = { 31, 28, 31, 30, 31, 30, 31, 31, 30, 31, 30, 31 };
time_t now;
struct tm *date;
int month,today,weekday,year,first,day,d;
```

Third, the *time()* and *localtime()* functions are called to obtain details about the current date:

```
time(&now);
date = localtime(&now);
```

Fourth, the current date info is packed into the variables month, today, weekday, and year. February's days are updated with a call to the *february()* function, and variable first is set to the day of the week upon which the first of the month falls:

```
month = date->tm_mon;
today = date->tm_mday;
weekday = date->tm_wday;
year = date->tm_year+1900;
mdays[1] = february(year);
first = thefirst(weekday,today);
```

Fifth, the *printf()* statement to output the current month and year is updated:

```
printf("%s %d\n",months[month],year);
```

And finally, the mdays variable in the original source code file must be replaced by mdays[month] in the final version.

This update to the code is titled month02.c, available in the online repository. Unlike the original, static program, this version outputs the current month.

EXERCISE 13.3

The *month* program's output lists the current month and year as the top heading but right-justified. Update the code to create a new function, center(). The function's purpose is to output a string of text centered within a certain width. Here is the prototype to use:

```
void center(char *text,int width);
```

The function calculates the length of string text and then does the fancy math to center the string within the given width. If the string is longer than the width, it's output and truncated to the width.

Making this update to the month02.c code involves more than just writing the *center()* function. Ensure that the function is called with the proper string arguments and that the result is output atop the calendar. My solution is titled month03.c, and it's available in the online repository.

EXERCISE 13.4

No, you're not quite done with the *month* program. Your final task is to modify the *main()* function from month03.c (see the preceding exercise) so that any command-line arguments are parsed as a month-and-year value. Both values must be present and valid; otherwise, the current month is output. My solution is available in the online repository as month04.c.

13.3.3 Displaying a full year

The issue with outputting a full year has nothing to do with fancy date coding; the math and functions required are already presented so far in this chapter. The problem is getting the output correct—rows and columns.

Figure 13.2 shows the output from a *year* program that uses the same format as the *months* program, shown earlier in this chapter. You see three columns by four rows of months. Steam output generates the text, one row at a time. Some coordination is required to produce the visual effect you see in the figure. Further, the output is far too wide for a typical 80-column text screen. So, while the math and functions might be known, fine-tuning the output is the big issue.

Rather than go hog-wild and attempt to code a multicolumn year program all at once, I sought to first code a long vertical column for the current year. The code, year01.c, is available in the online repository. It uses the existing *center()* and *february()* functions.

The *main()* function consists of two parts. The first part initializes all variables to a specific year. I chose the year 2000. The code sets the weekday for January 1, which

```
13_calendar$ ./year
          January 2021            February 2021             March 2021
Sun Mon Tue Wed Thu Fri Sat   Sun Mon Tue Wed Thu Fri Sat   Sun Mon Tue Wed Thu Fri Sat
                     1   2       1   2   3   4   5   6         1   2   3   4   5   6
 3   4   5   6   7   8   9     7   8   9  10  11  12  13     7   8   9  10  11  12  13
10  11  12  13  14  15  16    14  15  16  17  18  19  20    14  15  16  17  18  19  20
17  18  19  20  21  22  23    21  22  23  24  25  26  27    21  22  23  24  25  26  27
24  25  26  27  28  29  30    28                            28  29  30  31
31

           April 2021               May 2021                  June 2021
Sun Mon Tue Wed Thu Fri Sat   Sun Mon Tue Wed Thu Fri Sat   Sun Mon Tue Wed Thu Fri Sat
                 1   2   3                             1             1   2   3   4   5
 4   5   6   7   8   9  10     2   3   4   5   6   7   8     6   7   8   9  10  11  12
11  12  13  14  15  16  17     9  10  11  12  13  14  15    13  14  15  16  17  18  19
18  19  20  21  22  23  24    16  17  18  19  20  21  22    20  21  22  23  24  25  26
25  26  27  28  29  30        23  24  25  26  27  28  29    27  28  29  30
                              30  31

            July 2021              August 2021             September 2021
Sun Mon Tue Wed Thu Fri Sat   Sun Mon Tue Wed Thu Fri Sat   Sun Mon Tue Wed Thu Fri Sat
                 1   2   3     1   2   3   4   5   6   7                 1   2   3   4
 4   5   6   7   8   9  10     8   9  10  11  12  13  14     5   6   7   8   9  10  11
11  12  13  14  15  16  17    15  16  17  18  19  20  21    12  13  14  15  16  17  18
18  19  20  21  22  23  24    22  23  24  25  26  27  28    19  20  21  22  23  24  25
25  26  27  28  29  30  31    29  30  31                    26  27  28  29  30

          October 2021             November 2021            December 2021
Sun Mon Tue Wed Thu Fri Sat   Sun Mon Tue Wed Thu Fri Sat   Sun Mon Tue Wed Thu Fri Sat
                     1   2       1   2   3   4   5   6                     1   2   3   4
 3   4   5   6   7   8   9     7   8   9  10  11  12  13     5   6   7   8   9  10  11
10  11  12  13  14  15  16    14  15  16  17  18  19  20    12  13  14  15  16  17  18
17  18  19  20  21  22  23    21  22  23  24  25  26  27    19  20  21  22  23  24  25
24  25  26  27  28  29  30    28  29  30                    26  27  28  29  30  31
31
```

Figure 13.2   Output from a *year* program that uses the same format as the *month* program

starts the entire year. Once established, the second part of the *main()* function consists of a loop to output the months.

The following listing shows the initialization portion of the *main()* function. The code is cobbled together from the *month* series of programs, though the program doesn't scan command-line input.

> **Listing 13.11   Initialization in the *main()* function from `year01.c`**

```
const char *months[] = {                      ◁──   Constants and
    "January", "February", "March", "April",         stuff from earlier
    "May", "June", "July", "August",                 date code
    "September", "October", "November", "December"
};
int mdays[] = { 31, 28, 31, 30, 31, 30, 31, 31, 30, 31, 30, 31 };
struct tm date;
```

```
int month,weekday,year,day,dow;
const int output_width = 27;
char title[output_width];
```
Y2K is hardcoded here, minus 1900 for the `tm` structure.
```
date.tm_year = 2000-1900;
date.tm_mon = 0;
date.tm_mday = 1;
date.tm_hour = 0;
```
Remember to set hours, minute, and seconds.
```
date.tm_min = 0;
date.tm_sec = 0;
putenv("TZ=GMT");
tzset();
```
You must set the time zone, or else January 1 may fall in the previous year.
```
mktime(&date);
```

Uses `weekday` for readability and to save typing molecules
```
weekday = date.tm_wday;
year = date.tm_year+1900;
mdays[1] = february(year);
```
Adjusts the `year` value

Updates the `tm` date structure, specifically with the weekday value

Sets the proper number of days in February

It's important that the time zone be set to GMT, as shown in listing 13.11. In my original code, I forgot to do this step—even though I warned about doing so earlier in this chapter—and the oversight caused lots of grief. As I was testing the code late in the evening, the years and dates were off. Only by asserting GMT as the time zone does the calendar year properly render, no matter what your time zone.

The *main()* function's nested loops are shown next. They consist of an outer *for* loop to process the months and an inner *while* loop to process days of the month. Variable `dow` counts weekdays. It's updated manually as opposed to being in a loop because the first weekday of the month isn't the same for every month.

Listing 13.12 The output loop from the *main()* function in `year01.c`

The weekday loop variable, day-of-the-week

The outer loop pages through months of the year.
```
dow = 0;
for( month=0; month<12; month++ )
{
    sprintf(title,"%s %d",months[month],year);
    center(title,output_width);
    printf("Sun Mon Tue Wed Thu Fri Sat\n");
```
Outputs the month and year, centered, and the weekday header row

Initializes the day of the month, the first
```
    day = 1;
    while( day<=mdays[month] )
    {
```
Loops through the days of the month
```
        if( dow<weekday && day==1 )
        {
            printf("    ");
            dow++;
        }
    }
```
The first week is special; variable `weekday` holds the first weekday of the month. Outputs blanks before then.

```
        else
Outputs   {
the date      printf(" %2d ",day);          Increments the day of
              dow++;                         the week, Sunday (0)
Checks for    if( dow > 6 )                  through Saturday (6)
weekday       {
overflow          dow = 0;                   Resets the day of the
                  putchar('\n');             week back to Sunday (0)
              }
Tests for     day++;                         Outputs a newline
the end of    if( day>mdays[month] )         for the next week
the month         break;
          }                                  Increments the day
      }                                      of the month counter
      weekday = dow;                Sets the first day of the
      dow = 0;                      month for next month
      printf("\n\n");
}                            Resets the day of the week back
                             to Sunday for the next month
```

Variable dow works with variable weekday to output the first week of January. Afterward, variables weekday and dow are updated so that the following month's start day is properly set.

The full code is available in the online repository as year01.c. Here is the first part of the output:

```
        January 2000
Sun Mon Tue Wed Thu Fri Sat
                              1
  2   3   4   5   6   7   8
  9  10  11  12  13  14  15
 16  17  18  19  20  21  22
 23  24  25  26  27  28  29
 30  31

        February 2000
Sun Mon Tue Wed Thu Fri Sat
              1   2   3   4   5
  6   7   8   9  10  11  12
. . .
```

Each month follows, all down one long page of text. The output is accurate for the year 2000, but who wants to relive that?

EXERCISE 13.5

Modify the year01.c code so that it accepts a command-line argument for the year to output. When a command-line argument isn't available, the current year is output. The changes necessary all take place in the *main()* function. Remember that the year input and the tm_year value differ by 1900.

My solution is named year02.c and is found in the online repository. Comments in the code explain my approach.

13.3.4 *Putting the full year into a grid*

To output a full year of months in a grid on a text screen requires that it be output one row at a time. The approach used in the year01.c code just won't work; stream output doesn't let you back up or move the cursor on the text screen. Each line must be processed one a time, with multiple steps required to output different dates for different months. So, I threw out most of the year01.c code to start over.

The calendar still progresses month by month. But the months are organized into columns. For each column, individual rows for each month are output. Figure 13.3 illustrates this approach, with each month output a row at a time: two header rows, a special first week of the month row, and then the remaining weeks in the month. Each month must output six weeks, even when the month has only five weeks of dates.

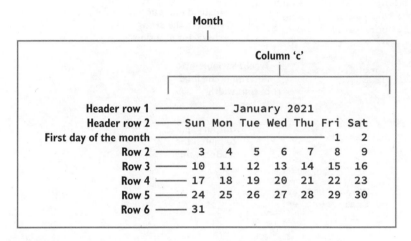

Figure 13.3 The approach to output a multicolumn display

To start working on the code, I copied the *center()* and *february()* functions from the existing *year* source code files. The *main()* function retains most of the setup required for the year02.c update to read a command-line argument. From this base, I built the rest of the code.

From the top down, the first change is to add a defined constant, COLUMNS:

```
#define COLUMNS 3
```

This symbolic constant sets the number of columns wide for the output, but it's not a value the user should change: valid values for COLUMNS are limited to factors of 12. You can change the definition to two, three, four, six, or even 12. But if you use another value, the arrays in the code will overflow.

The next update required is to the *center()* function. As used earlier in this chapter, the function centers the month and year within a given width but doesn't pad out the rest of the row of text. To line up the months in a grid, the header row one must be output at a consistent size. The next listing shows the required updates to the *center()* function for row-by-row output. The `width` argument centers the text *and* sets the number of spaces to pad on both sides.

Listing 13.13   The updated *center()* function

```
void center(char *text,int width)
{
    int s,length,indent;

    length = strlen(text);
    if( length < width )
    {
        indent = (width-length)/2;
        for(s=0;s<indent;s++)
            putchar(' ');
        while( *text )
        {
            putchar(*text);
            text++;
            s++;
        }
        for(;s<width;s++)
            putchar(' ');
    }
    else
    {
        for(s=0;s<width;s++)
            putchar(*text++);
    }
}
```

Instead of a *puts()* function, outputs the string one character at a time

Outputs each character

Increments the pointer

Tracks variable s to determine the final output width

Outputs spaces to match the width value

With the *center()* function updated, my approach is to output only the first row by itself—just to see whether it works. The program outputs header row one, the month and year. I used this code:

```
for( month=0; month<12; month+=COLUMNS )
{
    for( c=0; c<COLUMNS; c++ )
    {
        sprintf(title,"%s %d",months[month+c],year);
        center(title,output_width);
        printf("   ");
    }
    putchar('\n');
}
```

Skips over every COLUMN month to output rows

Three spaces

The *prntf()* statement outputs three spaces to keep each month/year header separated in the grid. This program serves as a test to ensure that the grid is output in the order I want. Here's a sample run, minus a few spaces to fit on this page:

```
    January 2021          February 2021             March 2021
      April 2021               May 2021              June 2021
       July 2021            August 2021         September 2021
    October 2021          November 2021          December 2021
```

Adding the weekday header row is the next step. It requires a second *for* loop inside the outer `month` loop. In fact, each row of output represents a *for* loop in the code. These statements are inserted after the `putchar('\n')` statement ending the previous *for* loop, which also adds spaces to separate the columns:

```
for( c=0; c<COLUMNS; c++ )
{
    printf("Sun Mon Tue Wed Thu Fri Sat    ");
}
```

At this point, I became confident that I could output the year calendar in a grid. The key was to use sequential *for* loops, one for each row in the month. The last statement in each *for* loop pads spaces to keep the month grids separate in each column.

The most difficult row to output is the first week of the month. As with the other calendar programs in this chapter, the first day of the month starts on a specific weekday. I could use the *first()* function to determine each month's starting weekday, but instead I created an array in the *main()* function:

```
int dotm[12];
```

The `dotm[]` (day of the month) array holds the starting day for each month in the year. Its values are the same as the `weekday` variable, 0 through 6. The `weekday` variable already holds the day of the week for January 1. It's stored in element 0 of the `dotm[]` array. A *for* loop then fills in values for the remaining months:

```
dotm[0] = weekday;

for( month=1; month<12; month++ )
{
    dotm[month] = (mdays[month-1]+dotm[month-1]) % 7;
}
```

The statement in the *for* loop totals the values of the number of days in the previous month, `mdays[month-1]`, with the starting day of the week for the previous month, `dotm[month-1]`. This total is modulo 7, which yields the starting day of the week for the month represented by variable `month`. When the loop is complete, the `dotm[]` array holds the starting weekday for the first of each month in the given year.

Listing 13.14 shows the next nested *for* loop that generates the first row for each month of the year. The starting value in the `dotm[]` array determines which weekday starts the month. The day of the month, starting with one, is stored in variable `day`.

Listing 13.14   The third nested *for* loop, outputting the first week of each month

```
for( c=0; c<COLUMNS; c++ )
{
    day = 1;                                    Initializes the
    for( dow=0; dow<7; dow++ )                  day of the month
    {
        if( dow<dotm[month+c] )                 Loops through
        {                                       days of the week
            printf("    ");
        }                                       If the first of the month
        else                                    weekday hasn't happened,
        {                                       outputs a space
            printf(" %2d ",day);
            day++;                              Otherwise, outputs the
        }                                       day, as was done in the
    }                                           other calendar programs
    printf("  ");
    dotm[month+c] = day;
}                                               After the month's
putchar('\n');                                  week is output,
                                                pads two spaces
```

Increments
the day of
the month

Saves the day of the
month for output
on the next row's
Sunday position

Most of the *for* loop shown in listing 13.14 is borrowed from code presented earlier in this chapter. What's different is saving the day of the month for the next row's output: dotm[month+c] = day. This value, available in variable day, replaces the starting day of the month in the dotm[] array. It's used to output the next row, to set the day of the month value for the next Sunday.

The final *for* loop is responsible for outputting rows two through six for each month. It includes a nested *for* loop for each day of the week, with the outer *for* loop processing each week. The following listing shows the details, which again use the dotm[] array to hold the starting day for each subsequent week.

Listing 13.15   The final *for* loops for the *main()* function

Six weeks for each month, regardless of
whether the month has a sixth week

Output is by column first—
each column and then each
week (outer loop).

```
for( week=1; week<6; week++ )
{
    for( c=0; c<COLUMNS; c++ )              Updates the day
    {                                       of the month for
        day = dotm[month+c];                Sunday output
        for( dow=0; dow<7; dow++ )
        {
            if( day <= mdays[month+c] )     For valid days of the
                printf(" %2d ",day);        current month, outputs
            else                            the day number
                printf("    ");
            day++;                          Outputs blanks for days
        }                                   beyond the last day of
    }                                       the month
```

The innermost
(fourth-nested)
loop outputs
weekdays.

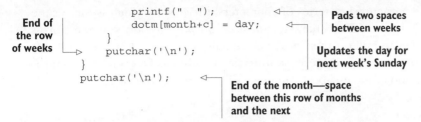

Because the starting day of the week is saved in the dotm[] array, the triple nested loops shown in listing 13.15 have an easy time outputting weeks for each row and then each month in the larger grid row.

The updated code for the *year* program is available in the online repository as year03.c. The output is shown in figure 13.2. I've adjusted the COLUMNS value to 2 and then 4, and the code still performs well. It also handles the year as a command-line argument. But it's just too wide!

Yes, you can adjust the terminal window for your operating system. Still, I like a cozy 80-by-24 window, just like grandpa used. Though I could adjust the output width for days of the week, making it narrower like the *cal* program, a better way to condense things might be to color-code the output.

13.4 A calendar in color

Text mode need not be as boring as it was at the height of its unpopularity in the early 1980s. Yes, many people had text-only displays because it was cheaper. Early graphics systems, primitive beyond belief by today's standards, were pricey. Early PC monochrome monitors could output text in normal or high intensity (brightness), inverse, and underline. Some data terminals output text in color, as did a few home computers.

As costs came down, color text became more common. Early word processors highlighted onscreen text in various colors to show different attributes and fonts. Colorful text programs, databases, spreadsheets, and such were all the rage—until graphical operating systems took over. Then color text took the backseat, where it's been ever since.

Color text can aid in program visibility. It's easier to identify different parts of the screen when the text is colored differently. Add in Unicode fancy characters, and the text terminal has a potential for output more interesting than just letters and numbers.

13.4.1 Understanding terminal colors

Text output in the terminal windows can be whatever the boring default is, such as green on black, but your options aren't limited to the terminal window's settings. Your programs can generate a variety of colors—eight foreground and eight background for up to 64 combinations, many of them annoying or invisible. To make this rainbow magic happen, the program outputs ANSI color sequences. As most terminals are ANSI-color compatible, all you need to know are the proper ANSI escape sequences.

An ANSI escape sequence is a series of characters, the first of which is the escape character, ASCII 27, hex 1B. This character must be output directly; you can't press the keyboard's Esc key to pull off this trick. The remainder of the characters follow a pattern, which are numerical codes representing various colors. The final character is m, which signals the end of the escape sequence, as illustrated in figure 13.4.

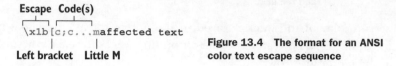

Figure 13.4   The format for an ANSI color text escape sequence

Text output that follows the ANSI sequence appears in the specified attributes or colors. To change colors, issue a new escape sequence. To restore terminal colors, a reset escape sequence is given.

Table 13.1 lists the basic character effects or attributes available with ANSI escape sequences. The escape character is listed as hex value \x1b, how it appears as a character in C.

Table 13.1   ANSI text effects

Effect	Code	Sequence
Reset	0	\x1b[0m
Bold	1	\x1b[1m
Faint	2	\x1b[2m
Underline	4	\x1b[4m
Blinking	5	\x1b[5m
Inverse	7	\x1b[7m

Not all attributes shown in table 13.1 are available in every terminal window. Just in case, the test program shown in the next listing creates defined constant strings for the escape sequences and then outputs each one a line at a time.

Listing 13.16   Source code for `ansi01.c`

```c
#include <stdio.h>

#define RESET "\x1b[0m"
#define BOLD "\x1b[1m"
#define FAINT "\x1b[2m"
#define UNDERLINE "\x1b[4m"
#define BLINK "\x1b[5m"
#define INVERSE "\x1b[7m"
```

```
int main()
{
    printf("%sBold text%s\n",BOLD,RESET);
    printf("%sFaint text%s\n",FAINT,RESET);
    printf("%sUnderline text%s\n",UNDERLINE,RESET);
    printf("%sBlinking text%s\n",BLINK,RESET);
    printf("%sInverse text%s\n",INVERSE,RESET);

    return(0);
}
```

Running the program for ansi01.c yielded mixed results on my various computers. The Mac Terminal window shows the output the best, including blinking text, which is most annoying. Ubuntu Linux in Windows 10/11 shows underlined text well. The rest of my computers were a mixed bag. Again, remember that you can obtain another terminal program if the one your OS provides shows less than spectacular results.

The ANSI color code sequences are shown in table 13.2. Codes in the 30s represent foreground colors; codes in the 40s are background colors.

Table 13.2 ANSI color-code escape sequences

Color	Foreground Code	Background Code	Foreground Sequence	Background Sequence
Black	30	40	\x1b[30m	\x1b[40m
Red	31	41	\x1b[31m	\x1b[41m
Green	32	42	\x1b[32m	\x1b[42m
Yellow	33	43	\x1b[33m	\x1b[43m
Blue	34	44	\x1b[34m	\x1b[44m
Magenta	35	45	\x1b[35m	\x1b[45m
Cyan	36	46	\x1b[36m	\x1b[46m
White	37	47	\x1b[37m	\x1b[47m

Codes can be combined in a single sequence, as shown back in figure 13.4. For example, if you want red text on a blue background, you can use the sequence \x1b[31;44m, where 31 is the code for red foreground and 44 is the code for blue background.

The code for ansi02.c in the next code listing cycles through all the permutations of foreground and background colors. Run the program to ensure that the terminal window is capable of outputting colors, plus to see how nifty it is to do color text output in C. (Well, it's a terminal feature, not really part of the C programming language.)

Listing 13.17   Source code for `ansi02.c`

```
#include <stdio.h>

int main()
{
    int f,b;                              Loops through
                                          foreground values

    for( f=0 ; f<8; f++ )                 Loops through
    {                                     background values
        for( b=0; b<8; b++ )
        {                                 Outputs the escape
            printf("\x1b[%d;%dm %d:%d ",  sequence and the
                                          two values
                f+30,b+40,f+30,b+40
                );                        Updates the
        }                                 numbers here
        printf("\x1b[0m\n");
    }                                     Resets and
                                          starts a new line

    return(0);
}
```

The generated output from `ansi02.c`—which I won't show here because this book isn't in color—is a grid of all the color combinations. Output with the same foreground and background colors makes the text invisible, but it's there.

This color output can be used in your text mode programs to spice up the screen or to call attention to one part of the output or another. Keep in mind that the output is still streaming, one character after another. Also, not all terminals properly render the character attributes.

13.4.2 *Generating a tight-but-colorful calendar*

It's possible to squeeze more months on a text screen if you eliminate the space between the days. On a plain text screen, such a move would render the month's data output useless to all but the most insane nerd. Yet it's possible to output a month with no spaces between the days—if you change each day's colors.

In figure 13.5, you see single month output from my *year* program (so far), the *cal* program, and then from a version of my *year* program with no spaces between the dates. Which is easiest to read?

I would offer that the calendars shown in figure 13.5 rank, from left to right, in order of easiest to read. However, the easier the calendar is to read, the more text screen real estate it occupies. You can always adjust the terminal window size, but a larger window is often impractical for many of the fun times to be had in text mode.

The year configuration on the right in figure 13.5 allows for more months to pack into a typical 80-by-24 character terminal window. In fact, you can march four columns of months across the terminal window when using this dense format. You can almost

```
        January 2000                    January 2000             Jan 2021
   Sun Mon Tue Wed Thu Fri Sat       Su Mo Tu We Th Fr Sa      SuMoTuWeThFrSa
                             1                         1                   1 2
     2   3   4   5   6   7   8        2  3  4  5  6  7  8        3 4 5 6 7 8 9
     9  10  11  12  13  14  15        9 10 11 12 13 14 15       10111213141516
    16  17  18  19  20  21  22       16 17 18 19 20 21 22       17181920212223
    23  24  25  26  27  28  29       23 24 25 26 27 28 29       24252627282930
    30  31                           30 31                      31

        My year program                 The cal program        The year program,
                                                                no spaces
```

Figure 13.5   Comparing output from various calendar programs

see all 12 months as well, though not the complete bottom row. The problem is that
the numbers all run together—unless you color-code them.

Figure 13.6 shows a full year's worth of output with no spaces between dates in
each month. The dates are color-coded, as are the weekday headers. You can't see the
colors in this book, but even in grayscale, it's far easier to visually separate the days in
a month.

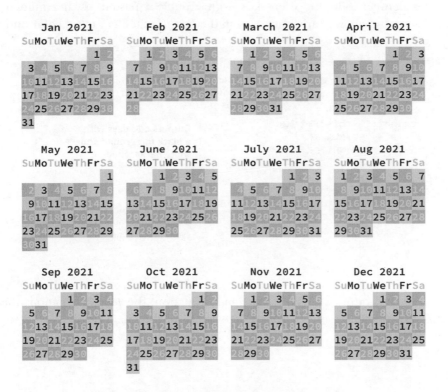

Figure 13.6   Color-coded days allow the tight calendar to be useful.

To update the *year* series of programs to output a tighter annual calendar, start with the year03.c source code. Color output requires no additional headers or libraries—just that you add the ANSI escape sequences to output color. These updates are found in the source code file year04.c, available in the online repository. Follow along as I review each update to the code.

First, I added the following defined constants, which help output colors, foreground and background:

```
#define BOLD 1
#define BLACK 0
#define CYAN 6
#define WHITE 7
#define FG 30
#define BG 40
```

The updated year program uses only the colors listed. Constants FG and BG are added to the other values to create the various foreground and background color combinations.

Second, to output dates, I added the *color_output()* function, shown in the next listing. Its job is to output every other date of the month in a different color. The *if* decision alternates between odd and even days, with variable d passed as an argument. The defined constants shown earlier are used in the *printf()* statement to set color output.

Listing 13.18   The *color_output()* function from year04.c

```
void color_output(int d)
{
    if( d%2 )                           ◁    The condition is true
        printf("\x1b[%d;%dm%2d",              for odd-numbered
                FG+BLACK,                     values of d.
                BG+WHITE,           ◁─┐  Outputs odd days with
                d                     │  a black foreground and
              );                      │  white background
    else
        printf("\x1b[%d;%dm%2d",
                FG+WHITE,           ◁─┐  Outputs even days with
                BG+CYAN,              │  a white foreground and
                d                     │  cyan background
              );
}
```

Along with the addition of the *color_output()* function, the *printf()* functions that output the current day must be replaced. They go from this:

```
printf(" %2d ",day);
```

to this:

```
color_output(day);
```

I also changed the length of the month and day strings. The month names are shortened to better fit in the tighter layout:

```
const char *months[] = {
    "Jan", "Feb", "March", "April",
    "May", "June", "July", "Aug",
    "Sep", "Oct", "Nov", "Dec"
};
```

The weekday headings are reset to two characters long. Like the days of the month, the weekday headings must be color-coded. I couldn't think of a clever way to code the weekday header without creating another array, so a series of *printf()* statements output the days, alternating bold and normal attributes:

```
printf("\x1b[%dm%s",BOLD,"Su");
printf("\x1b[0m%s","Mo");
printf("\x1b[%dm%s",BOLD,"Tu");
printf("\x1b[0m%s","We");
printf("\x1b[%dm%s",BOLD,"Th");
printf("\x1b[0m%s","Fr");
printf("\x1b[%dm%s",BOLD,"Sa");
printf("\x1b[0m   ");
```

Finally, the space between months is reduced to two. Various `putchar('\n')` statements are replaced by *printf()* statements that also output the ANSI escape sequence to reset the colors back to normal. This change avoided color spill at the end of each line of output. In fact, color spill is something you must be aware of when coding color output: always terminate the color output, resetting it when colored text is no longer required. The reset sequence is `\x1b[0m;`.

Output for the program generated by `year04.c` appears earlier, in figure 13.6. The BOLD attribute looks faint in the image because of how the terminal window sets bold color. Again, color output differs from terminal to terminal.

EXERCISE 13.6

What is missing from the output for the `year04.c` code, and missing in figure 13.6 as well, is a highlight for the current day of the year.

Your task for this exercise is to modify the source code for `year04.c` to detect the current day of the year and output this one specific day in a special color. Obviously, if the calendar isn't showing the current year, your code won't highlight today's date. So, your solution must detect whether the current year is shown.

My solution is named `year05.c`, available in the online repository. Comments in the text explain what I did. My chosen colors for the current day of the year are red text on a black background.

13.4.3 *Coloring holidays*

The final step to the *year* series of programs, and for both this and the preceding chapter, is to generate an annual calendar with highlighted holidays. This program requires an update to the year04.c source code but also the inclusion of the *isholiday()* function from chapter 12. The output uses the return value from *isholiday()* to color-code holiday dates, making them visible in the output.

To accomplish this task, three separate files are required:

- The new source code file, year05.c, which calls the *isholiday()* function and color-codes holiday dates
- A source code file, isholiday.c, containing the *isholiday()* function and its support functions
- A header file, holiday_year.h, which contains resources for the final program: header files to include, defined constants, the holiday structure definition, and the function prototype for *isholiday()*

These files are available in the online repository. Review them as I cover the changes to the code.

To update the year04.c source code to year05.c, several updates are required. The first is the addition of the *color_holiday()* function, which outputs a holiday's value with white text on a red background:

```c
void color_holiday(int d)
{
    printf("\x1b[%d;%dm%2d",
            FG+WHITE,
            BG+RED,
            d
          );
}
```

Next, the *for* loop that outputs the first day of the month is updated to scan for any holidays. The following listing shows the updates—specifically, how holiday structure h is filled to make the *isholiday()* function call. Also note that if a holiday falls on today's date, the color used is for the holiday, not the color for today's date.

Listing 13.19 The updated *for* loop for the first day of the week in year 06.c

```
for( c=0; c<COLUMNS; c++ )          These items are
{                                   consistent throughout
    h.month = month+c;              the first week.
    h.year = year;
    h.name = NULL;                  The month starts
    day = 1;                        on day 1.
    for( dow=0; dow<7; dow++ )      Loops through the first
    {                               week, Sunday through
        if( dow<dotm[month+c] )     Saturday
        {
            printf("   ");
        }
        else                        Updates holiday structure h
        {                           with the current day and
            h.day = day;            day of the week
```

Outputs blanks before the first of the month starts

```
                              h.wday = dow;
              Tests for  ┌─▷  if( isholiday(&h)==1 )                    │ Colors the
              holidays   │       color_holiday(day);            ◁────── │ holiday
                         │    else if( today->tm_year+1900==year &&  ◁────┐
                         │        today->tm_mon==month+c &&              │ Tests for
                         │        today->tm_mday==day                    │ today's date
                         │        )                                      │ and color
              Increments │       color_today(day);
              the day    │    else
              counter  └─▷       color_output(day);      ◁──── │ Outputs a
                         └─▷  day++;                            │ regular date
                         }
                    }
  Resets                    printf("\x1b[0m   ");       ◁──── │ Resets the
  the color                 dotm[month+c] = day;        ◁──── │ color output
  output             }                                        │ Updates the first
         └──────────────▷  printf("\x1b[0m\n");                │ day of next week
```

Changes similar to those shown in listing 13.19 are made in the next *for* loop, which outputs the remaining days of the month.

To build the program, you must build both `year06.c` and `isholiday.c` into a single program. I use the following command, which generates a program file named year. Also, don't forget to link in the math library, shown as the last argument:

```
clang -Wall year06.c isholiday.c -o year -lm
```

The program's output shows the current year—or any year specified at the command prompt—highlighting all the holidays and today's date, providing today isn't a holiday. It's compact, with nearly the entire year fitting in a standard terminal window. This type of output works well only when you color-code the dates.

Lotto picks 14

Back when I was a C programmer hatchling, I returned from a trip to Las Vegas eager to write my own keno program. Keno is a random-number game, a cross between the lottery and bingo. You pick several numbers in the range from 1 through 80. Payouts depend on how many numbers you choose and guess correctly.

In the process of writing the code, it became apparent that the payouts offered in the casino were nowhere close to the true odds. For example, if you pick 10 numbers and guess correctly, you win $200,000. But the odds of picking 10 out of 10 numbers in a range of 80 numbers are 1:8,911,712. You should win $8,911,712, right? But at least they have killer shrimp cocktail for a dollar. Or they once did.

The process of programming games of chance clues you in to several interesting and useful coding areas, including these:

- Understanding the odds and probability
- Calculating the odds
- Exploring random numbers
- Simulating drawing lotto balls
- Running simulations to test the odds

I acknowledge that I'm not a math genius. I understand math, but I got a D in calculus, which was a passing grade, so that's my limit. I'm not up to par when it comes to the realms of probability and such. After all, it's the computer that does the math. Your job is to plug in the proper equation and do all those programming things that keep the computer from crashing. The odds on this skill are pretty good.

14.1 A tax for those who are bad at math

I play the Powerball, even though my rational brain knows that I have scant chance of winning. My emotional brain argues, "Well, someone has to win!" Satisfied, I dump $20 on a sheaf of random lotto picks and fantasize about what I'll do with my never-to-appear loot.

It's this hope that keeps people playing games of chance. Whether it's the lotto, keno, or any casino game (except for poker and perhaps blackjack), people rely upon desire more than a clean understanding of the math. That's because the math isn't in your favor.

14.1.1 Playing the lottery

Rumor has it that a lottery financed the Great Wall of China. Even if the rumor is untrue, governments have used lotteries for centuries to finance various projects. The early United States used a lottery to fund defense.

Lotteries are used for other purposes as well. The Great Council of Genoa used a lottery to choose its members, drawing several names from a larger pool. Citizens would wager on the winners, calling the game *lotto*. It eventually grew so popular that lotteries were held by drawing numbers instead of names.

The goal of a good lottery is to raise funds, either for a project or to distribute as prize money. A portion of the funds always goes to pay the winners. To keep the lottery successful and popular, the prize money is typically spread across many winners. For most humans, seeing a return of two or three dollars after buying $20 worth of tickets is "winning."

In the multistate Powerball lottery, numbers are printed on palm-size balls and drawn sequentially from a machine. After five white balls are drawn, with a range from 1 through 69, a single red "power ball" is drawn, with a range from 1 to 26. Various side bets are available, but the desire is to match all five numbers drawn, plus the red power ball, to win the grand prize. If no one guesses all six numbers, the prize money rolls over—sometimes accumulating to the hundreds of millions of dollars.

The kind of lottery simulated for the programs in this chapter is a random-number lottery, like Powerball. Random numbers are drawn to represent the balls from the Powerball lottery. Important to the simulation is not to draw the same number twice, which is impossible in a physical lottery. Two methods of preventing duplicate numbers from being drawn are offered in this chapter.

14.1.2 Understanding the odds

To dampen your glee over potential lottery winnings, I must discuss the odds. These are the numbers that explain the ratio of the probability of something happening or not happening. I desire not to get too heavily into the math, nor to discuss the difference between statistical odds and gambling odds. Just stare at figure 14.1.

$$\text{Probability of winning} = \frac{\text{Chances of winning}}{\text{Chances of winning + Chances of losing}}$$

Odds of winning = Chances of losing : Chances of winning

Figure 14.1   Some math formula-things explain the odds.

Suppose that you're betting on the roll of a die. Here is how you would calculate your odds of guessing the right number, one out of six:

```
odds = 1 / (1+5) = 1/6 = 0.166...
```

You have a 16.6% chance of guessing correctly. To calculate your odds of losing, change the numerator in the top equation in figure 14.1 so that *Chances of losing* replaces *Chances of winning*. Here's the math for the dice roll:

```
odds = 5 / (1+5) = 5/6 = 0.833...
```

You have an 83.3% chance of losing. See how much stating the odds in this manner dashes all hope? It's depressing.

Odds are also expressed as a colon ratio, as shown on the bottom in figure 14.1. For the dice example, your odds of winning are 1 in 5, often expressed as 5:1 or "five to one." The odds aren't 1:6 because one of the choices wins but five lose. Therefore, the odds are expressed 5:1 with the same win/lose percentages: 16.6 and 83.3.

For a game like Powerball, the odds are calculated as numbers are drawn but also considering that the balls aren't drawn in any order. These items must be considered to properly calculate the odds.

For example, if you could bet on only one ball (and the minimum bet for Powerball is three numbers), the odds are 68:1 or 1/(68+1), which is a 1.45 percent chance of winning. If you bet on drawing two balls, the odds for the second ball become 67:1, and then 66:1 for the third ball, and so on. If you do the math, you get a very small number:

```
1/69 * 1/68 * 1/67 * 1/66 * 1/65 = 7.415e-10
```

Inverting the result, you see that your probability of winning is 1:1,348,621,560. The problem with this value is that the permutations of the numbers drawn must also be considered. If your guesses are 1, 2, 3, 5, and 8, the first ball could be any of those numbers. The second ball could be any four of those numbers, and so on. The number of balls from which the numbers are drawn—69, 68, 67, 66, 65—must be divided by 5 * 4 * 3 * 2 * 1, or 5! (five factorial):

```
( 69 * 68 * 67 * 66 * 65 ) / (5 * 4 * 3 * 2 * 1 ) = 11,238,513
```

Your chance of correctly picking five numbers from a 69-ball lottery is 1:11,268,513. Incidentally, the Powerball lottery pays $1 million if you succeed in accurately picking the five numbers. The probability is 11 times that.

14.1.3 Programming the odds

At university, I avoided computers because I thought you had to be a math genius to understand them. Poppycock! It's the computer that does the math. The preceding section introduced the formulas for calculating the odds. The next step is to program them.

The next listing shows the code for a simple odds calculator. You input the chances of something happening, such as guessing the correct roll of a dice. Then you input the chances of it not happening. The computer uses the formula shown earlier (refer to figure 14.1) to output the results. The source code is available in the online repository as odds01.c.

Listing 14.1 Source code for odds01.c

```
#include <stdio.h>

int main()                      ow = odds of
{                               winning, ol =
    int ow,ol;            <─┘   odds of losing

    printf("Chances of happening: ");
    scanf("%d",&ow);                          Two percent signs are
    printf("Chances of not happening: ");     used in the format
    scanf("%d",&ol);                          string to output a
                                              single percent sign.
    printf("Your odds of winning are[CA] %2.1f%%, or %d:%d\n",   <─
            (float)ow/(float)(ow+ol)*100,      <─┐
            ow,                                  │  The
            ol                                   │  equation
        );

    return(0);
}
```

To test the program, use the dice example shown earlier in this section:

```
Chances of happening: 1
Chances of not happening: 5
Your odds of winning are 16.7%, or 1:5
```

If you guess one of the six sides of a die, the chances of it happening are one, and the chances of it not happening are five. The odds of winning are 16.7%, or one in five.

Say you want to calculate the odds of drawing a heart from a deck of cards:

```
Chances of happening: 13
Chances of not happening: 39
Your odds of winning are 25.0%, or 13:39
```

Because hearts is one of four suits, your odds are 25% or one in four—though the program doesn't reduce the ratio. Even so, the answer is accurate.

To calculate multiple draws, as in a lottery, more math is required: The decreasing number of balls must be multiplied, as well as permutations of the number guessed. This formula is shown earlier, but coded in the following listing. The product of the total items is calculated in variable i; the product of the items to draw is calculated in variable d.

Listing 14.2   Source code for `odds02.c`

```c
#include <stdio.h>

int main()
{
    int items,draw,x;
    unsigned long long i,d;


    printf("Number of items: ");
    scanf("%d",&items);
    printf("Items to draw: ");
    scanf("%d",&draw);

    i = items;
    d = draw;
    for(x=1;x<draw;x++)
    {
        i *= items-x;
        d *= draw-x;
    }
    printf("Your odds of drawing %d ",draw);
    printf("items from %d are:\n",items);
    printf("\t1:%.0f\n",(float)i/(float)d);

    return(0);
}
```

- Even an unsigned `long` value may not be large enough to handle the odds for some calculations.
- Loops through the number of draws
- Obtains the product of each item, decreasing in value
- Obtains the product of each drawing permutation, decreasing in value
- Casts the variables to obtain an accurate result

I had to keep enlarging the storage space for variables i and d in the code, from *int* to *long*, to *unsigned long*. The product of multiple values grows quickly. Still, the code renders accurate results for the Powerball odds (not counting the Powerball itself):

```
Number of items: 69
Items to draw: 5
Your odds of drawing 5 items from 69 are:
    1:11238513
```

This result matches the value shown earlier, 11,238,513. As usual, many modifications to the code are possible.

EXERCISE 14.1

One thing that's missing from the source code for `odds02.c` is error-checking. What happens if the user inputs 10 items but 12 to draw? What happens when 0 is input for either value? Your task for this exercise is to modify the code to confirm that the input of either value isn't 0, and that the number of items drawn doesn't exceed the number of items available.

My solution, chock-full of comments, is available in the online repository as `odds03.c`. Use the source code for `odds02.c` as your starting point.

EXERCISE 14.2

Another good improvement to the code is to add commas to the output. After all, which is better: 1:11238513 or 1:11,238,513? Human eyeballs appreciate commas.

Your task for this exercise is to add commas to the odds numeric output. I recommend that you write a function to accept a floating-point value as input. Assume that the value has no decimal portion. Return a string that represents the value, but with commas placed every three positions, as shown earlier. My solution is the *commify()* function, available in the source code file `oddsd04.c`, found in the online repository.

14.2   Here are your winning numbers

Those lottery numbers you find on a fortune cookie fortune were most likely computer generated. I find this development disappointing. Instead, wouldn't it be charming to imagine some wise old Chinese woman sitting in an incense-filled room, actively consulting with the spirit world for inspiration? But, no. The truth is that the numbers were spewed forth from a computer—randomly generated. Sure, they could be correct guesses and win you a fortune, but the odds are against it.

To have the computer pick your lottery winners requires programming random numbers. These must simulate the randomness of the magical lottery-ball machine that generates the actual numbers drawn in Powerball. Unlike in the real world, your lottery simulation must ensure that the values drawn are in range. Further, you can't draw the same number twice. Your lottery picks must be unique, just like in the real world.

14.2.1   Generating random values

I can't think of a computer game that doesn't rely upon random numbers. Even complex chess-playing software must still decide its first move. A spin of the old random-number generator is what makes the decision.

Computers don't generate truly random numbers. The values are referred to as *pseudo random* because, if you had all the data, you could predict the values. Still, random-number generation is central to setting up an interesting game—or picking lottery numbers. The required tool is the *rand()* function, prototyped in the `stdlib.h` header file:

```
int rand(void);
```

The function takes no arguments and returns an integer value in the range zero through RAND_MAX. This value for most compilers is set to 0x7fffffff or 2,147,483,647. An improved version of the function, *random()*, works similarly to *rand()*, though this function isn't a part of the standard C library.

The source code shown next works like one of the first programs I ever wrote in BASIC, years ago. It spews out a grid of random numbers, five rows by five columns. The *rand()* function generates the value saved in variable r and output in a *printf()* statement.

Listing 14.3   Source code for `random01.c`

```
#include <stdio.h>
#include <stdlib.h>                    For the rand()
                                       function
int main()
{
    const int rows = 5;
    int x,y,r;
                                       Nested loop to
    for( x=0; x<rows; x++ )            process the grid
    {
        for( y=0; y<rows; y++ )        Obtains the
        {                              random integer
            r = rand();
            printf("%d ",r);           Outputs the
        }                              random integer
        putchar('\n');
    }                                  Ends the row
    return(0);
}
```

The code shown in listing 14.3 serves its purpose. It generates 25 random values, and the output is completely ugly:

```
1804289383 846930886 1681692777 1714636915 1957747793
424238335 719885386 1649760492 596516649 1189641421
1025202362 1350490027 783368690 1102520059 2044897763
1967513926 1365180540 1540383426 304089172 1303455736
35005211 521595368 294702567 1726956429 336465782
```

The numbers are huge, which is within the range generated by the *rand()* function, from zero through RAND_MAX. To output values in a different range, you can employ the modulo operator. Here is the expression I use:

```
value = rand() % range;
```

The variable value is between 0 and the value of range. If you want the value to be between 1 and range, I use this version of the expression:

```
value = rand() % range + 1;
```

To set the random-number output to values from 1 through 100, change two statements to modify the source code for random01.c:

```
r = rand() % 100 +1;
printf("%3d ",r);
```

The first statement limits the *rand()* function's output to the range of 1 through 100. The second statement aligns output, restricting the value to a three-character-wide frame, followed by a space. These changes are incorporated into the source code file random02.c, available in the online repository. Here is the updated output:

```
84  87  78  16  94
36  87  93  50  22
63  28  91  60  64
27  41  27  73  37
12  69  68  30  83
```

Alas, if you run the program twice, the same numbers are generated. This result doesn't bode well for your lottery picks because the desire is to be random.

If you've ever coded random numbers, you know that the solution is to seed the randomizer. The *srand()* function, also prototyped in the stdlib.h header file, handles the task:

```
void srand(unsigned int seed);
```

The seed argument is a positive integer value, which the *rand()* function uses in its random-number calculations. The *srand()* function needs to be called only once. It's often used with the *time()* function, which returns the current clock-tick value as a seed:

```
srand( (unsigned)time(NULL) );
```

The *time()* function is typecast to *unsigned* and given the NULL argument. This format ensures that the clock-tick value is properly consumed by the *srand()* function, and a new slate of random numbers is generated every time the program runs.

(If you use the *random()* function, it has a similar seed function, *srandom()*.)

Improvements to the random02.c code are included with random03.c, available in the online repository. The time.h header file is also included. Here is a sample run:

```
 8  53  95  12  93
76  92  59  45  21
32  65  73  95  85
62  55   9  89  16
59  13  33  61  74
```

And here's another sample run, just to show a different slate of random numbers:

```
14  49  92  92  56
80  95  41  57  66
 8  99  62  86  73
26  32  23  55  38
98  66  94  20  98
```

By the way, because a *time_t* value (returned from the *time()* function) is used, if you run the program rapidly in succession, you see the same values generated. This is a weakness of seeding the randomizer with a clock-tick value, but it shouldn't be a problem for most applications.

14.2.2 *Drawing lotto balls*

Into the tumbler fall 69 balls, numbered 1 through 69. The balls are agitated, popping up and down as they stir for a few tense moments. Using some sort of magic, a single ball is drawn from the lot, rolling down a tube onto a slide. Eager but stupid people tighten their focus to witness the number revealed. No, it probably wasn't one of their picks—but they have four more chances! Hope remains high. This process is how the Powerball lottery works.

For my lottery simulation, I use the basic premise of the Powerball: randomly draw five numbers in the range from 1 through 69. The sixth, the Powerball, adds another level of complexity, and it can be programmed later, but not in this chapter.

Drawing lottery numbers is like drawing any random sequence of items, such as playing cards. My first attempt at the simulation is shown in the next listing, the source code for `lotto01.c`. It borrows from the random series of programs shown earlier in this chapter but uses a *for* loop to output five random numbers in the range from 1 through 69.

> **Listing 14.4　Source code for `lottt01.c`**

```c
#include <stdio.h>
#include <stdlib.h>
#include <time.h>

int main()
{
    const int balls = 69, draw = 5;     // Sets the constants to represent total balls and number to draw
    int x,r;

    srand( (unsigned)time(NULL) );      // Seeds the randomizer

    printf("Drawing %d numbers from %d balls:\n",    // Informs the user
            draw,
            balls
        );

    for( x=0; x<draw; x++ )             // Loops to draw the given number of balls
    {
        r = rand() % balls+1;          // Generates a random value in range
        printf("%2d\n",r);             // Outputs the value
    }

    return(0);
}
```

Sometimes I think the code used to generate lottery winners on fortune cookie fortunes is just as simple as that presented in listing 14.4. Here is the output:

```
Drawing 5 numbers from 69 balls:
17
64
38
 1
26
```

True, the output could be prettier. An update is presented in a few pages. But if you run the code often enough, you eventually see output like this:

```
Drawing 5 numbers from 69 balls:
44
19
19
10
33
```

Because the code doesn't check previous numbers drawn, values can repeat. Such output it not only unrealistic—it's unlucky.

The code can't determine whether a value drawn is a repeat unless the values drawn are stored and examined. To do so, an array is necessary, dimensioned to the number of balls drawn. Each random value drawn must be stored in the array, and then the array is examined to ensure that no two values repeat.

For my first approach to this problem, I use the winners[] array, shown next, an update to the lotto01.c code. A *for* loop fills the array with random values. Next, a nested *for* loop works like a bubble sort to compare each value in the array with other values. When two values match, the second is replaced with a new random value, and the loop is reset to scan again.

Listing 14.5   Source code for `lottt02.c`

```c
#include <stdio.h>
#include <stdlib.h>
#include <time.h>

int main()
{
    const int balls = 69, draw = 5;      Dimensions the
    int x,y;                             array to hold the
    int winners[draw];      ◄———————     number of draws

    srand( (unsigned)time(NULL) );

    printf("Drawing %d numbers from %d balls:\n",
            draw,
            balls
          );                             Fills the array with
                                         random values, one
    for( x=0; x<draw; x++ )   ◄————      through balls
    {
        winners[x] = rand()%balls+1;
    }
```

**The outer loop moves through the array
to the next-to-last element, `draw-1`.**

**The inner loop moves
through the array from
the `x+1` element to the
last element.**

**Compares each
value to the rest
of the values**

**For a match, draws the
repeated value again**

**Forces the `y` loop to stop by
setting the termination value**

**Resets the `x` loop back to start
(−1 because the loop increments
`x` each time it runs)**

Outputs the results

```
    for( x=0; x<draw-1; x++ )
        for( y=x+1; y<draw ; y++ )
            if( winners[x]==winners[y] )
            {
                winners[y] = rand()%balls + 1;
                y = draw;
                x = -1;
            }

    for( x=0; x<draw; x++ )
        printf("%2d\n",winners[x]);

    return(0);
}
```

The improved version of the lotto program checks for repeated values and replaces them. The output looks the same as for the first version of the program, but no numbers repeat. You're all ready to plunk down your money for a chance at riches, yet the code presents room for improvement.

EXERCISE 14.3

The output from the existing rendition of the *lotto* program is tacky. It looks nothing like the back of a fortune cookie fortune. Two ways to improve it are to sort the numbers and output them on a single line to improve readability. For example:

```
Drawing 5 numbers from 69 balls:
 5 - 10 - 14 - 19 - 33
```

The output is now linear, ready for printing and saving that old Chinese woman time that she can spend with her grandkids. My solution for this exercise is titled `lotto03.c`, and it's available in the online repository.

14.2.3 Avoiding repeated numbers, another approach

The key to any lottery simulation is to ensure that no two numbers are drawn twice. The preceding section offered one method. Another method, one that I've used many times, is to simulate all the numbers or balls in an array. As random numbers are generated, elements of the array are updated to reflect that the ball is no longer available. I find this approach much easier to code, though perhaps not as easy to explain.

Figure 14.2 illustrates an array `numbers[]` that's been initialized with all zeros. The array's elements represent balls in a lottery. When an element has the value zero, it means that the ball hasn't yet been drawn. When a ball is drawn, its corresponding element in the array is set to 1, as shown in the figure. For example, if the random number generator returns 12, the 12th element of the array is set to one.

To confirm that a number is available to draw, the code tests the related array element. If the element is 0, the number is available and it's set to 1. If the element is 1,

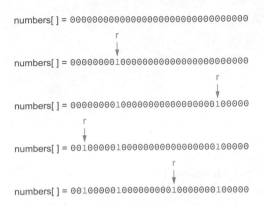

numbers[ ] = 00000000000000000000000000000000

numbers[ ] = 00000000100000000000000000000000

numbers[ ] = 00000000100000000000000000100000

numbers[ ] = 00100000100000000000000000100000

numbers[ ] = 00100000100000000010000000100000

Figure 14.2   Elements in an array representing lotto balls

it's skipped and another random number is generated. The following code performs this test:

```
for( x=0; x<draw; x++ )
{
    do
        r=rand()%balls;
    while( numbers[r]==1 );
    numbers[r] = 1;
}
```

The numbers[] array represents the simulated lotto balls. It's dimensioned to the number of balls available, 69. Variable draw is the number of balls to draw—five, in this instance.

The *do-while* loop repeats whenever the random array element numbers[r] is equal to 1. This test ensures that a ball isn't drawn twice. Otherwise, if the element is zero, meaning that the ball is available, it's "drawn" by setting its value to one: numbers[r] = 1. This statement flags the ball as drawn *and* prevents it from being drawn again.

The variable balls helps to truncate, via the modulus operator, the *rand()* function's return value: r=rand()%balls. However, this value isn't increased by 1. Because the code deals with an array, the first value must be 0. Therefore, the numbers drawn are in the range of 0 to balls-minus-1, or 68 in this example. This result can be adjusted during output to reflect the true lottery ball number.

The rest of the code to simulate a lottery drawing is presented in the following listing. The numbers[] array is initialized, the balls are drawn, and then the result is output. Because the numbers[] array is processed sequentially in the final *for* loop, the winning numbers need not be sorted before they're output.

Listing 14.6   Source code for `lotto04.c`

```
#include <stdio.h>
#include <stdlib.h>
#include <time.h>
```

```
int main()
{
    const int balls = 69, draw = 5;
    int x,r,count;
    int numbers[balls];

    srand( (unsigned)time(NULL) );

    printf("Drawing %d numbers from %d balls:\n",
            draw,
            balls
        );
    for( x=0; x<balls; x++ )          ◁─┐ Initializes
    {                                     the array
        numbers[x] = 0;
    }

    for( x=0; x<draw; x++ )           ◁─┐ Selects the
    {                                     random values
        do
            r=rand()%balls;
        while( numbers[r]==1 );
        numbers[r] = 1;
    }

    count = 0;                            Processes the array
    for( x=0; x<balls; x++ )          ◁─  to cull the winning
    {                                     numbers
        if( numbers[x] )              ◁─  If the element is nonzero
        {                                 (1), the ball was drawn.
            printf(" %d",x+1);        ◁─  Outputs the ball number,
            count++;                      plus one to account for the
            if( count<draw )          ◁─  array starting at element 0
                printf(" -");
        }                                 After all but the last
    }                                     number, outputs a
    putchar('\n');                        dash separator

    return(0);
}
```

The lotto04.c source code file shown in listing 14.6 is available in the online repository. Here is the output:

```
Drawing 5 numbers from 69 balls:
 1 - 25 - 37 - 39 - 40
```

No numbers are repeated, and the output is sorted. Good luck!

14.3   *Never tell me the odds*

If only you could play the lottery forever. Or perhaps you're eccentric enough to believe that you can purchase 11,238,513 tickets, each with a different number combination, and somehow come out ahead. But the system just doesn't work that way. Oh, I could wax on about the various techniques to "win" the lottery, but foo on all that.

Fortunately, you don't need to purchase a bunch of lottery tickets to see how well you would fare playing a game. The computer can not only generate lotto picks but also match those picks with other picks. You can run simulations to determine how many random draws it takes before the computer guesses which numbers the computer chose. As long as the coding is proper, you can put the odds to the test. Alas, you just don't win any money.

14.3.1   *Creating the lotto() function*

To simulate multiple draws in a lottery, you must modify the existing *lotto* code so that the balls are drawn in a function, which I call *lotto()*. This improvement to the code allows the function to be called repeatedly, representing the original numbers to match as well as the guesses made.

I toiled a few times writing the *lotto()* function: should it return the random numbers drawn, or should they be passed in an array? I finally chose to pass an array, which works as a pointer within the function. This method allows the array's elements to be modified directly, so the function returns nothing.

The *lotto()* function, shown next, uses similar statements as the *main()* function in the *lotto* series of programs shown earlier in this chapter: the numbers[] array now dwells within the *lotto()* function because its contents need not be retained between calls. After the array is initialized, a *for* loop sets the random element values representing numbers drawn. This operation is followed by a second *for* loop that processes the entire numbers[] array, filling elements from the passed array.

Listing 14.7   The *lotto()* function from `lotto05.c`

```
void lotto(int *a)              ←┤  The array is referenced as
{                                   a pointer in this function.
    int numbers[BALLS];         ←   This array stays local to
    int x,y,r;                      the lotto() function.

    for( x=0; x<BALLS; x++ )    ←   Initializes the
    {                               numbers[] array
        numbers[x] = 0;
    }

    for( x=0; x<DRAW; x++ )     ←┤  Randomly draws
    {                               items in the array
        do
            r=rand()%BALLS;         Variable y serves as an index
        while( numbers[r]==1 );     into the passed array.
        numbers[r] = 1;
    }
                                    Fills the passed array's
    y = 0;                      ←   elements with the random
    for( x=0; x<BALLS; x++ )    ←   numbers drawn
```

```
        {
            if( numbers[x] )                    ◁──    If the ball has
            {                                           been drawn . . .
                *(a+y) = x;                     ◁──    . . . sets the element number
                y++;                                    in the passed array
            }
            if( y==DRAW )                       ◁──    If the passed array
                break;                                  is full, breaks the
        }                                               loop early
    }
```

Increments the index (arrow pointing to `y++;`)

The defined constants BALLS and DRAW are the same as the *const int* values shown in early versions of the lotto programs. These are made into defined constants so that their values are available to all functions in the source code file.

The *main()* function calls the *lotto()* function, and then it outputs the contents of the array passed. The next listing shows the *main()* function, which again is based on parts of the *lotto* series shown earlier in this chapter.

Listing 14.8 The *main()* function from `lotto05.c`

```
int main()
{
    int x;
    int match[DRAW];                        ◁──   Uses an array as
                                                    the argument for
                                                    the lotto function
    srand( (unsigned)time(NULL) );

    printf("Trying to match:");             ◁──   Calls the lotto()
    lotto(match);                                   function, filling
    for( x=0; x<DRAW; x++ )                 ◁──    array match
    {
        printf(" %d",match[x]+1);                  Outputs the array's
        if( x<DRAW-1 )                              elements, the lottery
            printf(" -");                           "winners"
    }
    putchar('\n');

    return(0);
}
```

The full source code for `lotto05.c` is available in the online repository. Here is a sample run:

```
Trying to match: 32 - 33 - 45 - 55 - 61
```

The output looks like all the other *lotto* programs so far, though with the *lotto()* function set, it's now possible to draw multiple lottery numbers in the same code. After all, the prompt above says, "Trying to match." The next step in the program's generation is to obtain another set of random lottery ball picks to see whether they match the first numbers drawn.

14.3.2 Matching lottery picks

The *lotto()* function allows the code to repeatedly pull lottery numbers over and over, trying to match the original draw. To do so, I duplicated the *for* loop and output statements in the `lotto05.c` code, but with a second array, `guess[]`. This change appears in the source code file `lotto06.c`, which outputs a second round of lottery numbers to see whether the two draws match. Here is sample output:

```
Trying to match: 2 - 18 - 38 - 47 - 69
    Your guess: 6 - 10 - 34 - 35 - 49
```

I'm not showing the full source code here because it doesn't do anything new—it just repeats the same block of code but with a new array, `guess[]`. This array is passed to the *lotto()* function and then output, as shown earlier. The result is two lottery number draws. Do they match? Probably not.

Even if the two arrays matched, you must perform a visual inspection to confirm. In the previous sample output, they don't. But why do the work yourself when the computer is not only bored but all too eager?

To make the comparison between two sets of lottery ball draws, I use the *winner()* function, shown here. As arguments, it consumes two arrays, referenced as integer pointers. Nested *for* loops compare each array value from the first array with each array value in the second array. Pointer notation is used to make the comparison. When a match is found, variable c is incremented. The total number of matches, ranging from zero through DRAW, is returned.

Listing 14.9   The *winner()* function from `lotto07.c`

Both arrays are passed as integer pointers, m for match and g for guess.

Initializes the matching count to 0

Loops through all DRAW numbers in the first array

Loops through each DRAW number in the second array

Compares each element value

Increments the variable y if two values match

Returns the number of matches

```c
int winner(int *m, int *g)
{
    int x,y,c;

    c = 0;
    for( x=0; x<DRAW; x++ )
        for( y=0; y<DRAW; y++ )
        {
            if( *(m+x) == *(g+y) )
                c++;
        }
    return(c);
}
```

The *main()* function calls the *winner()* function immediately after array guess[] is filled by the *lotto()* function:

```
lotto(guess);
c = winner(match,guess);
```

The arrays are passed by name. In the *winner()* function, these arrays are recognized as integer pointers. Back in the *main()* function, the values for array *guess[]* are output, along with a final *printf()* statement that reports the number of matches.

   The full code is available in the online repository as lotto07.c. Here is a sample run:

```
Trying to match: 20 - 27 - 34 - 41 - 59
    Your draw: 1 - 19 - 27 - 33 - 48
You matched 1 numbers
```

As luck would have it, one of the values matched between the two simulated lottery drawings the first time I ran the code (shown above). The *winner()* function returned one in variable c, as both arrays share the value 27. I'm pleased that I didn't need to run the code several times to show a match. Yet, it's this step of repeatedly running the program that inspired me to code the program's final version, covered in the next section.

14.3.3 *Testing the odds*

In the Powerball game, you can't just match a single ball to win. No, you must match a single ball *and* the Powerball to win some paltry amount. Ditto for two balls: two balls plus the Powerball equals some modest payout. You can, however, match three main numbers to win $7 on a $2 bet. Garsh! Of course, I didn't code any of the Powerball nonsense, so my *lotto* programs are straightforward, and the prize money is consistently zero.

   The odds of matching one number and the Powerball are 1:92. This value means that if you play the game 92 times, you'll probably match one value and the Powerball at least once—but it's not a guarantee. I won't get into the math, but it could take you several hundred times to see a match or you could match the first time. It's this unpredictability that entices people to gamble—even when the odds are stupidly high.

   Rather than run the *lotto* program over and over, I decided to program a loop to output guesses until at least two numbers match. The next listing shows the *main()* function from an updated—the final—version of the *lotto* series of programs. The *lotto()* and *winner()* functions are unchanged, but to the *main()* function I added a constant, tomatch. It sets the minimum number of balls to match before a *do-while* loop stops drawing random lotto balls. Nothing is output until a match is found, which shaves several seconds from the processing time.

Listing 14.10   The *main()* function from `lotto08.c`

```
int main()
{
    const int tomatch = 2;            ←  Determines how
                                         many balls to match
    int x,c,count;
    int match[DRAW],guess[DRAW];      ←  The two arrays—one to hold
                                         the numbers to match and
    srand( (unsigned)time(NULL) );       the other the guesses

    printf("Trying to match:");       ←  Outputs the
    lotto(match);                        numbers to
    for( x=0; x<DRAW; x++ )              match
    {
        printf(" %d",match[x]+1);
        if( x<DRAW-1 )
            printf(" -");
    }
    putchar('\n');                    Tracks how many
                                      draws are attempted
    count = 0;                     ←
    do
    {                                 Grabs the simulated
        lotto(guess);             ←  lottery draw
        c = winner(match,guess);
        count++;                      Keeps looping as long as the
    } while( c<tomatch );         ←  number of balls matching is
                                      less than the goal
    printf("It took %d times to match %d balls:\n",     ←  Informs the user
            count,                                          of the result, how
               c                                            many draws were
           );                                               required
    for( x=0; x<DRAW; x++ )       ←  Outputs the
    {                                winning draw
        printf(" %d",guess[x]+1);
        if( x<DRAW-1 )
            printf(" -");
    }
    putchar('\n');

    return(0);
}
```

Sees whether any balls match — points to `c = winner(match,guess);`

Increments the count — points to `count++;`

The complete code for `lotto08.c` is available in the online repository. The program keeps drawing random lottery picks until the minimum match value, stored in variable `tomatch`, is met. Here is a sample run:

```
Trying to match: 1 - 5 - 21 - 33 - 37
It took 5 times to match 2 balls:
 1 - 30 - 37 - 63 - 66
```

The computer took five loops to find two matches—1 and 37, according to the output. You can run the program multiple times to see how many loops it takes to match at least two balls from five out of a total of 69. Again, I don't know the precise odds, but it's less than 100.

The fun part comes when you modify the code: alter the `tomatch` constant to the value 5, and then run the program. Here is sample output after I made this modification:

```
Trying to match: 15 - 33 - 47 - 59 - 60
It took 5907933 times to match 5 balls:
 15 - 33 - 47 - 59 - 60
```

Above, it took 5,907,933 spins of the *do-while* loop before an exact match of the five balls was achieved.

I don't know whether this code convinces anyone of the futility of playing a lottery. The issue is never the math; it's the human misunderstanding of odds and probability. The notion that "someone's gotta win" trumps logic and common sense every time.

EXERCISE 14.4

The computer mindlessly and effortlessly simulates as many lottery ball draws as you're willing to let it perform. The `lotto08.c` code shows that even when attempting to match five out of five balls, the program runs rather quickly. Yet, more coding can always be done, especially to sate the curious mind.

Your task for this exercise is modify the `lotto08.c` code with the goal of determining the average number of plays required to match all five balls from 69 possible numbers. Run the simulation 100 times, each time recording how many repeated calls to the *lotto()* function were required to achieve a match. Store each value, and then report the average number of plays it took to make a match.

Here is sample output from my solution, which is available in the online repository as `lotto09.c`:

```
Trying to match: 9 - 32 - 33 - 42 - 64
For 100 times, the average count to match 5 balls is 11566729
```

On average, it took 11,566,729 calls to the *lotto()* function to match the original numbers drawn. Remember from earlier in this chapter that the calculated odds of drawing the same five numbers from 69 lotto balls is 11,238,513. Darn close.

Comments in my solution explain my approach, though please attempt this exercise on your own before you see what I did. The modifications aren't that involved, because most of the coding necessary is already in the `lotto08.c` source code file.

Oh! And the solution program takes a while to run. On my fastest system, I timed it at almost 9 minutes to churn out the results. Be patient.

Tic-tac-toe

At the climax of the 1983 film *WarGames,* the computer that's about to start World War III is directed to play a game of tic-tac-toe with itself. Recognizing that the game is silly because experienced players often end play in a draw, the computer determines that nuclear war is futile. It decides not to blow up the world. This conclusion should add some excitement to this chapter, because you can equate any game of tic-tac-toe—even one simulated on a computer—to nuclear war.

Game play for tic-tac-toe is simple. It's easy to code. If you haven't yet done so, now is the time to write your own version of the game. Of course, it's made more complex when you consider such tasks as:

- Coding a game loop
- Programming turns for players
- Determining when the game is over
- Adding the computer as a player
- Giving the computer some intelligence

The biggest hurdle you face when programming a text-mode game like tic-tac-toe is that I/O in C isn't interactive. Unless you use a third-party library, such as Ncurses, you must rely upon stream I/O for your programs. It can work, but stream I/O brings potential problems to the table that the code must deal with, lest everything get hinky for the user.

15.1 A silly kids' game

No one knows the exact origins of the game tic-tac-toe, so I thought I'd make up some interesting facts: in ancient Egypt, a game similar to tic-tac-toe was played on a wooden peg board with tokens carved from the severed toes of enemy soldiers. The Romans enjoyed a game of *tria ordine*, which involved lining up pebbles on a marble tablet. The prize was to slap your opponent in the face. And in medieval Europe, Norwegian children played a game of tossing fish into baskets, which has nothing to do with tic-tac-toe, but it smelled terrible.

Yes, I made all that up.

The earliest written reference to tic-tac-toe comes from the late 1800s using the name *noughts and crosses*. Even today, that is the game's name in the Commonwealth outside America. The US name tic-tac-toe, originally tick-tack-toe, came about in the early 20th century. The first tic-tac-toe computer program was programmed in the early 1950s.

That's your history lesson for today—some parts true, but others mostly false.

15.1.1 *Playing tic-tac-toe*

I'm obligated by the Computer Authors Guild to explain the game of tic-tac-toe despite your complete familiarity with it. Even so, remember that—unlike playing on a piece of paper, in the dirt, or on a fogged mirror—coding the game requires that you review the game play.

Figure 15.1 shows the standard tic-tac-toe grid: two vertical lines intersecting two horizontal lines. This grid holds nine squares, which become the battlefield. These are numbered in the figure, one through nine, also with handy mnemonics for each square's location: top, middle, and bottom with left, center, and right.

```
1 TL     2 TC     3 TR


4 ML     5 MC     6 MR


7 BL     8 BC     9 BR
```

Figure 15.1   The tic-tac-toe game grid, squares numbered and labeled

Players take turns setting a mark into one of the nine grid squares. After choosing who goes first (an advantage), the players alternatively mark an X or O in the squares. Traditionally, the first player marks X, though this choice isn't a rule.

The winner is the first player to place three of their marks in a row. If this goal fails, the game is a tie, or "cat's game." All but the stupidest humans can achieve a tie, so desperate adults play with small kids to make themselves feel victorious.

Experienced players know that going first is advantageous. Further, marking the center square during the first turn, or *ply,* is the best strategy. Otherwise, good players attempt to set a triangle of squares, as illustrated in figure 15.2, which guarantees a win because their opponent can block only one of the legs.

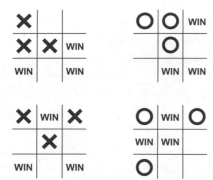

Figure 15.2   Arrangements for a winning triangle

Regardless of the strategy, tic-tac-toe has only eight paths to victory: three rows, three columns, or two diagonals. Despite the variety of games, only these eight possibilities define a winner. Because of the nine squares in the grid, victory is achieved in nine or fewer moves, making the game easy to learn, quick to play, and fun for a short measure of time.

15.1.2   *Approaching the game mathematically*

As a nerd, I'm compelled to discuss the mathematical details regarding the game of tic-tac-toe. Some of these details come into play when you code your own game—specifically, if you dare to code a computer opponent and make it somewhat intelligent.

The total number of permutations possible for a game of tic-tac-toe is 19,683. Don't trust me; someone else did the math. The number accounts for each of nine grid squares holding either an X or an O or being blank. Keep in mind that the game grid is ternary, not binary. I touch upon this point again at the end of this section.

The 19,683 number doesn't account for actual game play, because X and O follow each other and eliminate squares; the number of permutations is reduced as play moves forward. In practice, the game has 3,200 possible permutations. Removing those situations where the game is already won or tied drops the number further to 2,460.

A final reduction is made by eliminating duplicates due to rotating or mirroring the game grid. When these repetitions are removed, the total number of tic-tac-toe game permutations drops to 120. As this value is a lot easier to handle than 19,683, many programmers opt to create all 120 permutations in memory and use this database to guide the computer during game play.

The coding approach to handle 120 permutations is to create a game tree. This structure contains all possible game plays from which the program can choose a path to victory. In a way, this approach works like a giant cheat sheet, with the computer cribbing its next move based on all the possibilities, with a bias toward exploring only those paths to victory or a tie.

My approach to the computer's game play isn't as smart as following a game tree. Instead, I chose to emulate the way people play the game: move to win or move to block. Later in this chapter, I expand upon this technique.

Finally, it's important to remember that the game gird is ternary: blank, X, or O. Obviously, you use an array to store values in the grid. I originally used values 0, 1, and 2 for blank, X, and O, respectively. This approach made the math more difficult when examining rows, columns, and diagonals. So, I instead used 0 for blank, but −1 for O and +1 for X. You can read more about these choices in the next section.

15.2   The basic game

For my implementation of tic-tac-toe, I began by coding the game grid. In fact, I've written many programs that output tic-tac-toe grids, but never bothered writing any game play, probably because the game itself isn't rewarding to play.

At the core of any interactive text mode game is a game play loop. It accepts input for new moves, updates the grid, and determines when a winning condition occurs. It's the winning condition that breaks the loop, though other options for bailing out are also provided.

For this first round, I'm coding a human-versus-human version of the game. It features functions that output the game grid, prompt for input, and determine a winner. An updated version that adds the computer as an opponent is covered later in this chapter.

15.2.1   Creating the game grid

Programming a tic-tac-toe grid is one of the basic duties beginners perform when learning C programming. After all, the grid represents a real-life example of a two-dimensional array, with rows and columns. It can be implemented in several ways, as shown in figure 15.3.

```
1 | 2 | 3              1   2   3
---+---+---              |   |
4 | 5 | 6              4   5   6
---+---+---              |   |
7 | 8 | 9              7   8   9
ASCII line art        Wide character
                      line art


 1 2 3                  1 2 3                  1 2 3
 4 5 6                  4 5 6                  4 5 6
 7 8 9                  7 8 9                  7 8 9
Characters            Characters, spaces,    Color-coded
and spaces            and indents            squares
```

Figure 15.3   Various options for presenting a text-mode tic-tac-toe game grid

I experimented with each of the varieties shown in figure 15.3 before I decided it would be more fun to use color text to show the grid. Color text output is covered in chapter 13. It involves sending ANSI escape sequences to standard output, which are interpreted by most terminals as color. The grid I chose is shown in the lower right in figure 15.3, the color-coded squares.

Seven color constants are created to achieve the colors I want, as shown in table 15.1. Two different values are used for each of the three square possibilities: blank, X, and O. The alternating values help set a checkerboard pattern, which helps me avoid adding ugly ASCII line art to build the game grid.

Table 15.1   Color constants and their values used to create the tic-tac-toe game grid

Constant Name	Code	For Output
bfwb[]	\x1b[32;47m	Blank square, green foreground/white background
bf[]	\x1b[32m	Blank square, green foreground
xfwb[]	\x1b[31;47m	X square, red foreground/white background
xf[]	\x1b[31m	X square, red foreground
ofwb[]	\x1b[34;47m	O square, blue foreground/white background
of[]	\x1b[34m	O square, blue foreground
reset[]	\x1b[0m	Color values off

Each sequence sets a foreground or foreground-background combination. The background colors are used, every other square, to create the checkerboard pattern. The final reset[] sequence removes color from the output, which avoids color spill between lines in the output.

The next listing shows the source code for ttt01.c, the foundation upon which all code in this chapter is built. The *showgrid()* function outputs the game grid with alternating colors, numbering each position, one through nine. A *switch-case* test determines whether the square is occupied with an O (–1), an X (+1), or a blank (0). In the *main()* function, the grid is initialized in the grid[] array and then output. The purpose of this tiny program is to ensure that the output looks good.

Listing 15.1   Source code for ttt01.c

```
#include <stdio.h>

void showgrid(int *g)
{
    const char bfwb[] = "\x1b[32;47m";
    const char bf[] = "\x1b[32m";
    const char xfwb[] = "\x1b[31;47m";
    const char xf[] = "\x1b[31m";
```

The grid[] array is passed as an integer pointer.

Constants to define colors for grid output

```
const char ofwb[] = "\x1b[34;47m";
const char of[] = "\x1b[34m";
const char reset[] = "\x1b[0m";
int x;

for( x=0; x<9; x++ )
{
    switch( *(g+x) )
    {
        case -1:
            if( x%2 )
                printf("%s O %s",ofwb,reset);
            else
                printf("%s O %s",of,reset);
            break;
        case 1:
            if( x%2 )
                printf("%s X %s",xfwb,reset);
            else
                printf("%s X %s",xf,reset);
            break;
        default:
            if( x%2 )
                printf("%s %d %s",bfwb,x+1,reset);
            else
                printf("%s %d %s",bf,x+1,reset);
    }
    if( (x+1)%3==0 )
        putchar('\n');
}
putchar('\n');
}

int main()
{
    int grid[] = {
        0, 0, 0,
        0, 0, 0,
        0, 0, 0
    };

    puts("Tic-Tac-Toe");

    showgrid(grid);

    return(0);
}
```

Annotations:
- Loops through the entire grid, nine squares
- O occupies the square.
- Tests the value of each square: −1 for O, +1 for X, and 0 for blank
- Outputs the square with a background (and the O)
- Outputs the square without a background
- Repeats the same output for X
- Numbers the unoccupied squares, adding 1 for human eyeballs
- Every third square, adds a newline
- The game grid is initialized here.
- Outputs the grid

The *showgrid()* function processes squares in the game grid. For each possible value—−1, +1, or 0—two options are available for output. The first is triggered for odd-numbered squares, where a background color is applied. For even squares, no background color is used. The effect is to output the current state of play in a consistent pattern, with no extra text characters required to build the grid.

Here is a sample run:

```
Tic-Tac-Toe
 1  2  3
 4  5  6
 7  8  9
```

The numbers in the grid help reference squares as the game progresses. Eventually, they're replaced by X and O characters, which not only informs the user that the same square can't be played twice but also shows the game's progress.

You can stop here and just admire your work. But no. The next step is to add game play.

15.2.2 Adding game play

I'm unsure whether every game works this way, but all the text-mode games I've written contain a primary game play loop. The loop checks for input, updates the game field, and determines when the game is over.

Generally, the game play loop is endless. The terminating condition is winning the game, losing the game, or the player giving up.

To update the existing ttt01.c code, the game play loop must display the grid, prompt for input, and then update the grid[] array. This loop is shown in the next listing, added just below the *puts()* statement that outputs the game title. Two integer variables must be declared: ply and p.

Listing 15.2 The game play loop in the *main()* function

Turns, or plies, start at zero.

The loop is endless, relying on a win or exit command to break.

Outputs the grid

Accepts input, returning the square to place a token

```
ply = 0;
while(1)
{
    showgrid(grid);
    p = prompt(ply);
    if( p==0 )
        break;
    grid[p-1] = ply%2 ? -1 : 1;
    ply++;
}
```

Sets the token on the grid, subtracts one from p to obtain the array offset, and uses the current ply to determine whether O (–1) or X (+1) has played

Increments the ply to the next turn

If the user inputs zero, the game quits.

The *prompt()* function obtains user input, either the square in which to place a mark or zero to exit the game. The zero return value is tested to break the loop, ending the game. Otherwise, the grid[] array is updated.

The value of variable ply (the current turn) determines whether X or O is playing. It's assumed that X goes first. When ply%2 is 0, then O or –1 is generated in the grid; otherwise, X or +1 is set.

A text mode game must rely upon stream I/O to do its thing. Such a trick is possible if input is limited and makes sense to the user. For my tic-tac-toe game, numeric input is all that's allowed. I rely upon the *scanf()* function, which I detest, but it does the job.

The following listing shows the *prompt()* function, which is called from the *main()* function in the endless *while* loop, shown earlier in listing 15.2. The function's argument is the current ply, the game's next turn. This value is tested to determine whether X or O is playing. Input ranges from 1 through 9 (human numbers, not the actual array offsets), with 0 indicating the player wants to quit. Out-of-range values are interpreted as 0.

Listing 15.3 The *prompt()* function

```
int prompt(int p)
{
    int square;

    printf("%c's turn: Pick a square, 0 to quit: ",
            p%2 ? 'O' : 'X'
          );
    scanf("%d",&square);
    if( square<0 || square>9 )
        return(0);
    return(square);
}
```

Uses the `ply` value in variable `p` to determine which is the current play, X or O

Obtains numeric input

For out of range values, returns 0 (exit)

The *main()* function uses the return value from *prompt()* to set X or O into the grid. The complete source code is available in the online repository as `ttt02.c`. Here's a sample run:

```
Tic-Tac-Toe
 1  2  3
 4  5  6
 7  8  9

X's turn: Pick a square, 0 to quit: 5
 1  2  3
 4  X  6
 7  8  9

O's turn: Pick a square, 0 to quit: 1
 O  2  3
 4  X  6
 7  8  9

X's turn: Pick a square, 0 to quit: 2
 O  X  3
 4  X  6
 7  8  9
```

```
O's turn: Pick a square, 0 to quit: 5
  O  X  3
  4  O  6
  7  8  9

X's turn: Pick a square, 0 to quit: 0
```

The code successfully places an X or O on the grid, taking turns. What's missing from the code is the capability to determine when a square is already occupied. As you can see from this sample run, O was able to capture the center square after it was already taken by X. The code also lacks a method to determine when the game is over; game play continues until the user inputs zero to quit.

15.2.3   Limiting the input to free squares

The `ttt02.c` code has plenty of room for improvement. The priority for me at this point is to restrict play to only blank squares in the grid. For example, if the center square is occupied by an X, player O is unable to choose the square. This update requires a few modifications. To prevent squares from being retaken, the *prompt()* function must be updated as well as the game play loop in the *main()* function.

The updated *prompt()* function is shown next. The `grid[]` array must be passed as an argument so that the function can determine whether a square is occupied. Further, −1 is added as a return value to flag that a square is occupied or an input value is out of range. Otherwise, the return values are 1 through 9 to select an open square, or 0 to quit.

Listing 15.4   The updated *prompt()* function

```
int prompt(int p, int *g)                    ←     Array grid[] is
{                                                  used as pointer
    int square;                                    variable g here.

    printf("%c's turn: Pick a square, 0 to quit: ",
            p%2 ? 'O' : 'X'
        );
    scanf("%d",&square);

    if( square<0 || square>9 )                          Informs the user
    {                                                   that the value is
        puts("Value out of range");          ←         out of range
        return(-1);
    }
                                         Tests for the 0 to quit here; otherwise,
                                         the value is returned and used
    if( square==0 )               ←      improperly on array grid[]
        return(square);
                                      If the value chosen is occupied, or not zero; note that 1
                                      is subtracted because the input is 1 through 9, though
    if( *(g+square-1) != 0 )      ←   the array elements are numbered 0 through 8.
    {
        printf("Square %d is occupied, try again\n",
                square
            );
```

Returns −1 for invalid input

Informs the user that the square is occupied and to try again

```
        return(-1);
    }
    return(square);
}
```

◁— **Returns –1 for invalid input**

◁— **Returns the square chosen, which is unoccupied**

To make the updated *prompt()* function work, the statement that calls the function must be modified. Bad input must be dealt with right away. Therefore, I chose to set the function into a *while* loop, where the return value from *prompt()* is the condition:

```
while( (p = prompt(ply,grid)) == -1 )
    ;
```

The *while* loop repeatedly calls the *prompt()* function as long as the value returned is –1. Only valid input—0 or an open square number—breaks the loop. The remainder of the *main()* function is unchanged.

The updated source code is found in the online repository as `ttt03.c`. Here is a sample run:

```
Tic-Tac-Toe
 1  2  3
 4  5  6
 7  8  9

X's turn: Pick a square, 0 to quit: 5
 1  2  3
 4  X  6
 7  8  9

O's turn: Pick a square, 0 to quit: 5
Square 5 is occupied, try again
O's turn: Pick a square, 0 to quit: 1
 O  2  3
 4  X  6
 7  8  9

X's turn: Pick a square, 0 to quit: 9
 O  2  3
 4  X  6
 7  8  X

O's turn: Pick a square, 0 to quit: 0
```

At the second move, the program successfully prevents O from choosing X's square. It outputs a message displaying the issue and urges the player to try again.

15.2.4 *Determining the winner*

The game works so far, with players able to go back-and-forth choosing squares and setting their marks. But the code doesn't know when you've won. Further, because the game play loop is infinite, eventually you run out of open squares and the game doesn't stop, nor does the program know when to call a tie, or cat's game. Fixing is in order.

To determine a winner, I wrote the *winner()* function. It examines the eight slices through the game grid where a win is possible, as illustrated in figure 15.4. For a slice to identify as a winner, all of its squares must contain the same value—+1 for X or –1 for O. The total for a given slice must be either +3 or –3 to win the game.

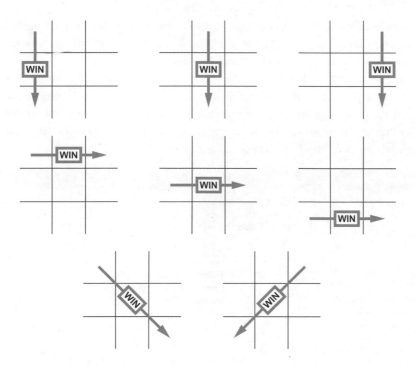

Figure 15.4   The eight slices defining a win in tic-tac-toe

The *winner()* function accepts the game grid as an argument. Each square is examined as columns, rows, and diagonals, as shown in figure 15.4. The notation to do the math was clunky in the function's original version. For example, to test the left column, I used the following statement:

```
slice[0] = *(g+0) + *(g+3) + *(g+6);
```

Element 0 of the `slice[]` array holds the total for the first column—squares 0, 3, and 6. However, I find the `*(g+n)` notation to be clumsy and confusing: each square is represented by integer pointer g, plus an offset into the array. Because I constantly had to refer to a map (see figure 15.1) when writing the code, I opted to create some defined constants to reference the various squares more easily:

```
#define TL *(g+0)
#define TC *(g+1)
#define TR *(g+2)
#define ML *(g+3)
#define MC *(g+4)
#define MR *(g+5)
#define BL *(g+6)
#define BC *(g+7)
#define BR *(g+8)
```

The mnemonics of these defined constants, also appearing in figure 15.1, make it easier to define the slices. They also play a role later in the program's development, when the computer is attempting to block or make a win.

The next listing shows the *winner()* function. Its argument is the game grid. The slice[] array contains the totals of the eight possible winning combinations, totaling the values in each of the three squares for each slice. If a slice contains all the same tokens, its value is –3 for an O win or +3 for an X win. A *for* loop tests these possibilities. When a win occurs, the function returns 1, or 0 otherwise.

Listing 15.5   The *winner()* function

```
int winner(int *g)                          Eight possible ways
{                                           to win; the slice[]
    int slice[8];                           array holds the totals.
    int x;

    slice[0] = TL + ML + BL;                Tallies the columns,
    slice[1] = TC + MC + BC;                rows, and diagonals
    slice[2] = TR + MR + BR;                for each slice
    slice[3] = TL + TC + TR;
    slice[4] = ML + MC + MR;
    slice[5] = BL + BC + BR;
    slice[6] = TL + MC + BR;
    slice[7] = TR + MC + BL;

    for( x=0; x<8; x++ )
    {                                       Checks for
        if( slice[x]==-3 )                  an O victory
        {
            showgrid(g);                    Informs
            puts(">>> O wins!");            the user
            return(1);                      Exits with 1,
        }                                   meaning a player
        if( slice[x]==3 )                   has 1
        {
            showgrid(g);
            puts(">>> X wins!");
            return(1);
        }
    }
    return(0);                              Returns 0 if
}                                           no one has 1
```

Reviews the totals

Outputs the winning game grid

Repeats the same sequence for an X victory

The *winner()* function must be integrated into the *main()* function within the game play loop to report a victory. It also provides another way to terminate the loop beyond the user typing zero to quit the game.

After the *winner()* function is added, another change to the game play loop is to set a termination condition for the *while* loop. After all, only nine plies (turns) are possible for a game of tic-tac-toe, assuming it's a draw.

After the game play loop, I added another *if* test to determine whether the game was a draw. These items are called out in the next code listing, which shows the updated code from the *main()* function.

Listing 15.6   Updating the game play loop in the *main()* function

```
ply = 0;
while(ply<9)              ◄──┤  Limits the loop
{                            │  to nine turns

    showgrid(grid);
    while( (p = prompt(ply,grid)) == -1 )
        ;
    if( p==0 )                     Calls the winner() function,
        break;                     which returns 1 when a win
    grid[p-1] = ply%2 ? -1 : 1;    is detected
    if( winner(grid) )      ◄──┘
        break;
    ply++;
}                          Tests to see whether
if( ply==9 )           ◄──┤ the loop terminated
{                          in a no-win
    showgrid(grid);
    puts("Cat's game!");    ◄───┐
}                               │  Informs
                                   the user
```

Halts the loop ⟶ (points to `break;`)

Outputs the grid to show the draw ⟶ (points to `showgrid(grid);`)

The complete update is found in the online repository as `ttt04.c`. The game now allows two players to compete. It accurately reports a winner and determines when the game ends in a draw. Here is sample output:

```
Tic-Tac-Toe
 1   2   3
 4   5   6
 7   8   9

X's turn: Pick a square, 0 to quit: 5
 1   2   3
 4  .X   6
 7   8   9

O's turn: Pick a square, 0 to quit: 2
 1   O   3
 4   X   6
 7   8   9
```

```
X's turn: Pick a square, 0 to quit: 1
  X  O  3
  4  X  6
  7  8  9

O's turn: Pick a square, 0 to quit: 9
  X  O  3
  4  X  6
  7  8  O

X's turn: Pick a square, 0 to quit: 4
  X  O  3
  X  X  6
  7  8  O

O's turn: Pick a square, 0 to quit: 7
  X  O  3
  X  X  6
  O  8  O

X's turn: Pick a square, 0 to quit: 6
  X  O  3
  X  X  X
  O  8  O

>>> X wins!
```

Think of all the paper you can save when you play tic-tac-toe on the computer! Of course, most users don't want to play against a human challenger, probably because they have no friends. The true foe for a game of tic-tac-toe is . . . a computer.

15.3   *The computer plays*

In the movie *WarGames*, the genius programmer is asked whether his game of tic-tac-toe has a configuration where the computer can play itself. It does. The key is to enter zero for the number of players. The computer plays itself, realizes that the game is futile, and we go to DEFCON 5.

Obviously, anyone who codes a computer version of tic-tac-toe is compelled to provide the same "number of players equals zero" option available to our intrepid cinematic heroes. Who doesn't want to see the computer battle wits with itself? This feature not only makes the game more interesting but also tests the programmer's logic: when the computer plays against itself, does the game always end in a draw?

15.3.1   *Choosing the number of players*

The decision tree required to set the number of players for the tic-tac-toe program certainly is ugly. I tried making it beautiful, but with three options to sift through, the coding choices are limited.

The prompt is easy enough to code:

```
Number of players (0, 1, 2):
```

Set in the *main()* function, immediately after the program's title is output, the prompt asks for the number of players: 0, 1, or 2. If an invalid number is input, the program quits.

In the game play loop, however, decisions are made based on the number of players:

- When the number of players is 0, the computer plays every turn.
- When the number of players is 1, the computer alternates every other turn.
- When the number of players is 2, humans take turns, as in the `ttt04.c` version of the game.

The following listing shows the updated *main()* function. The number of players is input, and then an *if-else* contraption sifts through the players, ensuring that human and computer take their turns. If the player count is 1, play alternates between computer and player, with the player going first.

Listing 15.7 The updated *main()* function

```
int main()
{
    int grid[] = {
        0, 0, 0,
        0, 0, 0,
        0, 0, 0
    };
    int ply,p,players;          ◁——  Variable players
                                      tracks the number of
                                      players: 0, 1, or 2.

    srand( (unsigned)time(NULL) );   ◁——  Seeds the randomizer
                                           for computer play

    puts("Tic-Tac-Toe");
    printf("Number of players (0, 1, 2): ");   ◁——┐ Prompts
    scanf("%d",&players);                          │ for input
    if( players<0 || players>2 )   ◁——┐ Exits the
        return(1);                      │ program upon
                                        │ invalid input

    ply = 0;
    while(ply<9)
    {
        showgrid(grid);          ┌── Zero players
        if( players==0 )   ◁──   └── are specified.
        {
            p = computer(grid);  ◁——┐ The computer always
        }                            │ plays itself, every turn.
        else if( players==1 )
        {
            if( ply%2 )    ◁——┐ On odd turns, the
            {                  │ computer plays.
                p = computer(grid);
            }
            else     ◁——┐ The prompt() function
            {           │ handles the player's turn.
                while( (p = prompt(ply,grid)) == -1 )
                    ;
```

One player is specified. ⌐——▷ (pointing to `else if( players==1 )`)

```
            }
        }
        else            ◄──┐ For two players, the prompt()
        {                  └ function handles both turns.
            while( (p = prompt(ply,grid)) == -1 )
                ;
        }
        if( p==0 )
            break;
        grid[p-1] = ply%2 ? -1 : 1;
        if( winner(grid) )
            break;
        ply++;
    }
    if( ply==9 )
    {
        showgrid(grid);
        puts("Cat's game!");
    }

    return(0);
}
```

The *computer()* function handles the computer's play, even when both players are the computer. The *prompt()* function deals with human player interaction.

The code isn't done. The *computer()* function must be written, which is covered in the next section. To complete the update from this section, however, you must add directives to include the stdlib.h and time.h header files, which support the *srand()* statement in the *main()* function, as well as the *rand()* statement in the *computer()* function.

15.3.2   *Coding a dumb opponent*

At this point in the game's development, the *computer()* function need not harbor insidious intelligence nor an intimate knowledge of how to win the game. So, I coded a purely random selection routine, as shown in the next listing. The function tests for an available random square in the grid and sets its token at that location. The random value is returned—in a range compatible with the human player's choice—where the token is set in the *main()* function.

Listing 15.8   The *computer()* function

```
int computer(int *g)
{
    int r;                    Generates a         Confirms that the square
                              random value,       is empty, or keeps looping
    do                        0 through 8         otherwise
    {
        r = rand() % 9;    ◄────┘              ┌
    } while( *(g+r) != 0 );  ◄─────────────────┘ Increments the square value for
                                                 humans as well as for consistency
                                                 with the prompt() function
    r++;                   ◄──────────────────┘
    printf("The computer moves to square %d\n",r);
```

Informs
the user └──►

```
        return(r);
}
```

The complete code, including the updated *main()* function from the preceding section as well as the *computer()* function, is available in the online repository as ttt05.c.

At this point in the program's evolution, the computer always goes second, playing O for its moves. Here is some sample output:

```
Tic-Tac-Toe
Number of players (0, 1, 2): 1
  1  2  3
  4  5  6
  7  8  9

X's turn: Pick a square, 0 to quit: 5
  1  2  3
  4  X  6
  7  8  9

The computer moves to square 6
  1  2  3
  4  X  O
  7  8  9

X's turn: Pick a square, 0 to quit: 3
  1  2  X
  4  X  O
  7  8  9

The computer moves to square 2
  1  O  X
  4  X  O
  7  8  9

X's turn: Pick a square, 0 to quit: 7
  1  O  X
  4  X  O
  X  8  9

>>> X wins!
```

It's possible to attribute some intelligence to the admittedly dumb *computer()* function, but nothing of the sort exists. I'd provide a sample run that makes you believe the computer is smart, but instead run the code on your own, setting 0 as the number of players, and review the output. Occasionally, it seems like the computer is being smart. Trust me—it's not.

EXERCISE 15.1
The computer complains that it's unfair that it always goes second in a one-on-one battle. To remedy this situation, update the *main()* function from ttt05.c so that a random choice is made, determining which player goes first: computer or human.

Here is the first part of the output from my solution:

```
Tic-Tac-Toe
Number of players (0, 1, 2): 1
A flip of the bitcoin says that the computer goes first

  1  2  3
  4  5  6
  7  8  9

The computer moves to square 3
  1  2  X
  4  5  6
  7  8  9
```

The random choice of who goes first is required only when one player is selected, a human-versus-computer battle. My solution is found in the online repository as ttt06.c.

15.3.3 Adding some intelligence

Most of the nerds who program a computer to play tic-tac-toe use a game tree. They plot every move and its consequences, all 120 or so permutations of the game. I looked into this approach, but it seemed like a lot of work. Being lazy, I instead rolled my own approach for the computer to play, and hopefully win, tic-tac-toe.

My code has three pieces of intelligence for the computer player. First, if it's the first turn (ply zero) and the computer moves first, it should snag the center square. This update is made to the *computer()* function:

```
if( p==0 )
{
    puts("The computer snags the center");
    return(5);
}
```

Variable p is the current ply value from the game play loop in the *main()* function. When its value is 0, the computer is taking the first turn and all squares are open. A message is output, and the function returns 5, the center square. The value should be 4, because this is the offset in the grid[] array, but the *computer()* function must be compatible with the user's *prompt()* function and return values in the range 1 through 9. (Remember that *prompt()* returns 0 to quit the game.)

This *if* test can be improved to check the center square during the second ply: if the computer goes second but its human opponent is too stupid to grab the center square, it should take it. Here is the update to the *if* decision:

```
if( p==0 || (p==1 && MC==0) )
{
    puts("The computer snags the center");
    return(5);
}
```

The *if* condition reads, "If it's the first turn—or if it's the second turn and the center square (MC) remains empty—grab the center square." The center square is a position of strength in this game. In fact, taking the center is one of the first tricks a kid learns when first playing tic-tac-toe.

The second iota of intelligence is to play a corner square when the center square is taken. This move provides the best defense when moving second. The *if* decision here is an easy one:

```
if( p==1 && TL==0 )
{
    puts("The computer moves to square 1");
    return(1);
}
```

The *if* condition reads, "If it's the second ply (turn) and the top-left (TL) square is empty, take it." The value 1 is returned. At this point in the *computer()* function, the center square has already been taken—guaranteed. The preceding *if* condition rules out MC as anything other than 0. Therefore, on the second ply, p==1, the top-left (TL) square is most likely empty. The *if* condition tests for it anyway and defensively moves to the top-left square.

The third piece of intelligence consists of a game grid scan for moves to block or moves to win. Before the computer resorts to a random move, it scans all eight possible winning slices on the game grid. If any of these slices contains two of the same tokens plus an empty square, the empty square is filled so that the computer wins or blocks a win.

I originally wrote two functions, *towin()* and *toblock()*, to carry out the game grid scan. Eventually, it dawned on me that both functions work the same, just look for different values. The *towin()* function wants the computer's tokens to add up to 2 or –2; the *toblock()* function wants the opponent's tokens to add up to 2 or –2. I wrote the *three()* function to handle both conditions:

```
int three(int *g, int p)
```

The function's arguments are g, the game grid, and p, the token to look for: –1 for O and +1 for X.

The *three()* function's statements are repetitive, with each block representing one of the eight slices that establish a win. Defined constants shown earlier in this chapter represent the specific squares. Here is a typical block:

```
if( TL + ML + BL == p*2 )
{
    if( TL==0 ) return 0;
    if( ML==0 ) return 3;
    if( BL==0 ) return 6;
}
```

Defined constants TL, ML, and BL represent the first column in the grid. If their total is equal to two times variable p, the column contains two matching tokens and a blank. This result holds true whether p is –1 for O or +1 for X.

After a slice is identified as a potential win or block, the function returns a value representing the blank square: If it's the top-left square, TL, 0 is returned. If the middle-left square is blank, ML==0, its offset is returned. This logic allows the computer to either win or block, depending on the value of variable p.

The *three()* function continues with similar tests for each of the eight slices. The value returned is the square to choose, reported to the *computer()* function shown in the next listing. The code first checks for a win, and then for a block. If neither test is successful (–1 is returned), the computer randomly chooses an available square, as before.

Listing 15.9   The updated *computer()* function

```
int computer(int p,int *g)          ←——  Variable p is the current
{                                          ply and g is the game grid.
    int r;

    if( p==0 || (p==1 && MC==0) )   ←——|  Grabs the center
    {                                      square if it's empty
        puts("The computer snags the center");
        return(5);
    }                                   ——|  On the second turn,
                                            grabs the corner
    if( p==1 && TL==0 )             ←——|    square if it's empty
    {
        puts("The computer moves to square 1");
        return(1);                      ——|  Detects a win using the
    }                                        ply value: 0 means it's
    if( p%2 )                       ←——      O's turn, 1 for X.
        r = three(g,-1);
    else
        r = three(g,1);                 ——|  If a win isn't detected, three()
                                            returns –1; checks for a block (you
    if( r==-1 )                     ←——|    want to win before you block).
    {
        if( p%2 )                   ←——|  Determines
            r = three(g,1);               whether X or O is
        else                              moving next
            r = three(g,-1);
    }                                   ——|  If r is equal to –1e, the computer
                                            hasn't won or blocked; time for a
    if( r==-1 )                     ←——      random square pick.
    {
        do
        {
            r = rand() % 9;
        } while( *(g+r) != 0 );
    }
```

Checks for a win for O (–1) — `if( p%2 )` / `r = three(g,-1);`

Checks for a win for X (+1) — `r = three(g,1);` / `if( r==-1 )`

Blocks for X — `r = three(g,1);`

Blocks for O — `r = three(g,-1);`

```
    r++;
    printf("The computer moves to square %d\n",r);

    return(r);
}
```

Informs the user →

Increments r to represent the proper offset, 1 through 9

The smarts in the *computer()* function work from the top down: first comes the center square check, and then the computer tries to grab the corner square. After that, the *three()* function is checked first to win and then to block. When these efforts fail, shown by the value −1 returned, the computer uses the randomizer.

The *main()* function must also be updated, reflecting the new argument for the *computer()* function. Two updates are required to modify this statement:

```
p = computer(grid);
```

into this statement:

```
p = computer(ply,grid);
```

The `ply` argument is used in the *computer()* function for its call to the *three()* function. It's this variable's value that determines whether the function is blocking or winning because, in the program, X always moves first.

All changes, including the full *three()* function, are found in the online repository in the source code file `ttt07.c`. The computer player isn't perfectly intelligent, but it's smart enough to prove a challenge—for at least a few games and definitely to defeat a small child or stupid adult.

The true test, of course, is when the computer plays itself. In theory, it should tie each time. But the program still uses random-number generation to plot its initial game. Specifically, in the computer-to-computer output shown here, see how the computer grabs the center square as well as the upper-left square? These are advantageous and defensive moves, respectively:

```
Tic-Tac-Toe
Number of players (0, 1, 2): 0
   1  2  3
   4  5  6
   7  8  9

The computer snags the center
   1  2  3
   4  X  6
   7  8  9

The computer moves to square 1
   O  2  3
   4  X  6
   7  8  9
```

```
The computer moves to square 3
   O  2  X
   4  X  6
   7  8  9

The computer moves to square 7
   O  2  X
   4  X  6
   O  8  9

The computer moves to square 4
   O  2  X
   X  X  6
   O  8  9

The computer moves to square 6
   O  2  X
   X  X  O
   O  8  9

The computer moves to square 9
   O  2  X
   X  X  O
   O  8  X

The computer moves to square 8
   O  2  X
   X  X  O
   O  O  X

The computer moves to square 2
   O  X  X
   X  X  O
   O  O  X
```

Cat's game!

From the output, you can see that the computer did well against itself. It's not exactly smart, but it's challenging enough—and the game ended in a tie.

Further updates to the code at this point would lead to a game tree strategy, where you map out the best second, third, and fourth moves in a complex tree decision structure-thing. At some point, however, playing the game employs the tactics of blocking and winning.

One devious improvement I considered was to have the computer cheat. It could, for example, replace an opponent's token with its own or prevent an opponent from selecting a winning square. Though such a modification would be fun, it involves rewriting a lot of the existing code. I leave this task up to you, though not as an official exercise.

index

Symbols

& (AND) bitwise logical operator 77
#include directives 133
| (OR) bitwise logical operator 77

A

ABBR option 184
add_noun() function 106
add_word() function 101–102, 105, 107
alfa int variable 182
ALPHA constant 277
alpha constant 160
AND operator 200
apt command 11
ar (archive) utility 134–135
ASCII (American Standard Code for Information
      Interchange)
   control codes 71–73
   conversion tricks 76–78
   generating noncharacter output 74–75
   overview 69–71, 145–147
-a switch 183, 185–187, 189
atexit() function 176

B

BALLS defined constant 326
balls variable 323
bash shell 11, 18–20, 130
Baudot code 141
BCD (Binary Coded Decimal) 141
BG constant 308
binString() function 74–75
bits, defined 164

BL defined constant 350
block buffering 53
BOLD attribute 309
bravo int variable 182
buf buffer 123, 208
buffer character array 54
BUFSIZ defined constant 208
build_vocabulary() function 103–105, 107
byte_sizes.c code 166
BYTES_PER_LINE constant 82
bytes variable 82
byte unsigned long variable 166

C

Caesarean ciphers 50–67
   devising variations 60–63
   filtering words 65–67
   hex output filters 63–64
   I/O filters 51–57
      stream I/O 51–54
      working filter at command prompt
         56–57
      writing simple filters 54–56
   NATO filter 64–65
   rot13 program 58–60
calendars 273–311
   calculating first day of month 280–282
   cal program 274–275
   color 303–311
      coloring holidays 309–311
      generating colorful calendar 306–309
      terminal colors 303–306
   creating constants and enumerating dates
         276–277
   finding day of week 277–280

calendars *(continued)*
  full year
    displaying 295–298
    putting into grid 299–303
  generating week 286–292
  leap years 282–283
  showing month 292–295
  time zones 283–285
cat command 86, 161
cd command 10
C development cycle 2–4
  building 3–4
  compiling 3–4
  editing source code 2–3
  linking 3–4
center() function 295, 299–300
changecwd.c source code 209
character encoding 141–163
  text representation 142–148
    ASCII 145–147
    early text formats 142–145
    Unicode 147–148
  wide character programming 148–163
    character types 150–152
    generating output 152–156
    locale settings 149–150
    receiving input 156–160
    working with wide characters in files 160–163
char array declaration 111
char data type 69–70, 74, 110, 137, 150–151, 157, 165–166
charlie int variable 182
char pointer 33, 44, 101, 257
char-sized chunks 169
char variables 74
ch character input 55
CHCP command 146
chdir() function 208–210, 215, 239
check_caps() function 108
checksum01.c program 88
checksum int variable 87
ch int variable 48, 74
chmod command 20, 199
chsh command 18
clang compiler 5, 12–13
closedir() function 203–204
code, writing 5–7
Code::Blocks IDE 5–7
code pages 146
code points 148
code space 148
color 303–311
  coloring holidays 309–311
  generating colorful calendar 306–309
  terminal colors 303–306

color_holiday() function 310
color_output() function 308
COLUMNS defined constant 299
command-line compiling 9–13
  accessing terminal window 9
  basic shell commands 10–11
  compiling and running 12–13
  GUI editor 12
  text screen editors 11–12
  using command-line compiler options 15–16
commify() function 317
computer() function 345–349, 351
constants, creating 276–277
const char arrays 143
const char pointers 137, 276
const char types 215
const classifier 276
core dump 171
COUNTRY command 146
count variable 128, 227, 235
cp command 10
C Programming Language, The (Kernighan and Dennis) 130
Csh shell 19
-c switch 134–135
ctime() function 23–24, 26, 196, 283
curl libcurl library 15
cwd[] char array 208
cypher program 13

D

Dan Gookin's Guide to Ncurses Programming 53
data[] array 175
data[] buffer 175
date tm structure 278
day member 257
dayoftheweek() function 279, 281
day variable 286, 292, 294, 301–302
DELTA constant 277
depth indent level 221
depth variable 221
dest buffer 115
diff command 86
diff program 86
d_ino member 205
dir() function 213, 215, 217–218, 220–221, 225
directories
  monitoring depth 220–222
  names 218–220
  reading 203–207
directory char variable 215

directory tree utility 191–222
  directory trees 217–222
    directory name 218–220
    monitoring directory depth 220–222
  files and directories 194–207
    file types and permissions 197–203
    gathering file information 194–197
    reading directories 203–207
  filesystem 192–194
  subdirectories 207–217
    exploring 210–212
    recursion 212–217
    tools for 208–210
dirent structure 204–206
DIR handle 203–204
dirtree03.c online repository 222
dirtree program 220–221
dotm[] array 301–303
double data type 110
double-quad words 165
doublewords 165
do-while loop 323, 330
dow variable 297–298
doy variable 271
DRAW defined constant 326
draw variable 323
d_reclen member 205
dump 170–171
dumpfile04.c source code 185
dumpfile code 175, 180, 183
dumpfile utility 175–179
  command-line options 179–190
    activating octal output 187–190
    getopt() function 180–182
    setting abbreviated output
      185–187
    updating program code 182–185
  fixing uneven output 178–179
  reading file data 175–177

E

easter() function 267–269, 271
easter01.c online repository 268
EBCDIC (Extended Binary Coded Decimal
  Interchange Code) 145
echo command 57, 247
else condition 198
else portion 294
else statement 59
Emacs text mode editor 11
encoding and decoding 68–92
  hex encoder/decoder 79–89
    error-checking 87–89
    writing 79–86
  plain text 69–78
    ASCII 69–71
    control codes 71–73
    conversion tricks 76–78
    generating noncharacter output 74–75
  URL encoder 89–92
    creating 91–92
    encoding rules 89
    writing 90–91
entry pointers 35–36
cntry variable 33–35
enum keyword 276–277
EOF (end-of-file) marker 51, 54–55
EOF flag 43
EPSILON constant 277
errno variable 204, 208–209, 211
exit() function 84, 176, 247
exit command 10
EXIT_FAILURE status 249
exit status 246
EXIT_SUCCESS status 249
extended_ascii.c source code 147
Extended Binary Coded Decimal Interchange
  Code (EBCDIC) 145
extract() function 219–220

F

FALSE constant 277
fclose() function 203
february() function 282–283, 288, 294–295, 299
fflush() function 54
FG constant 308
fgetc() function 48, 54, 162, 176
fgets() function 41, 48, 84, 111, 114, 158, 161–162,
  176
fgetwc() function 162
fgetws() function 157–159, 161–163
file finder utilities 175, 223–244
  Find Dupe utility 234–244
    building file list 235–239
    locating duplicates 239–244
  Find File utility
    coding 225–228
    find and grep utilities 224–225
    globbing 228–232
    using wildcards to find files 232–234
FILE handle 203
fileinfo series of programs 201, 203
filename char pointer 176, 195
find() function 225, 227, 232, 236–240
find command 224
Find Dupe utility 234–244
  building file list 235–239
  locating duplicates 239–244

finddupe utility 234
findfile01.c source code 227–228
Find File utility 223–244
   coding 225–228
   find and grep utilities 224–225
   globbing 228–232
   using wildcards to find files 232–234
find utility 224–225
finfo structure 235, 239, 243
first() function 301
first variable 293–294
float data type 137
floor() function 269
fopen() function 160, 176, 179, 203
fork() function 249
fortune program 31
found int variable 241
fputc() function 54–55, 160
fputs() function 154
fputwc() function 160
fputws() function 154
fread() function 176, 205
free() statements 37

G

GAMMA constant 277
gcc compiler 5, 12
getchar() function 52, 54, 156, 170
getcwd() function 208–209
getcwd.c demo program 208
getopt() function 180–183
getopt_long() function 180
getwchar() function 156–157
glob() function 228, 230–232, 234
globbing 228–232
glob (global) 228
GREET.COM program 25–26
greetings program 21–23
   adding general time info to greeting code
     25–26
   adding moon phases to greeting code
     30–31
   adding name as argument 22–23
   adding phrases to greeting code 37
   adding specific time info to greeting
     code 26–27
   coding 21–22
grep command 224
grep utility 224–225
grid[] array 335, 337, 339, 348
guess[] array 328
GUI editor 12

H

hash char variable 151
hello[] array 153
Hello World program 21
hello_wworld01.c code 153
help() function 183–185
hexdecode program 84, 86, 88
hexd (hexdefilter01.c) program 81
hexdump utility 161, 164–190
   dumpfile utility 175–179
     command-line options 179–190
     fixing uneven output 178–179
     reading file data 175–177
   storage 164–175
     dumping data 170–175
     outputting byte values 169–170
     storage units and size 165–168
hexe (hexenfilter01.c) program 81
hexencode program 84, 86
hex encoder/decoder 79–89
   error-checking 87–89
   writing 79–86
hex integer variable 85
hex output filters 63–64
h holiday structure 310
High Performance File System (HPFS) 192
holiday detector utility 245–272
   calculating Easter 266–269
   holidays in UK 255–256
   holidays in US 254–255
   irregular holidays 261–266
   obtaining any date 251–254
   obtaining today's date 250–251
   regular date holidays 256–261
   return values 246–250
     exit status vs. termination status 246
     interpreting 247–249
     preset 249–250
     setting 246–247
   testing 270–272
holiday integer 261
holiday structure 257–259, 268, 310
hostage filter 57
hostage program 57
HPFS (High Performance File System) 192
-h switch 183

I

I/O (input/output) filters 51–57
   stream I/O 51–54
   working filter at command prompt 56–57
   writing simple filters 54–56

IDEs (integrated development environments) 4–9
  choosing 4–5
  Code 5–7
  linking libraries 14–15
  XCode IDE 7–9
if condition 184, 188, 349
if decision 178, 257, 288, 294, 308, 348–349
if-else conditions 66
if else-if else structure 201, 290
if-else structures 143, 188, 203
if tests 160, 172, 183, 186, 200, 266, 282, 289, 343, 348
index variable 176
inode 194
input buffer 158
input wide character buffer 158
ins pointer 126
int8_t integer type 168
int16_t integer type 168
int32_t integer type 168
int64_t integer type 168
int data type 110, 137, 168, 170
International Telegraph Alphabet No. 2 (ITA2) 144
int variable declarations 85
inword variable 128
isalnum() function 90
isalpha() function 41, 49, 59, 64
isholiday() function 256–257, 259–263, 266, 268–272, 310
isholiday package 271
isspace() function 66
isterm() function 46–47
ITA2 (International Telegraph Alphabet No. 2) 144
items int variable 34
items variable 34, 36

J

JANUARY enumerated constant 277

K

Kernighan, Brian 130
key[] array 100
kibibytes 168
kludge technique 54
Ksh shell 19

L

-L (big L) switch 135
LC_CTYPE category 149
-L. (dash-big L-period) switch 135

ld program 4
leap years 282–283
Learn Linux in a Month of Lunches (Ovadia) 11
left() function 121–122, 124
LEFT$ command 121
len characters 121, 124
length() method 137
LENGTH constant 186
length constant 162
len integer 123
len variable 119, 138
libraries
  linking 14–15
  string 132–136
    creating 134–135
    using 135–136
    writing source and header file 133–134
line[] buffer 83, 85, 162
line_out() function 174, 176–178, 184–186, 188
list_base pointer 35
list_base variable 34–36
-l (little L) switch 15–16, 135–136, 199
LLVM clang compiler 5
-lm switch 166, 267
locale command 149
locale variable 150
localtime() function 24, 250–251, 256–257, 276–278, 286, 288, 294
$LOGNAME environment variable 20
lotto() function 325–328, 330
lotto01.c code 321
lotto05.c code 327
lotto08.c code 330
lotto pick utility 312–330
  avoiding repeated numbers 322–324
  creating lotto() function 325–327
  drawing lotto balls 320–322
  generating random values 317–320
  matching lottery picks 327–328
  odds
    overview 313–314
    programming 315–317
    testing 328–330
  playing lotteries 313
lotto programs 325, 328
lowercase() function 98, 107
ls command 10, 194
ls -l command 284

M

madlib01.c program 103, 106
madlib02.c program 104, 106
Mad Libs program 108
make command 11

malloc() function 32, 111
man command 10
man fs command 192
man pages 27, 44, 69, 112, 115, 157–158, 162, 180, 195, 203–204, 208–209, 230, 252, 284–285
match char pointer 44
math (m) library 166
mday integer 261
mdays[] array 270, 283, 288, 294
mdays variable 294–295
message URL http
    //brew.sh 11
methods 137
mid() function 122–124
MID$ command 121
MinGW 5
mkdir command 10
mktime() function 252, 254, 256
ML constant 350
month[] array 276–277
month program 285, 292, 295
months program 295
month variable 286, 289, 294, 301
mood variable 156
moon_phase() function 29–30
moon phase program 27–31
    adding moon phases to greeting code 30–31
    observing moon phases 28–29
    writing moon phase algorithm 29–30
more filter 63–64
mp variable 30
mv command 10
mystring.o object code 135

N

n[] pointer array 268
name member 257
name members 240
-name switch 224
nato[] array 40–42, 64
nato03.c program 46
nato04.c progam 47
NATO (North Atlantic Treaty Organization) 38
NATO phonetic alphabet filter 64–65
NATO phonetic alphabet translator program 38–49
    alphabet 38–39
    from NATO to English 43–49
        converting NATO input to character output 44–47
        reading NATO input from file 47–49
    reading and converting file 42–43
    writing translator 41–42
ncal program 274–275

new buffer 127
noglob option 229
North Atlantic Treaty Organization. See NATO
no_sigma constant 160
now time_t variable 250
NULL constant 44, 104
number() function 98, 106
numbers[] array 322–323, 325

O

octal output 187–190
octet 199
OCT option 184
offset characters 126
offset integer 123, 125–126
ohex() function 80
omega constant 160
on_exit() function 176
OOP (object-oriented programming) approach for strings 136–140
    adding function to structure 137–139
    creating string 139–140
opendir() function 203–204, 208
opterr global variable 180
options01.c source code 181
options int variable 183–185
options series 183
org pointer 125–126
-o switch 13, 16, 183, 188–189
Ovadia, Steven 11

P

password[] buffer 99
password generators 93–108
    random password program 97–101
        adding conditions 98
        building 97
        improving password 99–101
    random word password generator 101–108
        building 106–108
        generating random words 101–106
    strategies 94–97
        avoiding basic and useless passwords 94–95
        complexity 95–96
        word strategy 96–97
PATH_MAX defined constant 208
permissions_out() function 203
pithy05.c code 105
pithy saying program 31–37
    adding phrases to greeting code 37
    creating phrase repository 31–32
    randomly reading phrases 32–37

plain text 69–78
  ASCII 69–71
  control codes 71–73
  conversion tricks 76–78
  generating noncharacter output 74–75
ply integer variable 337
pmonth variable 289
pointers (memory locations) 32
popen() function 249
pow() function 166
printf() function 13, 27, 30, 34–35, 64, 69, 76, 79, 85, 90, 100, 112, 114, 130, 146, 150, 152, 166, 186, 198, 205–206, 220–221, 241, 251–252, 283, 285, 291, 294, 308–309, 318
-print switch 224
prntf() function 300
prompt() function 337–340, 346, 348
pseudo random 317
putchar('\n') statement 301, 309
putchar() function 54–55, 69, 170, 172
putenv() function 284–285
puts() function 114, 337
putwchar() function 153, 163
putwchar(ch) statement 163
p variable 337, 348
pwd command 10, 208–209

Q

qsort() function 137
quadwords 165

R

rand() function 317–319, 346
random() function 317, 319
random02.c code 319
random password program 97–101
  adding conditions 98
  building 97
  improving password 99–101
randomp series of programs 106
random values, generating 317–320
random word password generator 101–108
  building 106–108
  generating random words 101–106
randwords01.c code 102
ransom program 57
readdir() function 204–207
readdir02.c source code 205
readdir04.c source code 207
realloc() function 32, 36
recursion 212–217
repeat member 240–241, 243
reset[] sequence 335

reset command 73
return01 program 248
return keyword 176
return values 246–250
  exit status vs. termination status 246
  interpreting 247–249
  preset 249–250
  setting 246–247
right() function 122–124
RIGHT$ command 121
Ritchie, Dennis 130
rot13 filter 58–60
rot13 program 58–60
-r switch 135, 225

S

say command 43
saying variable 37
scanf() function 158–159, 338
scramble() function 99–100, 107, 115
screen dump 171
set +o noglob command 229
set_abbr() macro 184
setbuf() function 53
setlocale() function 149–150, 152–153
set macro 184
set -o command 229
set_oct() macro 184
shell commands 10–11
shell startup 18–21
  overview 18
  scripts
    editing 20–21
    overview 18–19
shift variable 61
sholiday() function 263
showgrid() function 335 336
Sh shell 19
S_IRGRP defined constant 200–201
S_IROTH defined constant 200
S_IRUSR defined constant 200
S_ISBLK() macro 198
S_ISCHR() macro 198
S_ISDIR() macro 198
S_ISFIFO() macro 198
S_ISLNK() macro 198
S_ISREG() macro 197–198
S_ISSOCK() macro 198
S_IWGRP defined constant 200
S_IWOTH defined constant 200
S_IWUSR defined constant 200
S_IXGRP defined constant 200
S_IXOTH defined constant 200
S_IXUSR defined constant 200

size characters 208
SIZE constant 178
sizeof operator 112–113, 119, 166
slice[] array 341–342
srand() function 319, 346
srandom() function 319
sscanf() function 86
-s switch 135
start_day variable 271
stat() function 195–197, 203, 206–207, 211
statbuf structure 195
stat command 197
stderr (standard error device) 176
stdin input device 51, 158
stdin (standard input) 162
stdlib.h library 284
stdout device 154
st_mode member 197, 199–200, 203
storage 164–175
　dumping data 170–175
　outputting byte values 169–170
　storage units and size 165–168
str1.length function 138
strappend() function 115–116
strcaps() function 118, 128, 136
strcasecmp() function 45, 115
strcat() function 114–116, 125–126
strchr() function 114
strcmp() function 45, 113–115
strcoll() function 114
strcpy() function 34, 114, 125–126
strcpy() statement 35
strcspn() function 115
stream I/O 51–54
strfry() function 115
strftime() function 26–27, 291–292
string_create() function 139
string_destroy() function 140
string functions 116–132
　changing case 117–118
　converting tabs to spaces 130–132
　counting words in strings 128–130
　inserting one string into another
　　125–128
　reversing strings 118–120
　splitting strings 124–125
　trimming strings 121–124
string library 132–136
　creating 134–135
　using 135–136
　writing source and header file 133–134
strings 110–116
　counting words in 128–130
　inserting one into another 125–128
　measuring 112–114

overview 110–111
returning vs. modifying directly 115–116
reversing 118–120
splitting 124–125
string functions 114–115
trimming 121–124
string structure 139–140
string utilities 109–140
　OOP approach 136–140
　　adding function to structure 137–139
　　creating string 139–140
　string functions 116–132
　　changing case 117–118
　　converting tabs to spaces 130–132
　　counting words in strings 128–130
　　inserting one string into another
　　　125–128
　　reversing strings 118–120
　　splitting strings 124–125
　　trimming strings 121–124
　string library 132–136
　　creating 134–135
　　using 135–136
　　writing source and header file 133–134
　strings 110–116
　　measuring 112–114
　　overview 110–111
　　returning vs. modifying directly
　　　115–116
　　string functions 114–115
strinsert() function 126–128
strlen() function 112–114, 119, 124, 127
strlower() function 118
strncat() function 114–115
strncmp() function 84, 114
strncpy() function 114, 125
strpbrk() function 114
strrchr() function 115
strrev() function 119
strsplit() function 125
strspn() function 115
strstr() function 115
Str string variable 137
str structure 137
strtabs() function 131
strtabs.c program 132
strtok() function 44–45, 86, 115
strtol() function 247
struct finfo variable 240
struct term *t pointer 105
strupper() function 117–118
strwords() function 128, 130
strwords.c program 129
strxfrm() function 115
subdir01.c source code 211

subdirectories 207–217
  exploring 210–212
  recursion 212–217
  tools for 208–210
subdir program 212–213, 220
switch-case structure 180, 182
switches 179
syllables 165
symbol() function 98, 106
system() function 248

T

tabs command 130
terminal window, accessing 9
termination status 246
term structure 104
test_abbr() macro 185–186, 188
test macro 184
test_oct() macro 188
text representation 142–148
  ASCII 145–147
  early text formats 142–145
  Unicode 147–148
text screen editors 11–12
thefirst() function 282, 294
THETA constant 277
three() function 349–351
THURSDAY defined constant 262
tic-tac-toe 331–352
  approaching game mathematically 333–334
  basic game 334–344
    adding game play 337–339
    creating game grid 334–337
    determining winner 340–344
    limiting input to free squares 339–340
  computer plays 344–352
    adding intelligence 348–352
    choosing number of players 344–346
    coding dumb opponent 346–348
  playing 332–333
time() function 23, 250–251, 257, 278, 283, 286, 294, 319
time of day program 23–27
  adding general time info to greeting code 25–26
  adding specific time info to greeting code 26–27
  obtaining current time 23–25
timespec structure 196
time_t data type 23, 278
time_t defined constant 225
time_t pointer 196
time_t variable 23
time zones 283–285

time zone (TZ) environment variable 284–285
tm_day member 252
tm_hour member 252
tm_isdst member 252
tm_mday member 252, 257, 286
tm_min member 252
tm_mon member 252, 257, 276
tm_sec member 252
tm structure 252–254, 256–257, 259, 276, 286, 291
tm_wday member 252, 259, 276, 286
tm_wday tm structure member 291
tm_yday member 252, 291
tm_year member 252
toblock() function 349
today tm structure 250
today variable 294
tohex() function 81, 91–92
tolower() ctype function 78
tomatch constant 328, 330
tomatch variable 329
toMorse() function 143–144
toupper() function 59, 78
towin() function 349
TREE command 220, 222
TREE utility 217–218
Tsch shell 19
ttt01.c code 337
ttt02.c code 339
type data type 137
tzset() function 284–285
TZ (time zone) environment variable 284–285

U

Unicode 147–148
unlink command 10
unsigned char pointer 174
unsigned long value 137
uppercase() function 98, 107
url_decoder01.c source code 92
URL encoder 89–92
  creating 91–92
  encoding rules 89
  writing 90–91
urlencoder program 90
UTF (Unicode Transformation Format) 148

V

value variable 318
version() function 190
vi editor 11
VIM text mode editor 11
vocabulary[] array 102, 107
-v switch 190

W

wait() function 249
-Wall switch 13
wchar_t buffer 158
wchar_t data type 150–153
wday integer 261
wday variable 282
WEDNESDAY enumerated constant 281
week01.c program 286
weekday variable 286, 294, 298, 301
weekend() function 261, 268, 271
weekno variable 291
WEOF end-of-file marker 162
wide character programming 148–163
    character types 150–152
    generating output 152–156
    locale settings 149–150
    receiving input 156–160
    working with wide characters in files 160–163
wide_hello.c program 154
wide_in.c source code 158
wildcards,using to find files 232–234
winner() function 327–328, 341–343
winners[] array 321

wint_t ch single wint_t variable 162
wint_t data type 160, 162
word[] buffer 48, 66–67
words 165
wprintf() function 152–153, 155–156, 158, 162
wscanf() function 158–159
WSL (Windows Subsystem for Linux) 9, 17

X

XCode IDE 7–9

Y

year01.c code 295, 298–299
year03.c code 308
year04.c code 310
year program 295, 303, 306
year variable 294
yen wchar_t variable 151, 155
yen wide character 151

Z

zsh shell 11, 19, 130